Documenting a complete Java^{TM} application using OPEN

Documenting a complete Java™ application using OPEN

Donald G Firesmith
Scott A Krutsch
Marshall Stowe
Greg Hendley

 Addison-Wesley

Harlow, England • Reading, Massachusetts
Menlo Park, California • New York
Don Mills, Ontario • Amsterdam • Bonn
Sydney • Singapore • Tokyo • Madrid
San Juan • Milan • Mexico City • Seoul • Taipei

© Addison Wesley Longman 1998

Addison Wesley Longman Limited
Edinburgh Gate
Harlow
Essex CM20 2JE

and Associated Companies throughout the World.

Published in the United States of America by Addison Wesley Longman Inc., New York.

The right to be identified as authors of this Work has been asserted by the authors in accordance with the Copyright, Designs and Patents Act 1988.

Typeset by 32
Typeset in 10/12 Times
Printed and bound in the United States of America

First printed 1998

ISBN 0-201-34277-2

British Library Cataloguing-in-Publication Data
A catalogue record for this book is available from the British Library

Library of Congress Cataloguing-in-Publication Data is available

Trademarks
Java is a registered trademark of SUN Microsystems.
ObjectMaker is a registered trademark of Mark V Systems Ltd.
VisualWorks is a registered trademark of Object Share.

Contents

Foreword

'Gimme a spec. Gimme a complete spec!'

How often I've heard that cry from clients over the past twenty years. 'Training by bullet points' is good, but by itself it's rarely enough. People want a comprehensive template – an example, not theory – on which to base the specification for their next real system. Of course, a training workshop usually challenges the participants with a case study. But more often than not, at the end of the week, folks get just snippet examples of system requirements and design to take back to the ranch.

So, with a flourish, enter Donald Firesmith *et al.* with the book that you're reading now. This book provides a complete system example from start to finish, including requirements specification, design specification and running Java code. Unlike most books that cover analysis and design, this book also covers quality control and testing.

You'll notice immediately that Donald's book expresses its graphic models in the Common Object Modeling Notation (COMN). This intuitive notation is part of the OPEN Modeling Language (OML). (OML also includes a founding metamodel that defines both graphic and textual modeling components.) If you're more familiar with the Unified Modeling Language (UML), Don provides an appendix containing sample diagrams in UML for comparison.

OPEN, by the way, is a full development-method framework that addresses the big questions: Who does what, when, how, with what, to what end, and for how long? This is a glib way of saying that OPEN, in addition to OML, comprises: activities and tasks that generate recommended deliverables by means of recommended techniques; standards, procedures and guidelines; recommended development roles; and project and quality metrics.

OPEN was initially the work of Donald himself, along with Brian Henderson-Sellers and Ian Graham. It was immediately lauded by methodologists and practitioners around the world and today many others have joined the original three in working on OPEN.

And now back to the book at hand. I expect that many shops will use this book as a springboard for its OO documentation standards. Because you can see a realistic example, you can get a very good idea of how much documentation could and should be produced for a system. This, in turn, allows you to tailor out unnecessary documentation from a position of knowledge, without jeopardizing the quality or content of your specifications.

Models of a real application should (and typically do) evolve over time as requirements change and understanding improves. OPEN therefore recommends an iterative and incremental development cycle. Few authors are brave enough to publish their early mistakes, but Donald has wisely included the previous architectures of the running example along with the current models in the design chapter. He thereby makes an important statement: If highly experienced OO architects initially make mistakes and produce better designs through iteration, then managers should certainly not mandate schedules that assume developers who are new to object technology will create perfect models the very first time.

There are many purposes to which you may put this book. You may use it as an inspiration for your next OO project. Or you may use it as a benchmark for your current documentation standards. You may use it to learn the OPEN approach or just the OML notation. You may, I suppose, even use it to learn Java. But, whatever use you have in mind for this book, I'm sure it will be a valuable instrument in your project's orchestra.

Meilir Page-Jones

Preface

During the Summer of 1995, two of us – Donald Firesmith and Scott Krutsch – were tasked with producing the first internally-developed introductory course in object-oriented requirements analysis and design at Knowledge System Corporation (KSC). This course was intended to be the typical student's first exposure to object orientation and to be a prerequisite to KSC's introductory Smalltalk and Java courses.

Three key design decisions shaped the development of this course:

- The course would be hands-on.

- The students would analyze and design the software for a vending machine.

- The course would be based on the OPEN (Object-oriented Process, Environment, and Notation) method, the international standard object-oriented development method from the OPEN Consortium.

Hands-on

Our most important decision was to make the course a hands-on modeling exercise. Knowing that most students learn better by doing than by watching, we very much wanted to avoid producing merely a traditional lecture course consisting primarily of viewgraphs supported by a few simple exercises. Instead, we chose to produce a course consisting largely of a single, comprehensive exercise supported by a relatively small number of viewgraphs designed to introduce new topics and techniques just prior to having the student practice them. The current five-day course consists of roughly two days of lecture followed by three days of hands-on analysis and design.

Vending machine

The second key design choice during course development was to decide on the application to be analyzed and designed during the ongoing exercise part of the course. We chose to develop the controlling software for a relatively powerful vending machine for the following reasons:

- *Application size.* Because this was to be the student's first introduction to object orientation and we had only five days in which to cover all of the basic topics of object orientation and techniques of object-oriented requirements analysis and design, the application could be neither too large nor complex.

- *Application scope.* On the other hand, the application to be developed had to be complete enough to illustrate all of the basic topics to be covered in a first course. Although most of the objects making up the vending machine are easy to identify and understand because they correspond to relatively simple hardware devices, the vending machine also has complex logic and state behavior requiring significant thought and iteration. The application was sophisticated enough for its architecture to incorporate quite a few important and well-known design patterns. Yet the application did not require a graphical user interface, a database or a distributed client/server architecture, all topics best postponed to an advanced object-oriented analysis and design course.

- *Domain expertise.* The typical student would also need reasonable domain knowledge if we were to avoid wasting too much time explaining the requirements of the application. All of our students have been reasonably familiar with the workings of a vending machine.

- *Student corporate culture.* Another consideration was that the majority of our students typically develop management information systems (MIS) and come to us with a strong background in relational data modeling. We therefore had to break most of them of their strong tendency to think of objects as merely rows in a relational table and consequently to create designs consisting primarily of a few complex 'god objects' controlling numerous dumb data objects. As an embedded application, the vending machine was a new kind of application for most of our MIS students, thus making their transition to the object-oriented mindset easier because they could not use any preconceived architecture biases. Finally, the primary responsibilities of many of the vending machine's objects are behavioral rather than informational. This preponderance of service providers over information holders also helped the students understand the important benefits of a responsibility-driven approach over more traditional data-driven approaches.

OPEN method

The third primary design decision was to use the OPEN method. The decision to use OPEN rather than either UML or one of the more traditional OO development methods was also made for numerous reasons:

- *KSC culture.* Having formerly been primarily a Smalltalk organization, Knowledge System Corporation has been strongly influenced by the Smalltalk culture. Specifically, the staff at KSC tend to take a purist, revolutionary view of object modeling and appreciate the benefits of responsibility-driven design over data-driven approaches. We therefore wanted to avoid using an evolutionary, data-driven method that would make it more difficult for our students to achieve the object mindset. Like KSC, OPEN takes a pure, revolutionary, responsibility-driven view of object modeling.

- *KSC customer base.* Many of KSC's customers are relatively traditional MIS shops involved in, insurance, telecommunications and the like that are transitioning to objects and client/server technology. KSC's students therefore often come from a data processing background strongly influenced by the separation of procedural code from relational databases. Thus, they have a tendency to view classes as essentially relational tables with associated functions and objects as merely rows in these tables. A critical responsibility of the *Introduction to Object Technology through Analysis and Design* course was to break them of their data-driven mindset so that they would think of objects as models of business concepts. OPEN has proven highly effective in this regard.

- *Newness to object technology.* Most of our customer are still new to object technology and its associated development methods. We felt that it was more important to choose a modeling language that is easy for them to learn and remember, rather than a more traditional one that has accumulated a lot of obsolete baggage over the years.

- *Standardization.* In light of the drive to standardize object-oriented development methods, we felt that the method used should be an international standard that is supported by more than just a single methodologist. This left us with only two choices: Rational's UML and OPEN from the OPEN Consortium.

- *Relationship to UML.* When viewed from a marketing and hype prospective, the Unified Modeling Language from the Rational-led Unified Consortium clearly had a strong lead over the OPEN method. However, we felt that UML suffered from a large number of technical problems that for various reasons showed no signs of being addressed. First of all, UML was only a modeling language and lacked the process framework provided by OPEN. Secondly, UML was viewed as an evolutionary, hybrid notation that encouraged a low-level-of-abstraction, data-driven mindset and which required an unnecessarily large amount of rote memorization. Because KSC has had a long tradition of choosing quality over popularity (e.g. our emphasis of Smalltalk over C++), we decided to concentrate on OPEN first and support UML only as required by our customer base.

- *Donald Firesmith.* As a leading OO methodologist with over a dozen years of experience with most major OO development methods, Don Firesmith had strong professional opinions as to the relative strengths and weaknesses of the object-oriented development methods under consideration. He is also a leading member of the OPEN Consortium and was able to ensure that many of KSC's needs were met during the development of the OPEN OML.

Introduction to Object Technology through Analysis and Design has been taught many times since December 1995, and like any good application, the vending machine has evolved through iteration and use. The architecture and its formal documentation have become more sophisticated over time in the following ways:

- Originally, a complete set of high-quality textual requirements was provided to the students. However, requirements are typically incomplete, vague, inconsistent, obsolete or even missing completely on real projects. Currently, we provide a much shorter (and incomplete) set of informal requirements and encourage the students to elicit additional requirements from the instructor.

- The original architecture had fewer, more complex classes than the current architecture. As time passed, the classes making up the application exhibited better abstraction, modularity, cohesion and coupling characteristics.

- Over time, a layered architecture with more packages has evolved. The packages now exhibit better cohesion and coupling characteristics.

- The requirements have also changed over time, providing more capabilities and providing yet another example that object-oriented architectures are more extensible and maintainable than procedural or data-modeling designs.

- Although the early versions of the vending machine were implemented in Smalltalk, the third version has been redesigned for and reimplemented in Java 1.1.

This book is intended to provide developers with a realistic example of the formal products of object-oriented development. Far too often, books and training courses provide only design fragments and code snippets, making it difficult for developers to envision what a real-world object-oriented application might look like.

Similarly, most developers are not allowed the time in which to provide complete documentation. This object-oriented documentation includes all of the artifacts that would reasonably be produced if one had unlimited resources. By examining this documentation, one can more rationally decide which parts of the documentation to produce and which to omit.

Organization

This book consists of the following sections:

1. Front matter, consisting of the foreword, preface, organization, intended audience, guidance on how to read this book, and acknowledgements.

2. *Part I: Introduction to the OPEN method.* This part provides the foundation with which to read and understand the vending machine documentation in the second section. It consists of the following three sections.

   - *The OPEN Modeling Language (OML).* The first section summarizes the OPEN Modeling Language (OML) of the OPEN Method, with special emphasis on the Common Object Modeling Notation (COMN). This section familiarizes the reader with the modeling concepts, notation, and diagrams used to document the vending machine. See *The OPEN Modeling Language (OML) Reference Manual* (Firesmith *et al.*, SIGS Books, 1997) for complete documentation of OML, as well as a detailed comparison of OML and UML.

   - *The OPEN development process.* The second section summarizes the OPEN process used to perform the requirements analysis and design of the vending machine. This section documents the activities, tasks, techniques and associated products that make up the Firesmith instantiation of the OPEN process framework.

   - *Documentation standard.* The third section provides a content and format standard for an object-oriented software requirements specification and design document that is compliant with OPEN and OML.

3. *Part II: Object-Oriented Documentation of the Vending Machine.* This second part provides a complete object-oriented software requirements specification and design document for a non-trivial application.

4. Appendices, providing a glossary of OML terms, examples of UML and Smalltalk documentation, tailoring guidelines, and a list of the contents of the CD-ROM.

5. An attached CD-ROM, which contains the complete source code for the vending machine application, written in both IBM VisualAge Java and VisualWorks Smalltalk.

Intended audience

The intended audience for this book includes modelers (both analysts and designers), quality assurance personnel, class builders, technical managers and domain experts who wish to better understand the artifacts produced by the OPEN Method documented with the OPEN Modeling Language. Instructors and educators can also use this book as an input to an implementation language course, allowing the students to concentrate on language features as they implement the design in this book. (Although this book assumes Java as the implementation language, only relatively minor changes are needed to adapt the design to other OO languages such as Smalltalk, Eiffel, C++, and Ada95. Instructors can use the book as a starting point, making changes as needed (e.g. for language naming conventions, weak vs strong typing, single inheritance vs multiple inheritance and mixins, single vs multiple interfaces.)

How to read this book

Because the vast majority of this book consists of the object-oriented documentation of a realistic application, this must be treated primarily as a reference book. The entire book contains useful example material and insights into the artifacts produced by an object-oriented development process.

We recommend that this book be read in the following order:

Part I   **1. Introduction to the OPEN method**

   I-1   **The OPEN Modeling Language (OML).** Read this section first, especially if you have not yet read *The OPEN Modeling Language (OML) Reference Manual* (Firesmith *et al.*, SIGS Books, 1997).

   I-2   **The OPEN development process.** This section summarizes the major activities and tasks used to produce the models in the book. Remember that an iterative, incremental, and parallel development cycle was used to produce these models, even though the book is organized by activity and this organization could mislead the reader into thinking that a waterfall development cycle was used.

   I-3   **Documentation standard.** Skim this section to get a feel for the content and format of the following documentation.

Part II **Object-oriented documentation of the vending machine**

   1 **Overview.** This section will describe and provide the informal requirements for the vending machine application.

2.1 **Context diagrams.** Notice that context diagrams occur at both the system and software levels.

2.2 **Use case diagrams.** Skim this subsection, noting that use cases are functional in nature and have been functionally decomposed to avoid complexity and redundantly specifying requirements.

2.3 **Capability requirements organized hierarchically by externals.** Skim this subsection, reading the textual requirements associated with several of the external objects as well as a few of the use case specifications. Compare the level of detail of these more formal requirements with that of the informal requirements in the overview.

3.6 **Previous architectures.** Read this subsection to get a feel for how the design has evolved from its simple beginnings to the current more powerful (if also more complex) design.

   3 **Design documentation.** Read the first two pages of Section 3 and the summaries of each layer (3.1, 3.2, 3.3, 3.4 and 3.5) to get an overview of the current architecture.

3.X.1 **Package overviews.** Read the descriptions of each package (3.1.1, 3.2.1, 3.3.1, 3.4.1 and 3.5.1). Evaluate the package diagrams and package collaboration diagrams in terms of software engineering principles and the associated design decisions and rationales.

        Class specifications. To better understand the package designs, skim the associated class specifications. Make sure that you have reviewed at least one of each kind of diagram: internal collaboration diagram, inheritance diagram, and state transition diagram.

4.1.1 **Model verification using whitebox sequence diagrams.** Skim this subsection, comparing the whitebox sequence diagrams with the corresponding blackbox sequence diagrams in the requirements section and the cluster collaboration diagrams in the design section.

4.1.2 **Class/package testing.** Skim this subsection, noticing how classes can be developed to test themselves.

4.1.3 **Acceptance testing.** Skim this subsection, concentrating on how whitebox sequence diagrams are used to identify specific acceptance test cases.

CD-ROM

   1 **Java.** Run the Java application and use it to service the vending machine and buy items from it. Read selected parts of the Java source code, comparing it with the associated class specifications in the design documentation.

   2 **Smalltalk.** Run the Smalltalk application and use it to service the vending machine and buy items from it. Read selected parts of the Smalltalk source code, comparing it to the associated class specifications in the design documentation.

Acknowledgements

We authors would first of all like to thank our management at Knowledge Systems Corporation (KSC) for permitting us to largely replace learning by lecture with learning by doing and thereby change the way classes are taught at KSC. We also appreciate being allowed to iterate and produce a quality product and to share the fruits of our labor in the form of this book.

We would like to thank the OPEN Consortium for producing a modeling language that is easy to learn and is consistent with the object-oriented principles used and taught at KSC.

We would like to thank the numerous students in the *Introduction to Object Technology through Analysis and Design* courses who analyzed and designed the vending machine application, often asking good questions leading to great discussions resulting in the iteration of the vending machine requirements and design. This trial by fire led to a better architecture and documentation.

We would also like to acknowledge Mark V Systems Ltd, which generously provided ObjectMaker to our students and us. The majority of the models contained in the example object-oriented documentation were generated using version 4.4 of this tool. The remaining diagrams were generated using an Alpha release of version 5.0.

As team leader on this project, I must also acknowledge the fine work of my co-authors. Thank you Scott for being the perfect reviewer, leaving no red ink unused if improvements were possible. Thank you Greg for making my Smalltalk code look like a Smalltalker wrote it. And thank you Marshall for reimplementing the application in Java. Without your help, I would not be as proud as I am of this book and its production would have taken much longer. I would also like to thank Margery Pruessner, my new boss at StorageTek, for her generous support in completing this manuscript.

Donald Firesmith

About the authors

Donald G. Firesmith

Before joining Storage Technology Corporation as a senior advisory software engineer, Donald Firesmith was a senior member of the technical staff at Knowledge Systems Corporation. He has worked extensively with objects since 1984, concentrating in the areas of project management, development methods and testing. He has authored or been the principal co-author of four books on object technology including *Object-Oriented Requirements Analysis: a Software Engineering Approach* (John Wiley and Sons, 1993), the *Dictionary of Object Technology: the Complete Desk Reference* (SIGS Books, 1995), and *OPEN Modeling Language (OML) Reference Manual* (SIGS Books, 1997). He has published numerous articles in journals such as ROAD, JOOP and Object Magazine. He spoke at the first OOPSLA, has been a member of the OOPSLA and TOOLS program committees, and given presentations and tutorials at numerous international conferences including ObjectEXPO, Smalltalk Solutions, TOOLS, and others. Currently, he is authoring a book of OO testing incorporating PLOOT, his pattern language for testing OO software. Don Firesmith can be reached by phone at (303) 673-5151 or by e-mail at Donald_Firesmith@stortek.com.

Greg Hendley

An advisory software engineer at IBM, and prior to that a senior member of the technical staff at Knowledge Systems Corporation, Greg Hendley has over eight years' experience in Smalltalk and object-oriented design. He has acted as developer, mentor and trainer in all of the major dialects of Smalltalk, led the design of over a dozen object-oriented software systems, and co-authored the GUI Smalltalk column in *The Smalltalk Report*. Recent activities include the development of the Interface Control Model (ICM) framework and domain development in Java. Prior to OO, he accumulated six years of experience in high-level design, specification, and testing of real-time computer graphics systems for flight simulators. Greg Hendley can be reached by phone at (919) 543-2719 or by e-mail at either ghendley@raleigh.ibm.com or 72672.3330@compuserve.com.

Scott A. Krutsch

Scott Krutsch is the principal instructor and one of the developers of *Introduction to Object Technology through Analysis and Design*, Knowledge Systems Corporation's initial course for object newcomers. In this hands-on course, students analyze and design major sections of the vending machine software documented in this book. Scott has seven years' experience in course development and teaching, most of these in the object world. He has performed object-oriented software engineering with Smalltalk in the fields of telecommunications, insurance and manufacturing, and has worked on CASE tool development and reuse efforts. He was also a primary reviewer of the *OPEN Modeling Language (OML) Reference Manual*. He holds degrees from Rose-Hulman Institute of Technology and Pennsylvania State University. Scott Krutsch can be reached by phone at (919) 677-1119x509 or by e-mail at krutschs@acm.org.

Marshall Stowe

A software engineer at Gilbarco Inc., Marshall Stowe is a recent computer science graduate of North Carolina State University. He is a Sun-certified Java programmer, and as a co-op programmer at Knowledge Systems Corporation has helped to develop their *Introduction to Object-Oriented Programming in Java* course and Java Apprentice Practicum as well as having a hand in the *Application Development with VisualAge Web Connection* course. Marshall Stowe can be reached by phone at (336) 547-5846 or by e-mail at either marshall_stowe@gilbarco.com or mstowe@juno.com

Part I

Introduction to OPEN

I-1 Introduction to the OPEN Method

OPEN (Object-oriented Process, Environment and Notation) is an international *de facto* standard object-oriented development method framework. OPEN was created and is maintained by the OPEN Consortium, a consortium of over thirty internationally recognized OO methodologists, researchers, developers and CASE tool vendors.

OPEN is a complete development process consisting of the following:

- A development cycle/process framework consisting of activities which are decomposed into tasks that are performed using techniques to generate deliverables.

- The OPEN Modeling Language (OML) which in turn consists of:
  - an underlying metamodel
  - the Common Object Modeling Notation (COMN).

- Standards, procedures and guidelines.

- Recommended development roles.

- Metrics.

OPEN was initially created as the merger of the following three object-oriented development methods: MOSES (Brian Henderson-Sellers), SOMA (Ian Graham), and The Firesmith Method (Donald Firesmith). OPEN's metamodel has been derived largely from the COMMA project (Brian Henderson-Sellers, 1995) which evaluated 14 previous OO development methods. Much of the impetus for OML was generated by the Object Management Group (OMG) Analysis and Design Task Force Request for Proposal (RFP) for an industry standard metamodel to support upperCASE tool interoperability. OPEN also provides an improved, more object-oriented alternative to the Unified Modeling Language (UML) being promulgated by Rational and others.

OPEN embodies the following major principles:

- OPEN covers the entire development process. OPEN covers all major activities and tasks including initial requirements elicitation, analysis, and specification; logical and physical design; implementation; and testing. The OPEN Modeling Language is only a small, but important, part of OPEN. OPEN emphasizes modeling over coding and emphasizes a high rather than low level of abstraction.

- OPEN takes a pure rather than a hybrid approach to object-oriented development. OPEN emphasizes an object-oriented mindset and is responsibility driven rather than use-case driven or data driven. OPEN has

2

been more influenced by pure languages such as Smalltalk, Java[†], and Eiffel than by hybrid languages such as C++ and Ada. OPEN has also been more influenced by object databases than by relational database technology.

- OPEN is state-of-the-art. OPEN has abandoned obsolete techniques and notations; instead it uses the latest thinking in these areas.

- OML/COMN is easy to learn and use. It avoids rote memorization and strives to make all icons intuitive, consistent, and easy to remember.

I-1.1 The OPEN Modeling Language

As the name implies, the OPEN Modeling Language (OML) is the modeling language used by the OPEN method to perform requirements analysis and design. OML consists of the following two components:

- The OML metamodel, which defines the terminology, syntax, and semantics of the underlying concepts.

- The Common Object Modeling Notation, COMN (pronounced as 'common'), which defines the OML diagrams and associated icons.

This subsection summarizes the basic concepts, icons and diagrams of OML Version 1.1 that were used to document the requirements and design of the vending machine application. For a complete description of OML Version 1.0, see *The OPEN Modeling Language (OML) Reference Manual* by Donald Firesmith, Brian Henderson-Sellers and Ian Graham (SIGS Books, 1997 currently being republished by Cambridge University Press) and for a complete description of the OPEN process framework, see *The OPEN Process Framework* by Brian Henderson-Sellers, Ian Graham and H. Younessi (Addison Wesley Longman, 1997).

I-1.1.1 *Common nodes*

This subsection documents the common nodes that are used on multiple kinds of COMN diagrams. These include objects (both internal and external), classes, types, roles, packages and notes.

Objects

An *object* is any uniquely identified abstraction that uses its *characteristics* to model a single thing that is important in the current application. In order to be a complete abstraction, an object captures all of the essential characteristics (i.e. *properties*, *behavior* and *rules*) of the thing being modeled while ignoring the thing's non-essential, diversionary details.

Objects may be either internal or external. An *internal object* is any object

---

[†]Yes, we know that Java is not strictly 100% pure because it contains a small number of traditional data types (e.g. int for integer) and that the object-oriented wrappers provided for them are highly incomplete. However, Java is still much purer than hybrid object-oriented programming languages such as Ada95, C++ and COBOL.

that models a part of the current application, and is represented in COMN by a house-shaped pentagon. On the other hand, an *external object* is any object that is not part of the current application but is nevertheless important to document during modeling (e.g. because it interacts with the application or implies the existence of a corresponding object inside the application).

A *multiobject* is a shorthand way of representing a collection of internal objects. A multiobject is represented in COMN by a stack of two internal object icons, the front icon being placed below and to the left of the back icon.

As illustrated by Figure I.1, externals can be stereotyped by the kind of thing they model:

- An *actor* is any external that models a role played by a human. An actor is represented in COMN by a stick figure (but, unlike the Unified Modeling Language (UML), COMN restricts usage of the stick figure icon to represent roles played by humans).

- A *hardware external* is any external that models a hardware device, either with or without significant processing power. A hardware external is represented in COMN by a three-dimensional box.

- A *software external* is any external that models some software (e.g. a legacy application). A software external is represented in COMN by a rounded rectangle drawn with a dashed boundary (in fact, this icon is used in COMN to represent all software that is larger than a class).

- A *persistent memory external* is any external that models some persistent memory (e.g. a file, a database, a relational database table, a tape, a disk). A persistent memory external is represented in COMN by the traditional database icon, a cylinder.

- An *other external* is any external that does not fit into any of the above categories (e.g. a network, a substance, a document, a location, an organization). An other external is represented in COMN by a cloud.

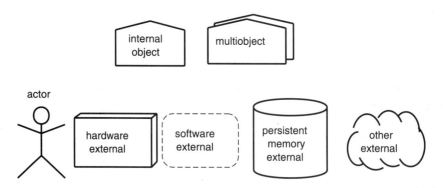

Figure I.1 COMN icons for internal and external objects.

As illustrated by Figure I.2, externals can be partitioned by the degree they are removed from the current application into either *direct externals*, which interact directly with the current application, or *indirect externals*, which interact indirectly with the current application via other externals.

As illustrated by Figure I.3, externals can also be partitioned by their direction of dependency with regard to the current application. A *client external* is any external that depends on the current application, and a *server external* is any external on which the application depends. A *peer external* is any external that is both a client external and a server external.

Objects may be either concurrent or sequential. A *sequential object* is any object that is not concurrent, and a *concurrent object* is any object that is inherently capable of running concurrently (i.e. simultaneously) with other objects because it contains, either directly or indirectly, one or more of its own threads of execution. Because actors are assumed to be concurrent, they do not need to be labeled as such. An object may be concurrent because:

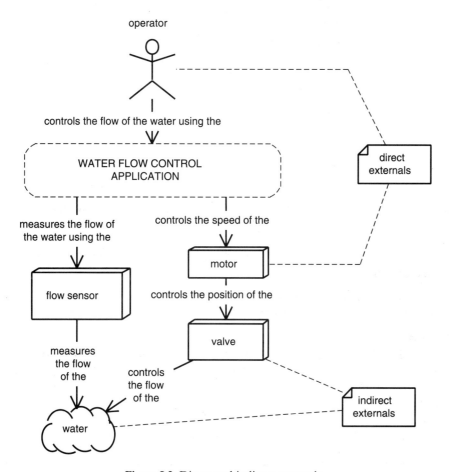

Figure I.2 Direct and indirect externals.

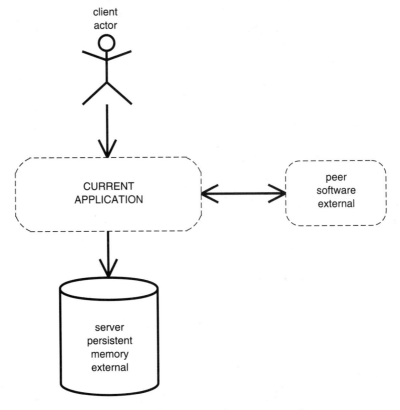

Figure I.3 Client, peer and server externals.

- it directly has its own thread of execution (e.g. an object in the Actor language),

- one or more of its properties are concurrent, or

- one or more of its operations are directly concurrent (i.e. have their own inherent thread of execution).

As illustrated in Figure I.4, a concurrent object is represented in COMN by placing two slashes, representing parallel processing, in front of the name of the object.

Classes and types

Objects in OML are instances of their defining object classes. A *class* is any definition of a single kind of instance (e.g. object, package instance, linkage, scenario). Optionally, a class can be used to instantiate instances that capture the same abstraction and have the same or similar characteristics. As illustrated by Figure I.5, a class consists of an interface of one or more types[†]

[†]Note that the terms type and class are not synonymous. Unlike a class, a type is not itself an instance and does not provide an implementation. A class is an instance of a metaclass, contains one or more types, and does provide an implementation.

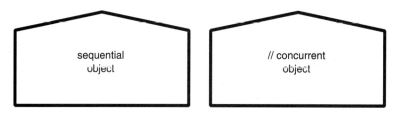

Figure I.4 Sequential and concurrent objects.

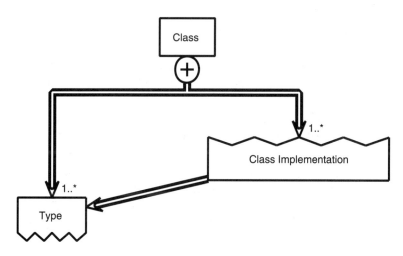

Figure I.5 COMN icons for classes, types and class implementations.

that are implemented by one or more implementations.[†] An *object class* is any object that is also a class, the instances of which are objects. In turn, an *object metaclass* is any class, the instances of which are object classes. As illustrated by Figure I.5, an object class is represented in COMN by a rectangle.

A *type* is any declaration of visible characteristics that form all or part of the interface of a single kind of instance that conforms to that type. An *object type* is any type, the instances of which are objects. An object conforms to an object type if and only if its interface is consistent with the type (i.e. the set of characteristics in the interface of the object is a superset of the set of characteristics declared by the type). As illustrated by Figure I.5, an object type is represented in COMN by a rectangle, the bottom edge of which is jagged.

A *class implementation* is any declaration of hidden characteristics that [partially] implements the associated class by implementing one or more of the types of a class. An *object class implementation* is any class implementation that [partially] implements an object class. As illustrated by Figure I.5, an object

---

[†]Few object-oriented programming languages clearly distinguish a class from its implementation. Ada clearly separates specification (type) from body (implementation) and Java clearly separates interface (type) from class. However, C++ and Smalltalk do not.

class implementation is represented in COMN by a rectangle, the top of which is jagged.

As illustrated by Figure I.6, the class icon can be divided horizontally by a jagged line to form the type icon and class implementation icon in order to symbolize that a class can be decomposed into its constituent types and implementations. The type icon is formed from the top half of the class icon because in COMN, client icons are typically drawn above server icons with referential relationships (e.g. associations) being drawn top-down and pointing at the top of the server icons. The interface of an icon is therefore naturally thought of as being on the top of the icon.

As illustrated by Figure I.7, classes can be partitioned by instantiability into the following three stereotypes:

- A *concrete class* is any complete class that therefore can be used to instantiate semantically meaningful instances. A concrete class in COMN is drawn with a solid boundary.

- An *abstract class* is any incomplete class that therefore cannot be used to instantiate semantically meaningful instances. An abstract class in COMN is drawn with a dotted boundary.

- A *deferred class* is any abstract class that declares the existence of one or more characteristics that must be implemented by its descendants prior to instantiation. A deferred class in COMN is further identified with the stereotype '{deferred}'.

Roles

A role is an abstraction of a partial object that is defined in terms of a cohesive collection of responsibilities and associated characteristics. All objects, regardless of their respective classes, that fulfil the same purpose within some pattern of collaborating objects are said to play the same role.

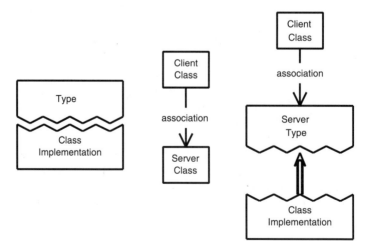

Figure 1.6 Decomposition of class icons into type and implementation icons.

Figure I.7 COMN icons for concrete, abstract and deferred classes.

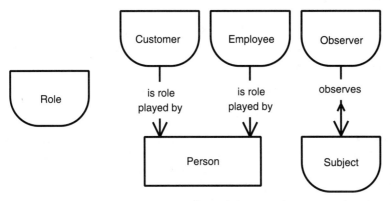

Figure I.8 COMN icons for roles.

Thus, objects of different classes and types can play the same role, and a single object can play multiple roles. For example, the role of customer can be played by either a person or an organization.

As illustrated by Figure I.8, the role icon is a rounded rectangle, the bottom two corners of which are rounded. Note that the role icon is reminiscent of the shape of masks used in ancient Greek plays.

Packages

Packaging is used to control size and complexity by providing a unit of modularity that is larger than a class. A package is usually used to encapsulate the software that is developed as a unit by a small team, but it is also used to capture the implementation of a pattern, a layer, a subdomain or a distribution unit.

A *package* [*class*] is any class that defines (and optionally can be used to instantiate) package instances. A package has an interface consisting of one or more package types and an implementation consisting of one or more package implementations. The characteristics of a package are usually object classes, but may also include types and other package classes. Packages may be related by package inheritance. Packages may be either logical or physical. As illustrated in Figure I.9, a package is represented in COMN by a dashed rectangle, the corners of which are rounded. A dashed boundary is used because a package is less concrete than an object class and because this is the traditional pen style used when drawing packages by hand.

Figure I.9 COMN icons for packages.

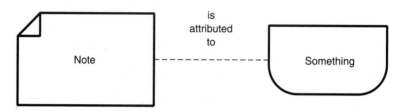

Figure I.10 COMN icons for notes.

A *package instance* is any uniquely identified instance of a package class. The characteristics of a package instance are usually objects but may also include object classes (which are themselves objects), roles and package instances. As illustrated in Figure I.9, a package instance is also represented in COMN by a dashed rectangle, the corners of which are rounded.

The following two advanced concepts are rarely used in practice and only completed for consistency and completeness sake:

- A *package type* is any type that declares the interface of a package. A package conforms to a package type if and only if its interface is consistent with the type (i.e. the set of visible characteristics in the interface of the package is a superset of the set of characteristics declared by the type). As illustrated in Figure I.9, a package type is represented in COMN as a dashed rectangle, the top two corners of which are rounded and the bottom of which is jagged.

- A *package implementation* is any class implementation that partially implements a package [class]. As illustrated in Figure I.9, a package implementation is represented in COMN as a dashed rectangle, the top of which is jagged.

Notes
A note is any developer-defined text providing a comment or listing a constraint about specific modeling element(s). As illustrated in Figure I.10, a note is represented by a rectangle with the upper left corner turned over; attribution (if any) is represented by a dashed line segment connecting the note to the relevant modeling element(s).

I-1.1.2 Common relationship arcs
All relationships in OML are inherently binary, unidirectional dependency relationships. All COMN relationship arcs are therefore directed from client to server with the direction signified by an arrowhead on the server end.

OML recognizes the following kinds of relationships:

- referential relationships
- definitional relationships
- scenario relationships
- transitional relationships

Referential relationships

A referential relationship is any relationship from one modeling element to another whereby the first modeling element refers to the second. OML recognizes the following kinds of referential relationships:

- association/linkage relationships
  - aggregation relationships
  - containment relationships
- interaction relationships

All referential relationships are represented in COMN by a single solid line with an arrowhead at the server end.

Association and linkage

An association is a general semantically meaningful relationship between two classes or types, and linkage is the corresponding relationship between two objects or roles.

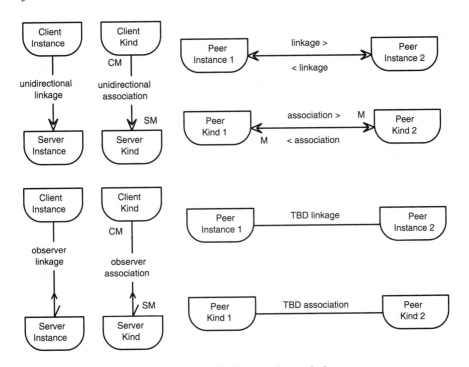

Figure I.11 Icons for links and associations.

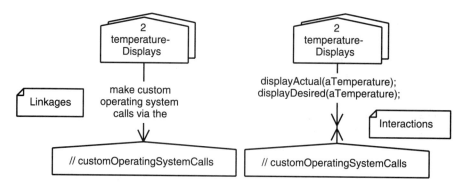

Figure I.12 Example linkages and associated interactions.

As illustrated in Figure I.11:

- A *unidirectional association/linkage* is represented in COMN as a solid line with an arrowhead at the server end. As illustrated in Figure I.12, associations and linkages are typically labeled with verb phrases which together with the labels of the nodes make semantically valid sentences when read in the direction of the arrow. Note that other kinds of association are more advanced, and that this is the only kind of association required by the digital thermostat example.

- A *bidirectional association/linkage* (which should be very uncommon) is represented in COMN as a solid line with an arrowhead at both the client and server ends. Remember that a bidirectional association/linkage is merely a short-hand notation for two unidirectional associations/linkages that are semi-strong inverses of one another, the referential integrity of which is ensured by operations in both the client and server nodes. Although included for completeness sake, this kind of association is not recommended because of the increased coupling, effort to implement, and probability of errors.

- An *observer association/linkage* is represented in COMN as a solid line with a normal sized arrowhead at the server end and a smaller arrowhead pointing the opposite direction near the server end. This is, in fact, a pattern documented in *Design Patterns* by Erich Gamma *et al.* (Addison Wesley, 1995) and is considered sufficiently common and important to deserve its own notation in OML.

- A *TBD association/linkage* is represented in COMN as a solid line without arrowheads. Note that this kind of association should only be used temporarily and should be replaced by one of the other kinds in the final documentation.

The abbreviations in Figure I.11 represent multiplicities as follows:

- CM = client multiplicity
- M = multiplicity
- SM = server multiplicity

Because all relationships in the object paradigm are directional and objects only know about other objects via properties that reference those objects:

- A *one-to-one association* is typically implemented as a property of the client object that references the server object.

- A *one-to-many association* is typically implemented as a property of the client object that contains a collection object that in turn contains one-to-one links to the server objects.

- A *many-to-many association* is often reified and modeled as an associative object that contains a collection object that in turn contains a pair of one-to-one links, one to each associated object.

- All associations/linkages are binary; any ternary or higher order associations/ linkages are reified and modeled as associative objects assuming that they represent real concepts and are not merely being treated as data tuples in entity-relationship modeling.

Aggregation and containment

Aggregation is the kind of association/linkage relationship that exists from a structure to its component parts. As illustrated in Figure I.13, aggregation is represented in COMN by attaching a circle labeled with a plus sign at the structure end of the association/linkage arc. COMN uses this notation because the arc points in the right direction (i.e. in the direction of object dependency rather than relational database table dependency) and because a whole can be thought of as being the sum of its component parts. In the rare cases where a part needs to know about its structure, a bidirectional arc may be used.

Containment is a kind of association/linkage relationship that exists from a collection to its component entries. As illustrated in Figure I.13, composition is represented in COMN by attaching a circle labeled with a ∪ at the collection end of the association/linkage arc. Containment is typically implemented by using standard collection classes that come with the implementation language (e.g. Vector and Hashtable in Java and Collection and Dictionary in Smalltalk).

Interactions

If linkages are considered the roads between objects, then interactions are the traffic on those roads. An interaction is either the sending of a message or the raising of an exception. As illustrated in Figure I.12, interactions are labeled with the messages and associated exceptions, typically written in the syntax of the implementation language, whereas associations/linkages are labeled with verb phrases so that the combination of the nodes and arc make a grammatically correct sentence. Thus, assertions/linkages are best used to communicate with domain experts and users, while interactions are used to communicate with developers.

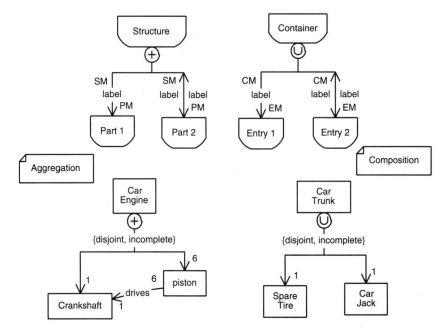

Figure I.13 Icons for aggregation and containment relationships.

A *sequential message* is any message (e.g. those in Smalltalk, C++) involving only one thread of control that is temporarily passed from the sender to the receiver, thereby blocking the sender until the receiver's operation(s) are completed.

A *synchronous message* is any message (e.g. Ada rendezvous) that synchronizes two threads of control, thereby potentially blocking either the sender or the receiver until both are ready to communicate.

An *asynchronous message* is any message involving two threads of control that do not synchronize during message passing so that neither the sender nor the receiver is blocked by having to wait for the other.

An *exception* is any abnormal interaction consisting of an object which models an exceptional or error condition. An exception is thrown (a.k.a. raised) by an operation in order to notify a client that the exception has occurred.

As illustrated by Figure I.14, the different kinds of messages are represented in COMN by different style arrowheads.

Definitional relationships

A definitional relationship is any relationship from one modeling element to another whereby the first modeling element depends on the definition provided by the second. OML recognizes the following kinds of definitional relationships:

- classification
- implementation
- inheritance

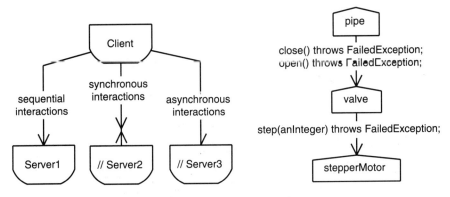

Figure I.14 Icons for interactions.

All definitional relationships are represented in COMN by a double solid line with an arrowhead at the server end. The double line clearly differentiates definitional relationships from the more common referential relationships and visually implies the strong coupling of the client to the server for its definition.

Classification

Classification is the 'is a' relationship from an instance to either its class, type or role. OML recognizes the following kinds of classification relationships:

- The *is an instance of* relationship is the classification relationship from an instance to a class, signifying that the instance is consistent to the complete definition (both interface and implementation) provided by the class.

- The *conforms to* relationship is the classification relationship from an instance to a type, signifying that the interface of the instance is consistent to the interface defined by the type.

- The *plays the role of* relationship is the classification relationship from an instance to a role, signifying that the object fulfills all of the responsibilities of the role.

As illustrated by Figure I.15, each classification relationship is represented in COMN by a double arrow. In fact, no label is required on classification arcs because the three different varieties can be disambiguated from each other and from implementation and inheritance by considering the metatypes of the client and server nodes. Thus, for example, an 'is instance of' relationship is from an instance to a class.

Implementation

An implementation relationship is any definitional relationship whereby one modeling element provides the implementation of another. As illustrated by Figure I.16, OML recognizes the following kinds of implementation relationships:

- The *implements* relationship is the implementation relationship from a class or a class implementation to one of the types that is implemented thereby.

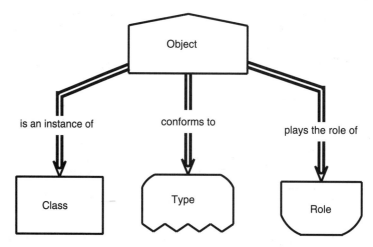

Figure I.15 Icons for classification relationships.

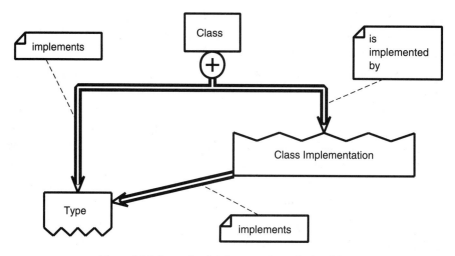

Figure I.16 Icons for implementation relationships.

- The *is implemented by* relationship is the implementation relationship from a class to one of its class implementations.

Because they are aggregation-like relationships, the implementation relationships from the class to its type(s) and implementation(s) are annotated with the aggregation symbol.

Inheritance

An inheritance relationship is any definitional relationship from a child to one of its parents, whereby the child is a new definition (e.g. class, type) created from one or more existing definitions provided by the parent(s). OML COMN recognizes the following three kinds of inheritance relationships based on purpose:

- *Specialization inheritance* is the 'a kind of' inheritance relationship, whereby the child (a.k.a. specialization) is a specialized kind of its more general parent (a.k.a. generalization).

- *Interface inheritance* is the blackbox inheritance relationship (i.e. subtyping) whereby the interface of the child conforms to the interface of its parent even though the child is not a specialization of that parent. Interface inheritance usually should be replaced with specialization inheritance and is included here primarily for completeness sake.

- *Implementation inheritance* is the whitebox inheritance relationship whereby the implementation of the child reuses the implementation of its parent even though the child's interface does not conform to that of its parent (i.e. polymorphic substitutability is lost). OPEN does not recommend the use of implementation inheritance, which should almost always be replaced by some form of association. It should be used rarely and is included here for completeness sake.

As illustrated in Figure I.17, specialization inheritance requires no further annotation because it should be the most common type of inheritance. However, a blackbox and whitebox are used as annotations to signify interface and implementation inheritance. When inheritance and classification relationships are drawn on the same diagrams as referential relationships, we recommend that, where practical, they be drawn top-down in order to be consistent with the direction of the other dependency relationships, to emphasize control flow over data flow, and to support dependency-based testing.

Inheritance between classes may be specification, interface or implementation. Inheritance between types may be either specialization or interface. Inheritance between class implementations is always implementation inheritance.

OML COMN recognizes the following two kinds of inheritance relationships based on the number of parents:

- *Single inheritance* is the kind of inheritance whereby the child has only a single parent.

- *Multiple inheritance* is the kind of inheritance whereby the child may have multiple parents.

The following terms are based on the position of a class within an inheritance structure:

- A *root class* is any class that has descendants but no ancestors.

- A *branch class* is any class that has both ancestors and descendants.

- A *leaf class* is any class that has no descendants. Although there is actually nothing that would prevent someone from subclassing a leaf class and thus turning it into a branch class, the distinction between the two may be

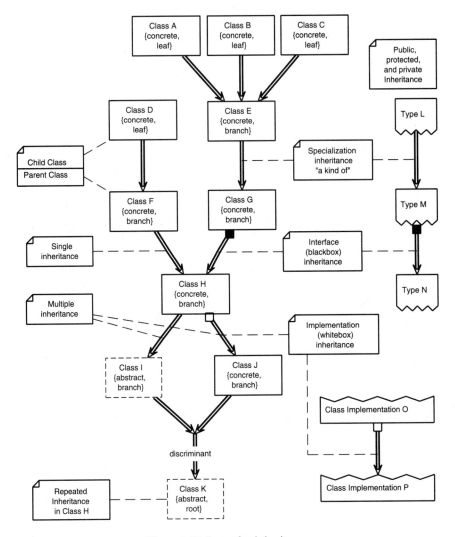

Figure I.17 Icons for inheritance.

nonetheless useful when discussing an inheritance structure and the position of classes within it.

Scenario relationships

A *scenario* is any specific functional abstraction that cannot be modeled as a single operation of a single object, but rather requires the collaboration of multiple objects.

A *scenario class* is any class of scenarios that captures a general abstraction that cannot be modeled as a single operation of a single class, but rather requires the collaboration of multiple classes. OML recognizes the following three kinds of scenario classes:

- A *mechanism* is any scenario class which captures the associations between a collection of collaborating classes.

- A *use case* is any scenario class which captures the associations between externals and an application whereby the application is treated as a blackbox.

- A *task script* is any scenario class which captures interactions among externals.

A *scenario relationship* is any relationship involving scenarios or scenario classes. OML recognizes the following kinds of scenario relationships:

- relationships between scenarios
  - invokes relationships
  - precedes relationships
- uses relationships

An *invokes relationship* is any scenario relationship between two scenarios or scenario classes whereby the server is invoked at a specific point in the execution of the client. As illustrated in Figure I.18, an invokes relationship is represented in COMN as a solid line with an arrowhead on the end pointing at the server and labeled with the word 'invokes'.

A *precedes relationship* is any scenario relationship between two scenarios or scenario classes whereby the client must complete execution before the server may begin execution. As illustrated in Figure I.18, a precedes relationship is represented in COMN as a solid line with an arrowhead on the end pointing at the server and labeled with the word 'precedes'.

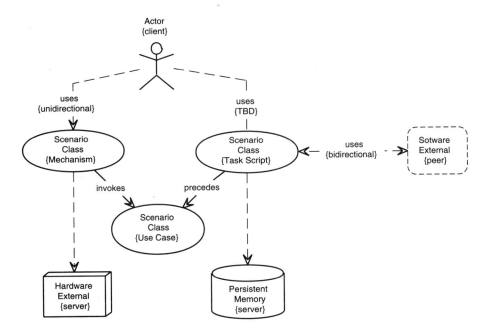

Figure I.18 Icons for scenario relationships.

A *uses relationship* is any scenario relationship between an external object and a scenario [class] whereby the client uses the server. As illustrated in Figure I.18, a uses relationship is represented in COMN as a dotted line with an arrowhead on the end pointing at the server.

Transitional relationships

A *state* is any mode or condition of an object, during which specific qualitative rules of behavior apply, and which is characterized by a collection of [state] property values. For example, a stack may be either empty, partially full, or full; when a stack is empty, no element may be popped off of the stack, and when a stack is full, no element may be pushed onto the stack. A *substate* of a *superstate* is a state that inherits all of the rules of the superstate, that may add additional rules, and which is characterized by a subset of the property values of the superstate.

A *transition relationship* is any relationship involving states. As illustrated in Figure I.19, a transition in COMN is represented by a line with an arrowhead pointing at the subsequent state(s) and labeled with the trigger (e.g. operation, exception) that causes it to fire. OML recognizes the following kinds of scenario relationships:

- A *normal transition* is triggered by an operation. As illustrated in Figure I.19, a normal transition is represented in COMN by a solid line.

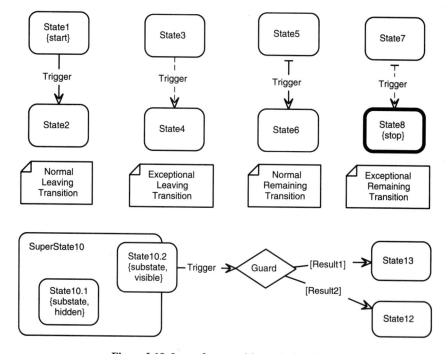

Figure I.19 Icons for transition relationships.

- An *exceptional transition* is triggered by the handling of an exception. As illustrated in Figure I.19, an exceptional transition is represented in COMN by a dotted line.

- A *leaving transition* causes the object to leave the previous state and transition to the subsequent state. As illustrated in Figure I.19, a leaving transition is represented in COMN by a solid line connected to the previous state.

- A *remaining transition* causes the object to remain in the previous state while also transitioning to the subsequent state. As illustrated in Figure I.19, a remaining transition is represented in COMN by a solid line with a small cross bar that does not touch the previous state. Remaining transitions are typically rare in most applications.

- A *guarded transition* transitions the object to the appropriate subsequent state determined by the value of the guard upon firing. If the guard condition is Boolean and the false result is not explicitly stated, then the object remains in the previous state. As illustrated in Figure I.19, a guard result is labeled with the appropriate enumeration value.

- A *group transition* involves a superstate. For example, a group transition from a superstate is equivalent to individual transitions from all associated substates, including their substates (if any). A group transition is represented in COMN by a solid line connected to the superstate state.

I-1.1.3 Diagrams

OML COMN uses the following four kinds of diagrams to document static architecture and dynamic behavior models developed during requirements analysis and design:

- semantic nets
- interaction diagrams
- scenario class diagrams
- state transition diagrams

In order to illustrate encapsulation and emphasize dependency relationships, the following guidelines apply to all relevant diagrams:

- Visible nodes are drawn so that they straddle the upper boundary of the node that contains them, whereas hidden nodes are drawn nested inside the node that encapsulates them.

- Arcs are generally drawn top-down from client nodes to server nodes. Client nodes are drawn above server nodes, whereas peer nodes are drawn side by side.

A simple digital thermostat will be used as a common example to illustrate the different kinds of diagrams.

Semantic nets

A semantic net is any directed graph which documents the static structure of a cohesive collection of related things (e.g. objects including externals, classes, types, roles and packages) connected by semantically meaningful relationships (e.g. association, aggregation, inheritance).

OML COMN recognizes the following six kinds of semantic nets:

- context diagrams
- layer diagrams
- configuration diagrams
- package diagrams
- inheritance diagrams
- deployment diagrams

Context diagrams

A context diagram is any specialized semantic net which documents the scope and environment of an application, layer, or subdomain treated as a blackbox in terms of itself, its externals and the semantically meaningful relationships (e.g. association, aggregation, inheritance) between them.

The primary intended audience for a context diagram consists of domain experts, business analysts, customers, managers, architects and modelers.

OML COMN recognizes the following two kinds of context diagrams:

- A *system context diagram* is any context diagram which documents the context of an entire system potentially consisting of hardware and software as well as wetware (people) and paperware (documentation). Figure I.20 documents the system context diagram of a digital thermostat system. The digital thermostat has one client external object (the user actor) and two server external objects (the air conditioner and furnace).

- A *software context diagram* is any context diagram which documents the context of a cohesive collection of software (e.g. an entire software application, a layer, or a subdomain within an application). Figure I.21 documents the software context diagram of the digital thermostat software. The software is indirectly controlled by three client external objects (the buttons) and indirectly controls seven server external devices (the two converters, the temperature sensor, the air conditioner and furnace, and the two displays). The custom operating system is a peer of the digital thermostat software, both sending software interrupts to it and being called by it.

Layer diagrams

A layer diagram is any specialized semantic net which documents the highest-level software architecture of an application.

The primary intended audience for a layer diagram consists of domain experts, business analysts, customers, managers, architects and modelers.

Figure I.22 documents the layer diagram of a digital thermostat. The software consists of only three layers: one containing four interfacer objects that capture user input, one containing coordinator and service provider objects implementing the control loop, and one containing interfacer objects providing output.

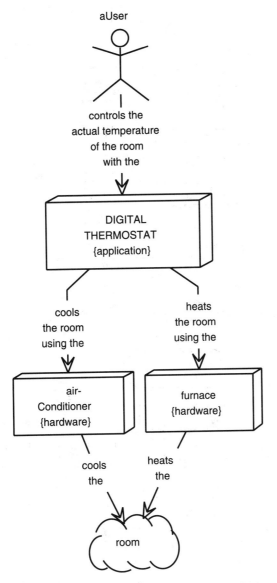

Figure I.20 Example system context diagram for the digital thermostat example.

Configuration diagrams

A configuration diagram is any specialized semantic net which documents the overall structure of an application, layer or subdomain in terms of its component layers, subdomains and packages, their visibility (i.e. encapsulation), and the semantically important relationships among the component parts. A configuration diagram typically shows more detail than a context diagram, but less detail than a package diagram.

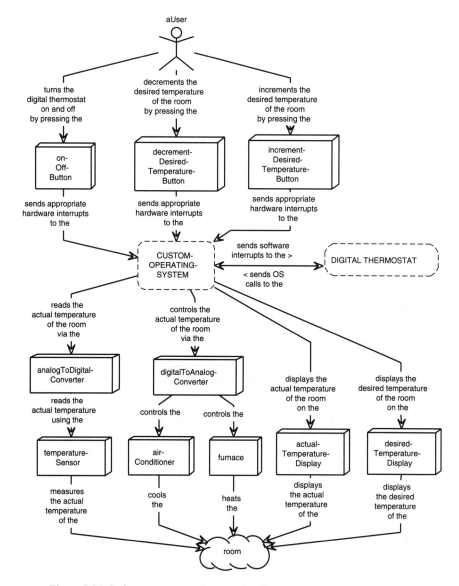

Figure I.21 Software context diagram for the digital thermostat example.

OML COMN recognizes the following two kinds of configuration diagrams:

- A *system configuration diagram* is any configuration diagram which documents an entire system consisting of hardware, software and possibly wetware (people) and paperware (documentation).

- A *software configuration diagram* is any configuration diagram which documents a software application, layer or subdomain.

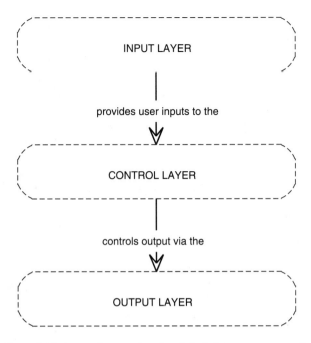

Figure I.22 Layer diagram for the digital thermostat example.

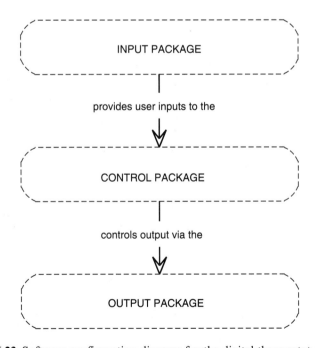

Figure I.23 Software configuration diagram for the digital thermostat example.

Figure I.23 documents the software configuration diagram of a digital thermostat. Because the digital thermostat software is so small and simple, each layer contains only a single package of the same name.

Package diagrams

A package diagram is any specialized semantic net which documents the static structure of a package, package instance, or mechanism in terms of its classes, types, roles and objects as well as the semantically meaningful relationships between them.

The primary intended audience for package diagrams consists of domain experts, architects, modelers and programmers.

Figure I.24 documents the overall package diagram of a digital thermostat. Because the software is so small and simple, a single package diagram is used to document all three packages. Whereas most of the objects were identified by the corresponding hardware objects that either control or are controlled by the software, the two custom operating system objects were introduced to provide independence from the actual custom operating system. The room object was introduced as the central coordinator object to encapsulate the attributes actualTemperature and desiredTemperature as well as the concurrent control-loop operation of the digital thermostat. In accordance with responsibility-driven design, the room object was also made proactive in that it actively seeks to maintain its actual temperature within an engineering tolerance of its desired temperature by controlling the air conditioner and furnace.

Inheritance diagrams

An inheritance diagram is any semantic net which documents the static structure of all or part (e.g. branch) of an inheritance graph.

The primary intended audience for inheritance diagrams consists of architects, modelers and programmers.

Figure I.25 documents the inheritance diagram of the Converter class hierarchy.

Deployment diagrams

A deployment diagram is any semantic net which documents the structure of hardware on which an application runs and the [static] allocation of the software (distribution units) to the hardware.

The primary intended audience for deployment diagrams consists of domain experts, architects and modelers.

Figure I.26 documents the deployment diagram of the digital thermostat including the computer on a chip and the client and server hardware devices. The rectangle attached to the bottom of the Digital Thermostat Computer node is a drop-down box used to document the distribution units allocated to it.

Use case diagrams

A use case diagram is any scenario class diagram[†] which documents one or more use cases, any associated externals that either use or are used by them, and the semantically important relationships between them.

[†] A *scenario class diagram* is any diagram which documents a set of collaborating scenario classes and invokes and precedes relationships between them. The other kinds of scenario class diagrams document the relationships between the other kinds of scenario classes (i.e. task scripts and mechanisms).

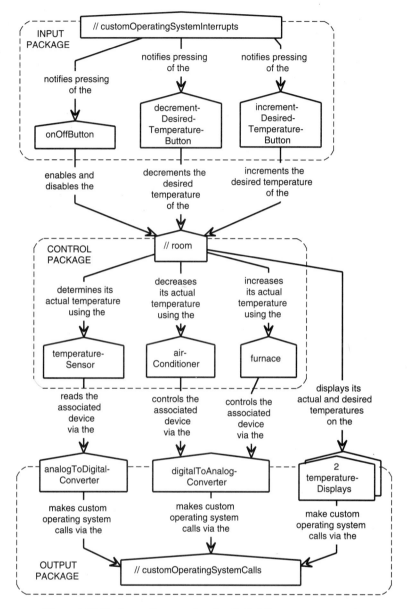

Figure I.24 Package diagram for the digital thermostat example.

The primary intended audience for use case diagrams consists of domain experts, users, customers, architects and modelers.

Figure I.27 documents the use case diagram of the digital thermostat including the single actor, the five use cases and the semantically important relationships between them. Because they are the only relationships that exist between externals and use cases, uses relationships do not need to be labeled.

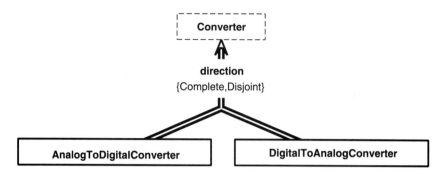

Figure I.25 Inheritance diagram for the Converter class.

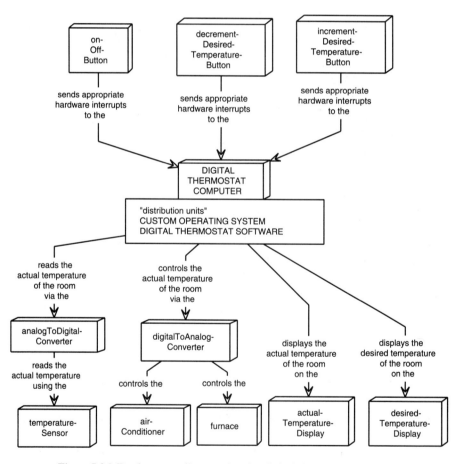

Figure I.26 Deployment diagram for the digital thermostat example.

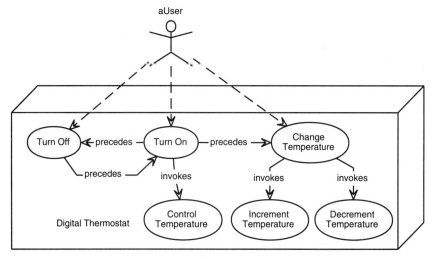

Figure I.27 Use case diagram for the digital thermostat example.

Interaction diagrams

An interaction diagram is any diagram which documents the interactions that are among externals and the application or among objects and classes within [part of] the application. The nodes of an interaction diagram represent either things or their timelines, and the arcs represent the interactions (messages, exceptions) between nodes. Interaction diagrams are either collaboration diagrams or sequence diagrams.

Collaboration diagrams

A collaboration diagram is any interaction diagram in the form of a graph, the purpose of which is to document the potential collaborations within a package of classes and objects in terms of the messages they may send and exceptions they may raise. Collaboration diagrams typically have the same nodes and topology as the corresponding package diagrams, but the arcs are labeled with messages and exceptions rather than with static relationships. If the associations, linkages, aggregation arcs and containment arcs on package diagrams are viewed as roads connecting the classes and objects, then the messages and exceptions on the collaboration diagrams can be viewed as the traffic on those roads.

In many cases, especially in concurrent situations, the ordering of this message and exception 'traffic' is important. Thus, the arcs on collaboration diagrams optionally can be labeled with sequence numbers. However, if the sequence of interactions is important, sequence diagrams are typically used instead of collaboration diagrams.

Package collaboration diagrams

A package collaboration diagram is any specialized collaboration diagram which documents the potential collaboration of a package of blackbox classes and objects in terms of the messages and exceptions they may send and throw.

The primary intended audience for package collaboration diagrams consists of modelers, architects, domain experts and programmers.

Figure I.28 documents the overall package collaboration diagram of the digital thermostat, including the objects in the three packages and the interactions (messages) between them.

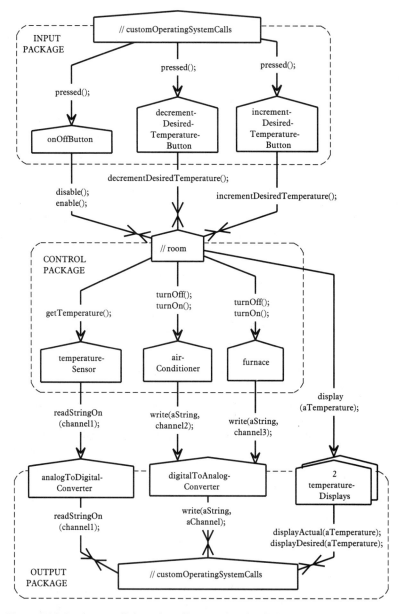

Figure I.28 Package collaboration diagram for the digital thermostat example.

Internal collaboration diagrams

An internal collaboration diagram is any collaboration diagram which documents the potential collaboration of operations within an individual class or object, in terms of control flow (i.e. message passing, exception throwing) and object flow (the reading and writing of properties within the class or object).

The primary intended audience for internal collaboration diagrams consists of modelers and programmers.

Figure I.29 documents the internal collaboration diagram for instances of the Room class, including operations, properties, and the interactions and object flows between them.

Sequence diagrams

A sequence diagram is any interaction diagram in the form of a 'fence' diagram which documents the sequence of interactions among either externals and the application or among objects within [part of] the application.

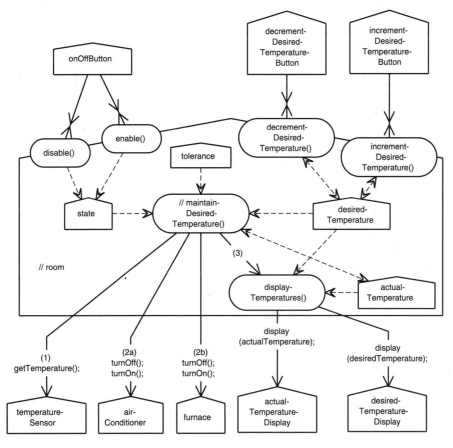

Figure I.29 Internal collaboration diagram for the instance of the Room class of the digital thermostat example.

Blackbox sequence diagrams

A blackbox sequence diagram is any sequence diagram which documents the sequence of interactions between externals and the blackbox system or software application involved in [part of] a use case. A blackbox sequence diagram treats the application as a blackbox and is used to capture user-oriented requirements, verify the context diagram and document an acceptance test case.

The primary intended audience for blackbox sequence diagrams consists of domain experts, users, architects and modelers.

Figure I.30 documents the blackbox sequence diagram of the Control Temperature use case, showing the collaborations between the user, the system and two server externals.

Whitebox sequence diagrams

A whitebox sequence diagram is any sequence diagram which documents the sequence of interactions among objects and classes involved in a single mechanism, design pattern, or [partial] path of a use case. A whitebox sequence diagram treats the application as a whitebox, showing the interactions among its internal objects. It is used to document dynamic behavior and document an integration test case.

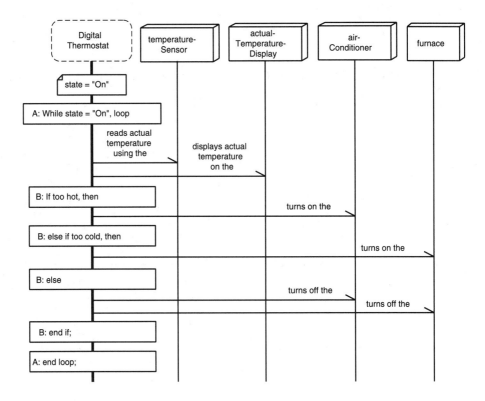

Figure I.30 Example blackbox sequence diagram for the use case: Control Temperature.

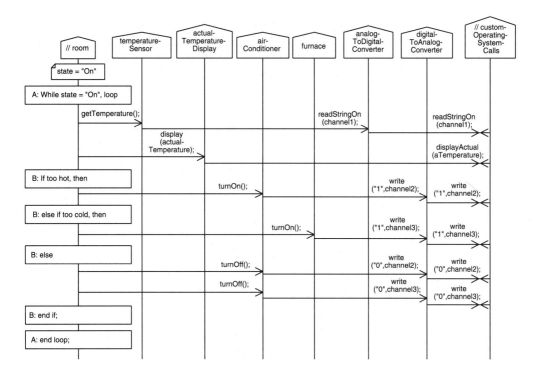

Figure I.31 Example whitebox sequence diagram for the use case: Control Temperature.

The primary intended audience for whitebox sequence diagrams consists of architects, modelers, and programmers.

Figure I.31 documents the whitebox sequence diagram of the Control Temperature use case, showing the interactions between the relevant objects.

State transition diagrams

A state transition diagram is any diagram consisting of a directed graph of states (nodes)[†] connected by transitions (directed arcs) which documents the common qualitative behavior (i.e. whether or not an operation executes or which path of a logic branch is taken) of the instances of a class. A state transition diagram describes the potential life history of objects of a given class, in terms of the ways they respond to interactions with (i.e. messages from, exceptions thrown by) other objects.

The primary intended audience for state transition diagrams consists of modelers and programmers.

[†]Although guard conditions are also graphed as nodes, they are better considered to be a part of the transition they control.

Figure I.32 documents the state transition diagram of the room object in the digital thermostat example. The operations disable, decrementDesired Temperature and incrementDesiredTemperature trigger group transitions, and maintainDesiredTemperature is a guarded transition.

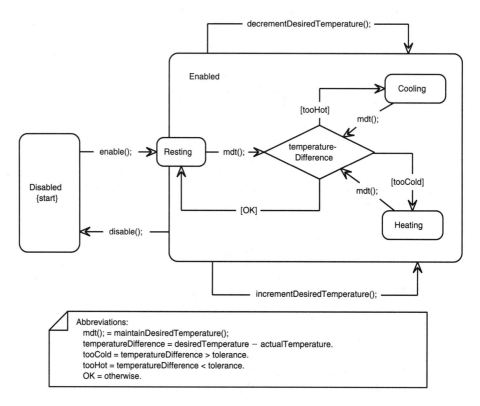

Figure I.32 State transition diagrams for the instance of the Room class of the digital thermostat example.

I-2 The OPEN development process

Object-Oriented Process, Environment and Notation, or OPEN as it is more commonly known, is a standard object-oriented development method that was developed and is maintained by the OPEN Consortium, an international organization of methodologists, commercial developers, academics and CASE tool vendors.

The OPEN process is actually a highly generic framework, consisting of large numbers of potential major *activities* which are decomposed into smaller *tasks* which are performed using *techniques* that produce *products*. Because of the large number of potential activities, tasks, techniques and products it provides, the OPEN process must be instantiated by selecting the specific activities, tasks, techniques and products best suited to meet the specific needs of the application and its development organization.

The vending machine software was analyzed, designed, coded and tested using the Firesmith Method, a compliant instantiation[†] of the OPEN Method. Because of the small size of the application, all of OPEN's development activities, tasks and techniques were not needed. The formal documentation of the vending machine software was documented in accordance with the OPEN Modeling Language (OML), as documented in the *OPEN Modeling Language Reference Manual*.

As illustrated in Figure I.33, the development cycle of the Firesmith Development Method uses an incremental, iterative and parallel development cycle. It is incremental in terms of builds and packages of classes, whereby packages are typically developed in a bottom-up dependency-based manner. It is iterative in that all of the models evolve through several iterations as knowledge increases and improvements are discovered. It is parallel in that layers, subdomains and packages are typically developed by different teams working in parallel.

The reader should recognize that there should be a great deal of overlap in the above activities and tasks due to the incremental, iterative and parallel nature of the object-oriented development cycle. For example, classes should be prototyped as they are designed. With experience, teams will learn to optimize the ordering of activities and tasks for the current work at hand.

I-2.1 Initial Planning and Development

The Initial Planning and Development activity occurs once at the beginning of the development of the application. The architecture team prepares for the Build Development activity by performing the following tasks:

[†]Although the Firesmith Method merged with SOMA and MOSES to create OPEN, it also lives on as OPEN/Firesmith, the name of the specific OPEN instantiation and tailoring recommended by Donald Firesmith.

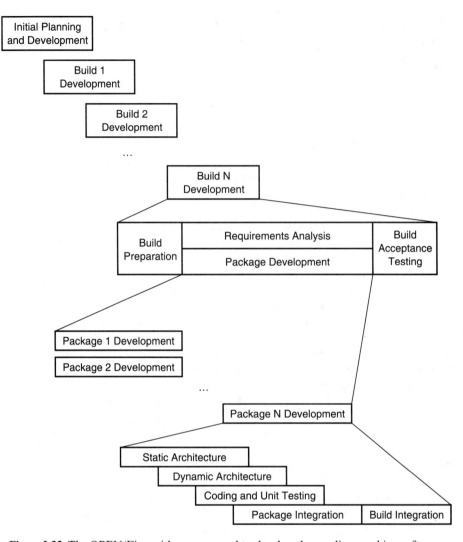

Figure I.33 The OPEN/Firesmith process used to develop the vending machine software.

1. *Document the Background.* During this task, the background of the application, its history and its business objectives are identified and documented. The kind of application (e.g. MIS, embedded), the kind of project (e.g. initial development, update, replacement of one or more existing applications), and the experience level of the development organization are determined.

2. *Initial Training.* During this task, the architecture team is trained in the OPEN Method including process, modeling language, implementation language, guidelines and metrics.

3. *Tailor the Method.* During this task, the architecture team selects the specific activities, tasks, techniques and products to be developed from those available within the OPEN framework.

4. *Model the Context.* During this task, the context of the application is developed and documented using the following subtask and technique:

   - *External object identification.* During this subtask, external objects are identified using techniques such as the following:
     - Identify an external object for each hardware device that either controls or is controlled by the application.
     - Identify an external object (actor) for each role played by a human that interacts with the application.
     - Identify an external object for each external system, application, or database that interacts with the application.

   - *Semantic modeling.* Using this technique, the context of the application is identified and documented in the following products:
     - System context diagram. This product documents the interface of the system in terms of its externals and the semantically important relationships between them.
     - Software context diagram. This product documents the interface of the software in terms of its externals and the semantically important relationships between them.
     - External specifications. These products document the individual external objects identified on the context diagrams.

5. *Capture the Initial Requirements.* During this task, the initial requirements are elicited and analyzed using the following techniques:

   - *JAD/RAD modeling.* Requirements are elicited, analyzed, and specified during joint application development (JAD)/rapid application development (RAD) sessions including domain experts, users and modelers.

   - *Interviews.* Requirements are elicited and analyzed during interviews with individual domain experts and users.

   - *Textual modeling.* This technique produces the following product:
     - Textual requirements. These products document the requirements of the application associated with non-actor externals.

   - *Use case modeling.* This technique produces the following products:
     - Use case diagrams. These products document the semantically important relationships between use cases and their associated externals.
     - Use case specifications. These products specify individual use cases including descriptions, associated externals, primary and alternative paths, preconditions, statements, and postconditions.
     - Blackbox sequence diagrams. These products document individual use cases as interactions between external objects and the application.

6. *Create the Initial Architecture.* The initial architecture forms the foundation for the following *Build Development* activity. During this task, an initial architecture of the application is developed and documented using the following subtasks and techniques:

- *Identify key abstractions.* During this subtask, objects, classes, types and roles are identified using object identification techniques such as the following:
  - Identify internal objects that correspond to and model each external object on a context diagram.
  - Identify an internal class, type, or role for each concept that is important to the application.
  - Identify objects, classes, types, and roles that correspond to the nouns and noun phrases in either textual requirements or descriptions.
  - Identify objects, classes, and types that correspond to the states of the application and its components.

- *Assign key abstractions to packages.* During this subtask, the key abstractions are assigned to initial packages based on cohesion and coupling characteristics.

- *Assign packages to layers.* During this subtask, the packages are assigned to layers.

- *Semantic modeling.* Using this technique, the initial architecture of the application is identified and documented in the following products:
  - Layer diagram. This product documents the overall configuration of the application in terms of its component packages.
  - Configuration diagram(s). These products document the overall configuration of each layer in terms of its component packages.
  - Deployment diagram. This product documents the overall configuration of the application in terms of its component hardware and the allocation of the software to the hardware.
  - Package diagrams. These products document the static architecture of the initial packages.

- *Responsibility-Driven Design (RDD).* Using this technique, the responsibilities and associated collaborators of components are identified and documented using the following products:
  - Class Responsibility Collaborator (CRC) cards. These products document the descriptions, responsibilities and collaborators of the classes or types, packages and roles of the application.

- *Interaction modeling.* Using this technique, the interactions are identified and documented using the following products:
  - Whitebox sequence diagrams. These products document the individual use cases as interactions between internal objects and roles.
  - Model verification. This technique is used to verify the products of semantic and collaboration modeling against the products of use case modeling. Specifically, the context diagrams are verified against the

blackbox sequence diagrams, and package diagrams and package collaboration diagrams are verified against the whitebox sequence diagrams for completeness and correctness.

7. *Document the Initial Products.* During this task, the initial requirements and architecture are specified and documented in the *requirements specification and design document* which, when completed, will document all of the requirements, design and testing information of the application.

8. *Scope the Application.* During this task, the scope of the application in terms of size (e.g. number of packages, number of classes) and required effort (e.g. number of person months) is estimated based on the initial architecture and the estimated productivity of the development team.

9. *Plan Build Development.* During this task, the initial builds and releases of the application are scheduled and documented in the *build plan*, which documents the planned schedule and capabilities of the upcoming builds.

Although the above tasks are listed in the rough order in which they occur, there is a great amount of overlap and iteration among them. This is especially true of the Capture the Initial Requirements and Create the Initial Architecture tasks. Due to the functional nature of use case modeling, use cases should be used more for verification purposes than for requirements analysis purposes.

I-2.2 Build Development

During the Build Development activity, the build development team performs the following tasks and subactivities:

1. *Build Preparation.* During this task, the build development team prepares to develop the build by performing the following subtasks:
   - Update the relevant requirements. During this task, any changes in requirements since the previous build are identified and analyzed for relevance to the current build.
   - Schedule the build. During this task, the development milestones of the current build are scheduled.
   - Update the build plan. During this task, the build plan is updated with information concerning the current build as well as the next few builds, as appropriate.

2. *Requirements Analysis.* This subactivity is performed in accordance with I-2.2.1 below.

3. *Package Development.* This subactivity is performed in accordance with I-2.2.2 below.

4. *Verify the Packages and Use Cases.* During this task, the consistency of the package and use case models is verified on an ongoing basis.

5. *Build Acceptance Testing*. During this task, acceptance testing of the build is performed using the following technique:
   - Use case testing. During this technique, the paths of the use cases are executed and the actual behavior is compared with the expected behavior.

I-2.2.1 Requirements Analysis

Precondition: Build Preparation has been started.
During the Requirements Analysis subactivity, the requirements team(s) perform the following tasks:

1. *Requirements Elicitation*. During this task, the relevant requirements are elicited using the following techniques:

   - *JAD/RAD sessions*. Requirements are elicited during joint application development / rapid application development sessions including domain experts, users, and modelers.

   - *Interviews*. Requirements are elicited and analyzed during interviews with individual domain experts and users.

2. *Requirements Analysis and Specification*. During this task, the relevant requirements are analyzed and specified using the following techniques:

   - *JAD/RAD sessions*. Requirements are analyzed and specified during joint application development/rapid application development sessions including domain experts, users, and modelers.

   - *Textual modeling*. This technique produces the following product:
     - Textual requirements. These products document the requirements of the application associated with non-actor externals.

   - *Use case modeling*. This technique produces the following products:
     - Use case diagrams. These products document the semantically important relationships between use cases and their associated externals.
     - Use case specifications. These products specify individual use cases including descriptions, associated externals, primary and alternative paths, preconditions, statements, and postconditions.
     - Blackbox sequence diagrams. These products document individual use cases as interactions between external objects and the application.

   - *Model verification*. This technique is used to verify the products of semantic and collaboration modeling against the products of use case modeling. Specifically, the context diagrams are verified against the blackbox sequence diagrams, and package diagrams and package collaboration diagrams are verified against the whitebox sequence diagrams for completeness and correctness.

I-2.2.2 Package Development

Precondition: Build Preparation has been started.
During the Package Development subactivity, the package teams develop,

document and integrate the packages in the build. The following tasks are performed in a highly iterative, incremental and parallel (i.e. different packages are concurrently developed by different package development teams) manner:

1. *Identify the packages.* This task is performed on an ongoing basis and consists of the following subtasks:

   - *Identify key abstractions.* During this subtask, objects, types, roles and classes are identified.

   - *Assign key abstractions to packages.* During this subtask, the key abstractions are assigned to packages using the following techniques:
     - Maximize package cohesion. Each package should capture a single abstraction.
     - Base packages on collaboration rather than inheritance. Packages should consist of collaborating classes rather than branches of inheritance hierarchies.
     - Minimize package to package coupling. Minimize the public interface of packages in terms of public components and the interactions across package boundaries.

2. *Model the Package Static Architecture.* This task is performed on a package by package basis, using the following techniques:

   - *Semantic modeling.* Using this technique, the components of a package, their visibility and the semantic relationships between them are identified and documented in the following products:
     - Package diagram. This product documents the static architecture of the package.
     - Inheritance diagram(s). These products document the inheritance structure of the package classes, types, object classes, and roles.

   - *Responsibility-Driven Design (RDD).* Using this technique, the responsibilities and associated collaborators of components are identified and documented using the following products:
     - Class Responsibility Collaborator (CRC) cards. These products document the descriptions, responsibilities, and collaborators of the classes or types, packages, and roles of the application.

   - *Patterns.* Patterns and frameworks are used where appropriate.

   Package diagrams and CRC cards are typically the first techniques used during package development and are best used in conjunction with one another. Inheritance diagrams are usually developed later in package modeling and are subject to extensive iteration due to refactoring.

3. *Model the Package Dynamic Architecture.*
   Precondition: Model the Static Architecture has started. This task is performed on a package by package basis, using the following techniques:

   - *Collaboration modeling.* Using this technique, the interactions between and within the classes are identified and documented in the following products:

- Package collaboration diagram. This product documents the collaboration of elements in the package or package instance. It is developed and verified against the package diagram and relevant CRC cards, possibly via role playing.
- Internal collaboration diagram(s). These products are developed for each class having adequate internal complexity in terms of operations and properties to justify their development and maintenance.
- Whitebox sequence diagrams. These products document the individual use cases as interactions between internal objects and roles.

- *Class modeling.* Using this technique, the classes are documented in the following product:
  - Class specifications. This product consists of class comments documenting the description, stereotypes, utility, responsibilities and characteristics of the class.

- *State modeling.* Using this technique, the state behavior of the classes is identified and documented in the following product:
  - State transition diagram(s). These products are developed for each class having significant state behavior.

4. *Coding and Unit Testing*
   Precondition: Model the Dynamic Architecture has started.
   This task is performed on a class by class basis and consists of the following subtasks:

   - *Class coding.* The package and its classes and interfaces are coded using the following techniques:
     - Coding standards. The software is developed using, and verified against, approved coding standards.
     - Idioms. The idioms of the implementation language are followed.
     - Dependency-based coding. The classes in the package are coded bottom-up in dependency order in accordance with the dependency-based coding pattern.

   - *Class testing.* The classes in the package are unit tested using the following techniques:
     - Dependency-based testing. The classes in the package are tested bottom-up in dependency order in accordance with the dependency-based testing pattern.
     - State-based testing. This technique uses state-based testing patterns (e.g. Every Operation in Every State) to develop class test cases.

5. *Package Integration.*
   Precondition: Coding and Unit Testing has started.
   This task is performed on a package by package basis. During this task, the classes in the package are integrated and tested as a unit.

6. *Build Integration.* During this task, the package is integrated into the growing build.

I-3 Documentation standard

The following is a content and format standard for the development/maintenance documentation of object-oriented software applications. This standard is strictly for development/maintenance documentation of software applications. It requires non-trivial tailoring when used for the documentation of:

- object-oriented *systems* consisting of software, hardware, wetware (i.e. personnel), and paperware (i.e. documentation),
- user documentation such as user manuals, and
- frameworks because the standard does not include subsections on how a framework is intended to be extended and instantiated for inclusion in an application.

It assumes that the documented software is developed in accordance with an instantiation of the OPEN Method and is modeled using the OPEN Modeling Language (OML) Common Object Modeling Notation (COMN).

This document covers requirements, design and testing, and is thereby consistent with the incremental, iterative and parallel OPEN/Firesmith development cycle with its highly overlapping activities. However, it organizes these topics into separate chapters based on activities as an aid for human understanding.

I-3.1 Cover page

The requirements specification and design document shall have a cover page that identifies the application documented, the date, the version number, the development organization, and the development team where practical.

I-3.2 Table of contents

The requirements specification and design document shall have a table of contents.

I-3.3 Overview

This section, numbered 1, shall provide an overview of the document.

I-3.3.1 *Description of the application*

This subsection, numbered 1.1, shall briefly describe the application documented.

I-3.3.2 *Purpose of this document*

This subsection, numbered 1.2, shall briefly describe the purpose of the document including scope (e.g. requirements, design, testing).

I-3.3.3 *Development method used*

This subsection, numbered 1.3, shall identify the object-oriented development method and CASE tools used to produce the contents of this document. This subsection may be included by reference to a separate organizational or project document.

I-3.4 Requirements specification

This section, numbered 2, shall specify the requirements of the application using context diagrams, use case diagrams, textual requirements and use case specifications. Additional diagrams, such as state transition diagrams, may be included where appropriate.

I-3.4.1 *Context diagrams*

This subsection, numbered 2.1, shall document the context of the application in terms of its externals and the semantically important relationships between the externals and the application.

System context diagram(s)

This subsection, numbered 2.1.1, shall contain the system context diagram(s) documenting the context of the system in terms of its externals and the semantically important relationships between the externals and the system. This subsection is optional if the application is totally software and the software is the system.

Software context diagram(s)

This subsection, numbered 2.1.2 (or 2.1.1 if the system context diagram(s) are omitted), shall contain the software context diagram(s) documenting the context of the software in terms of its externals and the semantically important relationships between the externals and the software.

I-3.4.2 *Scenario class diagram(s)*

This subsection, numbered 2.2, shall contain either the use case diagram(s) documenting the use cases or the task script diagram(s) documenting the task scripts of the application.

I-3.4.3 *Capability requirements*

This subsection, numbered 2.3, shall document the formal requirements (which may include system-level requirements, system-level design decisions and software-specific requirements) of the application in a user-oriented manner, organized hierarchically by the external to which they refer. For each external, this subsection shall include a description of the external, the responsibilities of the external, the formal requirements allocated to the external and, where appropriate, the corresponding blackbox scenario class (e.g. use case) specifications and state transition diagrams. Each use case specification shall include a description of the use case, the formal requirements allocated to the use case, the client, peer and server externals involved in the use case, any preconditions of the use case, the statements of the use case (either textual or in the form of blackbox sequence diagrams)[†], and the postconditions of the use case.

I-3.4.4 *Quality requirements*

This subsection, numbered 2.4, shall document the quality requirements of the application, organized into further subsections by the relevant quality factors such as reusability, extensibility and maintainability.

I-3.4.5 *Requirement trace to concrete classes*

This subsection, numbered 2.5, shall provide a trace of the requirements to the concrete classes.

I-3.5 Design document

This section, numbered 3, shall document the design of the application in terms of its layered architecture, its layers and their packages, classes and interfaces. It shall include a layer diagram and a comprehensive configuration diagram if the total number of packages is small.

I-3.5.1 *Layer L*

Each of these subsections, numbered 3.L (beginning with 3.1), shall document an individual layer of the application. It should include a configuration diagram if the layer contains more than two packages.

I-3.5.1.1 Packages

This subsection, numbered 3.L.1, shall document the packages comprising the layer.

Package P

Each of these subsections, numbered 3.L.1.P (beginning with 3.1.1.1), shall document an individual package in the corresponding layer. It shall document the static architecture of the package with a package diagram and the dynamic

---

[†]Because blackbox scenario class specifications may include structured text that duplicates some or all of the information on the blackbox sequence diagrams, the document may contain the structured text, the sequence diagram, or both.

architecture of the package with a package collaboration diagram. It shall also document the major design decisions of the package and the rationale behind them.

Class C

Each of these subsections, numbered 3.L.1.P.C (beginning with 3.1.1.1.1), shall document an individual class in the corresponding package. It shall include (possibly by reference to a javadoc-compliant class concept) a class specification documenting the description of the class, the class stereotypes and utilities, the superclass(es) of the class, the responsibilities of the class and the characteristics of the class. Where cost effective and appropriate, it shall include an inheritance diagram, an internal collaboration diagram, a state transition diagram and a screen shot (if a presentation class in a graphical user interface).

Requirement trace from the classes

This subsection, numbered 3.X.3, may provide a trace of the classes of the layer to the requirements that they completely or partially implement.

Distribution

This optional subsection, numbered 3.Y, shall document the distribution of the software including the allocation of distribution units to processors and processes in a distributed application. Where appropriate, it shall include one or more distribution diagrams.

Previous architectures

This optional subsection, numbered 3.Z, shall summarize the previous architectures (e.g. using configuration diagrams or package diagrams) and provide a discussion of both the major improvements it provided over older versions and its major known weaknesses corrected in more recent versions.

I-3.6 Testing

This section, numbered 4, shall document the testing approach, test harness architecture and test classes, used to test the application.

I-3.6.1 Testing approach

This subsection, numbered 4.1, shall document the approaches used to perform class, package, and acceptance testing.

Model verification using whitebox sequence diagrams

This subsection, numbered 4.1.1, shall document the approach used to verify the requirements and design models. This subsection may include a description, the requirements verified, the primary and secondary paths, any preconditions, implementation language-specific pseudocode, corresponding whitebox sequence diagrams, and any postconditions, as appropriate. (Because whitebox scenario class specification may include structured text that duplicates some or all of the information on the whitebox sequence diagrams, the document may contain either the structured text, the sequence diagram, or both.)

Class/package testing
This subsection, numbered 4.1.2, shall briefly describe the approach used to perform class and package testing.

Acceptance testing
This subsection, numbered 4.1.3, shall briefly describe the approach used to perform acceptance testing.

I-3.6.2 Test harness architecture
This subsection, numbered 4.3, shall document the architecture of the test harness used to test the application.

Test classes
This subsection, numbered 4.3.1, shall document the test classes.

I-3.6.3 Tests
This subsection, numbered 4.4, shall document the tests use to verify and validate the application.

I-3.7 Appendices

The appendices shall provide the following ancillary information, either directly or by reference to separate documents.

I-3.7.1 Summary of the development process
This appendix, labeled A, shall provide a brief summary of the development process used to create the document.

I-3.7.2 Summary of the modeling language
This appendix, labeled B, shall provide a summary of the modeling language used to capture the contents of the document.

I-3.7.3 Glossary
This appendix, numbered C, shall provide a glossary of terms used in the document.

I-3.7.4 Documentation standard
This appendix, numbered D, shall contain the content and format standards to which the document conforms.

Part II

Object-Oriented Documentation for the Mark I Vending Machine (MIVM) Software

4 March 1998

Version 3.0

Developed for:
MegaVending Corporation
123 Main Street, Gotham City, New York

Developed by:
Knowledge Systems Corporation
4001 Weston Parkway, Cary, North Carolina

Development team:
Donald G. Firesmith: team leader, modeler, Smalltalk and Java coder
Scott A. Krutsch: modeler and reviewer
Marshall Stowe: Java coder
Gregg Hendley: Smalltalk coder and reviewer

Overview

1.1 Description of the application

The Mark I Vending Machine (MIVM), MegaVending Corporation's pilot project using object technology, is a user-friendly vending machine supporting the needs of both customers and service representatives. Initially implemented in Smalltalk, it has been redesigned and implemented in Java.

The MIVM software permits customers to buy items and permits service representatives to both price items and display history information. Its software is controlled by and controls a large number of hardware devices. The MIVM houses an assembly of up to 80 item dispensers organized in a matrix of 10 columns (selected by number selection buttons) and 8 rows (selected by letter selection buttons). A refund button causes the refund of the customer's credit, and a mode button allows service representatives to change the mode (i.e. state) of the MIVM from 'Set Price' to 'Display History' to 'Dispense Item' and back. Change is dispensed by a coin dispenser assembly containing nickel, dime and quarter dispensers. Item displays on each item dispenser display the location and common price of the items, whereas the main display displays all other customer and service representative information.

1.1.1 Customers

The primary purpose of the vending machine is to sell items to customers. A customer may also request a refund from the vending machine.

1.1.1.1 Buying an item

A customer buys an item by performing the following actions:

- *Make a selection.* A customer makes a selection by selecting the corresponding column and row of the item dispenser assembly. A customer selects a column by pressing one of the ten number selection buttons labeled 1 through 10. A customer selects a row by pressing one of the eight letter selection buttons labeled A through H.
- *Make a payment.* A customer pays for a selection by inserting either dollar bills into the bill validator or nickels, dimes or quarters into the coin validator.

The preceding actions can be performed in any order and may even overlap. For example, a customer can select a column, select a row, insert some change, realize that he does not have enough money, select a new column, and select a new row. When an item has been selected and paid for, the vending machine dispenses the item, dispenses any change due the customer (if possible), thanks the customer and displays a greeting for the next customer.

1.1.1.2 Requesting a refund

At any time, the customer can request a refund by pressing the refund button, upon which the vending machine dispenses the customer's credit (if any), thanks the customer and displays a greeting for the next customer.

1.1.1.3 Displaying information to customers

The main display displays:

- The greeting 'HAVE A NICE DAY' until a customer interacts with the vending machine.
- The price of the item if both column and row have been selected, and no money has been inserted.
- The amount due (i.e. the price minus the customer's credit) if both column and row have been selected, money has been inserted, but the selection has not yet been paid for.
- Otherwise, the last customer action:
  — A customer's credit.
  — The column selected.
  — The row selected.
- 'THANK YOU' for two seconds once an item has been selected and paid for.
- The greeting 'HAVE A NICE DAY' after a customer has been thanked (if the vending machine could dispense all valid kinds of coins and all of the change due to the customer was dispensed).
- A customer's credit if the vending machine could not dispense all of the change due to the customer.
- The warning 'EXACT CHANGE ONLY' if the vending machine could not dispense all valid kinds of coins.

1.1.2 Service representatives

By unlocking the front door of the MIVM, service representatives can service the vending machine by loading the item dispensers, loading the coin dispensers, emptying the money boxes, pricing the items and displaying history information.

1.1.2.1 Changing the mode

The vending machine has three modes: 'Dispense Item', 'Set Price', and 'Display History'. A service representative changes the mode of the vending machine by pressing the mode button until the desired mode is displayed on the main display. In order to ensure that the service representative leaves the machine in the 'Dispense Item' mode, the vending machine is automatically set to the 'Dispense Item' mode when the door is closed and locked.

1.1.2.2 Pricing the items

A service representative prices the items in an item dispenser by:

1. Placing the vending machine in the 'Set Price' mode. The main display will display 'SET PRICE'.

2. Selecting a column. The main display will display the selected column.
3. Selecting a row. The main display will display the selected location.
4. Building a price by repeatedly pressing the number selection buttons. The corresponding main display will display the location and new price.
5. Entering the new price by pressing the 'E' letter selection button. The corresponding item display will display the new price and the main display will display 'ENTERED'.

The service representative may accept the old price by pressing the 'A' letter selection button immediately before building the new price. The main display will display 'ACCEPTED'.

The service representative may cancel the price change by pressing the 'C' letter selection button immediately after building the new price. The main display will display 'CANCELED'.

The vending machine will reject the new price if the new price would prohibit the coin dispenser assembly from being able to make change (e.g. the new price is not evenly divisible by five cents). The main display will display 'REJECTED'.

The vending machine shall ignore all inappropriate buttons during this process. If money is inserted into either money validator when the vending machine is in the 'Set Price' mode, the vending machine shall place itself into the 'Dispense Item' mode.

1.1.2.3 Displaying history information

A service representative may display history information by:

1. Placing the vending machine in the 'Display History' mode. The main display will display 'DISPLAY HISTORY'.
2. Pressing the 'A' letter selection button. The main display will display the total number of items sold by the vending machine.
3. Pressing the 'B' letter selection button. The main display will display the total income from the vending machine.

The vending machine shall ignore all inappropriate buttons during this process. If money is inserted into the money validators when the vending machine is in the 'Display History' mode, the vending machine shall place itself into the 'Dispense Item' mode.

1.2 Purpose of this document

The purpose of this document is to capture in one place the as-built requirements, design and testing information for the Mark I Vending Machine. It is intended to be a living document that evolves as the application evolves, supporting both initial development and ongoing maintenance. As such, its scope includes all information not readily obtained from lowerCASE tools such as javadoc and language-specific browsers.

1.3 Development method used

The MIVM software was developed using the Firesmith instantiation of the Object-oriented Process, Environment, and Notation (OPEN) Method and documented using the associated OPEN Modeling Language (OML) and its Common Object Modeling Notation (COMN).

2 Requirements specification

The purpose of this section is to specify the requirements of the MIVM software using context diagrams, use case diagrams, textual requirements and use case specifications including blackbox sequence diagrams. Although the requirements have been collected together into a single section of this document, this is for understandability and documentation purposes only! An iterative, incremental, parallel development cycle was used so that the requirements, design, coding and testing actually occurred in parallel.

2.1 Context diagrams

The purpose of this subsection is to document the context of the MIVM software in terms of its externals, whereby an external:

- is an object that is outside the MIVM software and
- interacts with the MIVM software, either directly or indirectly.

Context diagrams document the association/linkage relationships between the MIVM and its externals and any simplifying relationships (e.g. inheritance, aggregation, association/linkage) among the externals.

2.1.1 Context diagram of the MIVM system
The context of the MIVM system is illustrated in Figure 2.1 by a system context diagram, which documents the blackbox MIVM system and its two main externals: customers and service representatives. Notice that customers and service representatives are roles played by people interacting with the MIVM system.

2.1.2 Context diagram of the MIVM software
The context of the MIVM software is illustrated in Figure 2.2 by a software context diagram, which documents the context of the MIVM software and its externals: the custom operating system, the hardware input and output devices, and the human actors. Clients are drawn above servers to illustrate the top-down flow of control.

2.2 Use case diagrams

The functional requirements of the MIVM software are documented by the use case diagrams in Figures 2.3 and 2.4. Figure 2.3 documents the use cases involving customers of the MIVM, and Figure 2.4 documents the use cases involving the service representatives. Note that use case diagrams need not document all intermediate externals (e.g. the custom operating system).

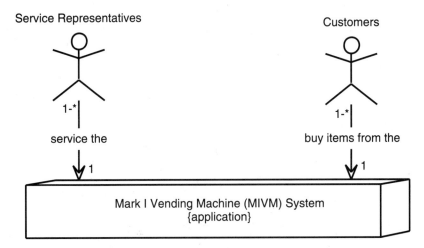

Figure 2.1 System context diagram for the Mark I Vending Machine.

In order to minimize redundancy, the main use cases have been functionally decomposed into lower-level sub-use cases. Because use cases are functional rather than object-oriented, this functional decomposition is reasonable for use cases. However, the functional decomposition of use cases can lead to a functional decomposition design if use cases drive the design. Therefore, the initial static architecture was developed before too much work was done on the use cases, and use cases were primarily used to verify and validate the object-oriented design rather than to derive it.

2.3 Capability requirements

The purpose of this subsection is to formally document the required capabilities of the MIVM software in an object-oriented manner, organized by the external object to which they refer.

The requirements for each *hardware external* are documented in terms of the following:

- A brief description describing the abstraction of the external.
- The high-level responsibilities and their corresponding collaborators allocated to the external.
- The formal textual requirements allocated to the external. These textual requirements are categorized into the following three varieties:
  - System-level requirements (SYS-R), which are blackbox requirements for the system as a whole and were developed during system requirements analysis.
  - System-level design decisions (SYS-D), which constrain the design of the software and were developed during system-level design.
  - Software requirements (SW-R), which are software-specific blackbox requirements and were developed during software requirements analysis.

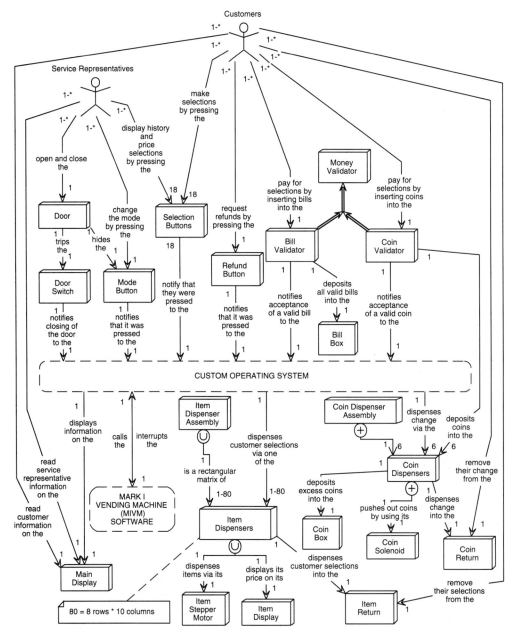

Figure 2.2 Software context diagram for the Mark I Vending Machine.

The requirements for each *actor external* are documented in terms of the following:

- A brief description describing the abstraction of the actor.
- The high-level responsibilities and their corresponding collaborators allocated to the actor.

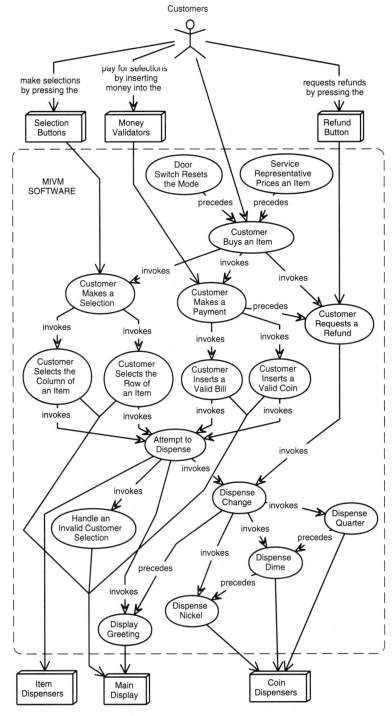

Figure 2.3 Partial use case diagram containing customer use cases of the Mark I Vending Machine Software.

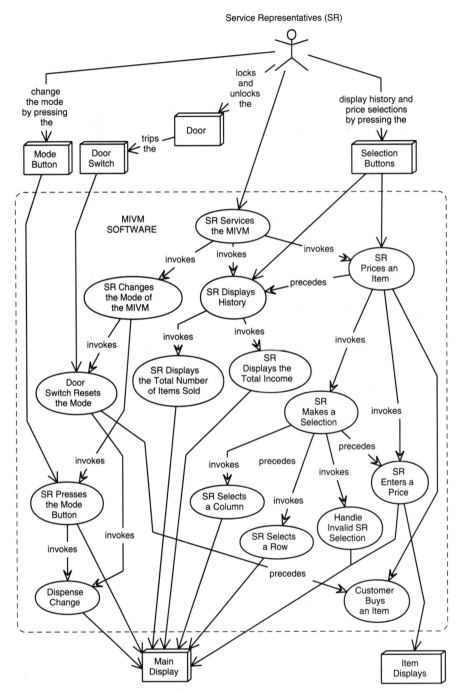

Figure 2.4 Partial Use Case Diagram containing the Service representative use cases of the Mark I Vending Machine Software.

- Use case specifications for each use case initiated by the actor. Each use case specification captures the following information:
  - A brief description of the functional abstraction of the use case.
  - The detailed, formal textual requirements allocated to the use case.
  - A list of the client, peer and server externals participating in the use case.
  - An identification of the primary and alternative paths through the use case, which will be used later to identify test case usage scenarios.
  - Any preconditions that must be satisfied before the use case can execute.
  - Statements in English with pseudocode specifying the logic of the use case.
  - A blackbox sequence diagram illustrating the interactions between the externals and the software that make up the use case.
  - A set of postconditions ensured by the execution of the use case, organized by path.

The software requirements for the MIVM software organized by direct and indirect externals[†] as follows:

2.3.1 Actuators:
2.3.1.1 Coin Solenoids
2.3.1.2 Item Stepper Motors
2.3.2 Buttons:
2.3.2.1 Letter Selection Buttons
2.3.2.2 Mode Button
2.3.2.3 Number Selection Buttons
2.3.2.4 Refund Button
2.3.3 Custom Circuit Board
2.3.4 Custom Operating System:
2.3.4.1 Custom Operating System Calls
2.3.4.2 Custom Operating System Interrupts
2.3.5 Dispensers:
2.3.5.1 Coin Dispensers
2.3.5.2 Item Dispensers
2.3.6 Dispenser Assemblies:
2.3.6.1 Coin Dispenser Assembly
2.3.6.2 Item Dispenser Assembly
2.3.7 Displays:
2.3.7.1 Item Displays
2.3.7.2 Main Display
2.3.8 Door
2.3.9 Door Switch
2.3.10 Money Validators:
2.3.10.1 Bill Validator
2.3.10.2 Coin Validator
2.3.11 Vending Machine Roles:
2.3.11.1 Customers
2.3.11.2 Service Representatives

[†] Note that the externals BillBox, CoinBox, CoinReturn and ItemReturn are not included because they have no associated software.

2.3.1 Actuators

Definition: a mechanical device for moving or controlling something.

Kind: indirect abstract server external[†].

Responsibility:
- Move something.
  Collaborator: none.

2.3.1.1 Coin Solenoids (CS)

Definition: an actuator that pushes coins out of a coin dispenser when electric current is applied.

Kind: indirect concrete server external.

Comment: The coin solenoids are the only parts of the coin dispenser assembly that are electrically connected to and directly controlled by software.

Responsibilities:
- Push the bottom coin out of the coin dispenser when requested by a custom operating system call.
  Collaborator: none.
- Throw a hardware exception if the coin dispenser was empty when the custom operating system makes a request.
  Collaborator: none.

Requirements:
  SYS-D) CS-1.
  If requested by a custom operating system call to push out the bottom coin of its coin dispenser, a coin solenoid shall do so if the coin dispenser is not empty.
  SYS-D) CS-2.
  If requested by a custom operating system call to push out the bottom coin of its coin dispenser, a coin solenoid shall throw an exception if the coin dispenser is empty. (When the coin solenoid touches the bottom coin, it completes an electrical circuit signaling the existence of the coin.) If that circuit is not made, then no coin exists and the coin dispenser is empty.)

2.3.1.2 Item Stepper Motors (ISM)

Definition: a stepper motor, the driveshaft of which rotates in small discrete steps, used for dispensing items.

Kind: indirect concrete server external.

Responsibility:
- Dispense an item if requested by a custom operating system call.
  Collaborator: none.

[†] Actually, externals are *models* of the corresponding real-world things and concepts, but this distinction is largely academic and irrelevant at this level of development.

Requirements:
SYS-D) ISM-1.
If requested by a custom operating system call, the item stepper motor shall push the next item out of its item dispenser by causing its spiral wire to rotate once, pushing the item off the end of the wire.
SYS-D) ISM-2.
Due to hardware cost considerations, there is no sensor allowing the item stepper motor to know if it has in fact dropped an item into the item return. It is possible that the item hung at the end of the wire or that the item dispenser was empty.

2.3.2 Buttons (B)

Definition: a button used as an input device of the MIVM.

Kind: indirect abstract client external.

Responsibility:
• Interrupt the custom operating system when pressed.
  Collaborator: Custom Operating System.

Requirements:
SYS-D) B-1.
When a button is pressed, it shall cause a button-specific interrupt to the custom operating system.

2.3.2.1 Letter Selection Buttons (LSB)

Definition: one of the eight buttons used by a customer or service representative to select a letter.

Kind: indirect concrete client external.

Responsibility:
• Interrupt the custom operating system when pressed, specifying the letter selected.
  Collaborator: Custom Operating System.

Requirements:
SYS-D) LSB-1.
There shall be 8 letter selection buttons labeled 'A' through 'H'.
SYS-D) LSB-2.
When a letter selection button is pressed, it shall interrupt the custom operating system, specifying the letter selected.

2.3.2.2 Mode Button (MB)

Definition: a button used by the service representative to change the mode of the vending machine.

Kind: indirect concrete client external.

Responsibility:
- Interrupt the custom operating system when pressed, specifying the mode button.
  Collaborator: Custom Operating System.

Requirements:

SYS-R) MB-1.
The modes of the MIVM shall be 'Dispense Item', 'Set Price' and 'Display History'.

SYS-R) MB-2.
Upon being plugged into an electrical outlet, the initial mode of the MIVM shall be 'Set Price'.

SYS-D) MB-3.
When the mode button is pressed, it shall interrupt the custom operating system, specifying that the mode button was pressed.

SYS-R) MB-4.
If the MIVM is in the 'Set Price' mode when the mode button is pressed, then the MIVM shall change to the 'Display History' mode.

SYS-R) MB-5.
If the MIVM is in the 'Display History' mode when the mode button is pressed, then the MIVM shall change to the 'Dispense Item' mode.

SYS-R) MB-6.
If the MIVM is in the 'Dispense Item' mode when the mode button is pressed, then the MIVM shall change to the 'Set Price' mode if all of the customer's credit (if any) is refunded.

2.3.2.3 Number Selection Buttons (NSB)

Definition: one of the ten buttons used by a customer or service representative to select a number.

Kind: indirect concrete client external.

Responsibility:
- Interrupt the custom operating system when pressed, specifying the number selected.
  Collaborator: Custom Operating System.

Requirements:

SYS-D) NSB-1.
There shall be 10 number selection buttons labeled '1' through '10'.

SYS-D) NSB-2.
When a number selection button is pressed, it shall interrupt the custom operating system, specifying the number selected.

2.3.2.4 Refund Button (RB)

Definition: the button used by the customer to request the refund of the customer's credit.

Kind: indirect concrete client external.

Responsibility:
- Interrupt the custom operating system when pressed, specifying the refund button.
  Collaborator: Custom Operating System.

Requirement:
  SYS-D) RB-1.
  When the refund button is pressed, it shall interrupt the custom operating system, specifying that the refund button was pressed.

2.3.3 Custom Circuit Board (CCB)

Definition: the circuit board designed specifically to execute the MIVM software (the custom circuit board is currently under development and the specific associated derived requirements are not yet available).

Kind: direct concrete peer external.

Responsibilities:
- Run the custom operating system.
  Collaborator: none.
- Run the MIVM software.
  Collaborator: none.

Requirements:
  SYS-D) CCB-1.
  All MIVM software shall run on a custom circuit board.
  SYS-D) CCB-2.
  The custom circuit board shall include the necessary standard 8-bit, 16-pin input and output registers for communicating with all input and output devices.

2.3.4 Custom Operating System

Definition: the minimal operating system specifically designed to support the MIVM software (the custom operating system is currently under development and its specific associated derived requirements are not yet available).

Kind: direct concrete peer external.

Responsibilities:
- Handle hardware interrupts from input registers (and associated devices).
  Collaborator: Custom Circuit Board.
- Provide operating system calls to control output registers (and associated devices).
  Collaborator: Custom Circuit Board.

2.3.4.1 Custom Operating System Calls (COSC)

Definition: that part of the custom operating system that handles calls that drive the output devices.

Kind: direct concrete server external.

Responsibility:
- Write to output registers via a specific port (and thereby control the associated devices).
  Collaborator: Custom Circuit Board.

Requirements:
> **SYS-D) COSC-1.**
> The custom operating system shall supply calls to drive all output registers (and associated devices).
> **SYS-D) COSC-1.1.** *Coin Dispensers*
> (a) The custom operating system shall provide the following call that causes the coin dispenser to dispense a coin: `dispenseCoinUsing (aPort)`.
> (b) If the coinDispenser detects that no coin is present, then the custom operating system shall raise the following exception to the MIVM software: `FailedException`.
> **SYS-D) COSC-1.2.** *Item Dispensers*
> (a) The custom operating system shall provide the following call that causes an item dispenser at a specified location to dispense an item: `dispenseItemUsing (aPort)`.
> (b) The custom operating system shall provide the following call that causes an item dispenser at a specified location to display its location and price on its item display: `displayItem(aString, aPort)`.
> (c) If the custom operating system detects that the item dispenser assembly does not hold an item dispenser at the corresponding location, then the custom operating system shall raise the following exception to the MIVM software: `FailedException`.
> **SYS-D) COSC-1.3** *Main Display*
> The custom operating system shall provide the following call that causes the main display to display a character string: `displayMain(aString)`.

2.3.4.2 Custom Operating System Interrupts (COSI)

Definition: that part of the custom operating system that produces software interrupts that drive the MIVM software.

Kind: direct concrete client external.

Responsibility:
- Transform input events from an input register (and associated device) into software interrupts to the MIVM software.
  Collaborator: Custom Circuit Board.

Requirements:

SYS-D) COSI-1.

General Behavior. The custom operating system shall be able to handle hardware interrupts from all input registers (and associated devices).

SYS-D) COSI-1.1.

Bill Validator. When the bill validator interrupts the custom operating system with the denomination of the validated bill, the custom operating system shall send a software interrupt to the MIVM software, specifying the denomination of the validated bill.

SYS-D) COSI-1.2.

Coin Validator. When the coin validator interrupts the custom operating system with the denomination of the validated coin, the custom operating system shall send a software interrupt to the MIVM software, specifying the denomination of the validated coin.

SYS-D) COSI-1.3.

Door Switch. When the door switch interrupts the custom operating system, the custom operating system shall send a software interrupt to the MIVM software, specifying that the door was locked.

SYS-D) COSI-1.4.

Letter Selection Buttons. When a letter selection button interrupts the custom operating system, the custom operating system shall send a software interrupt to the MIVM software, specifying the letter selected.

SYS-D) COSI-1.5.

Mode Button. When the mode button interrupts the custom operating system, the custom operating system shall send a software interrupt to the MIVM software, specifying that the mode button was pressed.

SYS-D) COSI-1.6.

Number Selection Buttons. When a number selection Button interrupts the custom operating system, the custom operating system shall send a software interrupt to the MIVM software, specifying the number selected.

SYS-D) COSI-1.7.

Refund Button. When the refund button interrupts the custom operating system, the custom operating system shall send a software interrupt to the MIVM software, specifying that the refund button was pressed.

2.3.5 Dispensers

Definition: a device that dispenses something to a customer.

Kind: indirect abstract server external.

Responsibility:
- Dispense something.
  Collaborator: Actuator.

2.3.5.1 Coin Dispensers (CD)

Definition: a dispenser that dispenses a single kind of coin to the customer.

Kind: indirect concrete server external.

Responsibilities:
- Dispense a single kind of coin.
  Collaborator: Coin Solenoid.
- Know when it fails to dispense a coin.
  Collaborator: Coin Solenoid.
- Hold up to a maximum number of coins.
  Collaborator: none.

Requirements:

SYS-D) CD-1.
Structure. Each coin dispenser shall consist of:
(a) a tube holding a stack of coins one foot high, and
(b) a coin solenoid that dispenses the coins, one at a time.

SYS-D) CD-2.
Maximum number of nickels. Each nickel coin dispenser shall be able to hold approximately the following maximum number of nickels: 160.

SYS-D) CD-3.
Maximum number of dimes. Each dime coin dispenser shall be able to hold approximately the following maximum number of dimes: 234.

SYS-D) CD-4.
Maximum number of quarters. Each quarter coin dispenser shall be able to hold approximately the following maximum number of quarters: 180.

SYS-D) CD-5.
Current number of coins. Due to hardware cost considerations, there is no way for the MIVM software to detect how many coins a coin dispenser currently holds.

SYS-R) CD-6.
Coin dispenser behavior. When requested by a custom operating system call, the coin dispenser shall either cause its coin solenoid to dispense a valid coin or raise a hardware exception if it cannot dispense a valid coin.

2.3.5.2 Item Dispensers (ID)

Definition: a dispenser that dispenses items having a common price to the customer.

Kind: indirect concrete server external.

Responsibilities:
- Dispense an available item.
  Collaborator: Item Stepper Motor.
- Display the location and common price of the items it contains.
  Collaborator: Item Display.

Requirements:
SYS-D) ID-1.
Structure. Each item dispenser shall consist of:
(a) an item display,
(b) a spiral wire that holds its items, and
(c) an item stepper motor for rotating the spiral wire.
SYS-D) ID-2.
Item display. The item display on the front of the item dispenser shall display its location in the item dispenser assembly and the common price of its items.
SYS-R) ID-3.
Stepper motor. When requested by a custom operating system call, the item dispenser shall cause its item stepper motor to cause its spiral wire to make one revolution, thereby dispensing the next item (if any). (Due to cost considerations, no hardware interrupt is raised if either the item dispenser is empty or it fails to dispense an item.)
SYS-D) ID-4.
Size. Large spiral wires shall hold up to 10 large items, whereas small spiral wires shall hold up to 20 small items. (Due to hardware cost considerations, there is no way for the MIVM software to detect whether an item dispenser has either a large or a small wire.)
SYS-D) ID-5.
Due to hardware cost considerations, there is no way for the MIVM software to detect how many items an item dispenser currently holds.
SYS-R) ID-6.
The price of all items stored in a single item dispenser shall be the same.

2.3.6 Dispenser Assemblies

Definition: an assembly of dispensers.

Kind: indirect abstract server external.

Responsibilities:
- Hold a number of dispensers.
  Collaborator: none.
- Dispense something.
  Collaborator: Dispenser.

2.3.6.1 Coin Dispenser Assembly (CDA)

Definition: an assembly of coin dispensers, arranged in a linear array.

Kind: indirect concrete server external.

Responsibilities:
- Hold the coin dispensers.
  Collaborator: none.

- Dispense available nickels, dimes, and quarters.
  Collaborator: Coin dispenser.
- Know when it fails to dispense a coin.
  Collaborator: Coin dispenser.

Requirements:

SYS-D) CDA-1.
The coin dispenser assembly shall contain two nickel dispensers.

SYS-D) CDA-2.
The coin dispenser assembly shall contain two dime dispensers.

SYS-D) CDA-3.
The coin dispenser assembly shall contain two quarter dispensers.

SYS-D) CDA-4.
Each coin validated by the coin validator shall be inserted by hardware into the tube of the first coin dispenser that holds that kind of coin and is not full; otherwise, the hardware shall insert the coin into the coin box.

2.3.6.2 Item Dispenser Assembly (IDA)

Definition: an assembly of item dispensers, arranged in a rectangular matrix.

Kind: indirect concrete server external.

Responsibilities:
- Hold up to 80 item dispensers.
  Collaborator: none.
- Dispense available items.
  Collaborator: Item Dispenser.
- Be configurable by the service representative.
  Collaborator: none.

Requirements:

SYS-D) IDA-1.
The item dispenser assembly shall consist of a rectangular matrix of item dispensers.

SYS-D) IDA-2.
The item dispenser assembly shall have 10 columns labeled '1' through '10'.

SYS-D) IDA-3.
The item dispenser assembly shall have 8 rows labeled 'A' through 'H'.

SYS-D) IDA-4.
In order to handle items that are too large to fit into a single location in the item dispenser assembly, not every location in the item dispenser assembly need have an item dispenser.

2.3.7 Displays

Definition: an electronic device for presenting visual information.

Kind: indirect abstract server external.

Responsibility:
- Display information.
  Collaborator: none.

Requirement:
SYS-R) DI-1.
When requested by a custom operating system call, the display shall display the associated string.

2.3.7.1 Item Displays (ID)

Definition: a display used to display the location of an item dispenser and the price of the items it contains.

Kind: indirect concrete server external.

Responsibilities:
- Display the location of the item dispenser in the item dispenser assembly.
  Collaborator: none.
- Display the common price of the items in the item dispenser.
  Collaborator: none.

Requirements:
SYS-D) ID-1.
Each item display shall be able to display up to 10 characters.
SW-R) ID-2.
Each item display shall display its information in the following format: row, column, space, and price. For example, '7A $1.75'.

2.3.7.2 Main Display (MD)

Definition: the primary display used to present general information to customers and service representatives.

Kind: indirect concrete server external.

Responsibility:
- Display general information to customers and service representatives.
  Collaborator: none.

Requirement:
SYS-D) MD-1.
The main display shall be able to display up to 22 characters.

2.3.8 Door (DO)

Definition: the door that protects the coin dispenser assembly, the item dispenser assembly, the mode button, and the money boxes from access by the customer.

Comment: Only a service representative can unlock the door.

Kind: indirect concrete client external.

Responsibility:
- Prevent customer access to MIVM internals: the coin dispenser assembly, the item dispenser assembly, the mode button and the money boxes.
  Collaborator: Door Switch.

Requirements:
  SYS-D) DO-1.
  When closed and locked, the door shall prevent access to the bill box, the coin box, the coin dispenser assembly, the item dispenser assembly and the mode button.
  SYS-D) DO-2.
  When closed and locked, the door shall *not* prevent direct access to the bill validator, the coin return, the coin validator, the main display, the item return, the letter selection buttons, the number selection buttons and the refund button.
  SYS-D) DO-3.
  The door shall trip the door switch when the closed door is locked.

2.3.9 Door Switch (DS)

Definition: the sensor that detects when the closed door is locked.

Kind: indirect concrete client external.

Responsibility:
- Interrupt the custom operating system when the closed door is locked.
  Collaborator: Custom Operating System.

Requirement:
  SYS-D) DS-1.
  When tripped by the door lock, the door switch shall interrupt the custom operating system specifying that the door was locked.

2.3.10 Money Validators (MV)

Definition: a device used to determine the validity of inserted money.

Kind: indirect abstract client external.

Responsibilities:
- Accept valid money that is inserted.
  Collaborator: Custom Operating System.
- Reject invalid money that is inserted.
  Collaborator: none.

Requirements:
> **SYS-R) MV-1.**
> When valid money is inserted, the money validator shall interrupt the custom operating system, specifying the denomination of the money it has validated.
> **SYS-D) MV-2.**
> The money validator shall reject invalid money without interrupting the custom operating system.

2.3.10.1 Bill Validator (BV)

Definition: a device used to determine the validity of inserted bills.

Kind: indirect concrete client external.

Responsibility:
- Validate inserted bills.
  Collaborator: Bill Box, Custom Operating System.

Requirements:
> **SYS-R) BV-1.**
> *Valid bills.* The bill validator shall validate United States one-dollar bills: $1.00.
> **SYS-D) BV-2.**
> *Validating bills.* Upon validating a bill, the bill validator shall interrupt the custom operating system, specifying the denomination of the validated bill.
> **SYS-D) BV-3.**
> *Storing valid bills.* Each bill validated by the bill validator shall be inserted by hardware into the bill box.
> **SYS-D) BV-4.**
> The bill validator shall reject invalid bills by ejecting them without interrupting the custom operating system.

2.3.10.2 Coin Validator (CV)

Definition: a device that determines the validity of inserted coins.

Kind: indirect concrete client external.

Responsibility:
- Validate inserted coins.
  Collaborator: Coin Dispenser Assembly, Custom Operating System.

Requirements:
> **SYS-R) CV-1.**
> *Valid coins.* The coin validator shall validate United States coins having the following denominations:
> – nickel: $0.05.
> – dime: $0.10.
> – quarter: $0.25.

SYS-D) CV-2.

Validating coins. Upon validating a coin, the coin validator shall interrupt the custom operating system, specifying the denomination of the validated coin.

SYS-D) CV-3.

Storing valid coins. Each coin validated by the coin validator shall be inserted by hardware into the tubes of the corresponding coin dispensers if there is room for that type of coin; otherwise, the hardware shall insert the coin into the coin box.

SYS-D) CV-4.

Invalid coins. The coin validator shall reject invalid coins by sending them by hardware to the coin return without interrupting the custom operating system.

2.3.11 Vending Machine Roles

Definition: the role of a person who interacts with the vending machine.

Kind: indirect abstract client actor.

Responsibility:
- Interact with the vending machine.
  Collaborators: Button, Door, Money Validator.

2.3.11.1 Customers (C)

Definition: the role played by a person when buying items from the vending machine.

Kind: indirect concrete client actor. (Note that whereas the customer is a peer of the MIVM system, the customer is only a client of the MIVM software.)

Responsibilities:
- Buy items from the vending machine.
  Collaborators: Money Validator, Refund Button, Selection Button.
- Take dispensed items from the item return.
  Collaborator: Item Return.
- Take dispensed coins from the coin return.
  Collaborator: Coin Return.

2.3.11.1.1 Customer Buys an Item

Description: This use case models the required interactions between the following externals and the MIVM software when a customer buys an item.

Requirement:

SYS-R) C-1.

Customer Buys an Item. If the MIVM is in the 'Dispense Item' mode, a customer shall be able to buy an item if the customer (in any order) selects the item and pays for the selection.

Externals:
- Client:
    1. a customer
    2. the bill validator
    3. the coin validator
    4. the letter selection buttons
    5. the number selection buttons
    6. the refund button
- Peer:
    7. the custom operating system
- Server:
    8. the coin dispensers
    9. the coin solenoids
    10. the item dispensers
    11. the item stepper motors
    12. the main display

Precondition: The mode of the MIVM is 'Dispense Item'.

Statements:
Concurrently[†]
    invoke use case: Customer Makes a Selection
and
    invoke use case: Customer Makes a Payment
and
    optionally invoke use case: Customer Requests a Refund
end concurrently.

Blackbox sequence diagram: See Figure 2.5.

Postconditions:
- Primary:
    - The postconditions of use case: Customer Makes a Selection.
    - The postconditions of use case: Customer Makes a Payment.
    - The mode of the MIVM is 'Dispense Item'.
- Alternative:
    - The postconditions of use case: Customer Requests a Refund.

2.3.11.1.1.1 Customer Makes a Selection

Description: This use case models the required interactions between the following externals and the MIVM software when a customer selects an item dispenser in the item dispenser assembly.

[†] The following statements can be executed in any order and may be interwoven in any manner.

aCustomer

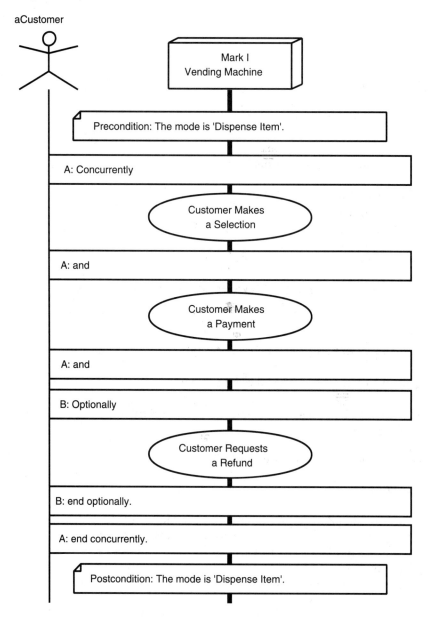

Figure 2.5 Blackbox sequence diagram for the use case: Customer Buys an Item (note that all interactions occur in the subordinate use cases).

Requirement:

SYS-R) C-1.1.

Customer Makes a Selection. If the MIVM is in the 'Dispense Item' mode, a customer shall be able to make a selection by selecting (in any order) the

corresponding column and row of the desired item dispenser in the item
dispenser assembly.

Externals:
- Client:
    1. a customer
    2. the letter selection buttons
    3. the number selection buttons
- Peer:
    4. the custom operating system
- Server:
    5. the coin dispensers (optional)
    6. the coin solenoids (optional)
    7. the item dispensers (optional)
    8. the item stepper motors (optional)
    9. the main display

Precondition: The mode of the MIVM is 'Dispense Item'.

Statements:
Concurrently
   invoke use case: Customer Selects the Column of an Item
and
   invoke use case: Customer Selects the Row of an Item
end concurrently.

Blackbox sequence diagram: See Figure 2.6.

Postconditions:
   The postconditions of the use case: Customer Selects the Column of an Item.
   The postconditions of the use case: Customer Selects the Row of an Item.
   The mode of the MIVM is 'Dispense Item'.

2.3.11.1.1.1.1 Customer Selects the Column of an Item

Description: This use case models the required interactions between the
following externals and the MIVM software when a customer selects a column
of the desired item dispenser in the item dispenser assembly.

Requirements:
   SYS-R) C-1.1.1.
   Customer Selects the Column of an Item. If the MIVM is in the 'Dispense
Item' mode, then a customer shall be able to select the column of the desired
item by pressing one of the corresponding number selection buttons which
are labeled 1 through 10.
   SW-R) C-1.1.1-1.
   Customer Selects the Column without Selecting the Item. If the MIVM is in
the 'Dispense Item' mode and neither column nor row has been selected,

aCustomer

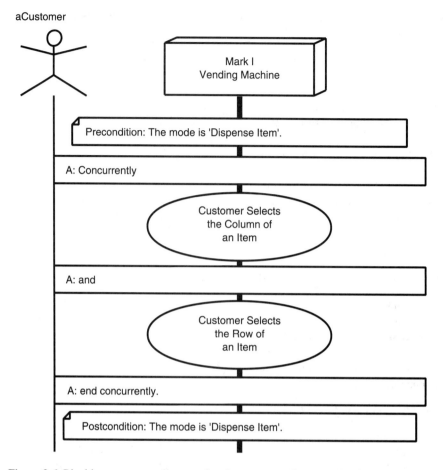

Figure 2.6 Blackbox sequence diagram for the use case: Customer Makes a Selection.

then a customer shall be able to select the column of the desired item dispenser in the item dispenser assembly by pressing the corresponding number selection button.

SW-R) C-1.1.1-2.

Customer Selects the Item by Selecting the Column. If the MIVM is in the 'Dispense Item' mode and a row has been selected but the column has not yet been selected, then a customer shall be able to select the desired item dispenser in the item dispenser assembly by selecting its column by pressing the corresponding number selection button.

SW-R) C-1.1.1-3.

Customer Reselects the Column. If the MIVM is in the 'Dispense Item' mode and a column has already been selected, then a customer shall be able to reselect the desired column and invalidate any prior selection of the row by pressing the corresponding number selection button.

Externals:
- Client:
  1. the number selection buttons
- Peer:
  2. a customer
  3. the custom operating system
- Server:
  4. the coin dispensers (optional)
  5. the coin solenoids (optional)
  6. the item dispensers (optional)
  7. the item stepper motors (optional)
  8. the main display

Paths:
- Primary:
  1. Customer Selects the Column without Selecting an Item
  2. Customer Selects an Item by Selecting the Column
- Alternative:
  3. Customer Reselects the Column

Precondition: The mode of the MIVM is 'Dispense Item'.

Statements:
A customer selects the column of an item dispenser by pressing a number
  selection button.
That number selection button interrupts the custom operating system, specifying
  the number selected.
The custom operating system interrupts the MIVM software, specifying the
  number representing the column of the customer's selection to the MIVM
  software.
If the MIVM software presently is not storing the column of the customer's
  selection, **then**
  If the MIVM software presently is not storing the row of the customer's
    selection, **then**
    // Primary Path 1. Customer Selects the Column without Selecting an Item:
      The MIVM software tells the custom operating system to display the
        column of the customer's selection on the main display.
      The custom operating system tells the main display to display the column
        of the customer's selection.
      The main display displays the column of the customer's selection to the
        customer.
  else
    // Primary Path 2. Customer Selects an Item by Selecting the Column:
      Invoke use case: Attempt To Dispense.
  end if.

else
// Alternative Path 3. Customer Reselects the Column:
> The MIVM software tells the custom operating system to display the new column of the customer's selection on the main display.
>
> The custom operating system tells the main display to display the column of the customer's selection.
>
> The main display displays the column of the customer's selection to the customer.

end if.

Blackbox sequence diagram: See Figure 2.7.

Postconditions:
1. Primary Path 1. Customer Selects the Column without Selecting an Item:
   - The MIVM software stores the column of the customer's selection.
   - The main display displays the column of the customer's selection.
   - The mode of the MIVM is 'Dispense Item'.
2. Primary Path 2. Customer Selects an Item by Selecting the Column:
   - The MIVM software stores the column of the customer's selection.
   - The postconditions of the use case: Attempt to Dispense.
   - The mode of the MIVM is 'Dispense Item'.
3. Alternative Path 3. Customer Reselects the Column:
   - The MIVM software stores the new column of the customer's selection.
   - The MIVM software no longer stores the previously selected row of the customer's selection.
   - The main display displays the column of the customer's selection.
   - The mode of the MIVM is 'Dispense Item'.

2.3.11.1.1.1.2 Customer Selects the Row of an Item

Description: This use case models the required interactions between the following externals and the MIVM software when a customer selects a row of the desired item dispenser in the item dispenser assembly.

Requirements:
SYS-R) C-1.1.2.
Customer Selects the Row of an Item. If the MIVM is in the 'Dispense Item' mode, then a customer shall be able to select the row of the desired item in the item dispenser assembly by pressing one of the corresponding letter selection buttons which are labeled A, B, C, D, E, F, G and H.

SW-R) C-1.1.2-1.
Customer Selects the Row without Selecting the Item. If the MIVM is in the 'Dispense Item' mode and neither column nor row has been selected, then a customer shall be able to select the row of the desired item dispenser in the item dispenser assembly by pressing the corresponding letter selection button.

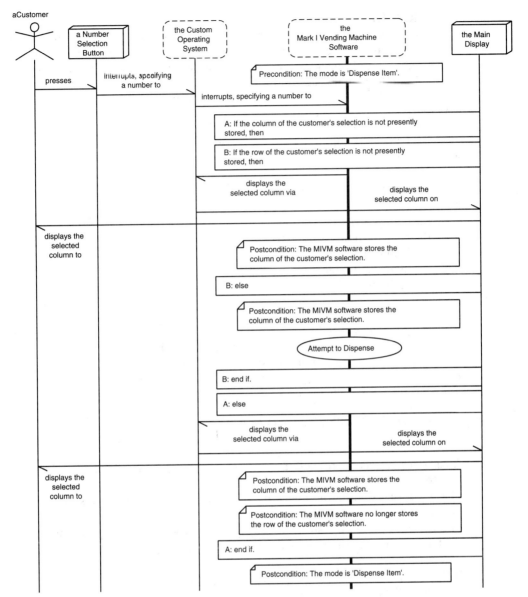

Figure 2.7 Blackbox sequence diagram for the use case: Customer Selects the Column of an Item.

Requirements:

SW-R) C-1.1.2-2.

Customer Selects the Item by Selecting the Row. If the MIVM is in the 'Dispense Item' mode and a column has been selected but the row has not yet been selected, then a customer shall be able to select the desired item dispenser in the item dispenser assembly by selecting its row by pressing the corresponding letter selection button.

SW-R) C-1.1.2-3.

Customer Reselects the Row. If the MIVM is in the 'Dispense Item' mode and a row has already been selected, then a customer shall be able to reselect the desired row and invalidate any prior selection of the column by pressing the corresponding letter selection button.

Externals:
- Client:
  1. the letter selection buttons
- Peer:
  2. a customer
  3. the custom operating system
- Server:
  4. the coin dispensers (optional)
  5. the coin solenoids (optional)
  6. the item dispensers (optional)
  7. the item stepper motors (optional)
  8. the main display

Paths:
- Primary:
  1. Customer Selects the Row without Selecting an Item
  2. Customer Selects an Item by Selecting the Row
- Alternative:
  3. Customer Reselects the Row

Precondition: The mode of the MIVM is 'Dispense Item'.

Statements:
A customer selects the row of an item dispenser by pressing a letter selection button.

That letter selection button interrupts the custom operating system, specifying the letter selected.

The custom operating system interrupts the MIVM software, specifying the letter representing the row of the customer's selection to the MIVM software.

If the MIVM software presently is not storing the row of the customer's selection, **then**

    If the MIVM software presently is not storing the column of the customer's selection, **then**

        // Primary Path 1. Customer Selects the Row without Selecting the Item:

        The MIVM software tells the custom operating system to display the row of the customer's selection on the main display.

        The custom operating system tells the main display to display the row of the customer's selection.

        The main display displays the row of the customer's selection to the customer.

else
// Primary Path 2. Customer Selects the Item by Selecting the Row:
   Invoke use case: Attempt To Dispense.
end if.
else
// Alternative Path 3. Customer Reselects the Row:
   The MIVM software tells the custom operating system to display the new
   row of the customer's selection on the main display.
   The custom operating system tells the main display to display the row of the
   customer's selection.
   The main display displays the row of the customer's selection to the
   customer.
end if.

Blackbox sequence diagram: See Figure 2.8.

Postconditions:
1. Primary Path 1. Customer Selects the Row without Selecting an Item:
   - The MIVM software stores the row of the customer's selection.
   - The main display displays the row of the customer's selection.
   - The mode of the MIVM is 'Dispense Item'.
2. Primary Path 2. Customer Selects an Item by Selecting the Row:
   - The MIVM software stores the row of the customer's selection.
   - The postconditions of the use case: Attempt to Dispense.
   - The mode of the MIVM is 'Dispense Item'.
3. Alternative Path 3. Customer Reselects the Row:
   - The MIVM software stores the new row of the customer's selection.
   - The MIVM software no longer stores the previously selected column of the
     customer's selection.
   - The main display displays the row of the customer's selection.
   - The mode of the MIVM is 'Dispense Item'.

2.3.11.1.1.2 Customer Makes a Payment

Description: This use case models the required interactions between the
following externals and the MIVM software when a customer pays for a
selection.

Requirement:
   SYS-R) C-1.2.
   Customer Makes a Payment. If the MIVM is in the 'Dispense Item' mode, then a
   customer shall be able to pay for an item (even if the item has not yet been
   selected) by inserting sufficient valid coins and/or bills to pay for the item.

Externals:
- Client:
  1. the bill validator
  2. the coin validator

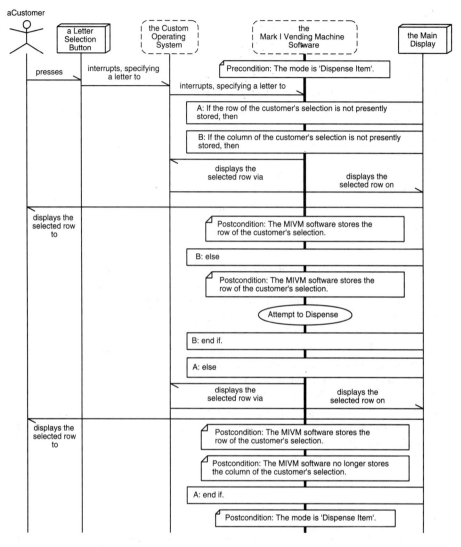

Figure 2.8 Blackbox sequence diagram for the use case: Customer Selects the Row of an Item.

- Peer:
  3. a customer
  4. the custom operating system
- Server:
  5. the coin dispensers (optional)
  6. the coin solenoids (optional)
  7. the item dispensers (optional)
  8. the item stepper motors (optional)
  9. the main display

Precondition: The mode of the MIVM is 'Dispense Item'.

Statements:
Concurrently
    invoke use case: Customer Inserts a Valid Bill
and
    invoke use case: Customer Inserts a Valid Coin
end concurrently.

Blackbox sequence diagram: See Figure 2.9.

Postconditions:
    The postconditions of the use case: Customer Inserts a Valid Bill.
    The postconditions of the use case: Customer Inserts a Valid Coin.

    The mode of the MIVM is 'Dispense Item'.

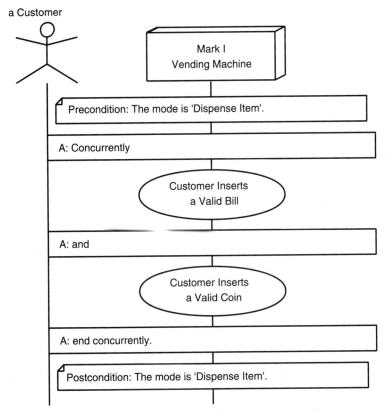

Figure 2.9 Blackbox sequence diagram for the use case: Customer Makes a Payment.

2.3.11.1.1.2.1 Customer Inserts a Valid Bill

Description: This use case models the required interactions between the following externals and the MIVM software when a customer inserts a valid bill into the bill validator.

Requirements:
   SYS-R) C-1.2.1.
   Customer Pays with Valid Bills. A customer shall be able to pay using valid dollar bills by inserting the bills into the bill validator.
   SW-R) C-1.2.1-1.
   Customer Inserts a Bill when the Item is Selected. If the customer has made a selection and the customer inserts a valid bill, then the MIVM software shall add the amount of the bill to the customer's credit (i.e. amount of money validated) and shall attempt to dispense the selection.
   SW-R) C-1.2.1-2.
   Customer Inserts a Bill when the Item is not Selected. If the customer has not yet made a selection and the customer inserts a valid bill, then the MIVM software shall add the amount of the bill to the customer's credit (i.e. amount of money validated) and display the amount of the customer's credit on the main display.

Externals:
- Client:
   1. the bill validator
- Peer:
   2. a customer
   3. the custom operating system
- Server:
   4. the coin dispensers (optional)
   5. the coin solenoids (optional)
   6. the item dispensers (optional)
   7. the item stepper motors (optional)
   8. the main display

Paths:
- Primary:
   1. An Item is Presently Selected
   2. An Item is not Presently Selected

Precondition: The mode of the MIVM is 'Dispense Item'.

Statements:
A customer pays for an item by inserting a valid bill into the bill validator.
The bill validator interrupts the custom operating system, specifying the valid bill.
The custom operating system interrupts the MIVM software, specifying the valid bill.

The MIVM software stores the customer's new credit, which is the customer's
old credit plus the amount of the validated bill.

If an item is presently selected, **then**

// Primary Path 1. An Item is Presently Selected:

Invoke use case: Attempt to Dispense.

else

// Primary Path 2. An Item is not Presently Selected:

The MIVM software tells the custom operating system to display the amount
of the customer's credit on the main display.

The custom operating system tells the main display to display the amount of
the customer's credit.

The main display displays the amount of the customer's credit to the customer.

end if.

Blackbox sequence diagram: See Figure 2.10.

Postconditions:

1. Primary Path 1. An Item is Presently Selected:
   - The MIVM software stores the customer's new credit.
   - The postconditions of the use case: Attempt to Dispense.
   - The mode of the MIVM is 'Dispense Item'.

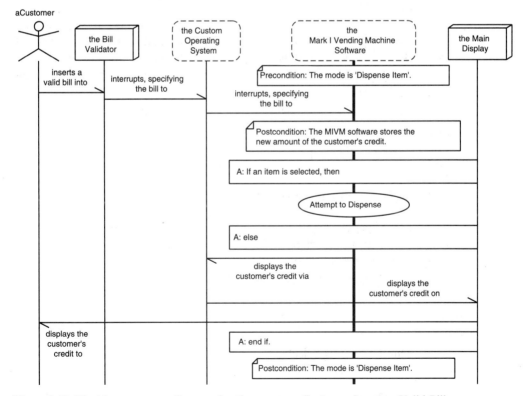

Figure 2.10 Blackbox sequence diagram for the use case: Customer Inserts a Valid Bill.

2. Primary Path 2. An Item is Not Presently Selected:
   - The MIVM software stores the customer's new credit.
   - The main display displays the amount of the customer's credit.
   - The mode of the MIVM is 'Dispense Item'.

2.3.11.1.1.2.2 Customer Inserts a Valid Coin

Description: This use case models the required interactions between the following externals and the MIVM when a customer inserts a valid coin into the coin validator.

Requirement:
   SYS-R) C-1.2.2.
   Customer Pays with Valid Coins. A customer shall be able to pay using valid coins by inserting the coins into the coin validator.
   SW-R) C-1.2.2-1.
   Customer Inserts a Coin when the Item is Selected. If the customer has made a selection and the customer inserts a valid coin, then the MIVM software shall add the amount of the coin to the customer's credit (i.e. amount of money validated) and shall attempt to dispense the selection.
   SW-R) C-1.2.2-2.
   Customer Inserts a Coin when the Item is not Selected. If the customer has not yet made a selection and the customer inserts a valid coin, then the MIVM software shall add the amount of the coin to the customer's credit (i.e. amount of money validated) and display the amount of the customer's credit on the main display.

Externals:
   - Client:
     1. the coin validator
   - Peer:
     2. a customer
     3. the custom operating system
   - Server:
     4. the coin dispensers (optional)
     5. the coin solenoids (optional)
     6. the item dispensers (optional)
     7. the item stepper motors (optional)
     8. the main display

Paths:
   - Primary:
     1. An Item is Presently Selected
     2. An Item is not Presently Selected

Precondition: The mode of the MIVM is 'Dispense Item'.

Statements:
A customer pays for an item by inserting a valid coin into the coin validator.
The coin validator interrupts the custom operating system, specifying the valid coin.
The custom operating system interrupts the MIVM software, specifying the
valid coin.
The MIVM software stores the customer's new credit, which is the customer's
old credit plus the amount of the validated coin.
The MIVM software stores the fact that the coin dispenser assembly can
dispense that kind of coin.[†]
If an item is presently selected, **then**
// Primary Path 1. An Item is Presently Selected:
Invoke use case: **Attempt to Dispense.**
else
// Primary Path 2. An Item is not Presently Selected:
The MIVM software tells the custom operating system to display the amount
of the customer's credit on the main display.
The custom operating system tells the main display to display the amount of
the customer's credit.
The main display displays the amount of the customer's credit to the customer.
end if.

Blackbox sequence diagram: See Figure 2.11.

Postconditions:
1. Primary Path 1. An Item is Presently Selected:
   - The MIVM software stores the customer's new credit.
   - The postconditions of the use case: Attempt to Dispense.
   - The mode of the MIVM is 'Dispense Item'.
2. Primary Path 2. An Item is Not Presently Selected:
   - The MIVM software stores the customer's new credit.
   - The main display displays the amount of the customer's credit.
   - The mode of the MIVM is 'Dispense Item'.

2.3.11.1.1.3 Customer Requests a Refund

Description: This use case models the required interactions between the following
externals and the MIVM software when a customer requests a refund.

Requirement:
SYS-R) C-1.3.
Customer Requests a Refund. When the customer presses the refund button,
the MIVM shall:

[†] Note that there is not enough information for the software to prevent the customer from inserting
more money than can be refunded by the coin dispenser assembly because (1) hardware costs
preclude the use of bill validators and coin validators that can reject valid money when told to do so
by the software and (2) the software only knows that the tube in a coin dispenser is empty when it
ries to dispense a coin from it. The software has no way of knowing for sure how many coins of
what types the coin dispensers hold.

aCustomer

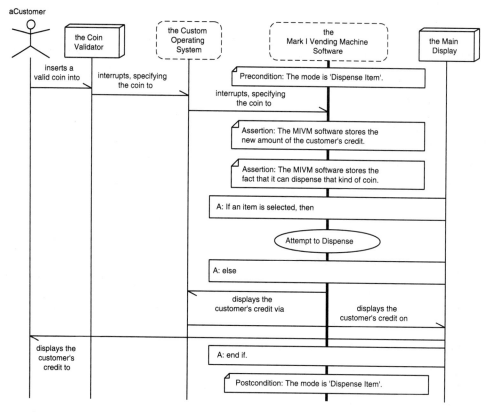

Figure 2.11 Blackbox sequence diagram for the use case: Customer Inserts a Valid Coin.

- reset the information it stores concerning the customer's selection (i.e. column no longer selected, row no longer selected, price of selection unknown) and the customer's credit (i.e. money validated set to zero), and
- refund the customer's credit. (If the coin dispenser cannot dispense a coin when requested to do so by the software, then it raises an exception to the software. See SYS-R) CD-6.)

Externals:
- Client:
  1. a customer
  2. the refund button
- Peer:
  3. the custom operating system
- Server:
  4. the coin dispensers
  5. the coin solenoids
  6. the main display

Precondition: The mode of the MIVM is 'Dispense Item'.

Statements:

A customer presses the refund button.

The refund button interrupts the custom operating system, specifying that the refund button was pressed.

The custom operating system interrupts the MIVM software, specifying that the refund button was pressed.

Invoke use case: Dispense Change.

Blackbox sequence diagram: See Figure 2.12.

Postconditions:

The postconditions of the use case: Dispense Change.

The mode of the MIVM is 'Dispense Item'.

2.3.11.1.1.4 Attempt To Dispense

Description: This use case models the required interactions between the following externals and the MIVM software when the machine attempts to dispense a customer's selection.

Requirements:

SYS-R) C-1.4.

Attempt to Dispense. The MIVM software shall dispense an item if the item has been selected (i.e. if both the column and row of the desired item dispenser in the item dispenser assembly have been selected) and paid for (i.e. if the money validated is sufficient to pay for the corresponding item).

SYS-R) C-1.4-1.

Item Selected and Paid For. If an item is selected and paid for, then the MIVM shall:

(a) subtract the price of the selection from the customer's credit,

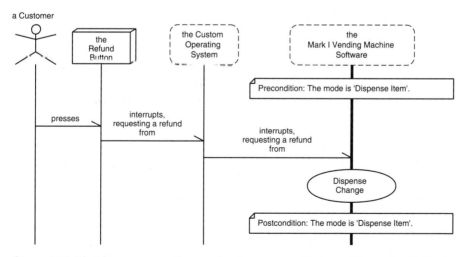

Figure 2.12 Blackbox sequence diagram for the use case: Customer Requests a Refund.

(b) dispense the selection,[†]

(c) clear the customer's selection, and

(d) dispense change equal to the customer's remaining credit, if any.

SYS-R) C-1.4-2.

Item Selected but Not Paid For. If an item is selected and has not yet been paid for, then the MIVM shall display the amount due (i.e. the price of the selection minus the customer's credit) on the main display.

Externals:

• Peer:

1. the custom operating system

• Server:

2. the coin dispensers (optional)

3. the coin solenoids (optional)

4. a customer

5. the item dispensers (optional)

6. the item stepper motors (optional)

7. the main display

Paths:

• Primary:

1. Item Paid For

2. Item Not Paid For

• Alternative:

3. Invalid Customer Selection

Preconditions:

The mode of the MIVM is 'Dispense Item'.

An item has been selected.

Statements:

If the selection is valid, **then**

　If the selection has been paid for, **then**

　// Path 1. Item Paid For:

　　The MIVM software stores the customer's remaining credit, which is the original credit minus the price of the selection.

　　The MIVM software tells the custom operating system to dispense the selection.

　　The custom operating system tells the appropriate item dispenser to dispense the selection.

　　The item dispenser tells its item stepper motor to make one revolution.

　　The item stepper motor drops an item into the item return.[‡]

[†] Due to hardware cost restrictions, the item dispenser has no sensor to determine whether or not it is empty. It shall therefore attempt to dispense an item even when it is empty. It is the customer's responsibility to only select item dispensers that visibly contain items.

[‡] Due to cost considerations, no hardware interrupt is raised if either the item dispenser is empty or it fails to dispense an item.

The item return delivers an item to the customer.
Invoke use case: Dispense Change.[†]
else
// Path 2. Item Not Paid For:
The MIVM software tells the custom operating system to display the
amount due on the main display.
The custom operating system tells the main display to display the amount
due.
The main display displays the amount due to the customer.
end if.
else
// Path 3. Invalid Customer Selection:
Invoke use case: Handle an Invalid Customer Selection.
end if.

Blackbox sequence diagram: See Figure 2.13.

Postconditions:
1. Primary Path 1. Item Paid For:
   - The postconditions of the use case: Dispense Change.
   - The mode of the MIVM is 'Dispense Item'.
2. Primary Path 2. Item Not Paid For:
   - The main display displays the amount due.
   - The mode of the MIVM is 'Dispense Item'.
3. Alternative Path 3. Invalid Customer Selection:
   - The postconditions of the use case: Handle an Invalid Customer Selection.
   - The mode of the MIVM is 'Dispense Item'.

2.3.11.1.1.4.1 Handle an Invalid Customer Selection

Description: This use case models the required interactions between the
following externals and the MIVM software when a customer makes an invalid
selection.

Requirement:
SW-R) C-1.4.1.
Handle Invalid Customer Selection. The MIVM software shall cause the main
display to display 'INVALID SELECTION' when a customer makes an invalid
selection (i.e. when either there is no item dispenser at the selected location or no
price has been set for the item dispenser at the selected location).

Externals:
- Peer:
  1. the custom operating system
- Server:
  2. the main display

[†] The use case is invoked, even if the customer's remaining credit is zero.

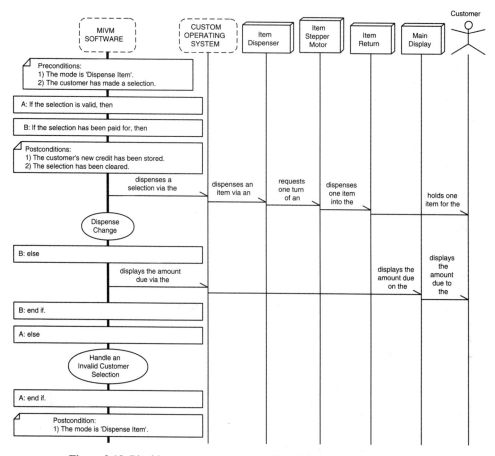

Figure 2.13 Blackbox sequence diagram for the use case: Attempt to Dispense.

Paths:
- Alternative:
  1. Invalid Selection

Preconditions:
The mode of the MIVM is 'Dispense Item'.
The MIVM software is presently storing the location (i.e. both the column and the row) of the customer's selection.
Either
    no item dispenser exists at that location
or
    no price has been set for the item dispenser at that location.

Statements:
// Invalid Selection.
The MIVM software tells the custom operating system to display 'INVALID SELECTION' on the main display.

The custom operating system tells the main display to display 'INVALID SELECTION'.

The main display displays 'INVALID SELECTION' to the customer.

Blackbox sequence diagram: See Figure 2.14.

Postconditions:

The MIVM software no longer stores either the column or row of the customer's selection.

The main display displays 'INVALID SELECTION'.

The mode of the MIVM is 'Dispense Item'.

2.3.11.1.2 Dispense Change

Description: This use case models the required interactions between the following externals and the MIVM software when the coin dispenser assembly dispenses change to the customer.

Requirements:

SYS-R) C-1.4.2.

Dispense Change. When dispensing change to the customer, the coin dispenser assembly shall dispense as much of the customer's credit as is possible.

SYS-R) C-1.4.2-1.

Credit for Undispensed Change. If all of the customer's credit cannot be dispensed, then any remaining credit shall remain available for another purchase.

SYS-D) C-1.4.2-2.

Coin Dispensing Policy. When dispensing change to the customer, the coin dispensing policy is that the coin dispenser assembly should dispense quarters first, then dimes, and finally nickels.

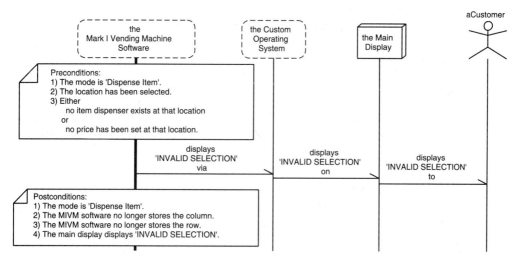

Figure 2.14 Blackbox sequence diagram for the use case: Handle an Invalid Customer Selection.

Externals:
- Peer:
  1. the custom operating system
- Server:
  2. the coin dispensers
  3. the coin solenoids
  4. the main display

Paths:
- Primary:
  1. Dispense Change

Precondition: The mode of the MIVM is 'Dispense Item'.

Statements:
Invoke use case: Dispense Quarters.
Invoke use case: Dispense Dimes.
Invoke use case: Dispense Nickels.
The MIVM software resets the information it stores concerning the customer's selection (i.e. column no longer selected, row no longer selected, and selection price unknown).
Invoke use case: Display Greeting.

Blackbox sequence diagram: See Figure 2.15.

Postconditions:
The MIVM software no longer stores information concerning the customer's selection (i.e. column no longer selected, row no longer selected, selection price unknown).
The postconditions of the use case: Dispense Quarters.
The postconditions of the use case: Dispense Dimes.
The postconditions of the use case: Dispense Nickels.
The postconditions of the use case: Display Greeting.
The mode of the MIVM is 'Dispense Item'.

2.3.11.1.2.1 Dispense Quarters

Description: This use case models the required interactions between the following externals and the MIVM software when the coin dispenser assembly dispenses quarters.

Requirement:
SYS-D) C-1.4.2.1.
Dispense Quarters. Each time the coin dispenser assembly dispenses a quarter, the MIVM shall subtract a quarter from the customer's credit.

Externals:
- Peer:
  1. the custom operating system

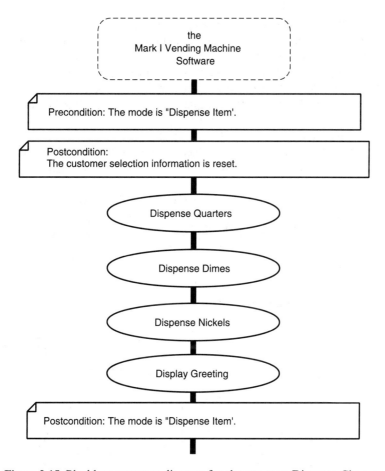

Figure 2.15 Blackbox sequence diagram for the use case: Dispense Change.

- Server:
  2. the quarter dispenser
  3. the quarter solenoid

Paths:
- Primary:
  1. Quarters Dispensed Without Problem
- Alternative:
  2. Could Not Dispense All

Precondition: The mode of the MIVM is 'Dispense Item'.

Statements:
Loop while the customer's credit is not less than a quarter and the quarter
  dispenser can dispense quarters:
    The MIVM software tells the custom operating system to dispense a quarter.

The custom operating system tells the quarter dispenser to dispense a quarter.
The quarter dispenser tells its quarter solenoid to push out a quarter.
If the quarter solenoid pushes out a quarter, **then**

    // Primary Path 1: Quarters Dispensed Without Problem:
    the quarter solenoid drops a quarter into the coin return, and
    the MIVM software subtracts a quarter from the customer's credit,

else

    // Alternative Path 2: Could Not Dispense All:
    the quarter solenoid raises the 'failed' exception to the quarter dispenser,
    the quarter dispenser raises the 'failed' exception to the custom operating
    system,
    the custom operating system raises the 'failed' exception to the MIVM
    software, and
    the MIVM software stores the fact that the quarter dispenser cannot
    dispense quarters.

    end if.
end loop.

Blackbox sequence diagram: See Figure 2.16.

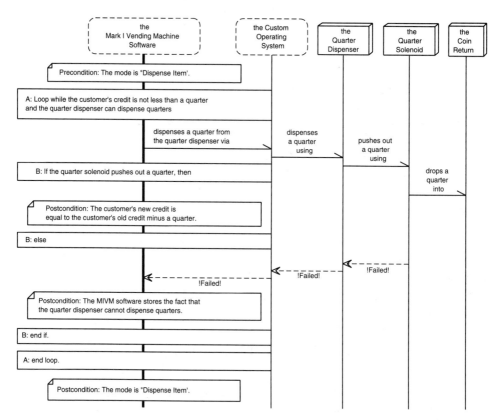

Figure 2.16 Blackbox sequence diagram for the use case: Dispense Quarters.

Postconditions:
The coin return holds zero or more quarters, and the customer's credit has been
  debited by the amount of the quarters.
If the coin return does not hold one or more quarters, **then**
    the MIVM software stores the fact that the quarter dispenser cannot dispense
      quarters.
The mode of the MIVM is 'Dispense Item'.

2.3.11.1.2.2 Dispense Dimes

Description: This use case models the required interactions between the following
externals and the MIVM software when the coin dispenser assembly dispenses
dimes.

Requirement:
  SYS-D) C-1.4.2.2.
  Dispense Dimes. Each time the coin dispenser assembly dispenses a dime, the
  MIVM shall subtract a dime from the customer's credit.

Externals:
- Peer:
  1. the custom operating system
- Server:
  2. the dime dispenser
  3. the dime solenoid

Paths:
- Primary:
  1. Dimes Dispensed Without Problem
- Alternative:
  2. Could Not Dispense All

Precondition: The mode of the MIVM is 'Dispense Item'.

Statements:
Loop while the customer's credit is not less than a dime and the dime dispenser
  can dispense dimes:
    The MIVM software tells the custom operating system to dispense a dime.
    The custom operating system tells the dime dispenser to dispense a dime.
    The dime dispenser tells its dime solenoid to push out a dime.
    If the dime solenoid pushes out a dime, **then**
      // Primary Path 1: Dimes Dispensed Without Problem:
      the dime solenoid drops a dime into the coin return, and
      the MIVM software subtracts a dime from the customer's credit,
    else
      // Alternative Path 2: Could Not Dispense All:
      the dime solenoid raises the 'failed' exception to the dime dispenser,
      the dime dispenser raises the 'failed' exception to the custom operating system,

the custom operating system raises the 'failed' exception to the MIVM software, and

the MIVM software stores the fact that the dime dispenser cannot dispense dimes.

end if.
end loop.

Blackbox sequence diagram: See Figure 2.17.

Postconditions:
The coin return holds zero or more dimes, and the customer's credit has been debited by the amount of the dimes.
If the coin return does not hold one or more dimes, **then**
the MIVM software stores the fact that the dime dispenser cannot dispense dimes.
The mode of the MIVM is 'Dispense Item'.

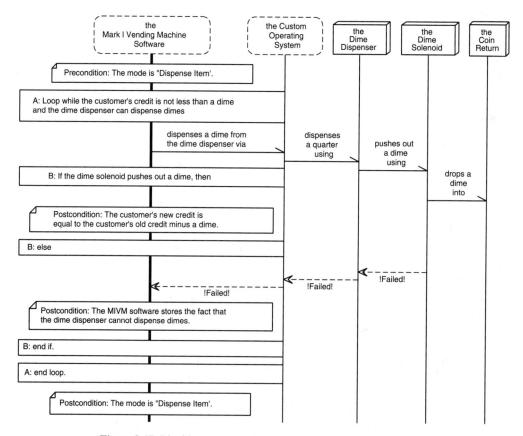

Figure 2.17 Blackbox sequence diagram for the use case: Dispense Dimes.

2.3.11.1.2.3 Dispense Nickels

Description: This use case models the required interactions between the following externals and the MIVM software when the coin dispenser assembly dispenses nickels.

Requirement:
SYS-D) C-1.4.2.3.
Dispense Nickels. Each time the coin dispenser assembly dispenses a nickel, the MIVM shall subtract a nickel from the customer's credit.

Externals:
- Peer:
  1. the custom operating system
- Server:
  2. the nickel dispenser
  3. the nickel solenoid

Paths:
- Primary:
  1. Nickels Dispensed Without Problem
- Alternative:
  2. Could not Dispense All

Precondition: The mode of the MIVM is 'Dispense Item'.

Statements:
Loop while the customer's credit is not less than a nickel and the nickel dispenser can dispense nickels:
   The MIVM software tells the custom operating system to dispense a nickel.
   The custom operating system tells the nickel dispenser to dispense a nickel.
   The nickel dispenser tells the nickel solenoid to push out a nickel.
   If the nickel solenoid pushes out a nickel, **then**
      // Primary Path 1: Nickels Dispensed Without Problem:
      the nickel solenoid drops a nickel into the coin return, and
      the MIVM software subtracts a nickel from the customer's credit,
   else
      // Alternative Path 2: Could Not Dispense All:
      the nickel solenoid raises the 'failed' exception to the nickel dispenser,
      the nickel dispenser raises the 'failed' exception to the custom operating system,
      the custom operating system raises the 'failed' exception to the MIVM software, and
      the MIVM software stores the fact that the nickel dispenser cannot dispense nickels.
   end if.
end loop.

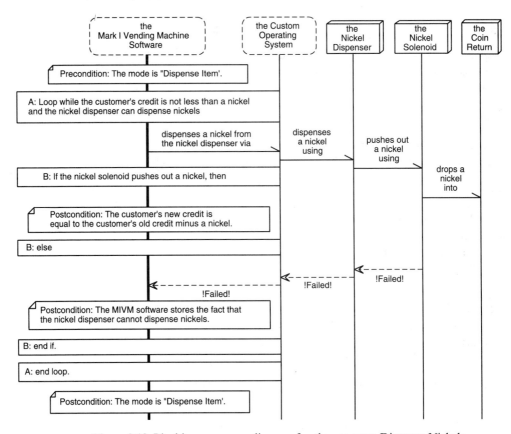

Figure 2.18 Blackbox sequence diagram for the use case: Dispense Nickels.

Blackbox sequence diagram: See Figure 2.18.

Postconditions:
The coin return holds zero or more nickels, and the customer's credit has been debited by the amount of the nickels.
If the coin return does not hold one or more nickels, **then** the MIVM software stores the fact that the nickel dispenser cannot dispense nickels.
The mode of the MIVM is 'Dispense Item'.

2.3.11.1.2.4 Display Greeting

Description: This use case models the required interactions between the following externals and the MIVM software when the machine displays a greeting.

Requirements:
SYS-D) C-1.4.2.4.
Display Greeting. After dispensing the customer's credit, the MIVM shall display an appropriate greeting to the next customer.

SYS-D) C-1.4.2.4-1.
Thank Customer. If all of the customer's credit was dispensed and the coin dispenser assembly could dispense all kinds of valid coins,[†] then the MIVM shall display 'THANK YOU' on the main display, wait 2 seconds, and then display 'HAVE A NICE DAY' on the main display.

SYS-D) C-1.4.2.4-2.
Display Exact Change Warning. If all of the customer's credit was dispensed but the coin dispenser assembly could not dispense all kinds of valid coins, then the MIVM shall display 'THANK YOU' on the main display, wait 2 seconds, and then display 'EXACT CHANGE ONLY' on the main display.

SYS-D) C-1.4.2.4-3.
Display Remaining Credit. If all of the customer's credit was not dispensed, then the MIVM shall display 'THANK YOU' on the main display, wait 2 seconds, and then display the amount of the remaining credit on the main display. (The customer can then use this amount to make another purchase.)

Externals:
- Peer:
  1. the custom operating system
- Server:
  2. the main display

Paths:
- Primary:
  1. Customer's Credit Dispensed Without a Problem
- Alternative:
  2. Could Not Dispense a Kind of Coin
  3. Could Not Dispense All of the Customer's Credit

Precondition: The mode of the MIVM is 'Dispense Item'.

Statements:
// Thank the customer:
The MIVM software tells the custom operating system to display 'THANK YOU' on the main display.
The custom operating system tells the main display to display 'THANK YOU'.
The main display displays 'THANK YOU' to the customer.
After 2 seconds:
   // Primary Path 1: Customer's Credit Dispensed Without a Problem:
   If the customer's credit is zero and the coin dispenser assembly could dispense all kinds of valid coins, **then**

[†] To minimize hardware costs, the MIVM system lacks hardware sensors to measure the actual number of coins remaining in the coin dispensers. Therefore, the MIVM software assumes that it can dispense a kind of coin if the associated coin dispensers have been loaded since the last time they all failed to push out a coin. The MIVM software assumes that all coin dispensers are loaded by the service representative whenever the mode is changed.

    // Greet the next customer:
    The MIVM software tells the custom operating system to display 'HAVE
      A NICE DAY' on the main display.
    The custom operating system tells the main display to display 'HAVE A
      NICE DAY'.
    The main display displays 'HAVE A NICE DAY' to the customer.
  end if.
  // Alternative Path 2: Could Not Dispense a Kind of Coin:
  If the customer's credit is greater than zero and the coin dispenser assembly
    could not dispense all kinds of valid coins, **then**
  // Warn the next customer that exact change is required:
    The MIVM software tells the custom operating system to display 'EXACT
      CHANGE ONLY' on the main display.
    The custom operating system tells the main display to display 'EXACT
      CHANGE ONLY'.
    The main display displays 'EXACT CHANGE ONLY' to the customer.
  end if.
  // Alternative Path 3: Could Not Dispense All of the Customer's Credit:
  If the customer's credit is greater than zero, **then**
  // Display the customer's credit:
    The MIVM software tells the custom operating system to display the
      customer's credit on the main display.
    The custom operating system tells the main display to display the
      customer's credit.
    The main display displays the customer's credit to the customer.
  end if.
end after.

Blackbox sequence diagram: See Figure 2.19.

Postconditions:
1. Primary Path 1. Customer's Credit Dispensed Without a Problem:
   - The coin return holds the customer's credit.
   - The main display displays 'HAVE A NICE DAY'.
   - The mode of the MIVM is 'Dispense Item'.
2. Alternative Path 2. Could Not Dispense a Kind of Coin:
   - The coin return holds the customer's credit.
   - The main display displays 'EXACT CHANGE ONLY'.
   - The mode of the MIVM is 'Dispense Item'.
3. Alternative Path 3. Could Not Dispense All of the Customer's Credit:
   - The main display displays the customer's remaining credit.
   - The mode of the MIVM is 'Dispense Item'.

2.3.11.2 Service Representatives (SR)

Definition: the role of a person when servicing the vending machine.

Kind: indirect concrete client actor.

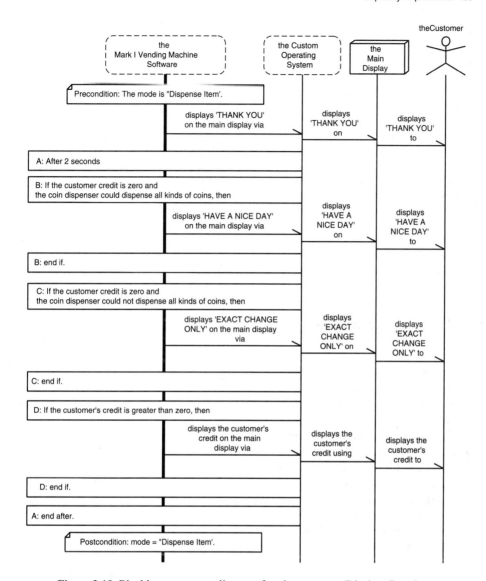

Figure 2.19 Blackbox sequence diagram for the use case: Display Greeting.

Responsibilities:
- Load each item dispenser with items having the same price.
  Collaborator: Item Dispenser.
- Load each coin dispenser with coins of appropriate value.
  Collaborator: Coin Dispenser.
- Set the prices of item dispensers in the item dispenser assembly.
  Collaborators: Item Dispenser, Letter Selection Button, Number Selection Button.

- Take bills from the bill box.
  Collaborator: Bill Box.
- Take coins from the coin box.
  Collaborator: Coin Box.
- Record the history of the MIVM.
  Collaborators: Letter Selection Button, Main Display, Mode Button.

2.3.11.2.1 Service Representative Services the MIVM

Description: This use case models the required interactions between the following externals and the MIVM software when a service representative services the MIVM.

Requirement:

SYS-R) SR-1.

Service Representative Services the MIVM. A service representative shall be able to service the MIVM.

Externals:
- Client:
  1. a service representative
  2. the door
  3. the door switch
  4. the letter selection buttons
  5. the mode button
  6. the number selection buttons
- Peer:
  7. the custom operating system
- Server:
  8. the bill box (hardware only)
  9. the coin box (hardware only)
  10. the coin dispensers
  11. the coin solenoids (optional)
  12. the item dispensers (hardware only)
  13. the item displays
  14. the main display

2.3.11.2.1.1 Initial State of the MIVM

Description: This requirement captures the initial state of the MIVM when a service representative plugs it into an electrical outlet.

Requirement:

SW-R) SR-1.1.

Initial State of the MIVM. Each time the service representative plugs the MIVM into an electrical outlet:[†]

[†] The service representative may therefore need to record the price and history information before unplugging the MIVM (e.g. in order to move it).

- the mode of the MIVM shall be set to 'Set Price',
- the customer information shall be initialized as follows:
  - the customer credit is zero, and
  - the column and row of the customer's selection are unselected.
- the service representative information shall be initialized as follows:
  - the price of the service representative' selection is undefined, and
  - the column and row of the service representative' selection are unselected.
- the coin dispenser assembly information shall be initialized as follows:
  - each coin dispenser is assumed to be able to dispense coins.
- the item dispenser assembly information shall be initialized as follows:
  - the price of each item dispenser is undefined.
- the history information shall be initialized as follows:
  - the total income from the MIVM is zero, and
  - the total number of items sold is zero.
- the main display shall display 'SET PRICE'.
- each item display shall display its location (i.e. row and column) but not its undefined price.

2.3.11.2.1.2 Service Representative Changes the Mode of the MIVM

Description: This use case models the required interactions between the following externals and the MIVM software when a service representative changes the mode of the MIVM.

Requirement:
SYS-R) SR-1.2.
Service Representative Changes the Mode of the MIVM. A service representative shall be able to change the mode of the MIVM.

Externals:
- Client:
  1. a service representative
  2. the door
  3. the door switch
  4. the mode button
- Peer:
  5. the custom operating system
- Server:
  6. the coin dispensers (optional)
  7. the coin solenoids (optional)
  8. the main display

Paths:
- Primary:
  1. Service Representative Presses the Mode Button
  2. Door Switch Resets the Mode

Precondition: None.

Statements:
Either
    invoke use case: Service Representative Presses the Mode Button
or
    invoke use case: Door Switch Resets the Mode.
end either.

Blackbox sequence diagram: See Figure 2.20.

Postconditions:
1. Primary Path 1. Service Representative Pressed the Mode Button:
   • The postconditions of the use case: Service Representative Presses the Mode Button.
2. Alternative Path 2. Door Switch Resets the Mode:
   • The postconditions of the use case: Door Switch Resets the Mode.

2.3.11.2.1.2.1 Service Representative Presses the Mode Button

Description: This use case models the required interactions between the following externals and the MIVM software when a service representative presses the mode button.

Requirements:
   SYS-R) SR-1.2.1.
   Service Representative Presses the Mode Button. A service representative shall be able to change the mode by pressing the mode button.
   SYS-R) SR-1.2.1-1.
   Change from 'Set Price' Mode. If the MIVM is in the 'Set Price' mode when the mode button is pressed, then:
   (a) the MIVM shall reset the information it stores concerning the service representative's selection (i.e. column not selected, row not selected, price unknown),
   (b) the MIVM shall be set to the new mode 'Display History', and
   (c) the main display shall display 'DISPLAY HISTORY'.
   SYS-R) SR-1.2.1-2.
   Change from 'Display History' Mode. If the MIVM is in the 'Display History' mode when the mode button is pressed, then:
   (a) the MIVM shall be set to the new mode 'Dispense Item', and
   (b) the main display shall display 'DISPENSE ITEM' for 2 seconds before displaying the appropriate greeting.
   SYS-R) SR-1.2.1-3.
   Change from 'Dispense Item' Mode. If the MIVM is in the 'Dispense Item' mode when the mode button is pressed, then:
   (a) the MIVM shall dispense the customer's credit (if any),
   (b) the MIVM shall reset the information it stores concerning the customer's selection (i.e. column not selected, row not selected, price unknown) and the customer's credit (i.e. to zero),

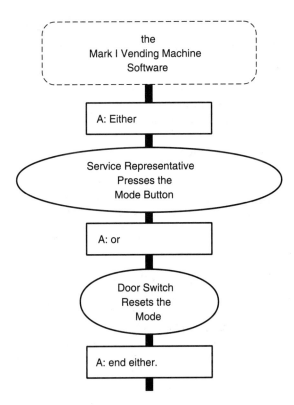

Figure 2.20 Blackbox sequence diagram for the use case: Service Representative Changes the Mode of the MIVM.

(c) the MIVM shall be set to the new mode 'Set Price', and
(d) the main display shall display 'SET PRICE'.

Externals:
- Client:
  1. a service representative
  2. the mode button
- Peer:
  3. the custom operating system
- Server:
  4. the coin dispensers (optional)
  5. the coin solenoids (optional)
  6. the main display

Paths:
- Primary:
  1. Change from 'Dispense Item' Mode
  2. Change from 'Set Price' Mode
  3. Change from 'Display History' Mode

- Alternative:
    4. Could Not Dispense All

Precondition: None.

Statements:
A service representative presses the mode button.
The mode button interrupts the custom operating system, specifying that it was pressed.
The custom operating system interrupts the MIVM software, specifying that the mode button was pressed.
Case:
    If the mode of the MIVM is 'Dispense Item', **then**
        // Primary Path 1. Change from 'Dispense Item' Mode:
        The customer's selection is reset (i.e., column not selected, row not selected, price unknown).
        Invoke use case: Dispense Change.
        If all of the customer's credit could be dispensed, **then**
            The mode is set to the 'Set Price' mode.
            The MIVM software tells the custom operating system to display 'SET PRICE' on the main display.
            The custom operating system tells the main display to display 'SET PRICE'.
            The main display displays 'SET PRICE' to the service representative.
        else
            // Alternative Path 4. Could Not Dispense All:
            // The mode remains 'Dispense Item'.
        end if.
    If the mode of the MIVM is 'Set Price', **then**
        // Primary Path 2. Change from 'Set Price' Mode:
        The MIVM software resets the information it stores concerning the service representative's selection (i.e., column no longer selected, row no longer selected, and selection price unknown).
        The mode is set to 'Display History'.
        The MIVM software tells the custom operating system to display 'DISPLAY HISTORY' on the main display.
        The custom operating system tells the main display to display 'DISPLAY HISTORY'.
        The main display displays 'DISPLAY HISTORY' to the service representative.
    If the mode of the MIVM is 'Display History, **then**
        // Primary Path 3. Change from 'Display History' Mode:
        The mode is set to 'Dispense Item'.
        The MIVM software tells the custom operating system to display 'DISPENSE ITEM' on the main display.
        The custom operating system tells the main display to display 'DISPENSE ITEM'.

The main display displays 'DISPENSE ITEM' to the service representative.
Invoke use case: Display Greeting.
end case.

Blackbox sequence diagram: See Figure 2.21.

Postconditions:
1. Primary Path 1. Change from 'Dispense Item' Mode:
   - The mode of the MIVM is 'Set Price' mode.
   - The main display displays 'SET PRICE'.
2. Primary Path 2. Change from 'Set Price' Mode:
   - The mode of the MIVM is the 'Display History'.
   - The main display displays 'DISPLAY HISTORY'.
3. Primary Path 3. Change from 'Display History' Mode:
   - The mode of the MIVM is the 'Dispense Item'.
   - The postconditions of the use case: Display Greeting.
4. Alternative Path 4. Could Not Dispense All:
   - The mode of the MIVM is the 'Dispense Item'.
   - The main display displays the customer's remaining credit.

2.3.11.2.1.2.2 Door Switch Resets the Mode

Description: This use case models the required interactions between the following externals and the MIVM software when a service representative closes and locks the door.

Requirements:
SYS-R) SR-1.2.2.
Door Switch Resets the Mode. If the door switch is tripped by the closing and locking of the door (when the door opens, the MIVM software ignores the open signal from the hardware door switch), then the MIVM software shall set the mode of the MIVM to 'Dispense Item'. (This is done to insure that customers can buy items but cannot reset the prices of items if a service representative forgets to use the mode button to reset the machine to 'Dispense Item' mode before closing the door.)
SYS-R) SR-1.2.2-1.
Door Switch Resets the Service Representative Information. If the MIVM is in the 'Set Price' mode when the door switch is tripped by the closing and locking of the door, then the MIVM software shall reset the information it stores concerning the service representative's selection (i.e. column not selected, row not selected, price unknown).
SYS-R) SR-1.2.2-2.
Door Switch Resets the Coin Dispenser Assembly Information. If the door switch is tripped by the closing and locking of the door, then the MIVM software shall reset the information it stores concerning the coin dispenser assembly (i.e. it assumes that the coin dispenser assembly has been loaded with all kinds of coins).

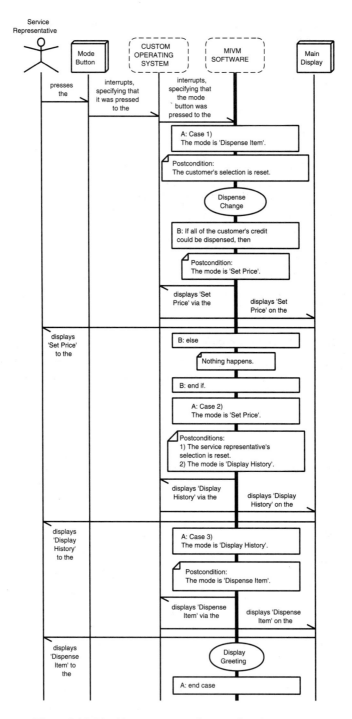

Figure 2.21 Blackbox sequence diagram for the use case: Service Representative Presses the Mode Button.

Externals:
- Client:
  1. a service representative
  2. the door
  3. the door switch
- Peer:
  4. the custom operating system
- Server:
  5. the main display

Paths:
- Primary:
  1. Change from 'Dispense Item' Mode
  2. Change from 'Set Price' Mode
  3. Change from 'Display History' Mode

Precondition: None.

Statements:
A service representative closes and locks the door.
The door trips the door switch.
The door switch interrupts the custom operating system, specifying that the door switch was tripped.
The custom operating system interrupts the MIVM software, specifying that the door switch was tripped.
Case
    If the mode of the MIVM is 'Dispense Item', **then**
        // Primary Path 1. Change from 'Dispense Item' Mode:
        nothing happens.
    If the mode of the MIVM is 'Set Price', **then**
        // Primary Path 2. Change from 'Set Price' Mode:
        the MIVM software resets the information it stores concerning the service representative's selection (i.e. column no longer selected, row no longer selected, and selection price unknown).
    If the mode of the MIVM is 'Display History', **then**
        // Primary Path 3. Change from 'Display History' Mode:
        nothing happens.
end case.
The MIVM software assumes that the coin dispenser assembly has been loaded.
The mode of the MIVM is set to 'Dispense Item'.
The MIVM software tells the custom operating system to display 'DISPENSE ITEM' on the main display.
The custom operating system tells the main display to display 'DISPENSE ITEM'.
The main display displays 'DISPENSE ITEM' to the service representative.
Invoke the use case: Display Greeting.

Blackbox sequence diagram: See Figure 2.22.

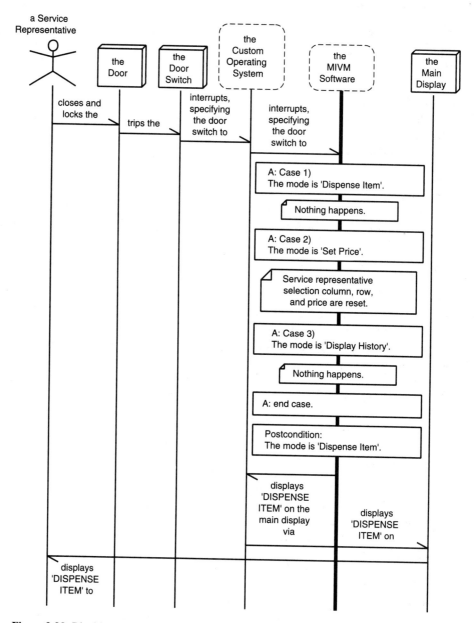

Figure 2.22 Blackbox sequence diagram for the use case: Door Switch Resets the Mode.

Postconditions:

1. Primary Path 1. Change from 'Dispense Item' Mode:
   - The mode of the MIVM is the 'Dispense Item'.
   - The postconditions of the use case: Display Greeting.

2. Primary Path 2. Change from 'Set Price' Mode:
   - The mode of the MIVM is the 'Dispense Item'.
   - The postconditions of the use case: Display Greeting.
3. Primary Path 3. Change from 'Display History' Mode:
   - The mode of the MIVM is the 'Dispense Item'.
   - The postconditions of the use case: Display Greeting.

2.3.11.2.1.3 Service Representative Prices an Item

Description: This use case models the required interactions between the following externals and the MIVM software when a service representative prices an item.

Requirement:

SYS-R) SR-1.3.

Service Representative Prices an Item. If the MIVM is in the 'Set Price' mode, a service representative shall be able to set the common price of all items in an item dispenser at a given valid location (i.e. row and column) in the item dispenser assembly.

Externals:
- Client:
  1. a service representative
  2. the letter selection buttons
  3. the number selection buttons
- Peer:
  4. the custom operating system
- Server:
  5. the item displays
  6. the main display

Precondition: The mode of the MIVM is 'Set Price'.

Statements:
Invoke use case: Service Representative Makes a Selection.
Invoke use case: Service Representative Enters a Price.

Blackbox sequence diagram: See Figure 2.23.

Postconditions:
The postconditions of use case: Service Representative Makes a Selection.
The postconditions of use case: Service Representative Enters a Price.
The mode of the MIVM is 'Set Price'.

2.3.11.2.1.3.1 Service Representative Makes a Selection

Description: This use case models the required interactions between the following externals and the MIVM software when a service representative makes a selection.

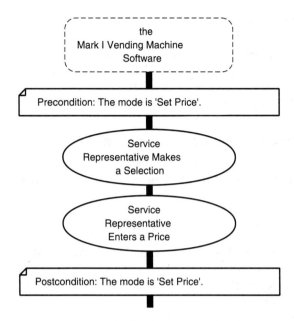

Figure 2.23 Blackbox sequence diagram for the use case: Service Representative Prices an Item.

Requirement:
SYS-D) SR-1.3.1.
Service Representative Makes a Selection. If the MIVM is in the 'Set Price' mode, a service representative shall be able to select an item dispenser at a given valid location (i.e. row and column) in the item dispenser assembly.

Externals:
● Client:
    1. a service representative
    2. the letter selection buttons
    3. the number selection buttons
● Peer:
    4. the custom operating system
● Server:
    5. the main display

Precondition: The mode of the MIVM is 'Set Price'.

Statements:
Concurrently
    invoke use case: Service Representative Selects a Column
and
    invoke use case: Service Representative Selects a Row.
end concurrently.

Blackbox sequence diagram: See Figure 2.24.

Postconditions:
The postconditions of use case: Service Representative Selects a Column.
The postconditions of use case: Service Representative Selects a Row.
The mode of the MIVM is 'Set Price'.

2.3.11.2.1.3.1.1 Service Representative Selects a Column

Description: This use case models the required interactions between the following externals and the MIVM software when a service representative selects a column.

Requirement:
  SYS-D) SR-1.3.1.1.
  Service Representative Selects a Column. If the MIVM is in the 'Set Price' mode, a service representative shall be able to select the column of an item dispenser to be priced.

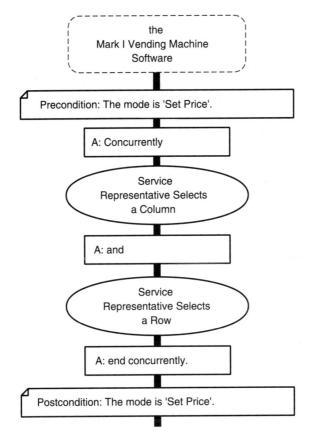

Figure 2.24 Blackbox sequence diagram for the use case: Service Representative Makes a Selection.

SYS-D) SR-1.3.1.1-1.

Service Representative Selects a Column when the Row is Not Selected. If a number selection button is pressed when the MIVM is in either the 'Nothing Selected' submode or the 'Column Selected' submode of the 'Set Price' mode, then the MIVM software shall:

(a) store the corresponding column of the service representative's selection,
(b) display the selected column on the main display, and
(c) be placed in the 'Column Selected' submode of the 'Set Price' mode.

SYS-D) SR-1.3.1.1-2.

Service Representative Selects a Column when the Row is Selected. If a number selection button is pressed when the MIVM is in the 'Row Selected' submode of the 'Set Price' mode, then the MIVM software shall:

(a) store the corresponding column of the service representative's selection,
(b) display the selected column, row, and selection price (if any) on the main display, and
(c) be placed in the 'Item Selected' submode of the 'Set Price' mode.

SW-R) SR-1.3.1.1-3.

Ignore the Refund Button. If the refund button is pressed when the MIVM is in the 'Set Price' mode, then the MIVM software shall ignore the input from the refund button.

SW-R) SR-1.3.1.1-4.

Handle Unexpected Money. If any money is validated when the MIVM is in the 'Set Price' mode, then the MIVM software shall:

(a) reset the location and price of the service representative's selection,
(b) set the mode of the MIVM to 'Dispense Item', and
(c) treat the unexpected money as if a customer had made a payment.

Externals:
- Client:
  1. a service representative
  2. the number selection buttons
- Peer:
  3. the custom operating system
- Server:
  4. the main display

Paths:
- Primary:
  1. Service Representative Selects the Column without Selecting an Item
  2. Service Representative Selects the Item by Selecting the Column
- Alternative:
  3. Press the Refund Button
  4. Handle Unexpected Money

Precondition: The MIVM is in the 'Set Price' mode.

Statements:
Case:
    If a service representative presses a number selection button, **then**
        The number selection button interrupts the custom operating system, specifying the number selected.
        The custom operating system interrupts the MIVM software, specifying the number selected.
        The MIVM software sets the column of the service representative to the number selected.
        Case:
            If the MIVM is in either the 'Nothing Selected' submode or the 'Column Selected' submode, **then**
                // Primary Path 1. Service Representative Selects the Column without Selecting an Item:
                The MIVM software is placed in the 'Column Selected' submode of the 'Set Price' mode.
                The MIVM software tells the custom operating system to display the column on the main display.
                The main display displays the column to the service representative.
            If a service representative presses a number selection button when the MIVM is in the 'Row Selected' submode, **then**
                // Primary Path 2. Service Representative Selects the Item by Selecting the Column:
                The MIVM software is placed in the 'Item Selected' submode of the 'Set Price' mode.
                The MIVM software tells the custom operating system to display the location and price on the main display.
                The main display displays the location and price to the service representative.
        end case.
    If a service representative presses the refund button, **then**
        // Alternative Path 3. Press the Refund Button:
        nothing happens.
    If a service representative inserts valid money, **then**
        // Alternative Path 4. Handle Unexpected Money:
        The MIVM software shall reset the location and price of the service representative's selection.
        The MIVM software shall set the mode of the MIVM to 'Dispense Item'.
        Invoke the use case: Customer Makes a Payment.
end case.

Blackbox sequence diagram: See Figure 2.25.

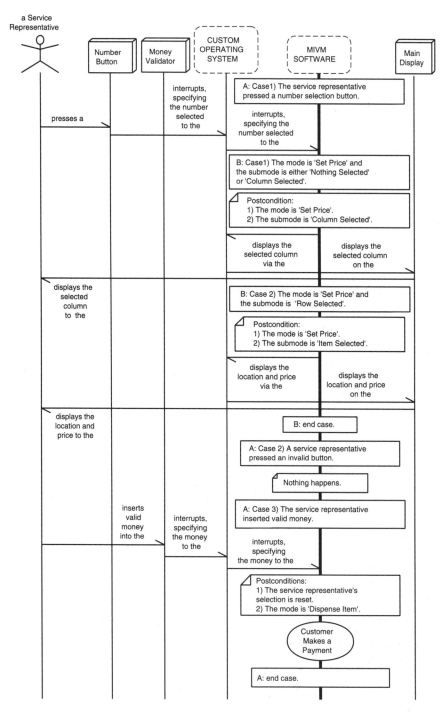

Figure 2.25 Blackbox sequence diagram for the use case:
Service Representative Selects a Column.

Postconditions:

1. Primary Path 1. Service Representative Selects the Column without Selecting an Item:
   - The MIVM software now stores the column of the service representative selection.
   - The MIVM is in the 'Column Selected' submode of the 'Set Price' mode.
2. Primary Path 2. Service Representative Selects the Item by Selecting the Column:
   - The MIVM software now stores the location and price of the service representative selection.
   - The MIVM is in the 'Item Selected' submode of the 'Set Price' mode.
3. Alternative Path 3. Press the Refund Button:
   - The MIVM is in the 'Item Selected' submode of the 'Set Price' mode.
4. Alternative Path 4. Handle Unexpected Money:
   - The mode of the MIVM is 'Dispense Item'.
   - The postconditions of the use case: Customer Makes a Payment.

2.3.11.2.1.3.1.2 Service Representative Selects a Row

Description: This use case models the required interactions between the following externals and the MIVM software when a service representative selects a row.

Requirement:
SYS-D) SR-1.3.1.2.
Service Representative Selects a Row. When the MIVM is in the 'Set Price' mode, a service representative shall be able to select the row of an item dispenser to be priced.
SYS-D) SR-1.3.1.2-1.
Service Representative Selects a Row when the Column is Not Selected. If a letter selection button is pressed when the MIVM is in either the 'Nothing Selected' submode or the 'Row Selected' submode of the 'Set Price' mode, then the MIVM software shall:
(a) store the corresponding row of the service representative's selection,
(d) display the selected row on the main display, and
(e) be placed in the 'Row Selected' submode of the 'Set Price' mode.
SYS-D) SR-1.3.1.2-2.
Service Representative Selects a Row when the Column is Selected. If a number selection button is pressed when the MIVM is in the 'Column Selected' submode of the 'Set Price' mode, then the MIVM software shall:
(a) store the corresponding column of the service representative's selection,
(b) display the selected column, row, and selection price (if any) on the main display, and
(c) be placed in the 'Item Selected' submode of the 'Set Price' mode.
SW-R) SR-1.3.1.1-3.
Ignore the Refund Button. If the refund button is pressed when the MIVM is in the 'Set Price' mode, then the MIVM software shall ignore the input from the refund button.

SW-R) SR-1.3.1.1-4.

Handle Unexpected Money. If any money is validated when the MIVM is in the 'Set Price' mode, then the MIVM software shall:
(d) reset the location and price of the service representative's selection,
(e) set the mode of the MIVM to 'Dispense Item', and
(f) treat the unexpected money as if a customer had made a payment.

Externals:
- Client:
  1. a service representative
  2. the letter selection buttons
- Peer:
  3. the custom operating system
- Server:
  4. the main display

Paths:
- Primary:
  1. Service Representative Selects the Row without Selecting an Item
  2. Service Representative Selects the Item by Selecting the Row
- Alternative:
  3. Press the Refund Button
  4. Handle Unexpected Money

Precondition: The MIVM is in the 'Set Price' mode.

Statements:

Case:

  If a service representative presses a letter selection button, **then**
    The letter selection button interrupts the custom operating system, specifying the letter selected.
    The custom operating system interrupts the MIVM software, specifying the letter selected.
    The MIVM software sets the row of the service representative to the letter selected.

    Case:

      If the MIVM is in either the 'Nothing Selected' submode or the 'Row Selected' submode, **then**
        // Primary Path 1. Service Representative Selects the Column without Selecting an Item:
        The MIVM software is placed in the 'Row Selected' submode of the 'Set Price' mode.
        The MIVM software tells the custom operating system to display the row on the main display.
        The main display displays the row to the service representative.
      If a service representative presses a number selection button when the MIVM is in the 'Column Selected' submode, **then**
        // Primary Path 2. Service Representative Selects the Item by Selecting the Row:

The MIVM software is placed in the 'Item Selected' submode of the 'Set Price' mode.
The MIVM software tells the custom operating system to display the location and price on the main display.
The main display displays the location and price to the service representative.
end case.
If a service representative presses the refund button, **then**
// Alternative Path 3. Press the Refund Button:
nothing happens.
If a service representative inserts valid money, **then**
// Alternative Path 4. Handle Unexpected Money:
The MIVM software shall reset the location and price of the service representative's selection.
The MIVM software shall set the mode of the MIVM to 'Dispense Item'.
Invoke the use case: Customer Makes a Payment.
end case.

Blackbox sequence diagram: See Figure 2.26.

Postconditions:
1. Primary Path 1. Service Representative Selects the Column without Selecting an Item:
   - The MIVM software now stores the row of the service representative selection.
   - The MIVM is in the 'Column Selected' submode of the 'Set Price' mode.
2. Primary Path 2. Service Representative Selects the Item by Selecting the Row:
   - The MIVM software now stores the location and price of the service representative selection.
   - The MIVM is in the 'Item Selected' submode of the 'Set Price' mode.
3. Alternative Path 3. Press the Refund Button:
   - The MIVM is in the 'Item Selected' submode of the 'Set Price' mode.
4. Alternative Path 4. Handle Unexpected Money:
   - The mode of the MIVM is 'Dispense Item'.
   - The postconditions of the use case: Customer Makes a Payment.

2.3.11.2.1.3.2 Service Representative Enters a Price

Description: This use case models the required interactions between the following externals and the MIVM software when a service representative enters a price.

Requirements:
SYS-D) SR-1.3.1.3.
Service Representative Enters a Price. If the MIVM is in the 'Building Price' submode of the 'Set Price' mode, a service representative shall be able to build the common price of the items in the item dispenser at the selected location in the item dispenser assembly.

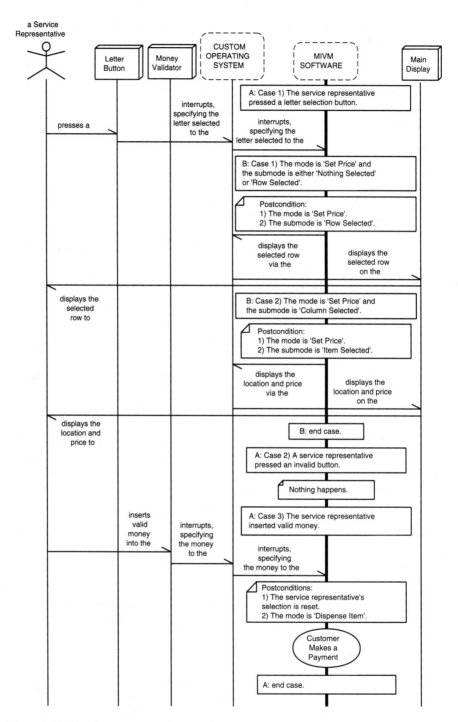

Figure 2.26 Blackbox sequence diagram for the use case: Service Representative Selects a Row.

SYS-D) SR-1.3.1.3-1.
Accept the Old Price. If the 'A' (for Accept) letter selection button is pressed when the MIVM is in the 'Item Selected' submode of the 'Set Price' mode, then the MIVM software shall.
(a) reset the location and price of the service representative's selection,
(b) display 'ACCEPTED' on its main display, and
(c) be placed in the 'Selecting Column' submode of the 'Set Price' mode.

SYS-D) SR-1.3.1.3-2.
Build the New Price. If a number selection button is pressed when the MIVM is in the 'Appending Price' submode of the 'Set Price' mode, then the MIVM software shall:
(a) incrementally build the new common price of items in the selected location whereby each number shall be added to the right of the preceding numbers with 10 being interpreted as 0, and
(b) display the new price on its main display.

SYS-D) SR-1.3.1.3-3.
Enter the New Price. If (a) the 'E' (for Enter) letter selection button is pressed when the MIVM is in the 'Appending Price' submode of the 'Set Price' mode and (b) a full coin dispenser assembly can theoretically dispense change after purchase (i.e., if the new price is evenly divisible by five cents), then the MIVM software shall:
(a) store the new common price of the item dispenser in the item dispenser assembly,
(b) display the new price on the item display of the item dispenser,
(d) display 'ENTERED' on the main display,
(e) reset the service representative selection (i.e. no longer store its location and price), and
(f) be placed in the 'Selecting Column' submode of the 'Set Price' mode.

SYS-D) SR-1.3.1.3-4.
Handle an Invalid Price. If (a) the 'E' (for Enter) letter selection button is pressed when the MIVM is in the 'Appending Price' submode of the 'Set Price' mode and (b) the coin dispenser assembly when full cannot theoretically dispense change after purchase (i.e. if the new price is not evenly divisible by five cents), then the MIVM software shall:
(a) no longer store new price of the service representative's selection,
(b) display 'REJECTED' on the main display, and
(c) remain in the 'Building Price' submode of the 'Set Price' mode.

SYS-D) SR-1.3.1.3-5.
Cancel the New Price. If the 'C' (for Cancel) letter selection button is pressed when the MIVM is in the 'Appending Price' submode of the 'Set Price' mode, then the MIVM software shall:
(a) reset the service representative selection (i.e. no longer store its location and new price),
(b) request the main display to display the message 'CANCELED', and
(c) be placed in the 'Selecting Column' submode of the 'Set Price' mode.

SW-R) SR-1.3.1.3-6.

Ignore Inappropriate Buttons. The MIVM software shall ignore all inputs from the refund button and the letter selection buttons B, D, F, G, and H.

SYS-D) SR-1.3.1.3-7.

Handle Unexpected Money. If any money is validated, then the MIVM software shall:

(a) reset the location and price of the service representative's selection,

(b) set the mode of the MIVM to 'Dispense Item', and

(c) treat the unexpected money as if a customer had made a payment.

Externals:

- Client:
    1. a service representative
    2. the 'A', 'C', and 'E' letter selection buttons
    3. the number selection buttons
- Peer:
    4. the custom operating system
- Server:
    5. the item displays
    6. the main display

Paths:

- Primary:
    1. Build and Enter the new Valid Price
- Alternative:
    2. Accept the old Price
    3. Build and Enter the new Invalid Price
    4. Build and Cancel the new Price
    5. Press an Inappropriate Button
    6. Handle Unexpected Money

Precondition: The MIVM is in the 'ItemSelected.SomethingSelected' submode of the 'Set Price' mode.

Statements:

Concurrently

// Alternative Path 2. Accept the Old Price:

A service representative presses the 'A' letter selection button.

The 'A' letter selection button interrupts the custom operating system, specifying the letter 'A' was selected.

The custom operating system interrupts the MIVM software, specifying the letter 'A' was selected.

The MIVM software resets the location of the service representative's selection.

The MIVM software sets the mode to the 'NothingSelected' submode of the 'Set Price' mode.

The MIVM software tells the custom operating system to display 'ACCEPTED' on the main display.

The custom operating system tells the main display to display 'ACCEPTED'.

The main display displays 'ACCEPTED' to the service representative.

and

(

The MIVM software sets the current price of the service representative selection to zero.

// Build the new price:

Until the 'C' or 'E' letter selection button or the refund button is pressed or money is validated **loop:**

>The service representative presses a number selection button.
>
>The number selection button interrupts the custom operating system, specifying the number selected.
>
>The custom operating system interrupts the MIVM software, specifying the number selected.
>
>The MIVM software sets the mode to the 'AppendingPrice.SomethingSelected' submode of the 'Set Price' mode.
>
>The MIVM software increments the price of the service representative selection by multiplying the previous price by 10 and adding the digit represented by the number selected.[†]
>
>// Display the new price on the main display:
>
>The MIVM software tells the custom operating system to display the new price on the main display.
>
>The custom operating system tells the main display to display the new price.
>
>The main display displays the new price to the service representative.

end loop.

Case

>**If** the service representative presses the 'C' letter button, **then**
>
>>// Alternative Path 4. Build and Cancel the New Price:
>>
>>The 'C' letter selection button interrupts the custom operating system, specifying the letter 'C' was selected.
>>
>>The custom operating system interrupts the MIVM software, specifying the letter 'C' was selected.
>>
>>The MIVM software resets the price and location of the service representative's selection.
>>
>>The MIVM software tells the custom operating system to display 'CANCELED' on the main display.
>>
>>The custom operating system tells the main display to display 'CANCELED'.
>>
>>The main display displays 'CANCELED' to the service representative.
>>
>>The MIVM software sets the MIVM to the 'NothingSelected' submode of the 'Set Price' mode.

[†] If the '10' number selection button is pressed, the digit added to the previous price to make the new price is zero.

> **Invoke use case:** Service Representative Selects a Column.
>
> **Invoke use case:** Service Representative Selects a Row.

If the service representative presses the 'E' letter button and the coin dispenser assembly when full cannot theoretically dispense change after purchase, **then**

> // Alternative Path 3. Build and Enter the New Invalid Price:
>
> The MIVM software resets the price of the service representative's selection to zero.
>
> The MIVM software tells the custom operating system to display 'REJECTED' on the main display.
>
> The custom operating system tells the main display to display 'REJECTED'.
>
> The main display displays 'REJECTED' to the service representative.
>
> The MIVM software sets the MIVM to the 'ItemSelected.SomethingSelected' submode of the 'Set Price' mode.

If the service representative presses the 'E' letter button and the coin dispenser assembly when full can theoretically dispense change after purchase, **then**

> // Primary Path 1. Build and Enter the New Valid Price:
>
> The MIVM software sets the price of the service representative's selection to the new price.
>
> The MIVM software tells the custom operating system to display new price on the main display.
>
> The custom operating system tells the main display to display the new price.
>
> The main display displays the new price to the service representative.
>
> The MIVM software sets the MIVM to the 'NothingSelected' submode of the 'Set Price' mode.

If a service representative presses the refund button or a number selection button, **then**

> // Alternative Path 5. Press an Inappropriate Button:
>
> Nothing happens.

> **end case.**
>
>)

and

> **If** a service representative inserts valid money, **then**
>
> > // Alternative Path 6. Handle Unexpected Money:
> >
> > The MIVM software resets the service representative's selection.
> >
> > The MIVM software shall set the mode of the MIVM to 'Dispense Item'.
> >
> > **Invoke the use case:** Customer Makes a Payment.
>
> **end if.**

end concurrently.

Blackbox sequence diagram: See Figure 2.27.

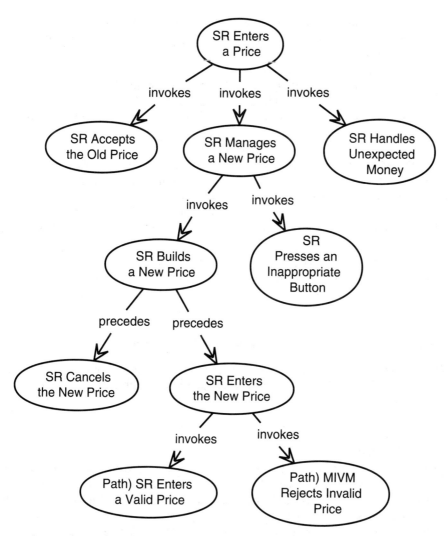

Figure 2.27 Use case diagram for the use case: Service Representative Enters a Price.

Postconditions:
1. Primary Path 1. Build and Enter the new Common Price:
   - The MIVM is in the 'Selecting Column' submode of the 'Set Price' mode.
   - The MIVM software stores the new location and new price of the service representative selection.
2. Alternative Path 2. Accept the old Common Price:
   - The MIVM is in the 'Selecting Column' submode of the 'Set Price' mode.
   - The MIVM software stores the old location and old price of the service representative selection.

3. Alternative Path 3. Build and Reject the new Common Price:
   - The MIVM is in the 'Building Price' submode of the 'Set Price' mode.
   - The MIVM software stores the new location and the old price of the service representative selection.
4. Alternative Path 4. Build and Cancel the new Common Price:
   - The MIVM is in the 'Building Price' submode of the 'Set Price' mode.
   - The MIVM software stores the new location and the old price of the service representative selection.
5. Alternative Path 5. Press an Inappropriate Button:
   - The MIVM is in the 'Building Price' submode of the 'Set Price' mode.
   - The MIVM software stores the new location and the partially built new price of the service representative selection.
6. Alternative Path 6. Handle Unexpected Money.
   - The MIVM software no longer stores the location or price of the service representative selection.
   - The mode of the MIVM is 'Dispense Item'.
   - The postconditions of the use case: Customer Makes a Payment.

2.3.11.2.1.4 Service Representative Displays History

Description: This use case models the required interactions between the following externals and the MIVM software when a service representative displays the history of the machine.

Requirements:
SYS-R) SR-1.4.
Service Representative Displays History. If the MIVM is in the 'Display History' mode, then a service representative shall be able to display the total number of items sold and the total vending machine income on the main display. (Note that the service representative typically displays the history of the machine each time that the machine is serviced. The service representative then subtracts the previous values from the currently displayed values in order to determine the machine's income and number of items sold since the last time that the machine was serviced.)
SYS-D) SR-1.4-3.
Ignore Inappropriate Buttons. The software shall ignore all inputs from the refund button, the number selection buttons, and the letter selection buttons 'C', 'D', 'E', 'F', 'G' and 'H'.
SYS-D) SR-1.4-4.
Handle Unexpected Money. If any money is validated, then the MIVM software shall:
(a) set the mode of the MIVM to 'Dispense Item', and
(b) treat the unexpected money as if a customer had made a payment.

Externals:
- Client:
  1. a service representative
  2. the 'A' and 'B' letter selection button
- Peer:
  3. the custom operating system
- Server:
  4. the main display

Paths:
- Primary:
  1. Display Total Items Sold
  2. Display Total Income
- Alternative:
  3. Ignore Inappropriate Buttons
  4. Handle Unexpected Money

Precondition: The mode of the MIVM is 'Display History'.

Statements:
Concurrently
  // Primary Path 1. Display Total Items Sold:
  Invoke use case: Service Representative Displays the Total Number of Items Sold.
and
  // Primary Path 2. Display Total Income:
  Invoke use case: Service Representative Displays the Total Income.
and
  // Alternative Path 3. Ignore Inappropriate Buttons:
  Ignore inappropriate buttons.
and
  // Alternative Path 4. Handle Unexpected Money:
  If money is validated, **then**
    The MIVM software stores the mode as 'Dispense Item', and
    Invoke use case: Customer Makes a Payment.
  end if.
end concurrently.

Blackbox sequence diagram: See Figure 2.28.

Postconditions:
1. Primary Path 1. Display Total Items Sold:
   - The main display displays the total number of items sold by the MIVM.
   - The mode of the MIVM is 'Display History'.

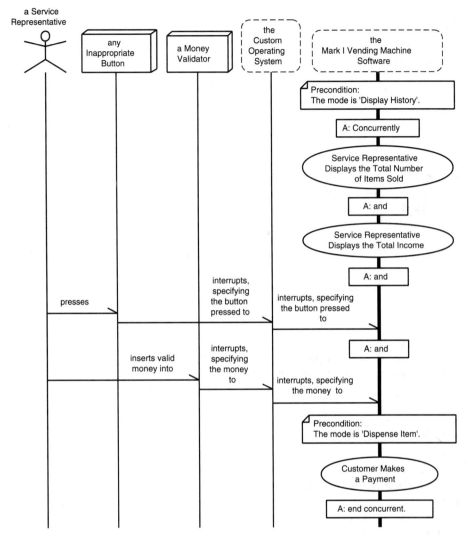

Figure 2.28 Blackbox sequence diagram for the use cse: Service Representative Displays History.

2. Primary Path 2. Display Total Income:
   - The main display displays the total income of the MIVM.
   - The mode of the MIVM is 'Display History'.
3. Alternative Path 3. Ignore Inappropriate Buttons:
   - The mode of the MIVM is 'Display History'.
4. Alternative Path 4. Handle Unexpected Money:
   - The postconditions of the use case: Customer Makes a Payment.
   - The mode of the MIVM is 'Dispense Item'.

2.3.11.2.1.4.1 Service Representative Displays the Total Number of Items Sold

Description: This use case models the required interactions between the following externals and the MIVM software when a service representative requests the display of the total number of items sold by the machine.

Requirement:
SYS-D) SR-1.4-1.
Service Representative Displays the Total Number of Items Sold. If the 'A' letter selection button is pressed, then the MIVM shall display on the main display the total number of items sold (i.e., dispensed) to date by the MIVM. (Because there is no way to reset this number, this is the grand total and not just the total number of items sold since the last time this use case was invoked.)

Externals:
- Client:
    1. a service representative
    2. the 'A' letter selection button
- Peer:
    1. the custom operating system
- Server:
    2. the main display

Paths:
- Primary:
    1. Display Total Items Sold

Precondition: The mode of the MIVM is 'Display History'.
1. Primary Path 2. Display Total Income:
    - The mode of the MIVM is 'Display History'.
    - The main display displays the total income of the MIVM.
2. Alternative Path 3. Ignore Inappropriate Buttons:
    - The mode of the MIVM is 'Display History'.

Statements:
A service representative presses the 'A' letter selection button.
The 'A' letter selection button interrupts the custom operating system, specifying that the letter 'A' was selected.
The custom operating system interrupts the MIVM software, specifying that the letter 'A' was selected.
The MIVM software tells the custom operating system to display the total number of items sold on the main display.
The custom operating system tells the main display to display the total number of items sold.

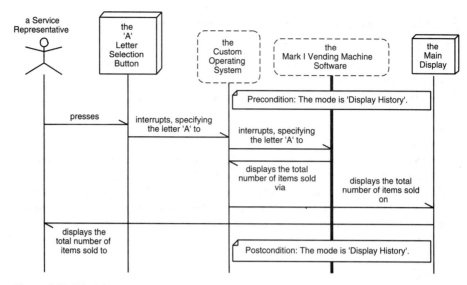

Figure 2.29 Blackbox sequence diagram for the use case: Service Representative Displays the Total Number of Items Sold.

The main display displays the total number of items sold to the service representative.

Blackbox sequence diagram: See Figure 2.29.

Postconditions:
The main display displays the total number of items sold from the MIVM.
The mode of the MIVM is 'Display History'.

2.3.11.2.1.4.2 Service Representative Displays the Total Income

Description: This use case models the required interactions between the following externals and the MIVM software when a service representative requests the display of the total income from the machine.

Requirement:
SYS-D) SR-1.4-2.
Service Representative Displays the Total Income. If the 'B' letter selection button is pressed, then the MIVM shall display on the main display the total income to date from all items sold by the MIVM. (Because there is no way to reset this number, this is the grand total and not just the income since the last time this use case was invoked.)

Externals:
• Client:
    1. a service representative
    2. the 'B' letter selection button
• Peer:
    3. the custom operating system

- Server:
  4. the main display

Paths:
- Primary:
  1. Display Total Income

Precondition: The mode of the MIVM is 'Display History'.

Statements:
A service representative presses the 'B' letter selection button.
The 'B' letter selection button interrupts the custom operating system, specifying that the letter 'B' was selected.
The custom operating system interrupts the MIVM software, specifying that the letter 'B' was selected.
The MIVM software tells the custom operating system to display the total income on the main display.
The custom operating system tells the main display to display the total income.
The main display displays the total income to the service representative.

Blackbox sequence diagram: See Figure 2.30.

Postconditions:
The main display displays the total income from the MIVM.
The mode of the MIVM is 'Display History'.

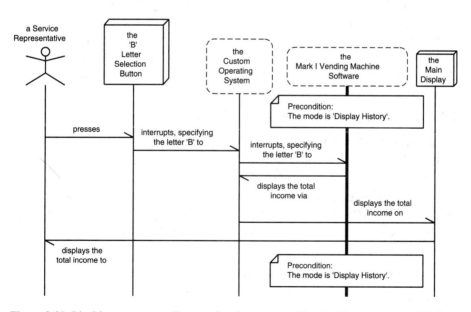

Figure 2.30 Blackbox sequence diagram for the use case: Service Representative Displays the Total Income.

2.4 Quality requirements

2.4.1 Extensibility requirements

Requirement: **SYS-R) E-1.**
Configuration of the Bill Validator. The design of the MIVM software shall make it easy to replace the current bill validator with one that validates different kinds of bills.

Requirement: **SYS-R) E-2.**
Configuration of the Coin Dispenser Assembly. The design of the MIVM software shall make it easy to replace the current coin dispenser assembly with one that dispenses different kinds of coins. For example, the current coin dispenser assembly may be replaced with one that dispenses 50 cent pieces, one that has different numbers of coin dispensers (e.g. one that has three dispensers for quarters), or one that has a different, more sophisticated coin dispensing policy.

Requirement: **SYS-R) E-3.**
Configuration of the Coin Validator. The design of the MIVM software shall make it easy to replace the current coin validator with one that validates different kinds of coins.

Requirement: **SYS-R) E-4.**
Configuration of the Customer Messages. The design of the MIVM software shall make it easy to replace the current customer messages (e.g. 'EXACT CHANGE ONLY', 'HAVE A NICE DAY', 'THANK YOU').

Requirement: **SYS-R) E-5.**
Configuration of the Item Dispenser Assembly. The design of the MIVM software shall make it easy to replace the current item dispenser assembly with one that has a different number of columns and/or a different number of rows.

2.4.2 User-friendliness requirements

Requirement: **SYS-R) UF-1.**
Order of Operations. Customers shall be able to perform any valid operation in any valid order.

Requirement: **SYS-R) UF-2.**
Feedback. The MIVM software shall acknowledge via the displays all valid inputs from the input devices (e.g. buttons, money validators).

2.4.3 Performance requirements

Requirement: **SYS-R) P-1.**
Response Time. The MIVM software shall take no longer than one second to respond to any input.

2.5 Requirements trace to concrete classes

Table 2.1 Requirements trace to concrete classes

Software requirements	Implemented by concrete classes*
C-1) Customer Buys an Item	BillValidator CoinDispenser CoinDispenserAssembly CoinDispensingPolicy CoinSolenoid CoinValidator CurrentModeProxy Customer CustomerCredit CustomerMessages CustomerSelection CustomOperatingSystemCalls CustomOperatingSystemInterrupts DispenseItemMode ItemDispenser ItemDispenserAssembly ItemStepperMotor LetterSelectionButton MainDisplay ModeButton NumberSelectionButton RefundButton
C-1.1) Customer Makes a Selection	CoinDispenser CoinDispenserAssembly CoinDispensingPolicy CoinSolenoid CurrentModeProxy Customer CustomerCredit CustomerMessages CustomerSelection CustomOperatingSystemCalls CustomOperatingSystemInterrupts DispenseItemMode ItemDispenser ItemDispenserAssembly ItemStepperMotor LetterSelectionButton Main Display NumberSelectionButton
C-1.1.1) Customer Selects the Column of an Item C-1.1.1-1) Customer Selects the Column without Selecting the Item C-1.1.1-2) Customer Selects the Item by Selecting the Column C-1.1.1-3) Customer Reselects the Column	CoinDispenser CoinDispenserAssembly CoinDispensingPolicy CoinSolenoid CurrentModeProxy Customer CustomerCredit CustomerMessages CustomerSelection CustomOperatingSystemCalls

* These classes are identified and documented in Chapter 3: Design Documentation.

Table 2.1 (continued)

Software requirements	Implemented by concrete classes
	CustomOperatingSystemInterrupts DispenseItemMode ItemDispenser ItemDispenserAssembly ItemStepperMotor MainDisplay NumberSelectionButton
C-1.1.2) Customer Selects the Row of an Item C-1.1.2-1) Customer Selects the Row without Selecting the Item C-1.1.2-2) Customer Selects the Item by Selecting the Row C-1.1.2-3) Customer Reselects the Row	CoinDispenser CoinDispenserAssembly CoinDispensingPolicy CoinSolenoid CurrentModeProxy Customer CustomerCredit CustomerMessages CustomerSelection CustomOperatingSystemCalls CustomOperatingSystemInterrupts DispenseItemMode ItemDispenser ItemDispenserAssembly ItemStepperMotor LetterSelectionButton MainDisplay
C-1.2) Customer Makes a Payment	BillValidator CoinDispenser CoinDispenserAssembly CoinDispensingPolicy CoinSolenoid CoinValidator CurrentModeProxy Customer CustomerCredit CustomerMessages CustomerSelection CustomOperatingSystemCalls CustomOperatingSystemInterrupts DispenseItemMode ItemDispenser ItemDispenserAssembly ItemStepperMotor MainDisplay
C-1.2.1) Customer Pays with Valid Bills C-1.2.1-1) Customer Inserts a Bill when the Item is Selected C-1.2.1-2) Customer Inserts a Bill when the Item is not Selected	BillValidator CoinDispenser CoinDispenserAssembly CoinDispensingPolicy CoinSolenoid CurrentModeProxy Customer CustomerCredit CustomerMessages CustomerSelection CustomOperatingSystemCalls CustomOperatingSystemInterrupts DispenseItemMode

Table 2.1 (continued)

Software requirements	Implemented by concrete classes
	ItemDispenser ItemDispenserAssembly ItemStepperMotor MainDisplay
C-1.2.2) Customer Pays with Valid Coins C-1.2.2-1) Customer Inserts a Coin when the Item is Selected C-1.2.2-2) Customer Inserts a Coin when the Item is not Selected	CoinDispenser CoinDispenserAssembly CoinDispensingPolicy CoinSolenoid CoinValidator CurrentModeProxy Customer CustomerCredit CustomerMessages CustomerSelection CustomOperatingSystemCalls CustomOperatingSystemInterrupts DispenseItemMode ItemDispenser ItemDispenserAssembly ItemStepperMotor MainDisplay
C-1.3) Customer Requests a Refund	CoinDispenser CoinDispenserAssembly CoinDispensingPolicy CoinSolenoid CurrentModeProxy Customer CustomerCredit CustomerMessages CustomerSelection CustomOperatingSystemCalls CustomOperatingSystemInterrupts DispenseItemMode MainDisplay RefundButton
C-1.4) Attempt to Dispense C-1.4-1) Item Selected and Paid For C-1.4-2) Item Selected but not Paid For	CoinDispenser CoinDispenserAssembly CoinDispensingPolicy CoinSolenoid CustomerCredit CustomerMessages CustomerSelection CustomOperatingSystemCalls ItemDispenser ItemDispenserAssembly ItemStepperMotor MainDisplay
C-1.4.1) Handle Invalid Customer Selection	CustomerSelection CustomOperatingSystemCalls ItemDispenser ItemDispenserAssembly MainDisplay
C-1.4.2) Dispense Change C-1.4.2-1) Credit for Undispensed Change	CoinDispenser CoinDispenserAssembly

Table 2.1 (continued)

Software requirements	Implemented by concrete classes
C-1.4.2-2) Coin Dispensing Policy	CoinDispensingPolicy CoinSolenoid CustomerCredit CustomerMessages CustomerSelection CustomOperatingSystemCalls MainDisplay
C-1.4.2.1) Dispense Quarters	CoinDispenser CoinDispenserAssembly CoinDispensingPolicy CoinSolenoid CustomerCredit CustomOperatingSystemCalls
C-1.4.2.2) Dispense Dimes	CoinDispenser CoinDispenserAssembly CoinDispensingPolicy CoinSolenoid CustomerCredit CustomOperatingSystemCalls
C-1.4.2.3) Dispense Nickels	CoinDispenser CoinDispenserAssembly CoinDispensingPolicy CoinSolenoid CustomerCredit CustomerMessages CustomOperatingSystemCalls
C-1.4.2.4) Display Greeting C-1.4.2.4-1) Thank Customer C-1.4.2.4-2) Display Exact Change Warning C-1.4.2.4-3) Display Remaining Credit	Customer CustomerCredit CustomerMessages CustomOperatingSystemCalls MainDisplay
SR-1) Service Representative Services the MIVM	CurrentModeProxy CustomOperatingSystemCalls CustomOperatingSystemInterrupts DisplayHistoryMode ItemDispenser ItemDispenserAssembly ItemDisplay MainDisplay ModeButton SetPriceMode Switch
SR-1.1) Initial State of the MIVM	CoinDispenser CurrentModeProxy CustomerCredit CustomerSelection ItemDispenser ItemDispenserAssembly ServiceRepresentativeSelection
SR-1.2) Service Representative Changes the Mode of the MIVM	CurrentModeProxy CustomOperatingSystemCalls

Table 2.1 (continued)

Software requirements	Implemented by concrete classes
	CustomOperatingSystemInterrupts DispenseItemMode DisplayHistoryMode MainDisplay ModeButton SetPriceMode Switch
SR-1.2.1) Service Representative Presses the Mode Button SR-1.2.1-1) Change from 'Set Price' Mode SR-1.2.1-2) Change from 'Display History' Mode SR-1.2.1-3) Change from 'Dispense Item' Mode	CurrentModeProxy CustomOperatingSystemCalls CustomOperatingSystemInterrupts DispenseItemMode DisplayHistoryMode MainDisplay ModeButton SetPriceMode
SR-1.2.2) Door Switch Resets the Mode of the MIVM SR-1.2.2-1) Door Switch Resets the Service Representative Information SR-1.2.2-2) Door Switch Resets the Coin Dispenser Assembly Information	CurrentModeProxy CustomOperatingSystemCalls CustomOperatingSystemInterrupts Door MainDisplay Switch
SR-1.3) Service Representative Prices an Item	CurrentModeProxy CustomOperatingSystemCalls CustomOperatingSystemInterrupts ItemDispenser ItemDispenserAssembly ItemDisplay LetterSelectionButton MainDisplay NumberSelectionButton ServiceRepresentative ServiceRepresentativeSelection SetPriceMode
SR-1.3.1) Service Representative Makes a Selection	CurrentModeProxy CustomOperatingSystemCalls CustomOperatingSystemInterrupts ItemDispenser ItemDispenserAssembly LetterSelectionButton MainDisplay NumberSelectionButton ServiceRepresentative ServiceRepresentativeSelection SetPriceMode
SR-1.3.1.1) Service Representative Selects a Column SR-1.3.1.1-1) Service Representative Selects a Column when the Row is Not Selected SR-1.3.1.1-2) Service Representative Selects a Column when the Row is Selected SR-1.3.1.1-3) Ignore the Refund Button SR-1.3.1.1-4) Handle Unexpected Money	CurrentModeProxy CustomOperatingSystemCalls CustomOperatingSystemInterrupts MainDisplay NumberSelectionButton ServiceRepresentative ServiceRepresentativeSelection SetPriceMode

Table 2.1 (continued)

Software requirements	Implemented by concrete classes
SR-1.3.1.2) Service Representative Selects a Row SR-1.3.1.2-1) Service Representative Selects a Row when the Column is Not Selected SR-1.3.1.2-2) Service Representative Selects a Row when the Column is Selected SR-1.3.1.2-3) Ignore the Refund Button SR-1.3.1.2-4) Handle Unexpected Money	CurrentModeProxy CustomOperatingSystemCalls CustomOperatingSystemInterrupts ItemDispenser ItemDispenserAssembly LetterSelectionButton MainDisplay ServiceRepresentative ServiceRepresentativeSelection SetPriceMode
SR-1.3.1.3) Service Representative Enters a Price SR-1.3.1.3-1) Accept the Old Price SR-1.3.1.3-2) Build the New Price SR-1.3.1.3-3) Enter the New Price SR-1.3.1.3-4) Handle an Invalid Price SR-1.3.1.3-5) Cancel the New Price SR-1.3.1.3-6) Ignore Inappropriate Buttons SR-1.3.1.3-7) Handle Unexpected Money	CoinDispenserAssembly CurrentModeProxy CustomOperatingSystemCalls CustomOperatingSystemInterrupts ItemDispenser ItemDispenserAssembly ItemDisplay LetterSelectionButton* MainDisplay NumberSelectionButton ServiceRepresentative ServiceRepresentativeSelection SetPriceMode
SR-1.4) Service Representative Displays History	CurrentModeProxy
SR-1.4-3) Ignore Inappropriate Buttons	CustomOperatingSystemCalls
SR-1.4-4) Handle Unexpected Money	CustomOperatingSystemInterrupts DisplayHistoryMode ItemDispenserAssembly LetterSelectionButton MainDisplay[†] ServiceRepresentative
SR-1.4-1) Service Representative Displays the Total Number of Items Sold	CurrentModeProxy CustomOperatingSystemCalls CustomOperatingSystemInterrupts DisplayHistoryMode ItemDispenserAssembly LetterSelectionButton[‡] MainDisplay ServiceRepresentative
SR-1.4-2) Service Representative Displays the Total Income	CurrentModeProxy CustomOperatingSystemCalls CustomOperatingSystemInterrupts DisplayHistoryMode ItemDispenserAssembly LetterSelectionButton[§] MainDisplay ServiceRepresentative

[*] C and E letter selection buttons.
[†] A and B letter selection buttons.
[‡] A letter selection button.
[§] B letter selection button.

3 Design documentation

The purpose of this section is to document the static and dynamic aspects of the architecture of the Mark I Vending Machine (MIVM) software in terms of its layers, packages, classes and interfaces.[†]

In order to maximize package cohesion and minimize cross-package coupling, the MIVM software has been decomposed into the following five layers, listed top-down by dependency:

1. *Client Interface Layer*. This layer contains all packages, classes and interfaces that model, are controlled by, and provide an interface to the input externals that are clients of (i.e. depend on) the MIVM software.
2. *Coordination Layer*. This layer contains all of the MIVM classes that are coordinator classes (i.e. classes that coordinate other classes).
3. *Model Layer*. This layer contains all of the MIVM classes that are primarily model classes (i.e. classes that model business objects).
4. *Server Interface Layer*. This layer contains all of the MIVM classes that model, control and provide an interface to the output externals that are servers of the MIVM software.
5. *Foundation Layer*. This layer contains all of the MIVM classes that are foundation classes (i.e. reusable, application-independent classes).

Figure 3.1 is a layer diagram that illustrates the layers of the MIVM software.

Due to the large number of packages and classes involved, the architecture of a typical application must be documented on a package by package basis. However, due to the small size of the MIVM software, the comprehensive configuration diagram on Figure 3.2 can summarize its entire static architecture. This diagram documents the object architecture rather than class architecture because objects are more important than classes in an embedded application. This is in contrast to a MIS architecture, which would typically focus on classes or types rather than objects.

3.1 Client Interface Layer

The purpose of this subsection is to document the design of the client interface layer in terms of its component packages and classes.

The rationale for creating this layer includes:

- The layer is cohesive, consisting of all classes that model, are controlled by, and provide an interface to the input externals that are clients of (i.e. depend on) the MIVM software.
- This cohesion supports efficient staffing by allowing scarce developer expertise in input devices to be concentrated on one team.

[†]On Java projects, much of the class level textual information in this chapter is best provided in the form of javadoc html files rather than in paper form.

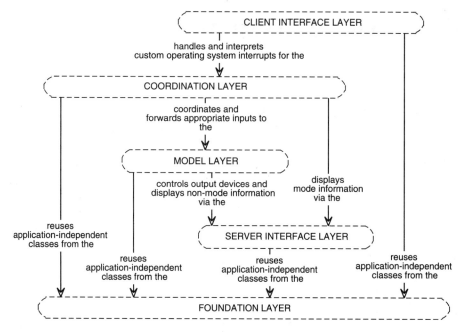

Figure 3.1 Layer diagram for the Mark I Vending Machine software.

- The layer is loosely coupled to other layers, in that it only contains one class as its interface and only interfaces with one other application-specific layer.
- The layer is modular, consisting of only 25 objects of 8 classes.
- The layer exhibits good encapsulation, hiding 24 of its 25 objects.

3.1.1 Packages in the Client Interface Layer

The purpose of this subsection is to document the packages that comprise the client interface layer. Due to the small size of the application, the client interface layer consists of only a single package: the client interface package.

3.1.1.1 Client Interface Package

The purpose of this subsection is to document the design of the client interface package. This package contains all classes that model, are controlled by, and provide an interface to the input externals that are clients of the MIVM software. This section includes a package diagram, a package collaboration diagram, and the design decisions and rationale for the package.

Because the client interface layer contains only this single package, they share the same rationale.

3.1.1.1.1 Static architecture of the Client Interface Package

Figure 3.3 illustrates the static architecture of the client interface package.

3.1.1.1.2 Dynamic architecture of the Client Interface Package

Figure 3.4 summarizes the dynamic architecture of the client interface package.

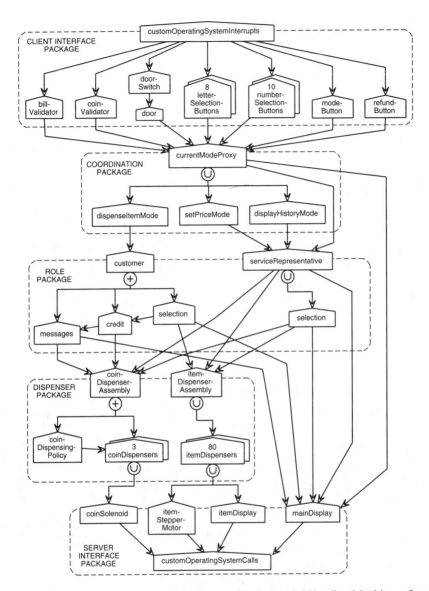

Figure 3.2 Comprehensive configuration diagram for the Mark I Vending Machine software.

3.1.1.1.3 Design decisions and rationale for the Client Interface Package
The following summarizes the important design decisions that were made during the modeling of the client interface package and the rationales behind them:

1. *Package identification.* In order to be cohesive, the client interface package was chosen to encapsulate all classes that are directly or indirectly involved with interfacing to the clients of the MIVM software. This choice also resulted in a well-encapsulated and modular package.

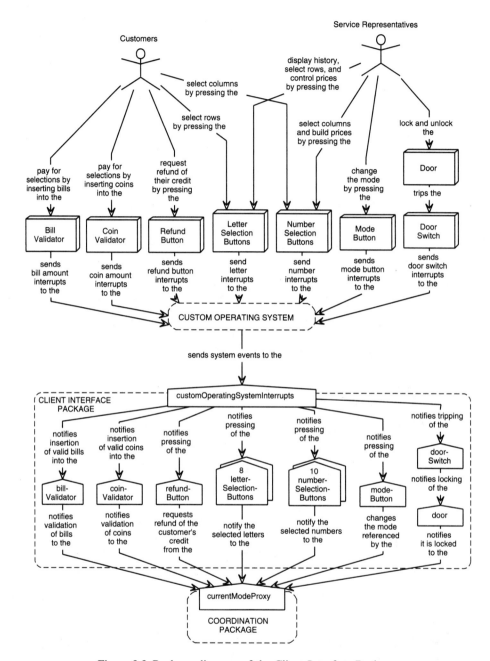

Figure 3.3 Package diagram of the Client Interface Package.

2. *Object identification.* Most of the objects in the instance of this package correspond to client external objects on the software context diagram illustrated in Figure 2.2. Most model hardware input devices. The custom

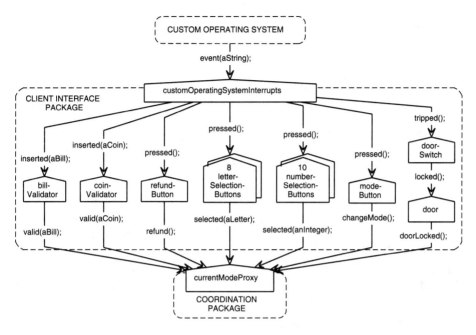

Figure 3.4 Package collaboration diagram of the Client Interface Package.

operating system, however, was decomposed into two objects representing interrupts and calls in order to:
- avoid having a bidirectional peer association between the custom operating system and MIVM software;
- cleanly separate client interface from server interface objects.

3. *Axis of symmetry.* As discussed in Barry Rubel's Pedestal pattern (Coplien J. and Schmidt D. (eds) (1995). *Pattern Languages of Program Design*, Addison-Wesley, Reading, p. 120) there is often an axis of symmetry separating the external hardware objects in the real world and the internal software objects that model them. For example, the external door trips the external door switch which interrupts the external custom operating system which sends an event to the software custom operating system which trips the software doorSwitch which notifies the currentModeProxy object of the closing and locking of the software door.

4. *Custom operating system interrupts.* The MIVM software should be decoupled from the custom operating system so that its other classes may be ported without change to new operating systems. Therefore, all inputs from the custom operating system are passed to the single instance of the CustomOperatingSystemInterrupts class, rather than being sent directly to the objects that model the hardware input devices.

5. *Hash table of buttons.* In order to organize and handle the large number of selection buttons, the letter selection buttons and the number selection buttons are grouped into two hash table objects.

6. *Switch.* In order to increase reusability and to more closely model the real world, the doorSwitch merely notifies the door that it has been tripped rather than directly notifying the currentModeProxy that the door has been locked.

7. *Door.* A door object is required to decouple the simple reusable door switch from the currentModeProxy and to interpret the tripping of the doorSwitch to mean the locking of the door. The Door class is therefore application-specific and probably will not be reusable in other application domains.

8. *Money validators.* A single MoneyValidator class was used instead of an inheritance hierarchy containing different classes for the coin validator and bill validator because:
   - all money validators have essentially the same behavior and properties, and
   - this minimizes the number of classes to be developed and maintained.

3.1.1.1.4 Classes of the Client Interface Package

The purpose of this subsection is to document the classes that comprise the Client Interface Layer. The following classes are organized alphabetically with inheritance indicated by indentation:

- **CustomOperatingSystemInterrupts**
  Definition: the part of the custom operating system that interrupts the vending machine software.
  Stereotype: Interfacer.
  Utility: Application-specific.
- **InputDevice**
  Definition: a hardware device providing input to the vending machine.
  Stereotype: Notifier.
  Utility: Domain-specific.
  - **Button**
    Definition: a button that notifies its server when pressed.
    Stereotype: Notifier.
    Utility: Domain-specific.
    - **ModeButton**
      Definition: the button used by the service representative to change the mode of the vending machine.
      Stereotype: Notifier.
      Utility: Domain-specific.
    - **RefundButton**
      Definition: the button used by the customer to request the refund of the customer's credit.
      Stereotype: Notifier.
      Utility: Domain-specific.
    - **SelectionButton**
      Definition: a button used to select a character.
      Stereotype: Notifier.
      Utility: Domain-specific.

  – **LetterSelectionButton**
  Definition: a button used to select a letter.
  Stereotype: Notifier.
  Utility: Domain-specific.
  – **NumberSelectionButton**
  Definition: a button used to select a number.
  Stereotype: Notifier.
  Utility: Domain-specific.
– **Door**
Definition: the door of the vending machine.
Stereotype: Notifier.
Utility: Domain-specific.
– **MoneyValidator**
Definition: a device used to validate money inserted into the vending machine.
Stereotype: Notifier.
Utility: Domain-specific.
– **Switch**
Definition: the switch that is tripped when the door is closed and locked.
Stereotype: Notifier.
Utility: Domain-specific.

3.1.1.1.4.1 CustomOperatingSystemInterrupts

Definition: the part of the custom operating system that interrupts the vending
machine software.

Superclass: `TestableObject`.

Stereotype: Interfacer.

Utility: Application-specific.

Responsibilities:
• Interpret input events.
  Collaborator: none.
• Forward interpreted input events on to the appropriate internal input object.
  Collaborators: `Button, MoneyValidator, Switch`.

Constructor:
• `CustomOperatingSystemInterrupts`
    `(MoneyValidator aBillValidator,`
    `MoneyValidator aCoinValidator,`
    `Hashtable letterSelectionButtons,`
    `Mode Button aModeButton,`
    `Hashtable numberSelectionButtons,`
    `DoorSwitch aDoorSwitch,`
    `RefundButton aRefundButton)`
    `{...};`

Characteristics:
  Operations:
    Public service:
      ● `event(aString);`
          `public void event(String aString) {...};`
          // Interpret the string and notify the appropriate internal input object.

Properties:
  Attribute:
    ● `Hashtable`   `interruptHandlers;` // Contains MessageSend
  Links:
    ● `MoneyValidator` `billValidator;`
    ● `MoneyValidator` `coinValidator;`
    ● `Switch`   `doorSwitch;`
    ● `Hashtable`   `letterSelectionButtons;`
    ● `ModeButton`   `modeButton;`
    ● `Hashtable`   `numberSelectionButtons;`
    ● `RefundButton`   `refundButton;`

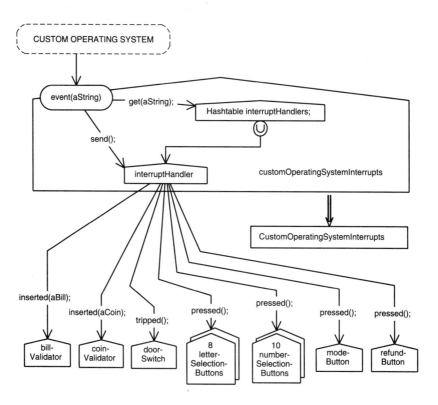

Figure 3.5 Internal collaboration diagram for the single instance of the
CustomOperatingSystemInterrupts class.

Parts: none.
Entries: none.
Exceptions thrown: none.

3.1.1.1.4.2 InputDevice

Definition: a hardware device providing input to the vending machine.

Superclass: `TestableObject`.

Stereotype: Notifier.

Utility: Domain-specific.

Responsibilities:
- Notify its server.
  Collaborator: `Object`.

Characteristics:
  Operations:
    Public services: none.
  Properties:
    Attributes: none.
    Link:
    - `Object server;`

  Parts: none.
  Entries: none.
  Exceptions thrown: none.

3.1.1.1.4.2.1 Button

Definition: a button that notifies its server when pressed.

Superclass: `InputDevice`.

Stereotype: Notifier.

Utility: Domain-specific.

Responsibilities:
- When pressed, send appropriate message to server.
  Collaborator: `Object`.

Characteristics:
  Operations:
    Public service:
    - `pressed();`
      ```
      public abstract void pressed();
      ```
      // When pressed, send appropriate message to the server.

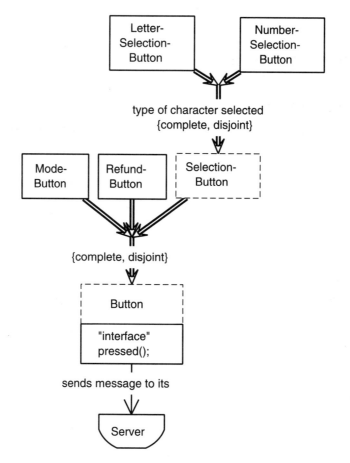

Figure 3.6 Inheritance diagram for the Button class.

Properties:
    Attributes: none.
    Links: none.
    Parts: none.
    Entries: none.
    Exceptions thrown: none.

3.1.1.1.4.2.1.1 ModeButton

Definition: the button used by the service representative to change the mode of the vending machine.

Superclass: `Button`.

Stereotype: Notifier.

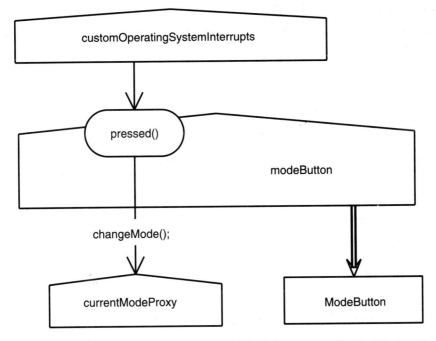

Figure 3.7 Internal collaboration diagram for the single instance of the ModeButton class.

Utility: Domain-specific.

Responsibilities:
- When pressed, request the server to change its mode.
  Collaborator: CurrentModeProxy.

Constructor:
- ModeButton(CurrentModeProxy aCurrentModeProxy) {...};

Characteristics:
  Operations:
    Public service:

    - pressed();
        public void pressed() {...};
        // When pressed, request the server to change its mode.

Properties:
  Attributes: none.
  Links: none.
  Parts: none.
  Entries: none.
  Exceptions thrown: none.

3.1.1.1.4.2.1.2 RefundButton

Definition: the button used by the customer to request the refund of the customer's credit.

Superclass: `Button`.

Stereotype: Notifier.

Utility: Domain-specific.

Responsibilities:
- When pressed, request a refund from the server.
  Collaborator: `CurrentModeProxy`.

Constructor:
- `RefundButton(CurrentModeProxy aCurrentModeProxy) {...};`

Characteristics:
  Operations:
    Public service:
      - `pressed();`
          `public void pressed() {...};`
          // When pressed, request a refund from the server.

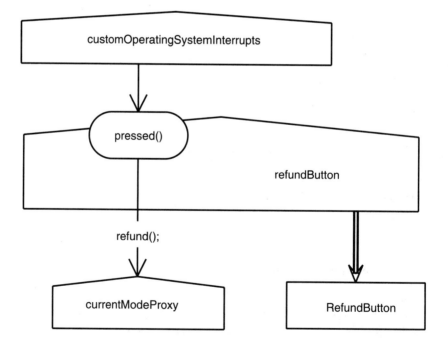

Figure 3.8 Internal collaboration diagram for the single instance of the RefundButton class.

Properties:
  Attributes: none.
  Links: none.
  Parts: none.
  Entries: none.
  Exceptions thrown: none.

3.1.1.1.4.2.1.3 SelectionButton

Definition: a button used to make a selection.

Superclass: `Button`.

Stereotype: Notifier.

Utility: Domain-specific.

Responsibilities:
● Know identifier of button.
  Collaborator: none.

Characteristics:
  Operations: none.
  Properties:
    Attributes: none.
    Links: none.
    Parts: none.
    Entries: none.
    Exceptions thrown: none.

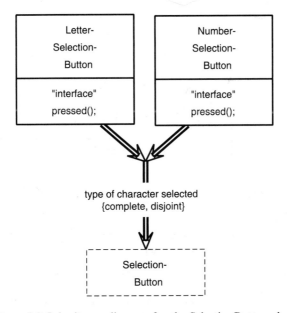

Figure 3.9 Inheritance diagram for the SelectionButton class.

3.1.1.1.4.2.1.3.1 **LetterSelectionButton**

Definition: a button used to select a letter.

Superclass: `SelectionButton`.

Stereotype: Notifier.

Utility: Domain-specific.

Responsibilities:
- When pressed, notify the server of the letter selected.
  Collaborator: `CurrentModeProxy`.

Constructor:
- `LetterSelectionButton(CurrentModeProxy aCurrentModeProxy,`
  `Character letterSelected) {...};`

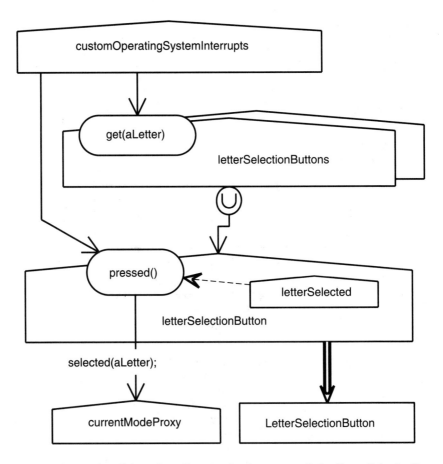

Figure 3.10 Internal collaboration diagram for instances of the LetterSelectionButton class.

Characteristics:
  Operations:
    Public service:
      ● pressed();
          public void pressed() {...};
          // When pressed, notify the server of the letter selected.

Properties:
  Attribute:
    ● Character letterSelected;
        // Invariant: (Character.isLetter(letter)).

Links: none.
Parts: none.
Entries: none.
Exceptions thrown: none.

3.1.1.1.4.2.1.3.2 NumberSelectionButton

Definition: a button used to select a number.

Superclass: SelectionButton.

Stereotype: Notifier.

Utility: Domain-specific.

Responsibilities:
● When pressed, notify the server of the number selected.
  Collaborator: CurrentModeProxy.

Constructor:
● NumberSelectionButton(CurrentModeProxy aCurrentModeProxy, int
  integerSelected)
  {...};

Characteristics:
  Operations:
    Public service:
      ● pressed();
          public void pressed(){...};
          // When pressed, notify the server of the number selected.

Properties:
  Attribute:
    ● int integerSelected;
        // Invariant: (0 < integerSelected && integerSelected < 11).

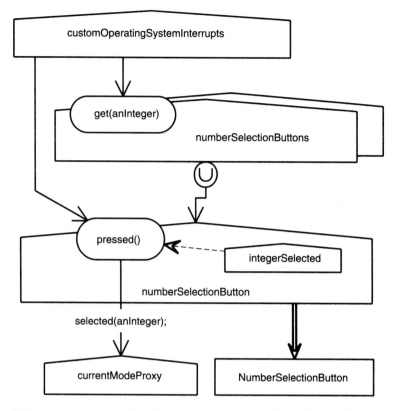

Figure 3.11 Internal collaboration diagram for instances of the NumberSelectionButton class.

Links: none.
Parts: none.
Entries: none.
Exceptions thrown: none.

3.1.1.1.4.2.2 Door

Definition: the door of the vending machine.

Superclass: InputDevice.

Stereotype: Notifier.

Utility: Domain-specific.

Responsibilities:
• Notify the server when closed and locked.
  Collaborator: CurrentModeProxy.

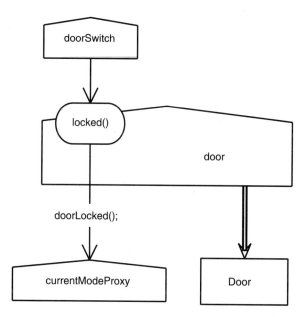

Figure 3.12 Internal collaboration diagram for the single instance of the Door class.

Constructor:
- `Door(CurrentModeProxy aCurrentModeProxy) {...};`

Characteristics:
  Operations:
    Public service:
    - `locked();`
      `public void locked(){...};`
      // Notify the server that the door has been closed and locked.

Properties:
  Attributes: none.
  Links: none.
  Parts: none.
  Entries: none.
  Exceptions thrown: none.

3.1.1.1.4.2.3 MoneyValidator

Definition: a device used to validate money inserted into the vending machine.

Superclass: `InputDevice`.

Stereotype: Notifier.

Utility: Domain-specific.

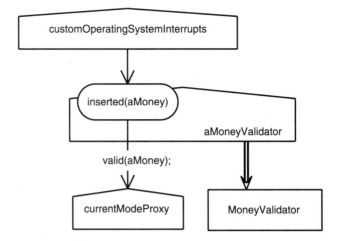

Figure 3.13 Internal collaboration diagram for instances of the MoneyValidator class.

Responsibilities:
● Notify the server of the amount of the money validated when interrupted by the associated hardware money validator.
   Collaborators: `CurrentModeProxy`.

Constructor:
● `MoneyValidator(CurrentModeProxy aCurrentModeProxy) {...};`

Characteristics:
   Operations:
      Public service:
      ● `inserted(aMoney);`
         `public void inserted(Money aMoney) {...};`
         // Notify the current mode coordinator that money was validated.

   Properties:
      Attributes: none.
      Links: none.
      Parts: none.
      Entries: none.
      Exceptions thrown: none.

3.1.1.1.4.2.4 Switch

Definition: the switch that is tripped when the door is closed and locked.

Superclass: `InputDevice`.

Stereotype: Notifier.

Utility: Domain-specific.

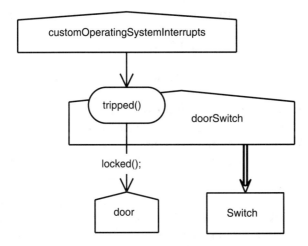

Figure 3.14 Internal collaboration diagram for the single instance of the Switch class.

Responsibilities:
- Notify the server when tripped.
  Collaborator: Door.

Constructor:
- Switch(Door aDoor){...};

Characteristics:
Operations:
  Public service:
  - tripped();
    public void tripped() {...};
    // Notify the door that the switch has been tripped.

  Properties:
  Attributes: none.
  Link:
  - Door door;
  Parts: none.
  Entries: none.
  Exceptions thrown: none.

3.2 Coordination Layer

The purpose of this subsection is to document the design of the Coordination Layer in terms of its component packages and classes.

The rationale for creating this layer includes:

- The layer is cohesive, consisting of classes that are primarily coordinator classes (i.e. classes that coordinate the interactions of other classes).

- This cohesion supports efficient staffing by allowing scarce developer expertise in mode issues to be concentrated on one team.
- The layer is loosely coupled to other layers, in that it only contains one class as its interface.
- The layer is modular, consisting of only four objects of four classes.

3.2.1 Packages in the Coordination Layer

The purpose of this subsection is to document the packages that comprise the Coordination Layer. Due to the small size of the application, the coordination layer consists of only a single package, the Coordination Package.

3.2.1.1 Coordination Package

The purpose of this subsection is to document the design of the coordination package. This package contains all of the MIVM software classes that are primarily coordinator classes. This section includes a package diagram, a package collaboration diagram, and the design decisions and rationale for the package. Instances of this package export one object and hide three objects.

Because the Coordination Layer contains only this single package, they share the same rationale.

3.2.1.1.1 Static architecture of the Coordination Package

Figure 3.15 illustrates the static architecture of the Coordination Package.

3.2.1.1.2 Dynamic architecture of the Coordination Package

Figure 3.16 summarizes the dynamic architecture of the Coordination Package.

3.2.1.1.3 Design decisions and rationale for the Coordination Package

The following summarizes the important design decisions that were made during the modeling of the Coordination Package and the rationales behind them:

1. *Package identification.* The coordination package encapsulates the mode classes, the only coordinator classes in the vending machine.
2. *Object identification.* All objects in the instance of this package were identified using the state pattern to model the modes of the vending machine.
3. *State Pattern.* Because the handling of input events strongly depends on the mode of the vending machine, all inputs are funneled through a single object, currentModeProxy, representing the current mode of the vending machine. The currentModeProxy object thus defines and provides cohesion to the coordination package by acting as the coordination package's central coordinator class. Based on the current mode of the vending machine, the currentModeProxy object delegates the input events to the encapsulated mode that represents the actual current mode of the vending machine. This design choice of the currentModeProxy containing concrete actual mode objects implements the state pattern from the book *Design Patterns* [Gamma *et al.*, 1995][†]. (In the state pattern, the

---

[†]Gamma E., Helm R., Johnson R. and Vlissides J. (1995). *Design Patterns: Elements of Reusable Object-Oriented Software.* Addison-Wesley.

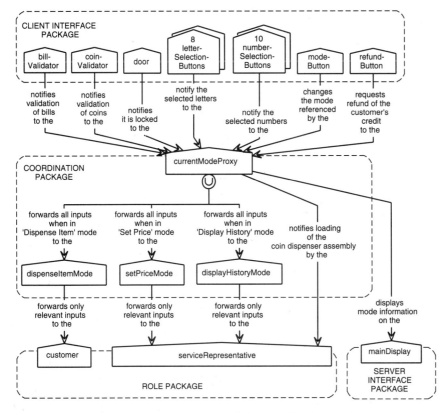

Figure 3.15 Package diagram of the Coordination Package.

currentModeProxy is called the context and the concrete mode objects are called concrete state objects.)

4. *Chain of Responsibility Pattern.* Most input messages are passed through the currentModeProxy object and the appropriate actualMode object to the appropriate VendingMachineRole object, which handles the message. This design choice implements the chain of responsibility pattern from the book *Design Patterns* [Gamma *et al.*, 1995].

5. *Actual modes.* The three actual modes (dispenseItemMode, displayHistoryMode, and setPriceMode) are completely polymorphic, in that they respond to the same messages, although the displayHistoryMode and setPriceMode objects ignore the following messages:

- DisplayHistoryMode:
  - `public void selected(int anInteger) {...};`
  - `public void refund() {...};`
  - `public void reset(){...};`
- SetPriceMode:
  - `public void refund() {...};`

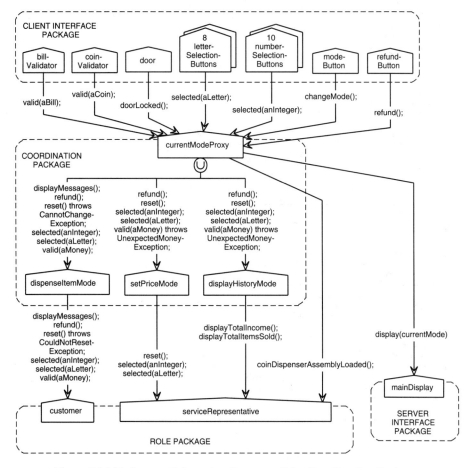

Figure 3.16 Package collaboration diagram of the Coordination Package.

6. *Handling unexpected money*. When money is unexpectedly validated during either the 'Display History' mode or 'Set Price' mode, the associated displayHistoryMode or setPriceMode object raises the UnexpectedMoneyException to the currentModeProxy. The currentModeProxy then (1) resets the actual mode, (2) sets the current mode to dispenseItemMode, and (3) notifies the dispenseItemMode object of the validated money. This is an example of the mediator pattern from the book *Design Patterns* [Gamma *et al.*, 1995] because all communication between the actual modes is mediated via the currentModeProxy object.

7. *HandleSelection interface*. The Handle Selection interface that defines the `selected(anInteger)` and `selected(aLetter)` messages is implemented by all mode objects as well as by all role objects.

8. *Loading the coin dispenser*. When the door object notifies the currentModeProxy object that the door has been locked, the

currentModeProxy object notifies the serviceRepresentative object that the human service representative should have loaded the coin dispenser assembly. The serviceRepresentative object therefore notifies the coinDispenserAssembly object that it has been loaded. The coinDispenserAssembly in turn notifies each of its coinDispenser objects that coins have been inserted.

The currentModeProxy object should not directly notify the coinDispenser object because:

- Loading the coin dispenser assembly is the responsibility of the service representative in the real world.
- That would increase package coupling by coupling the coordination package to the dispenser package.
- That would unnecessarily increase coupling because the serviceRepresentative object is already indirectly coupled to the coinDispenserAssembly via its serviceRepresentativeSelection (i.e. indirect coupling is better than the combination of direct and indirect coupling).

9. *Polymorphic refunding of change.* As an example of the Chain of Responsibility Pattern, the refundButton object sends the `refund()` message to the currentModeProxy object, which sends the same message to the actualMode object, and the dispenseItemMode object sends the same message to the customer object.

10. *Handle CannotDispenseAllException.* The currentModeProxy object can only transition from the 'Dispense Item' mode to the 'Set Price' mode if all of the customer's credit (if any) can be refunded. The currentModeProxy object sends the `reset()` message to the dispenseItemMode object which forwards it to the customer object which sends the `refundMinus(none)` message to the customerCredit object which in turn sends the `dispense(aMoney)` message to the coinDispenserAssembly object, etc. If all of the money cannot be dispensed, the coinDispenserAssembly object throws the CouldNotDispenseAllException to the customerCredit object which throws the CouldNotRefundAll exception to the customer object which throws the CouldNotResetException to the dispenseItemMode object which throws the CannotChangeException to the currentModeProxy object, thereby preventing the transition.

This is an example of how developer-defined exceptions should typically not be propagated outside of the scope in which they have meaning, but rather should be captured and translated into a new exception that has meaning in the new scope. Notice that at each level of abstraction, an exception that is appropriate for that level of abstraction is thrown.

3.2.1.1.4 Classes of the Coordination Package

The purpose of this subsection is to document the classes that comprise the Coordination Package. The following classes are organized alphabetically with inheritance indicated by indentation:

- **Mode**

  Definition: an overall mode of the vending machine.
  Stereotype: Coordinator, State.
  Utility: Domain-specific.

  – **ActualMode**

    Definition: an actual mode of the vending machine.
    Stereotype: Notifier, State.
    Utility: Domain-specific.

    – **DispenseItemMode**

      Definition: the mode of the vending machine that permits customers to buy items.
      Stereotype: Notifier, State.
      Utility: Domain-specific.

    – **ServiceRepresentativeMode**

      Definition: a mode of the vending machine used by service representatives.
      Stereotype: Notifier, State.
      Utility: Domain-specific.

      – **DisplayHistoryMode**

        Definition: the mode of the vending machine that permits service representatives to display history information.
        Stereotype: Notifier, State.
        Utility: Domain-specific.

      – **SetPriceMode**

        Definition: the mode of the vending machine that permits service representatives to set prices.
        Stereotype: Notifier, State.
        Utility: Domain-specific.

  – **CurrentModeProxy**

    Definition: the reference to the current actual mode.
    Stereotype: Coordinator, State.
    Utility: Domain-specific.

3.2.1.1.4.1 Mode

Definition: an overall mode of the vending machine.

Superclass: TestableObject.

Description: This class specifies the common protocol of all concrete mode objects.

Stereotype: Coordinator, State.

Utility: Domain-specific.

Interfaces Implemented:
- HandleMoney   // Handle inputs related to money.
- HandleSelection   // Handle inputs related to making a selection.

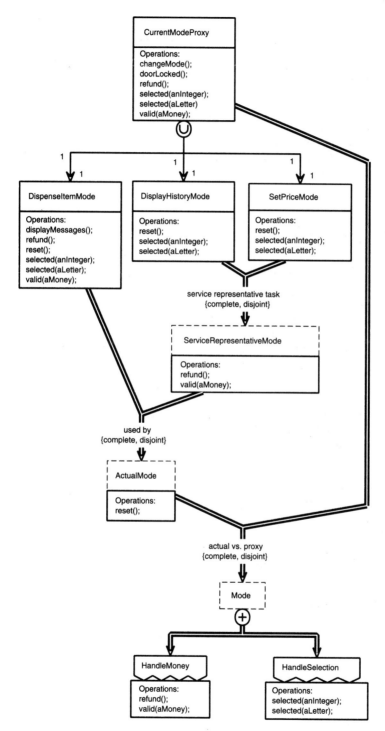

Figure 3.17 Inheritance diagram showing public protocol for the Mode class hierarchy.

Responsibilities:
- Standardize the common protocol of all modes.
  Collaborators: none.

Characteristics:
  Operations:
    Public services:
    - refund();
        ```
        public abstract void refund();
        /* Refund the customer's credit.
         * Interface: HandleMoney.
         */
        ```
    - selected(anInteger);
        ```
        public abstract void selected(int anInteger);
        /* Handle the selection of an integer.
         * Precondition: (0 < anInteger && anInteger < 11).
         * Interface: HandleSelection.
         */
        ```
    - selected(aLetter);
        ```
        public abstract void selected(Character aLetter);
        /* Handle the selection of a letter
         * Precondition: (Character.isLetter(aLetter)).
         * Interface: HandleSelection.
         */
        ```
    - valid(aMoney);
        ```
        public abstract void valid(Money aMoney);
        /* Handle the validation of money.
         * Interface: HandleMoney.
         */
        ```

  Properties:
    Attributes: none.
    Links: none.
    Parts: none.
    Entries: none.
    Exceptions thrown: none.

3.2.1.1.4.1.1 ActualMode

Definition: an actual mode of the vending machine.

Superclass: Mode.

Stereotype: Notifier, State.

Utility: Domain-specific.

Responsibilities:
- Know how to reset itself.

Characteristics:
   Operations:
     Public service:
       ● `reset();`
         `public void reset() throws CannotChangeException {...};`
         // Reset the associated vending machine role.

Properties:
   Attributes: none.
   Links: none.
   Parts: none.
   Entries: none.
   Exceptions thrown: none.

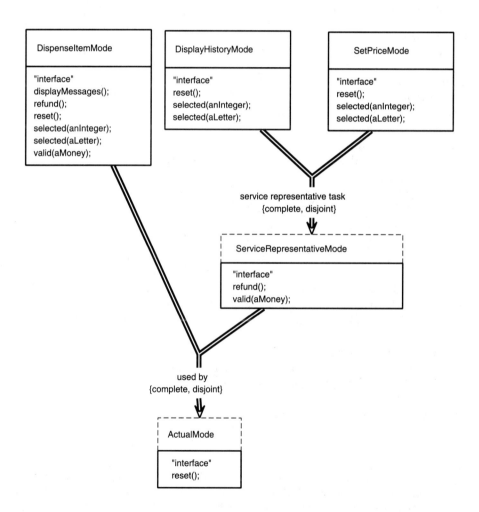

Figure 3.18 Inheritance diagram showing public protocol for the ActualMode class hierarchy.

3.2.1.1.4.1.1.1 DispenseItemMode

Definition: the mode of the vending machine that permits customers to buy items.

Superclass: `ActualMode`.

Stereotype: Notifier, State.

Utility: Domain-specific.

Responsibilities:
- Translate and forward all relevant customer inputs from the currentModeProxy to the customer object.
  Collaborators: `Customer`.

Constructor:
- `DispenseItemMode(Customer aCustomer) {...};`

Characteristics:
  Operations:
    Public services:
- `displayMessages();`
  `public void displayMessages(){...};`
  // Display the appropriate customer messages.
- `refund();`
  `public void refund() {...};`[†]
  /* Refund the customer's credit.
    * Interface: `HandleMoney`.
    */
- `reset();`
  `public void reset() throws CannotChangeException {...};`
  /* Reset the customer.
    * Handle `CouldNotResetException` by throwing
    * `CannotChangeException`.
    */
- `selected(anInteger);`
  `public void selected(int anInteger) {...};`
  /* Handle the selection of an integer.
    * Precondition: `(0 < anInteger && anInteger < 11)`.
    * Interface: `HandleSelection`.
    */

[†]Compare the signature of this operation with that of the same operation in the Mode class. The refund operation in the mode class is abstract, which is implied by the reserved word abstract and the missing implementation. The corresponding operation in this class is effective, having overridden the operation from the Mode class and provided an implied implementation.

● selected(aLetter);
  public void selected(Character aLetter) {...};
  /* Handle the selection of a letter.
   * Precondition: (Character.isLetter(aLetter)).
   * Interface: HandleSelection.
   */
● valid(aMoney);
  public void valid(Money aMoney) {...};
  /* Handle the validation of money.
   * Interface: HandleMoney.
   */

Properties:
  Attributes: none.
  Link:
● Customer customer;

Parts: none.
Entries: none.
Exceptions thrown:
● CannotChangeException
  /* Throw if the actual mode cannot be changed from dispenseItemMode
     because all of the customer's credit could not be refunded (i.e. if the
     customer throws the CouldNotResetException). */

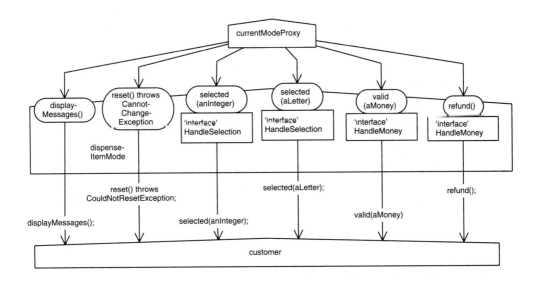

Figure 3.19 Internal collaboration diagram for the single instance of the
Dispense ItemMode class.

3.2.1.1.4.1.1.2 ServiceRepresentativeMode

Definition: a mode of the vending machine used by service representatives.

Superclass: `ActualMode`.

Stereotype: Notifier, State.

Utility: Domain-specific.

Responsibilities:
- Translate and forward all relevant service representative inputs to the serviceRepresentative object.
  Collaborator: `ServiceRepresentative`.
- Ignore requests for refunding money.
  Collaborator: none.
- Handle the unexpected validation of money.
  Collaborator: none.

Characteristics:
  Operations:
    Public services:
    - `refund();`
        ```
        public void refund() {...};
        ```
        /* Do nothing.
        * Interface: `HandleMoney`.
        */
    - `valid(aMoney);`
        ```
        public void valid(Money aMoney) throws
        UnexpectedMoneyException {...};
        ```
        /* Throw `UnexpectedMoneyException`.
        * Interface: `HandleMoney`.
        */

  Properties:
    Attributes: none.
    Link:
    - `ServiceRepresentative serviceRepresentative;`

    Parts: none.
    Entries: none.
    Exceptions thrown:
    - `UnexpectedMoneyException`
      // Throw if in an inappropriate state to validate money.

3.2.1.1.4.1.1.2.1 DisplayHistoryMode

Definition: the mode of the vending machine that permits service representatives to display history information.

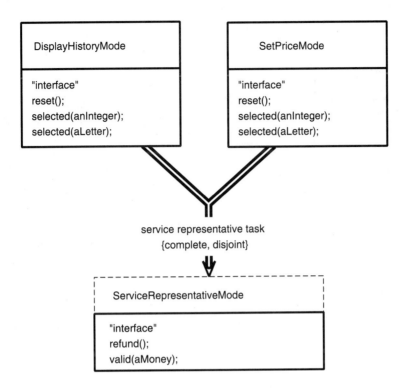

Figure 3.20 Inheritance diagram showing public protocol for the
ServiceRepresentativeMode hierarchy.

Superclass: `ServiceRepresentativeMode`.

Stereotype: Notifier, State.

Utility: Domain-specific.

Responsibilities:
- Translate and forward all relevant inputs to the serviceRepresentative when in 'Display History' mode.
  Collaborators: `ServiceRepresentative`.

Constructor:
- `DisplayHistoryMode(ServiceRepresentative aServiceRepresentative) {...};`

Characteristics:
  Operations:
    Public services:
    - `reset();`
        `public void reset() {...};`
        // Do nothing.

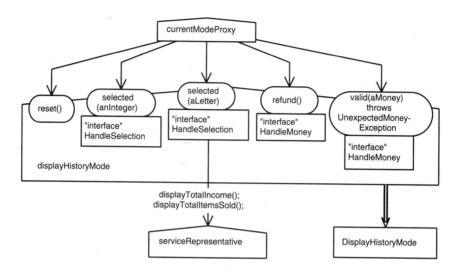

Figure 3.21 Internal collaboration diagram for the single instance of the DisplayHistoryMode class.

- `selected(anInteger);`
    ```
    public void selected(int anInteger) {};
    /* Do nothing.
    * Precondition: (0 < anInteger && anInteger < 11).
    * Interface: HandleSelection.
    */
    ```
- `selected(aLetter);`
    ```
    public void selected(Character aLetter) {...};
    /* Notify the service representative that he has selected aLetter.
    * Precondition: (aLetter == 'A' || aLetter == 'B').
    * Interface: HandleSelection.
    */
    ```

Properties:
Attributes: none.
Links: none.
Parts: none.
Entries: none.
Exceptions thrown: none

3.2.1.1.4.1.1.2.2 SetPriceMode

Definition: the mode of the vending machine that permits service representatives to set prices.

Superclass: `ServiceRepresentativeMode.`

Description: Unlike the displayHistoryMode object, the setPriceMode does not interpret inputs because this is the responsibility of the serviceRepresentativeSelection object.

Stereotype: Notifier.

Utility: Domain-specific.

Responsibilities:
- Forward all relevant inputs to the serviceRepresentative when in 'Set Price' mode.
  Collaborator: `ServiceRepresentative`.

Constructor:
- `SetPriceMode(ServiceRepresentative aServiceRepresentative)`
  `{...};`

Characteristics:
  Operations:
    Public services:
- `reset();`
  `public void reset() {...};`
  // Reset the service representative.
- `selected(anInteger);`
  `public void selected(int anInteger) {...};`
  /* Notify the service representative that he has selected anInteger.
  * Precondition: `(0 < anInteger && anInteger < 11)`.
  * Interface: `HandleSelection`.
  */
- `selected(aLetter);`
  `public void selected(Character aLetter) {...};`
  /* Notify the service representative that he has selected aLetter.
  * Precondition: `(Character.isLetter(aLetter))`.
  * Interface: `HandleSelection`.
  */

  Properties:
    Attributes: none.
    Links: none.
    Parts: none.
    Entries: none.
    Exceptions thrown: none.

3.2.1.1.4.1.2 CurrentModeProxy

Definition: the reference to the current actual mode.

Superclass: `Mode`.

Stereotype: Coordinator.

Utility: Domain-specific.

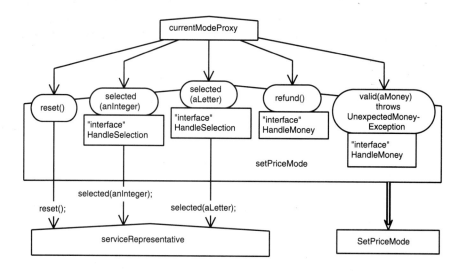

Figure 3.22 Internal collaboration diagram for the single instance of the SetPriceMode class.

Responsibilities:
- Know all three component actual modes.
  Collaborators: none.
- Know current actual mode.
  Collaborators: none.
- Display mode information.
  Collaborator: `MainDisplay`.
- Notify loading of the coin dispenser assembly.
  Collaborator: `ServiceRepresentative`.

Constructor:
- `CurrentModeProxy`
  ```
  (DispenseItemMode        aDispenseItemMode,
   DisplayHistoryMode      aDisplayHistoryMode,
   MainDisplay             aMainDisplay,
   ServiceRepresentative   aServiceRepresentative,
   SetPriceMode)           aSetPriceMode) {...};
  ```

Characteristics:
  Operations:
    Public services:
      - `changeMode();`
        ```
        public void changeMode() {...};
        ```
        /* Cycle the current mode of the vending machine to the next mode.

```
* Modes cycle from Dispense Item to Set Price to Display History
* and back to Dispense Item.
* Then display the new mode.
* Handle CannotChangeException by remaining in 'Dispense Item'
* mode and send displayMessages() to dispenseItemMode.
*/
```

- doorLocked();
  ```
  public void doorLocked() {...};
  /* Set the current mode of the vending machine to 'Dispense Item'
   * mode, and notify the service representative that the service
   * representative should have loaded the coin dispenser.
   */
  ```

- refund();
  ```
  public void refund() {...};
  /* Notify the current mode that a refund of the customer's credit has
   * been requested.
   * Interface: HandleMoney.
   */
  ```

- selected(anInteger);
  ```
  public void selected(int anInteger) {...};
  /* Notify the current mode that anInteger has been selected.
   * Precondition: (0 < anInteger && anInteger < 11).
   * Interface: HandleSelection.
   */
  ```

- selected(aLetter);
  ```
  public void selected(Character aLetter) {...};
  /* Notify the current mode that aLetter has been selected.
   * Precondition: (Character.isLetter(aLetter)).
   * Interface: HandleSelection.
   */
  ```

- valid(aMoney);
  ```
  public void valid(Money aMoney) {...};
  /* Notify the current mode that aMoney has been validated.
   * Handle UnexpectedMoneyException by setting currentMode to
   * dispenseItemMode.
   * Interface: HandleMoney.
   */
  ```

Properties:
Attributes:
- ActualMode   currentMode;

Links:
- MainDisplay   mainDisplay;
- ServiceRepresentative serviceRepresentative;

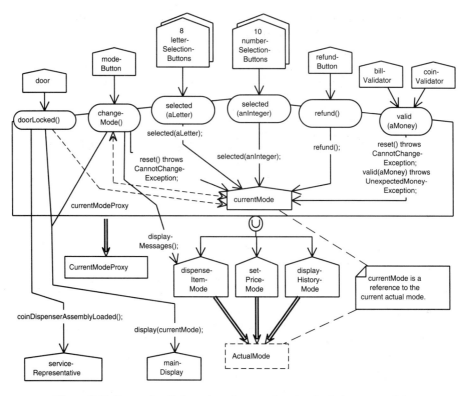

Figure 3.23 Internal collaboration diagram for the single instance of the
CurrentModeProxy class.

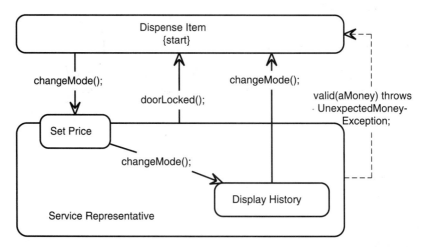

Figure 3.24 State transition diagram for the single instance of the CurrentModeProxy
class.

Parts: none.
Entries:
- DispenseItemMode   dispenseItemMode;
- DisplayHistoryMode   displayHistoryMode;
- SetPriceMode   setPriceMode;

Exceptions thrown: none.

3.3 Model Layer

The purpose of this subsection is to document the design of the Model Layer in terms of its component packages and classes.

The rationale for creating this layer includes:

- The layer is cohesive, consisting of all of the MIVM software classes that are primarily model classes (i.e. classes that model business objects).
- This cohesion supports efficient staffing by allowing scarce developer expertise in business objects to be concentrated on one team.
- The layer is loosely coupled, in that it only contains two classes as its interface.
- The layer is modular, consisting of only two packages.

3.3.1 Packages in the Model Layer

The purpose of this subsection is to document the following packages that comprise the Model Layer: the Role Package and the Dispenser Package.

3.3.1.1 Role Package

The purpose of this subsection is to document the design of the Role Package, which contains all classes related to vending machine roles. This section includes a package diagram, a package collaboration diagram, and the design decisions and rationale for the package. Instances of this package export two objects and hide four objects.

The rationale for creating this package includes:

- The package is cohesive, consisting of classes that model the roles that people play.
- This cohesion supports efficient staffing by allowing scarce developer expertise in role issues to be concentrated on one team.
- The package is loosely coupled to other packages, in that it only contains two classes as its interface.
- The package is modular, consisting of only five classes.

3.3.1.1.1 Static architecture of the Role Package

Figure 3.25 illustrates the static architecture of the Role Package.

3.3.1.1.2 Dynamic architecture of the Role Package

Figure 3.26 summarizes the dynamic architecture of the Role Package.

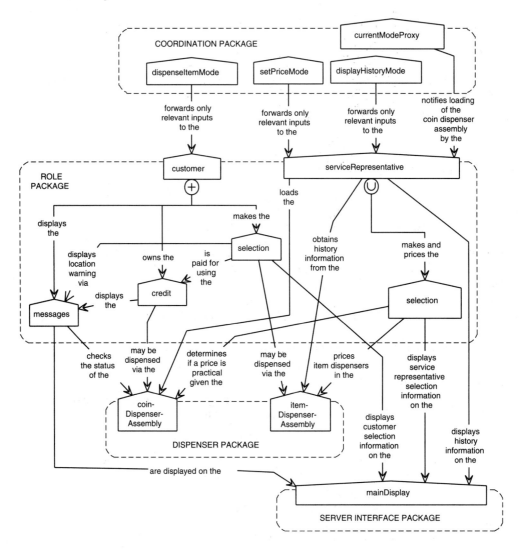

Figure 3.25 Package diagram of the Role Package.

3.3.1.1.3 Design decisions and rationale for the Role Package

The following summarizes the important design decisions that were made during the modeling of the Role Package and the rationales behind them:

1. *Package identification.* The role package was chosen to encapsulate all role-related classes. This resulted in it being cohesive, well-encapsulated and modular.
2. *Identification of objects.* All role objects in the instance of this package correspond to the actors on the software context diagram illustrated in Figure 2.2. The parts and entries of the role objects were identified to simplify the role objects by reifying their complex properties.

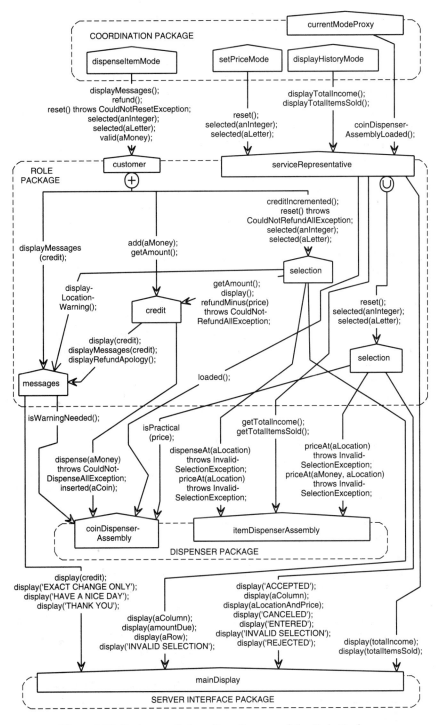

Figure 3.26 Package collaboration diagram of the Role Package.

3. *One customer.* Although many different external customers may buy items from the same vending machine, only one corresponding internal software object is needed. This is because only one customer at a time can buy items from the vending machine and the vending machine software has no way of knowing which customer is using it. Thus, the same internal customer object can be reused to represent each external customer.

4. *One service representative.* Although many different external service representatives may service the same vending machine, only one corresponding internal software object is needed. This is because only one service representative at a time can service a machine and the vending machine software has no way of knowing which service representative is servicing it. Thus, the same internal service representative object can be reused to represent each external service representative.

5. *Aggregation vs composition.* The customer object is a structure because its parts interact; aggregation relationships therefore connect it to its parts. However, the serviceRepresentative object only has a single entry and thus cannot have interacting parts; a composition relationship therefore connects it to its single entry.

6. *Displaying customer information.* Many different messages must be displayed to the customer on the main display. These messages have been localized into the messages object in order to provide flexibility and minimize coupling between the customer object and the mainDisplay object. This also makes the application more extensible by making it easy to change the messages that the customer object and its component parts display on the mainDisplay object. The messages object is made responsible for sending general messages to the mainDisplay object because:
   - It must handle the CouldNotRefundCreditException raised by the credit object regardless of original cause:
     - refundMinus(Money none) indirectly from the refundButton object.
     - refundMinus(price) directly from the customer selection object.
   - The need to display 'EXACT CHANGE ONLY' is not specific to either the customer credit object or the customer selection object.
   - In order to be complete, we also have the customer messages object display the customer credit.

7. *Customer selection.* In order to distribute the intelligence of the application among its component objects, the selection object actively tries to dispense a corresponding item whenever an input could make this possible. These inputs (and the situations in which an item can be dispensed) are:
   - A column is selected (when a row has already been selected and the customer's credit is greater than or equal to the corresponding price).
   - A row is selected (when a column has already been selected and the customer's credit is greater than or equal to the corresponding price).
   - A coin is validated (when both a column and row have already been selected and the customer's credit will become greater than or equal to the corresponding price).
   - A bill is validated (when both a column and row have already been

selected and the customer's credit will become greater than or equal to the corresponding price).

8. *Service representative selection.* The serviceRepresentativeSelection is analogous to the customerSelection in that both objects have location and price as properties. (Note that the price of an item should not be confused with the customer's credit.) The serviceRepresentativeSelection is considerably more complex because it must allow the service representative to build and enter new prices, whereas the customerSelection need only store the existing price of an item.

9. *Using the mediator pattern to minimize coupling inside customer.* The selection object needs to be notified when the customerCredit object is incremented, because the selection should attempt to dispense an item. However, having the customerCredit object directly notify the customerSelection object would increase the coupling between them via the resulting bi-directional linkage between them because the selection object is paid for using the customerCredit object. Therefore, the customer object sends the `creditIncremented()` message to the selection object after sending the `add(aMoney)` message to the customerCredit object so that only a unidirectional link from the selection object to the credit object exists. This is an example of the mediator pattern from the book *Design Patterns* [Gamma *et al.*, 1995][†].

10. *Minimizing the protocol of customer credit.* In order to minimize the interface of the CustomerCredit class, the single `refundMinus(price)` message was used to both:
    - Refund the entire amount of the customer's credit when the refund button is pressed, in which case aPrice is zero.
    - Dispense change (i.e. the customer's credit minus the price of the item dispensed) to the customer when the customer has inserted more than the price of the item dispensed, in which case `price` is the price of the customer's selection.

11. *Propagation of exceptions.* The currentModeProxy object can only transition from the 'Dispense Item' mode to the 'Set Price' mode if all of the customer's credit (if any) can be refunded. The currentModeProxy object sends the `reset()` message to the dispenseItemMode object which forwards it to the customer object which sends the `refund()` message to the customerCredit object which in turn sends the `dispense(aMoney)` message to the coinDispenserAssembly object. If all of the money cannot be dispensed, the coinDispenserAssembly object throws the CouldNot-DispenseAllException to the customerCredit object which throws the CouldNotRefundAllException to the customer object which throws the CouldNotResetException to the dispenseItemMode object which throws the CannotChangeException to the currentModeProxy object, thereby preventing the transition.

[†]Gamma E., Helm R., Johnson R. and Vlissides J. (1995). *Design Patterns: Elements of Reusable Object-Oriented Software*. Addison-Wesley, page 273.

This is an example of how developer-defined exceptions should typically not be propagated outside of the scope in which they have meaning, but rather should be captured and translated into a new exception that has meaning in the new scope. Notice that at each level of abstraction, an exception that is appropriate for that level of abstraction is thrown.

12. *Displaying history information.* Because displaying history information has nothing to do with the serviceRepresentativeSelection object, the Service Representative directly requests the history information from the itemDispenserAssembly object before displaying it on the mainDisplay. The itemDispenserAssembly does not directly display the history information because this would result in additional coupling (i.e. between the itemDispenserAssembly and the mainDisplay).

13. *Loading the coin dispenser.* When the door object notifies the currentModeProxy object that the door has been locked, the currentModeProxy object notifies the serviceRepresentative object that the human service representative should have loaded the coin dispenser assembly. The serviceRepresentative object therefore notifies the coinDispenserAssembly object that it has been loaded. The coinDispenserAssembly in turn notifies each of its coinDispenser object that coins have been inserted.

The currentModeProxy object should not notify the coinDispenser object directly because:

- Loading the coin dispenser assembly is the responsibility of the service representative in the real world.
- That would increase package coupling by coupling the coordination package to the dispenser package.
- That would unnecessarily increase coupling because the serviceRepresentative object is already indirectly coupled to the coinDispenserAssembly via its serviceRepresentativeSelection (i.e. indirect coupling is better than the combination of direct and indirect coupling).

3.3.1.1.4 Classes of the Role Package

The purpose of this subsection is to document the classes that comprise the Role Package. The following classes are organized alphabetically with inheritance indicated by indentation:

- **CustomerCredit**
  Definition: the customer's validated money that can be used to pay for the customer's selection.
  Stereotype: Information Holder.
  Utility: Domain-specific.
- **CustomerMessages**
  Definition: the messages displayed to the customer on the main display.
  Stereotype: Information Holder, Service Provider.
  Utility: Domain-specific.
- **Selection**
  Definition: the choosing of an item dispenser in the item dispenser assembly.
  Stereotype: Information Holder.

Utility: Domain-specific.
- **CustomerSelection**
  Definition: the customer's selection of an item dispenser in the item dispenser assembly.
  Stereotype: Information Holder.
  Utility: Domain-specific.
- **ServiceRepresentativeSelection**
  Definition: the service representative's selection of an item dispenser in the item dispenser assembly.
  Stereotype: Information Holder.
  Utility: Application-specific.
- **VendingMachineRole**
  Definition: a role that is played by a person when interacting with the vending machine.
  Stereotype: Coordinator.
  Utility: Domain-specific.
  - **Customer**
    Definition: the role that is played by a person when buying items from the vending machine.
    Stereotype: Coordinator.
    Utility: Domain-specific.
  - **ServiceRepresentative**
    Definition: the role that is played by a person when pricing items and displaying history information.
    Stereotype: Coordinator.
    Utility: Application-specific.

3.3.1.1.4.1 CustomerCredit

Definition: the customer's validated money that can be used to pay for the customer's selection.

Superclass: `TestableObject`.

Stereotype: Information Holder.

Utility: Domain-specific.

Responsibilities:
- Accumulate the amount of the customer's credit.
  Collaborator: `CustomerMessages`.
- Pay the price of the selected item.
  Collaborators: `CoinDispenserAssembly`, `CustomerMessages`.
- Refund itself upon demand using the coin dispenser assembly.
  Collaborator: `CoinDispenserAssembly`, `CustomerMessages`.

Constructor:
- `CustomerCredit(CoinDispenserAssembly aCoinDispenserAssembly,`
     `CustomerMessages customerMessages) {...};`

Characteristics:
  Operations:
    Public services:
- `add(aMoney);`
  `public void add(Money aMoney) {...};`
  // Increment the amount by aMoney and display the new amount.
- `display();`
  `public void display() {...};`
  // Display the amount of the customer's credit.
- `refundMinus(aPrice);`
  `public void refundMinus(Money aPrice) throws`
  `CouldNotRefundAllException {...};`
  /* Deduct aPrice from the amount and refund the balance using the
  * coinDispenserAssembly.
  * Handle `CouldNotDispenseAllException` by displaying the refund
  * apology and throwing the CouldNotRefundAllException.
  */

Public query:
- `getAmount();`
  `public Money getAmount() {...};`
  // Return the amount of the customer's credit.

Properties:
  Attribute:
- `Money`   `amount;` // the amount of the customer's credit.

Links:
- `CoinDispenserAssembly` `coinDispenserAssembly;`
- `CustomerMessages`   `customerMessages;`

Parts: none.
Entries: none.
Exceptions thrown:
- `CouldNotRefundAllException;`
  // Thrown if the coinDispenserAssembly throws the
  CouldNotRefundAllException.

3.3.1.1.4.2 CustomerMessages

Definition: the messages displayed to the customer on the main display.

Superclass: `TestableObject`.

Stereotype: Information Holder, Service Provider.

Utility: Domain-specific.

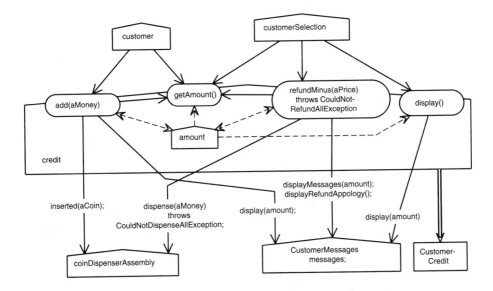

Figure 3.27 Internal collaboration diagram for the single instance of the CustomerCredit class.

Responsibilities:
- Display the appropriate customer messages based on the state of the coin dispenser assembly.
  Collaborators: `CoinDispenserAssembly`, `MainDisplay`.
- Know the exact change warning message.
  Collaborators: none.
- Know the greeting message.
  Collaborator: none.
- Know the location warning.
  Collaborators: none.
- Know the refund apology.
  Collaborators: none.
- Know the thanking message.
  Collaborators: none.

Constructor:
- `CustomerMessages(CoinDispenserAssembly aCoinDispenserAssembly,`
  `String exactChangeWarning,`
  `String greeting,`
  `String locationWarning,`
  `String refundApology,`
  `String thanks,`
  `MainDisplay aMainDisplay) {...};`

Characteristics:
 Operations:
  Public services:
   ● `display(credit);`
      `public void display(Money credit) {...};`
      // Display the customer's credit on the main display.
   ● `displayLocationWarning();`
      `private void displayLocationWarning() {...};`
      // Display the invalid selection warning message on the main
      // display.
   ● `displayMessages(credit);`
      `public void displayMessages(Money credit) {...};`
      /* Display the appropriate messages on the main display after the
       * customer buys an item or requests a refund based on the customer's
       * credit. */
   ● `displayRefundApology();`
      `private void displayRefundApology() {...};`
      // Display the refund apology message on the main display.

  Private services:
   ● `displayExactChangeWarning();`
      `private void displayExactChangeWarning() {...};`
      // Display the exact change message on the main display.
   ● `displayGreeting();`
      `private void displayGreeting() {...};`
      // Display the message that greets the next customer on the main
      // display.
   ● `displayThanks();`
      `private void displayThanks() {...};`
      // Display the thanks message on the main display.

 Properties:
  Attributes:
   ● `String`   `exactChangeWarning;`
   ● `String`   `greeting;`
   ● `String`   `locationWarning;`
   ● `String`   `refundApology;`
   ● `String`   `thanks;`

  Links:
   ● `CoinDispenserAssembly` `coinDispenserAssembly;`
   ● `MainDisplay`   `mainDisplay;`

 Parts: none.
 Entries: none.
 Exceptions thrown: none.

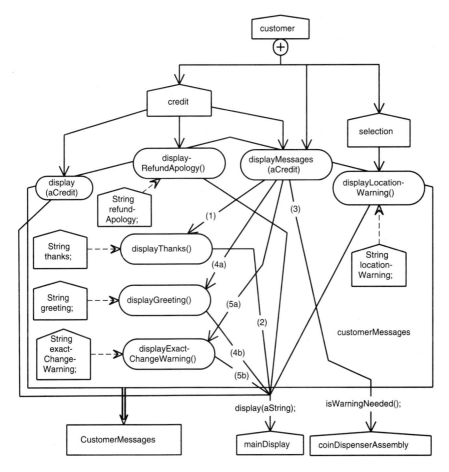

Figure 3.28 Internal collaboration diagram for the single instance of the
CustomerMessages class.

On Figure 3.28, the interaction arcs resulting from the
displayMessages(aCredit) method are labeled with sequence numbers that
capture the sequence in which these interactions occurred.

3.3.1.1.4.3 Selection

Definition: the choosing of an item dispenser in the item dispenser assembly.

Superclass: `TestableObject`.

Stereotype: Information Holder.

Utility: Domain-specific.

Interface implemented:
● `HandleSelection` // Handle inputs related to making a selection.

Responsibilities:
- Know the location of the item dispenser in the item dispenser assembly.
  Collaborators: `ItemDispenserAssembly,`
  `ItemDispenserAssemblyLocation.`
- Reset itself.
  Collaborators: none.
- Display selection information on the main display.
  Collaborators: `MainDisplay.`

Characteristics:
  Operations:
    Public services:
    - `reset();`
        ```
        public void reset(){...};
        ```
        // Clear the location of the selection.
    - `selected(anInteger);`
        ```
        public void column(int anInteger);
        ```
        /* Handle the selection of an integer.
        * Precondition: `(0 < anInteger && anInteger < 11).`
        * Interface: `HandleSelection.`
        */
    - `selected(aLetter);`
        ```
        public void selected(Character aLetter);
        ```
        /* Handle the selection of a letter.
        * Precondition: `(Character.isLetter(aLetter)).`
        * Interface: `HandleSelection.`
        */

  Properties:
    Attribute:
    - `ItemDispenserAssemblyLocation  location;`

    Links:
    - `ItemDispenserAssembly            itemDispenserAssembly;`
    - `MainDisplay                      mainDisplay;`

    Parts: none.
    Entries: none.
    Exceptions thrown: none.

3.3.1.1.4.3.1 CustomerSelection

Definition: the customer's selection of an item dispenser in the item dispenser assembly.

Superclass: `Selection.`

Stereotype: Information Holder.

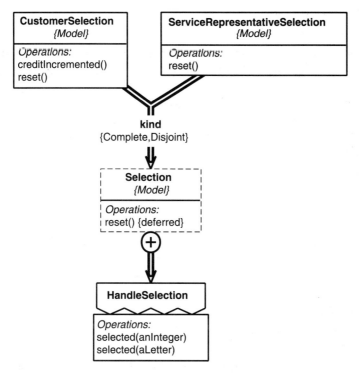

Figure 3.29 Inheritance diagram for the Selection class.

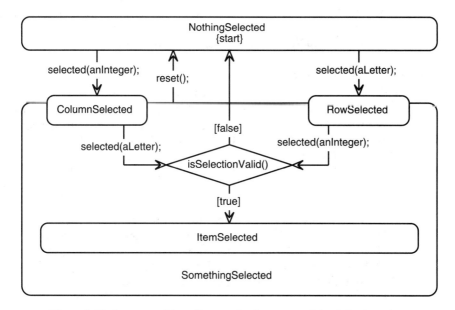

Figure 3.30 State transition diagram for instances of the Selection class.

Utility: Domain-specific.

Responsibilities:
- Actively attempt to dispense the corresponding item when notified that the customer credit was incremented or when notified of a newly selected column or row.
  Collaborators: `CustomerCredit`, `ItemDispenserAssembly`, `ItemDispenserAssemblyLocation`, `MainDisplay`.
- Display messages to the customer by controlling the main display.
  Collaborator: `MainDisplay`.

Constructor:
- `CustomerSelection`
  ```
  (CustomerCredit credit,
   CustomerMessages messages,
   ItemDispenserAssembly anItemDispenserAssembly,
   MainDisplay aMainDisplay) {...}.
  ```

Characteristics:
  Operations:
    Public services:
- `creditIncremented();`
  ```
  public void creditIncremented() {...};
  ```
  // Attempt to dispense when notified that the customer credit was
  // incremented.
- `reset();`
  ```
  public void reset()throws CouldNotRefundAllException {...};
  ```
  /* Clear the location of the customer's selection and refund the
  * customer's credit.
  * Handle CouldNotRefundAllException by rethrowing it.
  */
- `selected(anInteger);`
  ```
  public void selected(int anInteger) {...};
  ```
  /* Set the column of the location to anInteger and attempt to dispense.
  * Handle `InvalidLocationException` by asking customerMessages
  * to display 'INVALID SELECTION' on the main display.
  * Precondition: `(0 < anInteger && anInteger < 11)`.
  * Interface: `HandleSelection`.
  */
- `selected(aLetter);`
  ```
  public void selected(Character aLetter) {...};
  ```
  /* Set the row of the location to aLetter and attempt to dispense.
  * Handle `InvalidLocationException` by asking customerMessages
  * to display 'INVALID SELECTION' on the main display.
  * Precondition: `(Character.isLetter(aLetter))`.
  * Interface: `HandleSelection`.
  */

Private services:

- `attemptToDispense();`
    `private void attemptToDispense() {...};`
    // Dispense the customer's selection if the selection has been made and
    // there is sufficient credit.
- `dispenseSelection();`
    `private void dispenseSelection() {...};`
    /* Dispense a selection that has been made and paid for.
    * Handle `CouldNotRefundAllException` by ignoring it.
    * Handle `InvalidSelectionException` requesting the customer
    * messages to display the location warning on the mainDisplay.
    */
- `displayLocation();`
    `private void displayLocation() {...};`
    /* Display the column of the location on the main display if only the
    * column is selected.
    * Display the row of the location on the main display if only the row is
    * selected.
    */

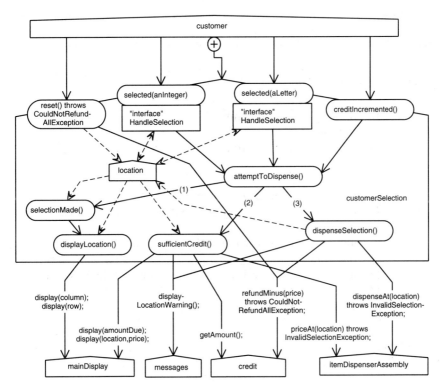

Figure 3.31 Internal collaboration diagram for the single instance of the
CustomerSelection class.

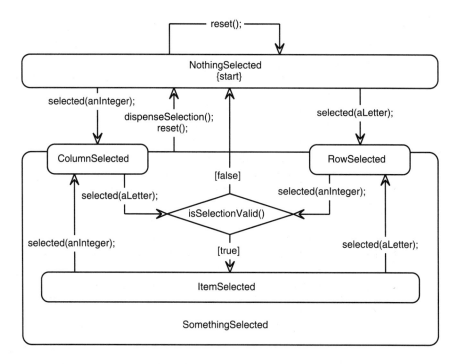

Figure 3.32 State transition diagram for the single instance of the CustomerSelection class.

- `selectionMade();`
  `private Boolean selectionMade() {...};`
  /* Return true if both column and row have been selected; otherwise,
  * return false.
  * Delegate to displayLocation.
  * /
- `sufficientCredit();`
  `private Boolean sufficientCredit() {...};`
  /* Return true if customer credit is not less than the price; otherwise,
  * return false.
  * Display amount due on the main display if the customer's credit is
  * less than the price.
  * Display the location and price if the customer's credit is zero.
  * Handle `InvalidSelectionException` by displaying 'INVALID
  * SELECTION' on the mainDisplay.
  * /

Properties:
Attributes: none.
Links:
- `CustomerCredit     credit;`
- `CustomerMessages   messages;`

Parts: none.
Entries: none.

Exceptions thrown: none.
- CouldNotRefundAllException
  //Thrown if credit throws CouldNotRefundAllException.

3.3.1.1.4.3.2 ServiceRepresentativeSelection

Definition: the service representative's selection of an item dispenser in the item dispenser assembly.

Superclass: Selection.

Stereotype: Information Holder.

Utility: Application-Specific.

Responsibilities:
- Select an item dispenser in the item dispenser assembly.
  Collaborators: ItemDispenserAssembly, ItemDispenserAssemblyLocation.
- Build and set the price of the selected item dispenser.
  Collaborators: CoinDispenserAssembly, ItemDispenserAssembly, ItemDispenserAssemblyLocation, MainDisplay.

Constructor:
- ServiceRepresentativeSelection
    (CoinDispenserAssembly aCoinDispenserAssembly,
    ItemDispenserAssembly anItemDispenserAssembly,
    MainDisplay aMainDisplay) {...}.

Characteristics
  Operations:
    Public services:
      - selected(anInteger);
          public void selected(int anInteger) {...};
          /* Either set the column to anInteger or build a price.
          * Precondition: (0 < anInteger && anInteger < 11).
          * Interface: HandleSelection.
          */
      - selected(aLetter);
          public void selected(Character aLetter) {...};
          /* Either set the row to aLetter or make a choice.
          * Precondition: (Character.isLetter(aLetter)).
          * Interface: HandleSelection.
          */

Private services:
- `accept();`

  ```
  private void accept() {...};
  ```
  // Accept the previous price.
- `appendToPrice(anInteger);`

  ```
  private void appendToPrice(int anInteger) {...};
  ```
  // Build the new price by concatenating anInteger to the end of the new
  // price.
- `cancel();`

  ```
  private void cancel() {...};
  ```
  // Cancel the new price.
- `enter();`

  ```
  private void enter() {...};
  ```
  /* Accept the new price.
  * Handle `InvalidSelectionException` by displaying 'INVALID
  * SELECTION' on the main display.
  */
- `setColumn(anInteger);`

  ```
  private void setColumn(int anInteger) {...};
  ```
  // Set the column of the location of the selection.
- `setRow(aLetter);`

  ```
  private void setRow(Character aLetter) {...};
  ```
  /* Set the row of the location of the selection.
  * Precondition: (`Character.isLetter(aLetter)`).
  * Handle `InvalidSelectionException` by displaying 'INVALID
  * SELECTION' on the main display.
  */

Properties:

  Attributes:
- `Money`   `price;`
- `String`   `state;`
  // NothingSelected, ColumnSelected, RowSelected, ItemSelected,
  // AppendingPrice.

  Link:
- `CoinDispenserAssembly`   `coinDispenserAssembly;`

Parts: none.

Entries: none.

Exceptions thrown: none.

3.3.1.1.4.4 VendingMachineRole

Definition: a role that is played by a person when interacting with the vending machine.

Superclass: `TestableObject`.

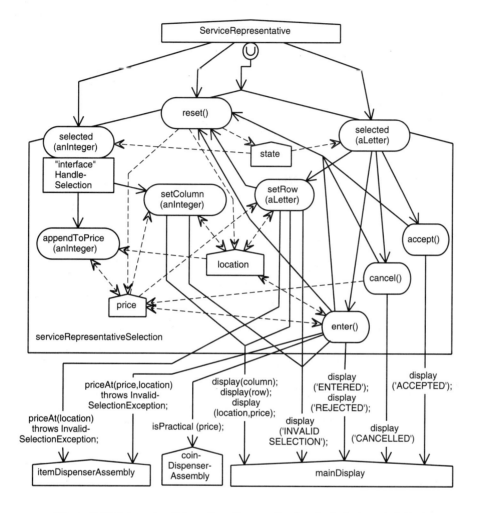

Figure 3.33 Internal collaboration diagram for the single instance of the ServiceRepresentativeSelection class.

Stereotype: Coordinator.

Utility: Domain-specific.

Interface implemented:
- `HandleSelection` // Handle inputs related to making a selection.

Responsibilities:
- Reset its component parts.
  Collaborators: none.

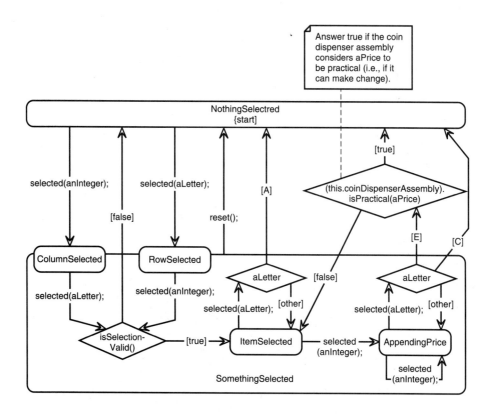

Figure 3.34 State transition diagram for the single instance of the
ServiceRepresentativeSelection class.

Characteristics:
  Operations:
    Public services:
      ● `reset();`
        `public abstract void reset()` throws
        `CouldNotResetException;`
        // Reset the component parts.

Properties:
  Attributes: none.
  Links: none.
  Parts: none.
  Entries: none.
  Exceptions thrown:
    ● `CouldNotResetException`
      // Thrown when the role could not be reset because some of the
      // customer's credit could not be refunded.

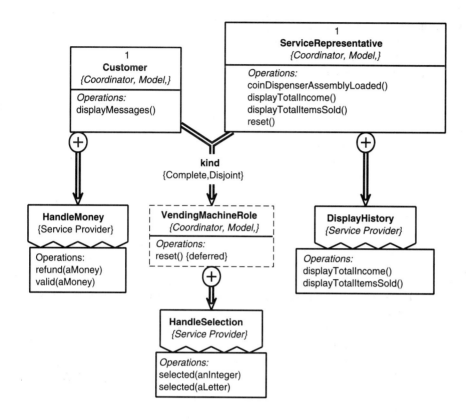

Figure 3.35 Inheritance diagram for the VendingMachineRole class.

3.3.1.1.4.4.1 Customer

Definition: the role that is played by a person when buying items from the vending machine.

Superclass: VendingMachineRole.

Stereotype: Coordinator.

Utility: Domain-specific.

Interface implemented:
• HandleMoney // Handle inputs related to money.

Responsibilities:
• Handle all inputs from the customer.
  Collaborators: CustomerCredit, CustomerMessages, CustomerSelection.
• Know the customer's credit.
  Collaborator: CustomerCredit.

- Display messages to the customer.
  Collaborator: `CustomerMessages`.
- Know the customer's selection.
  Collaborator: `CustomerSelection`.

Constructor:
- `Customer(CustomerCredit    aCustomerCredit,`
  `          CustomerMessages  aCustomerMessages,`
  `          CustomerSelection aCustomerSelection,`
  `          MainDisplay       aMainDisplay) {...};`

Characteristics:
  Operations:
    Public services:
      - `displayMessages();`
          `public void displayMessages() {...};`
          // Display the appropriate customer messages based on the amount of the
          // customer's credit.
      - `refund();`
          `public void refund() {...};`
          /* Refund the customer's credit.
           * Handle `CouldNotRefundAllException` by displaying appropriate
           * messages to the customer.
           * Interface: `HandleMoney`.
           */
      - `reset();`
          `public void reset() throws CouldNotResetException {...};`
          /* Reset the customer credit and customer selection and then display
           * messages.
           * Handle `CouldNotRefundAllException` by displaying appropriate
           * messages to the customer and by throwing
           * CouldNotResetException.
           */
      - `selected(anInteger);`
          `public void selected(int anInteger) {...};`
          /* Set the column of the customer selection to anInteger.
           * Precondition: `(0 < anInteger && anInteger < 11)`.
           * Interface: `HandleSelection`.
           */
      - `selected(aLetter);`
          `public void selected(Character aLetter) {...};`
          /* Set the row of the customer selection to aLetter.
           * Precondition: `(Character.isLetter(aLetter))`.
           * Interface: `HandleSelection`.
           */

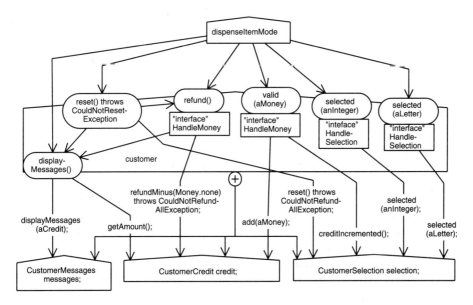

Figure 3.36 Internal collaboration diagram for the single instance of the Customer class.

- `valid(aMoney);`
    `public void valid(Money aMoney) {...};`
    /* Add aMoney to the customer's credit and then notify the customer
    * selection.
    * Interface: `HandleMoney`.
    */

Properties:
  Attributes: none.
  Links: none.
  Parts:
  - `CustomerCredit     credit;`
  - `CustomerMessages   messages;`
  - `CustomerSelection selection;`

Entries: none.
Exceptions thrown:
  - `CouldNotResetException`
    // Thrown when the customer could not be reset because some of the
    // customer's credit could not be refunded.

3.3.1.1.4.4.2 ServiceRepresentative

Definition: the role that is played by a person when pricing items and displaying
history information.

Superclass: `VendingMachineRole`.

Stereotype: Coordinator.

Utility: Application-specific.

Implements interfaces:
- `DisplayHistory` // Display the history of the vending machine.

Responsibilities:
- Know the service representative's selection including setting the price at a location.
  Collaborator: `ServiceRepresentativeSelection`.
- Display history information.
  Collaborators: `ItemDispenserAssembly`, `MainDisplay`.
- Load the coin dispenser assembly.
  Collaborator: `CoinDispenserAssembly`.

Constructor:
- `ServiceRepresentative(CoinDispenserAssembly, aCoinDispenserAssembly,ItemDispenserAssembly anItemDispenserAssembly, MainDisplay aMainDisplay Selection aServiceRepresentativeSelection) {...};`

Characteristics:
Operations:
  Public services:
  - `coinDispenserAssemblyLoaded();`
    `public void coinDispenserAssemblyLoaded() {...};`
    // Notify the coin dispenser assembly that it has been loaded.
  - `displayTotalIncome();`
    `public void displayTotalIncome() {...};`
    // Display to the service representative the total income of the vending
    // machine.
    // Interface: `DisplayHistory`.
  - `displayTotalItemsSold();`
    `public void displayTotalItemsSold() {...};`
    // Display to the service representative the total number of items sold
    // of the vending machine.
    // Interface: `DisplayHistory`.
  - `reset();`
    `public void reset() {...};`
    // Reset the service representative selection.
  - `selected(anInteger);`
    `public void selected(int anInteger) {...};`
    /* Set the column of the service representative selection to anInteger or
    * build the price of the service representative selection. */

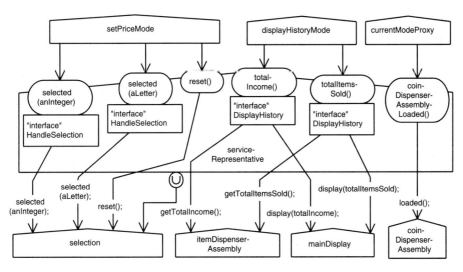

Figure 3.37 Internal collaboration diagram for the single instance of the ServiceRepresentative class.

```
    * Precondition: (0 < anInteger && anInteger < 11).
    * Interface: HandleSelection.
    */
● selected(aLetter);
    public void selected(Character aLetter) {...};
    /* Set the row of the service representative selection to aLetter or enter
    * the associated command.
    * Precondition: (Character.isLetter(aLetter)).
    * Interface: HandleSelection.
    */
```

Properties:
Attributes: none.
Links:

- `CoinDispenserAssembly`   `coinDispenserAssembly;`
- `ItemDispenserAssembly`   `itemDispenserAssembly;`
- `MainDisplay`   `mainDisplay;`

Parts: none.
Entries:
- `ServiceRepresentativeSelection selection;`

Exceptions thrown: none.

3.3.1.2 Dispenser Package

The purpose of this subsection is to document the design of the Dispenser Package. This section includes a package diagram, a package collaboration diagram, and the design decisions and rationale for the package. Instances of this package export two objects and hide 84 objects.

The rationale for creating this package includes:

- The package is cohesive, consisting of classes that model the hardware devices that dispense things.
- This cohesion supports efficient staffing by allowing scarce developer expertise in dispenser issues to be concentrated on one team.
- The package is loosely coupled to other packages, in that it only contains two classes as its interface.
- The package is modular, consisting of only five classes.

3.3.1.2.1 Static architecture of the Dispenser Package

Figure 3.38 illustrates the static architecture of the Dispenser Package.

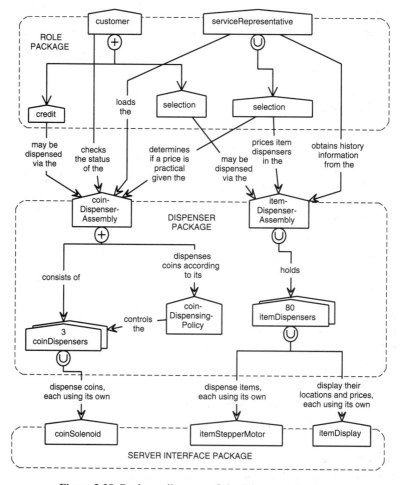

Figure 3.38 Package diagram of the Dispenser Package.

3.3.1.2.2 Dynamic architecture of the Dispenser Package
Figure 3.39 summarizes the dynamic architecture of the Dispenser Package.

3.3.1.2.3 Design decisions and rationale for the Dispenser Package
The following summarizes the important design decisions that were made during
the modeling of the Dispenser Package and the rationales behind them:

1. *Package identification.* The Dispenser Package was chosen to encapsulate all
   classes directly involved with dispensing coins and items.

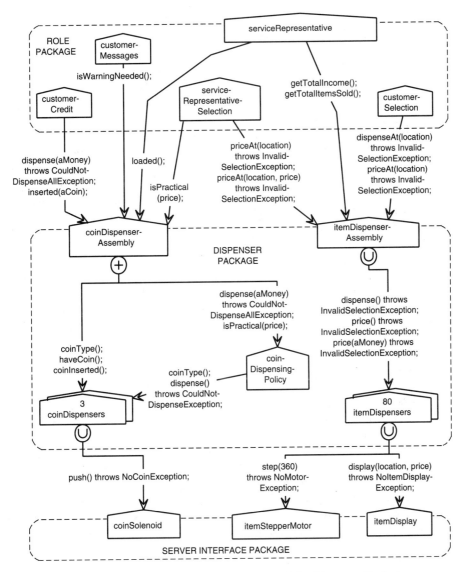

Figure 3.39 Package collaboration diagram of the Dispenser Package.

2. *Object identification.* Most of the objects in the instance of this package correspond to server external objects on the software context diagram illustrated in Figure 2.2. They represent output devices involved with dispensing coins and items. In order to provide flexibility, the dispensers are collected into dispenser assemblies that can be parameterized in terms of the number and kind of dispensers they contain.

3. *Coin dispenser assembly.* The coin solenoids are the only parts of the coin dispenser assembly that are electrically connected to, and controlled by, the MIVM software. Nevertheless, it was decided to create an aggregation hierarchy consisting of a coin dispenser assembly holding multiple coin dispensers, each containing its own coin solenoid. The rationale for this design decision is based on the following:
   - This aggregation structure mirrors the physical aggregation structure of the hardware.
   - Each coin dispenser and coin solenoid in the structure is a logical abstraction of something in the real world.
   - This design simplifies the resulting individual objects.
   - This design yields a better separation of concerns.
   - This design provides more extensibility to allow MegaVending Corp. to easily introduce new hardware coin dispenser assemblies in the future. For example, one that handles different kinds of coins or one that has multiple coin dispensers for the same kind of coin may be introduced because certain kinds of coins often run out before others.

4. *Item dispenser assembly.* The item stepper motors and the item displays are the only parts of the item dispenser assembly that are electrically connected to, and controlled by, the MIVM software. Nevertheless, it was decided to create an aggregation hierarchy consisting of an item dispenser assembly holding multiple item dispensers, each containing its own item stepper motor and item display. The rationale for this design decision is based on the following:
   - This aggregation structure mirrors the physical aggregation structure of the hardware.
   - Each object in the structure is a logical abstraction of something in the real world.
   - This design simplifies the resulting individual objects.
   - This design yields a better separation of concerns.
   - This design provides more extensibility to allow MegaVending Corp. to easily introduce new hardware item dispenser assemblies in the future (e.g. one that has sensors to tell when it is running low so that it can contact MegaVending to request restocking).

5. *Number of item dispensers.* Although the number of hardware item dispensers may vary from one to 80, depending on how many kinds of oversized items are to be dispensed, it was decided to have exactly 80 software item dispensers, whereby only some were valid. This design decision had the following benefits:
   - The number of software item dispensers did not have to be changed on the fly.

- The same concept of invalid selection could be used for either a software item dispenser that does not have a corresponding hardware item dispenser at the specified location or one for which no price has been set when it receives the message to dispense an item.
- The determination of whether a software item dispenser is invalid would happen only when required and exception handling.

6. *Coin dispensing policy.* The policy for making change was reified as an object in order to:
   - make the CoinDispenserAssembly class more modular, and thereby more reusable,
   - separate the dispensing algorithm from the coin dispensers, and
   - provide flexibility to handle multiple dispensing policies in the future.

7. *Loading the coin dispenser.* When the door object notifies the currentModeProxy object that the door has been locked, the currentModeProxy object notifies the serviceRepresentative object that the human service representative should have loaded the coin dispenser assembly. The serviceRepresentative object therefore notifies the coinDispenserAssembly object that it has been loaded. The coinDispenserAssembly in turn notifies each of its coinDispenser objects that coins have been inserted.

   The currentModeProxy object should not notify the coinDispenser object directly because:
   - Loading the coin dispenser assembly is the responsibility of the service representative.
   - That would increase package coupling by coupling the coordination package to the dispenser package.
   - That would unnecessarily increase coupling because the serviceRepresentative object already is indirectly coupled to the coinDispenserAssembly via its serviceRepresentativeSelection.

8. *Valid prices.* Because the coinDispenserAssembly object knows what kinds of coins it can dispense, it can tell the serviceRepresentativeSelection object whether or not a price is practical i.e. whether the coin dispenser assembly can make change regardless of the amount of the customer's credit. (We ignore the possibility that any coin dispensers are empty and we assume that the coin validator validates the same kind of coins that the coin dispenser assembly dispenses.)

9. *History information.* Because itemDispenserAssembly is the natural object to be responsible for keeping track of the total number of items that it has dispensed and the total resulting income from these items, it should also be responsible for informing the service representative of this information when requested.

10. *Handling the failed exception.* The customOperatingSystemCalls object raises the FailedException to a coinSolenoid object when the hardware solenoid fails to dispense a coin. This exception throws the NoCoinException to the appropriate coinDispenser, which rethrows it as the CouldNotDispenseException to the coinDispensingPolicy object.

Depending on where it is in the execution of its algorithm, the coinDispensingPolicy may throw the CouldNotDispenseAllException to the coinDispenserAssembly object. The coinDispenserAssembly throws the CouldNotDispenseException to the customerCredit object so that the customer may use the remaining credit to buy another item.

11. *Invalid selections.* The itemDispenserAssembly object always contains 80 itemDispenser objects even though the hardware item dispenser assembly may contain fewer hardware item dispensers (e.g. in order to accommodate larger-sized items). Exception handling is used when an invalid item dispenser is selected. (An invalid software item dispenser is one that either does not have a corresponding hardware item dispenser at the specified location or one for which no price has been set when it receives the message to dispense an item.) A message to an invalid itemDispenser object will throw the InvalidSelectionException because either no price has been set for that item dispenser or because a corresponding hardware item dispenser does not exist at that location (e.g. because of the need to store large items in a neighboring location.

12. *ItemDispenserAssemblyLocation.* Each itemDispenserAssemblyLocation object models a location within the itemDispenserAssembly object, and therefore knows its row and column. It also therefore enforces the range restrictions of the configuration of the itemDispenserAssembly (i.e. number of columns and number of rows). Unlike the other classes, instances of ItemDispenserAssemblyLocation do not appear on the diagrams because they represent hidden attributes of other objects that are on the diagram.

3.3.1.2.4 Classes of the Dispenser Package

The purpose of this subsection is to document the classes that comprise the Dispenser Package. The following classes are organized alphabetically with inheritance indicated by indentation:

- **CoinDispensingPolicy**
  Definition: the policy used to determine the order in which to dispense coins when making change.
  Stereotype: Service Provider.
  Utility: Domain-specific.
- **Dispenser**
  Definition: a hardware device used to dispense something.
  Stereotype: Service Provider.
  Utility: Domain-specific.
  - **CoinDispenser**
    Definition: a dispenser that dispenses coins.
    Stereotype: Service Provider.
    Utility: Domain-specific.
  - **ItemDispenser**
    Definition: a dispenser that dispenses items.
    Stereotype: Service Provider.
    Utility: Domain-specific.

- **DispenserAssembly**
  Definition: an assembly of dispensers.
  Stereotype: Structurer.
  Utility: Domain-specific.
  - **CoinDispenserAssembly**
    Definition: the dispenser assembly that holds the three coin dispensers.
    Stereotype: Structurer.
    Utility: Domain-specific.
  - **ItemDispenserAssembly**
    Definition: the dispenser assembly that holds a matrix of 80 item dispensers.
    Stereotype: Structurer.
    Utility: Domain-specific.
- **ItemDispenserAssemblyLocation**
  Definition: a possible location of an item dispenser in the item dispenser assembly.
  Stereotype: Information Holder.
  Utility: Domain-specific.

3.3.1.2.4.1 CoinDispensingPolicy

Definition: the policy used to determine the order in which to dispense coins when making change.

Superclass: `TestableObject`.

Stereotype: Service Provider.

Utility: Domain-specific.

Responsibilities:
- Know the correct order[t] in which to dispense coins.
  Collaborator: `CoinDispenser`.
- Determine whether a price is practical based on the coin dispenser assembly configuration.
  Collaborator: none.

Constructor:
- `CoinDispensingPolicy`
  `(Coin[] coinDispenserAssemblyConfiguration,`
  `CoinDispenser[] coinDispensers) {...};`

Characteristics:
  Operations:
    Public services:
    - `dispense(aMoney);`
      `public void dispense(Money aMoney) throws`
      `CouldNotDispenseAllException {...};`

---

[t]To minimize the number of coins dispensed, the current policy is to first dispense as many quarters as possible, then as many dimes as possible, and finally any remainder in nickels.

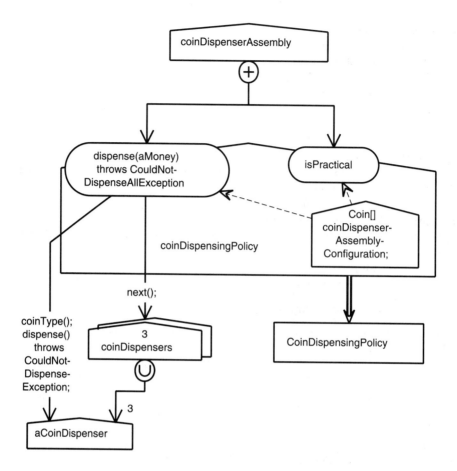

Figure 3.40 Internal collaboration diagram for the single instance of the
CoinDispensingPolicy class.

```
/* Dispense aMoney using the coin dispensers.
 * Handle CouldNotDispenseException by trying the next coin
 * dispenser holding coins of the desired type. If there are no other
 * dispensers, throw
 * CouldNotDispenseAllException.
 */
```
● isPractical(aPrice);
```
     public Boolean isPractical(Money aPrice) {...};
```
// Answer true if aPrice is practical based on the coin dispenser assembly
// configuration.

Properties:
  Attribute:
- `Coin[]`   `coinDispenserAssemblyConfiguration;`

  Link:
- `CoinDispenser[] coinDispensers;`

Parts: none.
Entries: none.
Exceptions thrown:
- `CouldNotDispenseAllException`
  // Thrown if all of the money could not be dispensed.

3.3.1.2.4.2 Dispenser

Definition: a hardware device used to dispense something.

Superclass: `TestableObject`.

Stereotype: Service Provider.

Utility: Domain-specific.

Responsibility:
- Dispense something.
  Collaborator: `Actuator`.

Characteristics:
  Operations:
    Public services:
- `dispense();`
    `public abstract void dispense() throws`
    `InvalidSelectionException;`
    // Dispense one thing using the actuator.

Properties:
  Attributes: none.
  Links: none.
  Parts: none.
  Entries:
- `Actuator actuator;` // Either a solenoid or a stepper motor.

Exceptions thrown:
- `InvalidSelectionException`
  /* Thrown by an item dispenser if there is no item stepper motor, no
  * item display, or the price has not been set.
  */

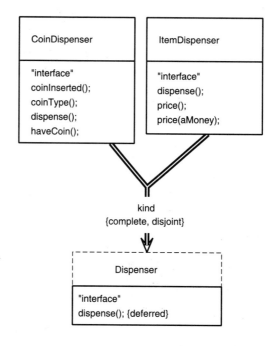

Figure 3.41 Inheritance diagram for the Dispenser class.

3.3.1.2.4.2.1 CoinDispenser

Definition: a dispenser that dispenses coins.

Superclass: Dispenser.

Stereotype: Service Provider.

Utility: Domain-specific.

Responsibilities:
• Dispense a coin.
  Collaborator: Solenoid.
• Know the type of the coins it stores.
  Collaborator: none.
• Know if it has any coins.
  Collaborator: none.

Constructors:
• CoinDispenser(Coin aCoinType, Solenoid aSolenoid) {...};

Characteristics:
  Operations:

Public services:
- coinInserted();
    public void inserted(){...};
    // Know that a coin can be dispensed.
- dispense();
    public void dispense() throws CouldNotDispenseException
    {...};
    /* Dispense a coin.
     * Handle NoCoinException by throwing
     * CouldNotDispenseException and by setting haveCoin to false.
     */

Public queries:
- coinType();
    public Coin coinType(){...};
    // Return the type of the coins it contains.

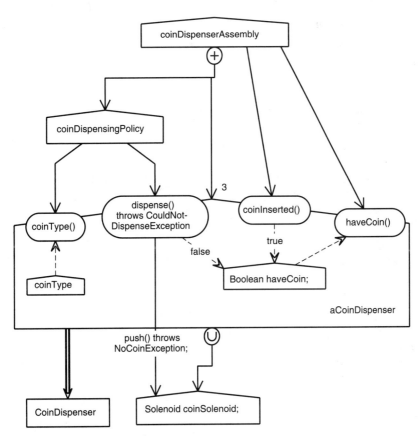

Figure 3.42 Internal collaboration diagram for the single instance of the CoinDispenser class.

- haveCoin();
    ```
    public Boolean haveCoin(){...};
    ```
    /* Return false if it has failed to dispense a coin and no coins have
    * been inserted since then. Otherwise, return true.
    */

Properties:
  Attributes:
  - `Boolean haveCoin;`
  - `Coin    coinType;`

  Links: none.
  Parts: none.
  Entries:
  - `Solenoid actuator;`

  Exceptions thrown:
  - `CouldNotDispenseException`
    // Thrown if the coin dispenser could not dispense a coin.

3.3.1.2.4.2.2 ItemDispenser

Definition: a dispenser for dispensing items.

Superclass: `Dispenser`.

Stereotype: Service Provider.

Utility: Domain-specific.

Responsibilities:
- Dispense an item.
  Collaborator: `StepperMotor`.
- Display the common location and price of the items it stores.
  Collaborators: `ItemDisplay`.
- Know location within the item dispenser assembly.
  Collaborators: none.

Constructor:
- `ItemDispenser`
    ```
    (ItemDispenserAssemblyLocation location,
    ItemDisplay                    anItemDisplay,
    StepperMotor                   aStepperMotor) {...};
    ```

Characteristics:
  Operations:
    Public services:
    - dispense();
        ```
        public void dispense() throws InvalidSelectionException
        {...};
        ```
        // Dispense an item.
        // Handle `NoMotorException` by throwing
        // `InvalidSelectionException`.

Public accessors:
- `price();`

    `public Money price() throws InvalidSelectionException`
    `{...};`
    // Return the common price of the contained items.
- `price(aMoney);`

    `public void price(Money aMoney)`
    `throws InvalidSelectionException {...};`
    /* Set the common price of the contained items and then display the
    * location and price on the corresponding item display.
    * Handle `NoPriceDisplayException` by throwing
    * `InvalidSelectionException`.
    */

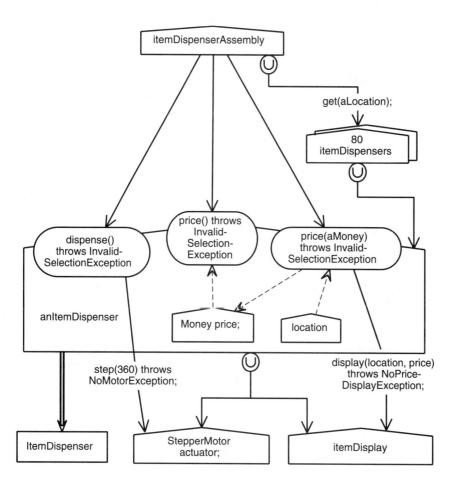

Figure 3.43 Internal collaboration diagram for the single instance
of the ItemDispenser class.

Properties:
  Attribute:
  - ItemDispenserAssemblyLocation location;
  - Money   price;

  Links: none.
  Parts: none.
  Entries:

  - StepperMotor   actuator;
  - ItemDisplay   itemDisplay;

  Exceptions thrown:
  - InvalidSelectionException
    /* Thrown if there is no corresponding item stepper motor or item
     * display, or if the price has not been set. (Note that prices cannot be set
     * if there is no hardware item dispenser.)
     * /

3.3.1.2.4.3 DispenserAssembly

Definition: an assembly of dispensers.

Superclass: TestableObject.

Stereotype: Structurer.

Utility: Domain-specific.

Responsibilities:
- Know its dispensers.
  Collaborator: none.

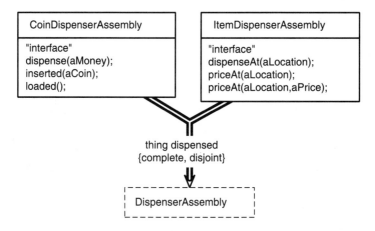

Figure 3.44 Inheritance diagram for the DispenserAssembly class.

Properties:
   Attributes: none.
   Links: none.
   Parts:
   ● Dispenser[] dispensers;

Entries: none.
Exceptions thrown: none.

3.3.1.2.4.3.1 CoinDispenserAssembly

Definition: the dispenser assembly that holds the three coin dispensers (i.e. nickelDispenser, dimeDispenser and quarterDispenser).[†]

Superclass: DispenserAssembly.

Stereotype: Structurer.

Utility: Domain-specific.

Responsibilities:
● Dispense a specified amount of money in coins.
   Collaborators: CoinDispensingPolicy, CoinDispenser.
● Know its policy for dispensing coins.
   Collaborator: CoinDispensingPolicy.
● Determine if the exact change warning is needed because all coin dispensers holding the same coin type are empty.
   Collaborator: CoinDispenser.
● Determine if change can be dispensed for a given price.
   Collaborator: CoinDispenser.

Constructors:
● CoinDispenserAssembly
```
   (Coin[]                  aCoinDispenserAssemblyConfiguration,
   CoinDispensingPolicy     coinDispensingPolicy,
   CustomOperatingSystemCalls aCustomOperatingSystemCalls) {...};
```

Characteristics:
   Operations:
   Public services:
   ● dispense(aMoney);
```
      public void dispense(Money aMoney) throws
      CouldNotDispenseAllException {...};
```
      // Dispense aMoney with available coins.

[†]This class is parameterized by the coinDispenser Assembly Configuration object so that it can dispense more coin types and have multiple dispensers for the same coin type.

- inserted(aCoin);

    public void inserted(Coin aCoin) {...};
    // Notify the appropriate coin dispenser(s) that aCoin has been
    // inserted.
- loaded();

    public void loaded() {...};
    // Notify the coin dispensers that they have been loaded.

Public queries:

- isPractical(price);

    public Boolean isPractical(Money price) {...};
    // Return true if change can be dispensed for an item with the given
    // price; otherwise return false.[†]

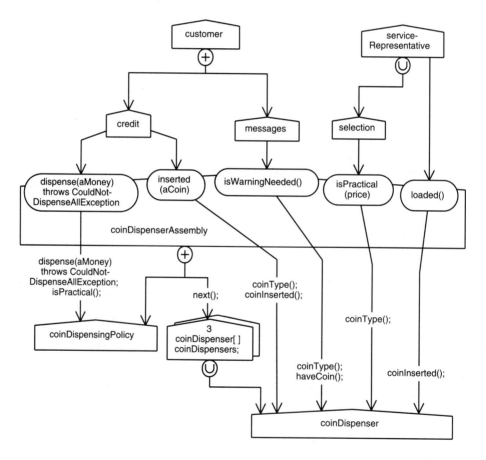

Figure 3.45 Internal collaboration diagram for the single instance of the
CoinDispenserAssembly class.

[†]This may be approximated (e.g. if price is divisible by a nickel).

- `isWarningNeeded();`
     `public Boolean isWarningNeeded() {...};`
     // Return true if the coin dispenser cannot dispense a type of coin;
     // otherwise, return false.

Properties:
   Attributes: none.
   Links: none.
   Parts:
- `CoinDispenser[]     dispensers;`
     // Determined from coinDispenserAssemblyConfiguration.
- `CoinDispensingPolicy coinDispensingPolicy;`

   Entries: none.
   Exceptions thrown:
- `CouldNotDispenseAllException`
     // Thrown if all money to be dispensed could not be dispensed.

3.3.1.2.4.3.2 ItemDispenserAssembly

Definition: the dispenser assembly that holds a matrix of 80 item dispensers.

Superclass: `DispenserAssembly`.

Stereotype: Structurer.

Utility: Domain-specific.

Responsibilities:
- Dispense an item from a requested item dispenser.
   Collaborator: `ItemDispenser`.
- Know the price associated with each item dispenser.
   Collaborator: `ItemDispenser`.
- Know the total number of items sold.
   Collaborators: none.
- Know the total income from the items it has dispensed.
   Collaborators: none.

Constructor:
- `ItemDispenserAssembly(int numberOfColumns, int numberOfRows)`
   `{...};`

Characteristics:
   Operations:

Public services:

- dispenseAt(aLocation);

  ```
  public void dispenseAt(ItemDispenserAssemblyLocation
  aLocation) throws InvalidSelectionException {...};
  ```
  /* Request the item dispenser at a location to dispense an item.
  * Handle InvalidSelectionException by rethrowing it.
  */

- priceAt(aLocation);

  ```
  public Money priceAt(ItemDispenserAssemblyLocation
  aLocation) throws InvalidSelectionException {...};
  ```
  /* Return the common price of items in the item dispenser at
  * aLocation.
  * Handle InvalidSelectionException by rethrowing it.
  */

- priceAt(aPrice, aLocation);

  ```
  public void priceAt(Money aPrice,
  ItemDispenserAssemblyLocation
  aLocation) throws InvalidSelectionException {...};
  ```
  /* Set the common price of items in the item dispenser at aLocation.
  * Handle InvalidSelectionException by rethrowing it.
  */

Public queries:

- numberOfColumns();

  ```
  public int numberOfColumns(){...};
  ```
- numberOfRows();

  ```
  public int numberOfRows(){...};
  ```
- getTotalIncome();

  ```
  public Money getTotalIncome(){...};
  ```
  // Return the sum of the prices of the items it has dispensed.
- getTotalItemsSold();

  ```
  public int getTotalIncome(){...};
  ```
  // Return the total number of items it has dispensed.

Properties:
Attributes:

- int   numberOfColumns; // Invariant: (numberOfColumns > 0).
- int   numberOfRows;   // Invariant: (numberOfRows > 0).
- int   totalItemsSold; // Invariant: (totalItemsSold ⩾ 0).
- Money totalIncome;   // Invariant: (totalIncome.amount() ⩾ 0).

Links: none.
Parts: none.

Entries:
● `Hashtable dispensers;`
    //Contains 80 itemDispensers keyed by location.

Exceptions thrown:
● `InvalidSelectionException`
    //Thrown when an invalid selection is made.

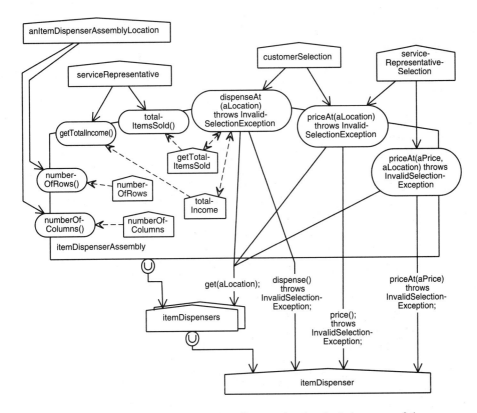

Figure 3.46 Internal collaboration diagram for the single instance of the
ItemDispenserAssembly class.

3.3.1.2.4.4 **ItemDispenserAssemblyLocation**

Definition: a possible location of an item dispenser in the item dispenser
assembly.

Superclass: `TestableObject.`

Stereotype: Information Holder.

Utility: Domain-specific.

Responsibilities:
- Know column.
  Collaborator: none.
- Know row.
  Collaborator: none.
- Determine if the location is possible.
  Collaborator: `ItemDispenserAssembly`.

Constructor:
- `ItemDispenserAssemblyLocation`
  `(ItemDispenserAssembly anItemDispenserAssembly) {...};`

Characteristics:
  Operations:
    Public accessors:
      - `column();`
          `public int column(){...};`
          // Return the column of the location.
      - `column(anInteger);`
          `public void column(int anInteger) throws`
          `InvalidLocationException {...};`
          // Set the column of the location.
      - `row();`
          `public int row(){...};`
          // Return the row of the location.
      - `row(aLetter);`
          `public void row(Character aLetter) throws`
          `InvalidLocationException {...};`
          // Set the row of the location (i.e. A → 1, B → 2, etc.).

  Properties:
    Attributes:
      - `int column;`
          // Invariant: `(0 < column).`
          // Invariant: `(column <= itemDispenserAssembly.`
          //   `numberOfColumns()).`
      - `int row;`
          // Invariant: `(0 < row).`
          // Invariant: `(row <= itemDispenserAssembly.numberOfRows()).`

    Links:
      - `ItemDispenserAssembly itemDispenserAssembly;`

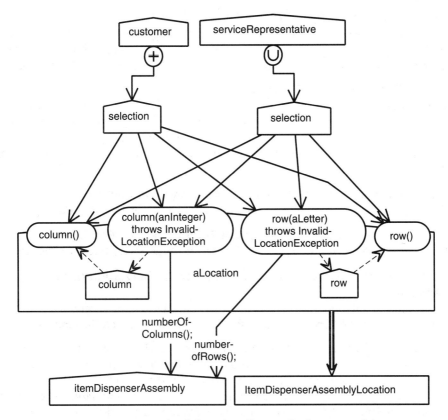

Figure 3.47 Internal collaboration diagram for instances of the
ItemDispenserAssemblyLocation class.

Parts: none.
Entries: none.
Exceptions thrown:
- `InvalidLocationException`
  // Thrown when an invariant is violated.

3.4 Server Interface Layer

The purpose of this subsection is to document the design of the Server Interface
Layer in terms of its component packages and classes.

The rationale for creating this layer includes:

- The layer is cohesive, consisting of all of the classes that model, control and
  provide an interface to the output externals that are servers of the MIVM software.
- This cohesion supports efficient staffing by allowing scarce developer
  expertise in output issues to be concentrated on one team.
- The layer is modular, consisting of only one package, five classes and 165 objects.

3.4.1 Packages in the Server Interface Layer

The purpose of this subsection is to document the packages that comprise the Server Interface Layer. Due to the small size of the application, the Server Interface Layer consists of only a single package, the Server Interface Package.

3.4.1.1 Server Interface Package

The purpose of this subsection is to document the design of the Server Interface Package. This section includes a package diagram, a package collaboration diagram, and the design decisions and rationale for the package.

Because the server interface layer contains only this single package, they share the same rationale.

3.4.1.1.1 Static architecture of the Server Interface Package

Figure 3.48 illustrates the static architecture of the Server Interface Package.

3.4.1.1.2 Dynamic architecture of the Server Interface Package

Figure 3.49 summarizes the dynamic architecture of the Server Interface Package.

3.4.1.1.3 Design decisions and rationale for the Server Interface Package

The following summarizes the important design decisions that were made during the modeling of the Server Interface Package and the rationales behind them:

1. *Package identification.* The Server Interface Package was chosen to encapsulate all classes directly involved in interfacing with server externals.
2. *Object identification.* Most of the objects in the instance of this package correspond to server external objects on the software context diagram illustrated in Figure 2.2. Most model hardware output devices. The custom operating system, however, was decomposed into two objects representing interrupts and calls in order to:
   - Avoid having a bidirectional peer association between the custom operating system and the vending machine software.
   - Cleanly separate client interface from server interface objects.
3. *Exception handling.* Exception handling was used to handle the situation in which the coin dispenser assembly could not dispense the entire amount due to the customer (i.e. change or refund of entire amount) because the hardware coin dispenser assembly ran out of one or more kinds of coins.
   - The coinDispenserAssembly throws a CouldNotDispenseAllException to the customer's credit object, which displays the customer's credit on the mainDisplay.
   - The customerCredit object raises a CouldNotRefundAllException to the customer's selection object so that it leaves the credit on the mainDisplay instead of displaying either 'HAVE A NICE DAY' or 'EXACT CHANGE ONLY'.
   - If any custom operating system call fails, it throws a FailedException to the custom-OperatingSystemCalls object, which passes it back to the output device. Specific exceptions are not needed because the output devices know what message they sent that resulted in the failure.

4. *Custom operating system calls.* This object is used to decouple the model objects from the custom operating system. If the common operating system changes, only this one object need be changed; all model objects will continue to function properly.

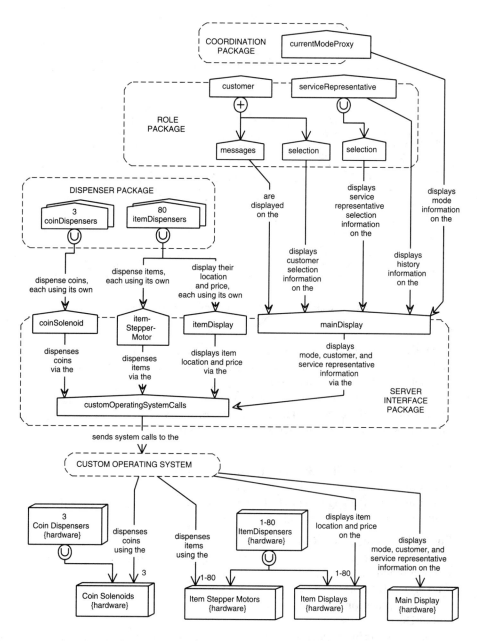

Figure 3.48 Package diagram of the Server Interface Package.

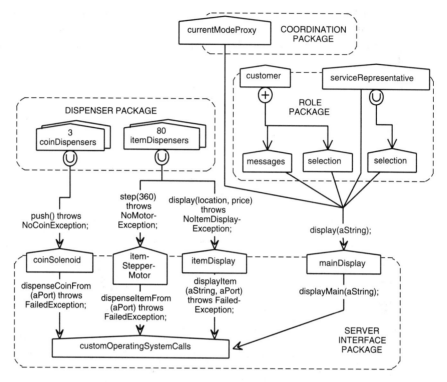

Figure 3.49 Package collaboration diagram of the Server Interface Package.

5. *Containment rather than aggregation.* Containment is used rather than aggregation because the itemStepperMotor and itemDisplay in each itemDispenser do not collaborate.
6. *Ports.* The real custom operating system will control the output devices by means of hardware ports. The customOperatingSystemCalls object therefore needs to know the port of each hardware output device.

3.4.1.1.4 Classes of the Server Interface Package

The purpose of this subsection is to document the classes that comprise the Server Interface Package. The following classes are organized alphabetically with inheritance indicated by indentation:

- **CustomOperatingSystemCalls**
  Definition: the part of the custom operating system that can be called by the vending machine software.
  Stereotype: Interfacer.
  Utility: Application-specific.
- **OutputDevice**
  Definition: a hardware device that is controlled by the vending machine software.
  Stereotype: Service Provider.

Utility: Domain-specific.
- **Actuator**
  Definition: a mechanical device for moving or controlling something.
  Stereotype: Service Provider.
  Utility: Domain-specific.
  - **Solenoid**
    Definition: a kind of motor that pushes something when electric current is applied.
    Stereotype: Service Provider.
    Utility: Domain-specific.
  - **StepperMotor**
    Definition: a kind of motor the driveshaft of which rotates in small discrete steps.
    Stereotype: Service Provider.
    Utility: Domain-specific.
- **Display**
  Definition: an electronic device for presenting visual information.
  Stereotype: Service Provider.
  Utility: Domain-specific.
  - **ItemDisplay**
    Definition: a display used to display the location of an item dispenser and the price of the items it contains.
    Stereotype: Service Provider.
    Utility: Domain-specific.
  - **MainDisplay**
    Definition: the primary display used to display customer and service representative information.
    Stereotype: Service Provider.
    Utility: Domain-specific.

3.4.1.1.4.1 CustomOperatingSystemCalls

Definition: the part of the custom operating system that can be called by the vending machine software.

Superclass: `TestableObject`.

Stereotype: Interfacer.

Utility: Application-specific.

Responsibilities:
- Make custom operating system calls.
  Collaborators: CUSTOM OPERATING SYSTEM.

Constructor:
- `CustomOperatingSystemsCalls`
  `(CustomOperatingSystem aCustomOperatingSystem) {...};`

Characteristics:

Operations:

Public services:

- `dispenseCoinFrom(aPort);`

   `public void dispenseCoinFrom(Port aPort) throws`
   `FailedException {...};`
   // Dispenses a coin using the coin solenoid connected to aPort.
   // Handles FailedException by rethrowing it.

- `dispenseItemFrom(aPort);`

   `public void dispenseItemFrom(Port aPort) throws`
   `FailedException {...};`
   // Dispenses an item using the item stepper motor connected to aPort.
   // Handles FailedException by rethrowing it.

- `displayItem(aString, aPort);`

   `public void displayItem(String aString, Port aPort)`
   `throws FailedException {...};`
   // Displays aString on the item display connected to aPort.
   // Handles FailedException by rethrowing it.

- `displayMain(aString);`

   `public void displayMain(String aString) {...};`
   // Displays aString on a main display.[†]
   // Handles FailedException by rethrowing it.

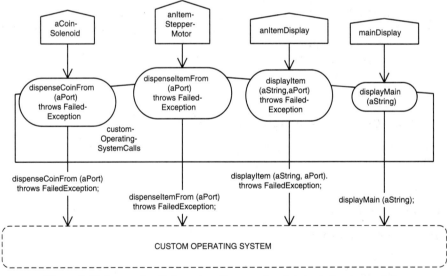

Figure 3.50 Internal collaboration diagram for the single instance of the CustomOperatingSystemCalls class.

[†] The port is not needed for displayMain( ) because only one exists and customOperatingSystemCalls knows the port.

Properties:
  Attributes: none.
  Link:
  ● `CustomOperatingSystem customOperatingSystem;`

  Parts: none.
  Entries: none.
  Exceptions thrown:
  ● `FailedException`
    // Raised when the custom operating system throws an exception.

3.4.1.1.4.2 OutputDevice

Definition: a hardware device that is controlled by the vending machine software.

Superclass: `TestableObject`.

Stereotype: Service Provider.

Utility: Domain-specific.

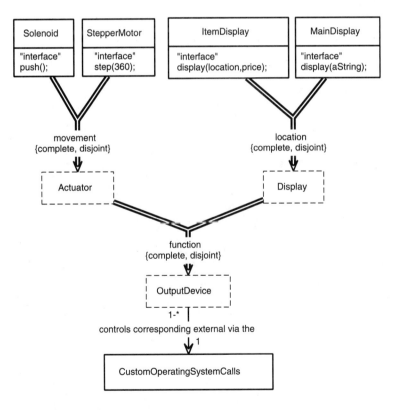

Figure 3.51 Inheritance diagram for the OutputDevice class.

Responsibilities:
- Control associated hardware output device.
  Collaborator: CustomOperatingSystemCalls.
- Know port connected to the corresponding hardware device.
  Collaborator: none.

Characteristics:
  Operations: none.
  Properties:
    Attribute:
    - `int`   `port;` // Hardware port connected to output device.

  Link:
  - `CustomOperatingSystemsCalls customOperatingSystemCalls;`

  Parts: none.
  Entries: none.
  Exceptions thrown: none.

3.4.1.1.4.2.1 Actuator

Definition: a mechanical device for moving or controlling something.

Superclass: `OutputDevice`.

Stereotype: Service Provider.

Utility: Domain-specific.

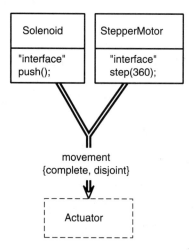

Figure 3.52 Inheritance diagram for the Actuator class.

Responsibilities:
- Control the corresponding hardware actuator.
  Collaborator: CustomOperatingSystemCalls.

Characteristics:
  Operations: none.
  Properties:
    Attributes: none.
    Links: none.
    Parts: none.
    Entries: none.
    Exceptions thrown: none.

3.4.1.1.4.2.1.1 Solenoid

Definition: a kind of actuator that pushes something when electric current is applied.

Superclass: `Actuator`.

Stereotype: Service Provider.

Utility: Domain-specific.

Responsibilities:
- Push out a coin.
  Collaborator: CustomOperatingSystemCalls.

Constructor:
- `Solenoid(CustomOperatingSystemsCalls`
  `aCustomOperatingSystemCalls,int aPort) {...};`

Characteristics:
  Operations:
    Public services:
    - `push();`
        `public void push() throws NoCoinException {...};`
        // Push a coin out of the associated hardware coin dispenser.
        // Throws NoCoinException when a FailedException is caught.

  Properties:
    Attributes: none.
    Links: none.
    Parts: none.

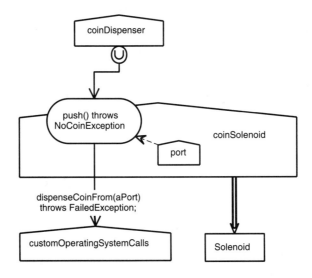

Figure 3.53 Internal collaboration diagram for instances of the Solenoid class.

Entries: none.

Exceptions thrown:

- NoCoinException
  // Raise only if the hardware coin solenoid fails to push out a coin when
  // requested.

3.4.1.1.4.2.1.2 StepperMotor

Definition: a kind of motor the driveshaft of which rotates in small discrete steps.

Superclass: Actuator.

Stereotype: Service Provider.

Utility: Domain-specific.

Responsibilities:

- Rotate the wire of the item dispenser.
  Collaborator: CustomOperatingSystemCalls.

Characteristics:

Constructor:

- StepperMotor(CustomOperatingSystemsCalls
  aCustomOperatingSystemCalls,int aPort) {...};

Operations:
  Public services:
- `step(degrees);`
    `public void step(int degrees) throws NoMotorException`
    `{...};`
    // Rotate the wire of the associated item dispenser degrees clockwise.
    // Handle FailedException by throwing NoMotorException.

Properties:
  Attributes: none.
  Links: none.
  Parts: none.
  Entries: none.
  Exceptions thrown:
- `NoMotorException`
    // Raise only if there exists no hardware stepper motor.

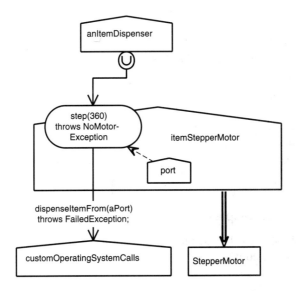

Figure 3.54 Internal collaboration diagram for the StepperMotor class.

3.4.1.1.4.2.2 Display

Definition: an electronic device for presenting visual information.

Superclass: `OutputDevice`.

Stereotype: Service Provider.

Utility: Domain-specific.

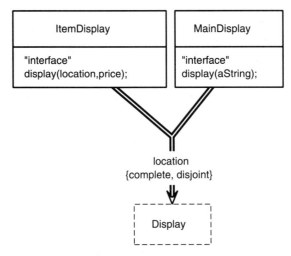

Figure 3.55 Inheritance diagram for the Display class.

Responsibilities:
● Display a string on the associated hardware display.
  Collaborators: CustomOperatingSystemCalls.

Characteristics:
  Operations: none.
  Properties:
    Attributes: none.
    Links: none.
    Parts: none.
    Entries: none.
    Exceptions thrown: none.

3.4.1.1.4.2.2.1 ItemDisplay

Definition: a display used to display the location of an item dispenser and the price of the items it contains.

Superclass: `Display`.

Stereotype: Service Provider.

Utility: Domain-specific.

Responsibilities:
● Display price at a location.
  Collaborator: CustomOperatingSystemCalls.

Constructor:
● `ItemDisplay(`
    `CustomOperatingSystemsCalls aCustomOperatingSystemCalls,`
    `int aPort) {...};`

Characteristics:
  Operations:
    Public services:
    ● display(location, price);
         public void display(ItemDispenserAssemblyLocation
         location, String price) throws NoItemDisplayException
         {...};
         // Display location and price on the item display.
         // Handle FailedException by throwing NoItemDispenserException.

  Properties:
    Attributes: none.
    Links: none.
    Parts: none.
    Entries: none.
    Exceptions thrown:
    ● NoItemDisplayException
         // Raise only if there is no hardware item display.

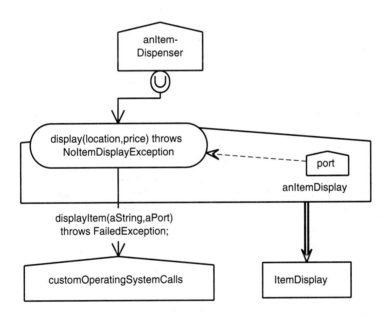

Figure 3.56 Internal collaboration diagram for instances of the ItemDisplay class.

3.4.1.1.4.2.2.2 MainDisplay

Definition: the primary display used to display customer and service representative information.

Superclass: `Display`.

Stereotype: Service Provider.

Utility: Domain-specific.

Responsibilities:
- Display customer information.
  Collaborator: CustomOperatingSystemCalls.
- Display service representative information.
  Collaborator: CustomOperatingSystemCalls.

Constructor:
- `MainDisplay(CustomOperatingSystemsCalls aCustomOperatingSystemCalls, int aPort) {...};`

Characteristics:
  Operations:
    Public services:
      - `display(aString);`
          `public void display(String aString) {...};`
          // Display aString on the main display.

  Properties:
    Attributes: none.
    Links: none.
    Parts: none.
    Entries: none.
    Exceptions thrown: none.

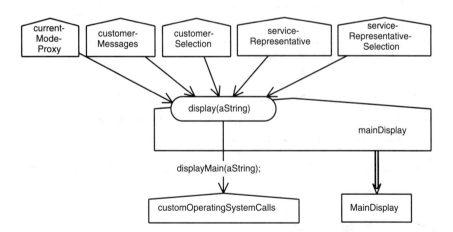

Figure 3.57 Internal collaboration diagram for the single instance of the MainDisplay class.

3.5 Foundation Layer

The purpose of this subsection is to document the design of the Foundation Layer in terms of its component classes. This layer contains all of the MIVM software classes that are foundation classes (i.e. reusable, application-independent classes).

3.5.1 Classes in the Foundation Layer

3.5.1.1 Money

Definition: Each instance of this concrete class models money.

Superclass: `TestableObject`.

Stereotype: Model.

Utility: General Purpose.

Responsibilities:
- Provide arithmetic operations on money.
  Collaborator: `int`.
- Know amount.
  Collaborator: none.
- Know currency.
  Collaborator: none.

Constructors:
- Money(String currency, BigDecimal amount).

Characteristics:
  Operations:
  Public services:
  - `add(aMoney);`
    `public Money add(Money aMoney) {...};`
    // Add aMoney to the amount and return the sum.
  - `subtract(aMoney);`
    `public Money subtract(Money aMoney) {...};`
    // Subtract aMoney from the amount and return the difference.
  - `multiply(anInteger);`
    `public Money multiply(int anInteger) {...};`
    // Multiply the amount by anInteger and return the product.
  - `divide(anInteger);`
    `public Money divide(int anInteger) {...};`
    // Divide the amount by anInteger and return the quotient.
    // Precondition: (anInteger is not zero).

Public queries:
- `amount();`
    `public BigDecimal amount() {...};`
    // Return the amount of money.
- `currency();`
    `public String currency() {...};`
    // Return the currency of the money.

Properties:
  Attributes:
  - `BigDecimal amount;` // Invariant: `amount.scale() = 2.`
  - `String       currency;`

Links: none.
Parts: none.
Entries: none.
Exceptions thrown: none.

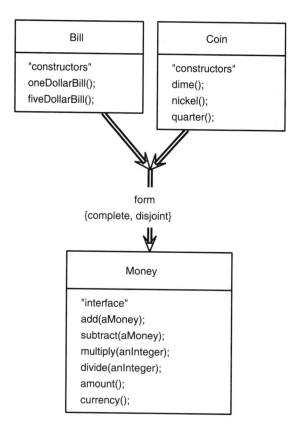

Figure 3.58 Inheritance diagram for instances of the Money class.

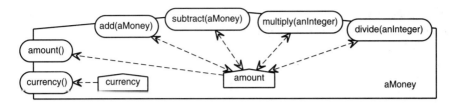

Figure 3.59 Internal collaboration diagram for instances of the Money class.

3.5.1.1.1 Bill

Definition: The two instances, oneDollarBill and fiveDollarBill, of this concrete flyweight class model valid US bills. (Because the MIVM software only deals with a single bill or coin at a time, there is only the need for a single instance of each bill or coin. Thus, the Bill and Coin classes are flyweight classes.)

Superclass: Money.

Stereotype: Model.

Utility: General Purpose.

Responsibilities:
• Construct valid bills.
  Collaborators: none.

Characteristics:
  Class operations:
  • `fiveDollarBill();`
      `public static Bill fiveDollarBill() {...};`
      // Return the five-dollar bill object.
  • `oneDollarBill();`
      `public static Bill oneDollarBill() {...};`
      // Return the one-dollar bill object.

  Properties:
    Attributes: none.
    Links: none.
    Parts: none.
    Entries: none.
    Exceptions thrown: none.

3.5.1.1.2 Coin

Definition: The three instances (dime, nickel, and quarter) of this concrete flyweight class model valid US coins.

Superclass: Money.

Responsibilities:
- Construct valid nickels, dimes, and quarters.
  Collaborators: None.

Characteristics:
  Class operations:
  - dime();
      ```
      public static Coin dime() {...};
      ```
      // Return the dime object.
  - nickel();
      ```
      public static Coin nickel() {...};
      ```
      // Return the nickel object.
  - quarter();
      ```
      public static Coin quarter() {...};
      ```
      // Return the quarter object.

Properties:
  Attributes: none.
  Links: none.
  Parts: none.
  Entries: none.
  Exceptions thrown: none.

3.6 Previous architectures

This subsection documents the previous architectures of the MIVM. This documentation includes a configuration diagram with a textual explanation of each architecture and a discussion including:

- the design rationale for the architecture,
- improvements over the preceding architecture,
- and weaknesses that prompted iteration of the architecture.

3.6.1 Initial architecture

As part of a scoping study completed in December 1995, the initial architecture was created and prototyped in Smalltalk. It was used to identify some of the key abstractions, give the developers some experience in the vending machine domain, and scope the size of the application.

3.6.1.1 Configuration diagram
The initial MIVM architecture consists of the following two packages:

1. *Selection Package.* Instances of this package contained all objects involved in selecting and dispensing items. It contained the column and row selection buttons that notified the selection of the selected column and row, respectively. The selection displayed customer messages on the display. The

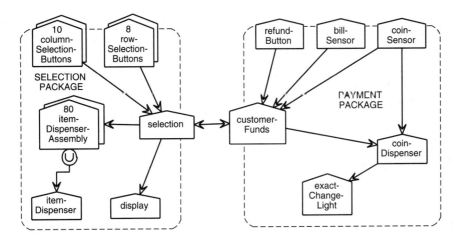

Figure 3.60 Configuration diagram for the initial architecture.

selection also queried its price and dispensed itself via the item dispenser assembly. The item dispenser assembly was a matrix of item dispensers, which stored the prices and dispensed the items. The selection queried and requested payment from the customerFunds.

2. *Payment Package.* Instances of this package contained all objects involved in paying for selections. It contained bill and coin sensors that incremented the customerFunds. It also contained a refundButton that requested the refund of the customerFunds. The customerFunds was refunded via the coinDispenser, which was notified of the type of inserted coin by the coinSensor. The coinDispenser controlled the exactChangeLight to signify that it was out of a specific kind of coin. The customerFunds notified the selection when it was incremented and reset the selection after it was refunded.

3.6.1.2 Discussion
The design rationale for the two packages was to support and implement the two main subordinate use cases of the Customer Buys an Item use case: Customer Makes a Selection and Customer Makes a Payment. It was also decided to ignore requirements involving the service representative in order to make the initial prototype simple.

The initial architecture had the following major weaknesses:

1. As a partial prototype, the initial architecture only covered customers buying items and completely ignored the servicing of the machine by the service representative. Therefore, its main weakness was that there was no way for the service representative to set or to change the price of the items or to display history information.

2. Because it was based on use cases, the decomposition of the architecture into packages was along functional lines rather than along object lines. This led to poor package cohesion and excessive coupling between the packages:
   - There was no customer object, and two of its properties (i.e. the selection and customerFunds) were not encapsulated and were even split across packages.
   - The third major weakness was that the selection and customerFunds objects were peers of one another, so that there was high coupling between them.
3. Due to ignorance of proper domain jargon, money *validators* were called *sensors*.

3.6.2 Version 1 architecture

In March 1996, version 1 of the MIVM architecture was completed and implemented in Smalltalk. It was the first architecture designed to implement all of the major requirements of the MIVM.

3.6.2.1 Configuration diagram

As illustrated in Figure 3.61, version 1 of the MIVM architecture consists of the following three packages:

1. *Input Package.* Instances of this package contained all objects that were directly involved in gathering input from the customer or serviceRepresentative. It contained buttons that notified the currentModeProxy, telling it to change its currentMode, refund the customerCredit, and which integer or letter was selected. It also contained a billValidator and coinValidator that notified the currentModeProxy of the money validated. The currentModeProxy implemented the state pattern via its actual mode objects: dispenseItemMode, displayHistoryMode and setPriceMode. The currentModeProxy also displayed mode information on the display.
2. *Customer Package.* Instances of this package contained all non-input objects that directly supported the customer. It contained the customer object, which had customerCredit and customerSelection as parts. The customer incremented, refunded and reset the customerCredit.

    The customer reset and selected the location of the customerSelection. The customerCredit and customerSelection were peers. The customerCredit notified the customerSelection when it was incremented and reset the customerSelection after it was refunded. The customerSelection queried and requested payment from the customerCredit.

    The customerCredit refunded itself to the customer via the coinDispenser, which was notified by the dispenseItemMode of each coin validated. The customerSelection queried its price and dispensed itself via the item DispenserAssembly. Both the customerSelection and the coinDispenser displayed relevant messages via the display.

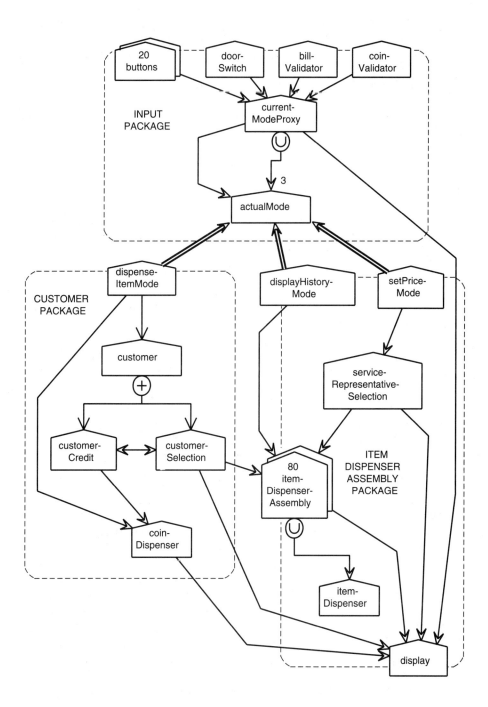

Figure 3.61 Configuration diagram for the version 1 architecture.

3. *Item Dispenser Assembly Package.* Instances of this package contained all objects that directly involved the itemDispenserAssembly. It contained the serviceRepresentativeSelection, which was passed input by the setPriceMode and the itemDispenserAssembly that was passed input by the displayHistoryMode. The serviceRepresentativeSelection queried and set the price of itemDispensers via the itemDispenserAssembly. The serviceRepresentativeSelection and itemDispenserAssembly also displayed relevant information on the display.

3.6.2.2 Discussion

The basic design rationale for the three packages was to move into a more object-oriented decomposition than that produced by basing packages on use cases. A major goal of the version 1 architecture was to support the service representative as well as the customer.

The version 1 architecture had the following major improvements over the initial architecture:

1. Support for the service representative, including the setting of prices and the displaying of history information, was provided.
2. The vending machine now handled the resulting mode issues.
3. A more object-oriented decomposition of the architecture into packages was produced, resulting in higher package cohesion and less coupling between packages.
4. The customerCredit and customerSelection objects were encapsulated within the customer object.
5. Class names were improved with *sensors* being renamed *validators* and *customerFunds* renamed *customerCredit*.

The version 1 architecture had the following major weaknesses:

1. The handling of modes was not adequately localized, being scattered across multiple packages.
2. The dispenseItemMode object directly tells the coinDispenser object about customer coins, thereby usurping one of the customer's responsibilities.
3. All of the buttons, regardless of purpose or type are grouped into a single collection. (This was actually somewhat of a backward step from the initial prototype, proving that iteration does not always bring improvements in practice.)
4. The item dispense assembly package is not cohesive in that it contains the serviceRepresentativeSelection, which is only indirectly related to item dispensing.
5. The customerCredit and the customerSelection objects are tightly coupled as peers.
6. There is no serviceRepresentative object corresponding to the customer object.

3.6.3 Version 2 architecture

In June 1996, version 2 of the MIVM architecture was completed and implemented in Smalltalk.

3.6.3.1 Configuration diagram

As illustrated in Figure 3.62, version 2 of the MIVM architecture consists of the following four packages:

1. *Input Package*. Instances of this package contained all objects that were directly involved in input from the customer or service representative. The doorSwitch object, the button objects and the money validator objects provided external inputs to the currentModeProxy object which forwarded them to the actual mode objects in the customer and service representative packages.

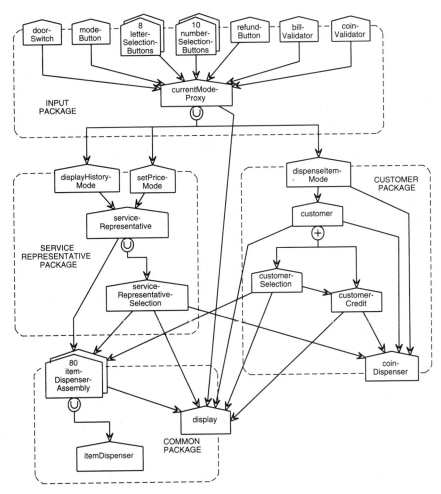

Figure 3.62 Configuration diagram for the version 2 architecture.

2. *Customer Package.* Instances of this package contained all objects that directly modeled the customer. The dispenseItemMode object forwarded customer inputs to the customer object and notified the coinDispenser that coins had been validated. The customer object updated the customerSelection and customerCredit objects and checked the status of the coinDispenser object prior to displaying its messages on the display.

3. *Service Representative Package.* Instances of this package contained all objects that directly modeled the service representative. The displayHistoryMode and setPriceMode objects forwarded service representative inputs to the serviceRepresentative object which either requested history information from the itemDispenserAssembly object or updated the serviceRepresentativeSelection object. The serviceRepresentative-Selection object queried and dispensed items from the itemDispenser-Assembly object, displayed service representative messages on the display, and checked the practicality of prices using the coinDispenser object.

4. *Common Package.* Instances of this package contained all objects that supported both of the customer and service representative packages. The itemDispenserAssembly object consisted of 80 itemDispenser objects and displayed history information on the display.

3.6.3.2 Discussion

The basic design rationale for the four packages was to create a more layered architecture with more cohesive packages. The version 2 architecture had the following major improvements over the version 1 architecture:

1. A service representative package including the service representative and its selection was introduced, thereby producing better package cohesion and a more layered architecture.
2. The itemDispenserAssembly and display objects were placed in their own package, which is used by both the customer and service representative packages.
3. The customerCredit was decoupled from the customer selection so that the two are no longer peers, thereby minimizing the coupling between them.
4. All actual modes collaborate only with roles. Before, the display history mode collaborated directly with the item dispenser assembly.
5. The letter and number selection buttons were separated, as they were in the initial prototype.

The version 2 architecture had the following major weaknesses, which have been fixed in version 3:

1. There was poor cohesion of the input package due to inclusion of both input devices and mode information.
2. Mode information was poorly localized, being split across three packages.
3. There was poor maintainability and extensibility due to:
   - Excessive coupling of the input and output devices to the custom operating system. Many objects had to understand custom operating system interrupts or make custom operating system calls, thereby making it

difficult to modify the custom operating system without adversely impacting too many other objects.

– The hardwiring of the customer messages.
– The hardwiring of the coin dispensing policy.

4. The customer package had poor cohesion due to inclusion of the coin dispenser. This also caused unnecessary coupling between the customer and service representative packages.

5. The itemDispenserAssembly and coinDispenser objects were treated inconsistently, because individual coinDispensers are actually localized in an assembly.

6. The use of paper price and location labels on the item dispensers allow the posted price to be inconsistent with the stored price.

The replacement of Smalltalk by Java resulted in the following changes:

- The messages on various diagrams and class specifications were changed to valid Java syntax.
- The design was modified to take advantage of Java's support for multiple interfaces per class.
- Java supports the overloading of messages based on the types of their arguments. For example, the Smalltalk messages `integer: anInteger` and `letter: aLetter` were replaced by the Java messages `selected(anInteger)` and `selected(aLetter)` respectively.
- The single Smalltalk Button class needed to be replaced by a small hierarchy of Java Button classes due to Java's inability to treat messages as objects.

The current version 3 architecture has the following major weaknesses, which will be fixed in future versions[†]:

1. Allow the service representative a way to enter new customer messages (e.g. using the letter, number and mode buttons).

2. Allow the service representative to obtain items sold and associated income on an item dispenser by item dispenser basis.

3. As a convenience, allow the service representative to set all item dispensers to the same price.

4. Replace the service representative with two new actors: price setter and auditor. This enables the replacement of the current mode proxy and actual mode objects with a single current role object. This redesign also eliminates the need for the Coordination Package and decreases the number of classes by four. This redesign is based on the fact that actors need not map one-to-one to job titles.

[†]The reader is encouraged to upgrade the design by iterating the package and collaboration diagrams and also the Java code.

4 Test documentation

This section documents the testing performed on the MIVM software. It covers the following four major topics:

1. Model verification
2. Test harness
3. Test classes
4. Class/package testing
5. Acceptance testing

4.1 Model verification

The design models were verified against their associated requirements models by means of whitebox sequence diagrams that show the interaction of internal objects that implement the use cases of the requirements specification.

4.1.1 Customers

This subsection documents all of the whitebox scenario diagrams involving the customer as the primary actor.

4.1.1.1 Customer Buys an Item

Description: This whitebox scenario diagram models the interactions between internal objects when a customer buys an item.

Requirement verified:
    SYS-R) C-1. Customer Buys an Item

Objects:
- Mandatory:
    - aLetterSelectionButton
    - anItemDispenser
    - anItemStepperMotor
    - aNumberSelectionButton
    - currentModeProxy
    - customer
    - customerCredit
    - customerMessages
    - customerSelection

- – customOperatingSystemCalls
  - – customOperatingSystemInterrupts
  - – dispenseItemMode
  - – itemDispenserAssembly
  - – mainDisplay
- ● Optional:
  - – If bill inserted:
    - – billValidator
  - – If coin inserted:
    - – coinDispenserAssembly
    - – coinValidator
  - – If change is due to the customer:
    - – aCoinDispenser
    - – aCoinSolenoid
    - – coinDispensingPolicy

Paths:
- ● Primary path:
  1. Customer Buys an Item
- ● Alternative path:
  2. Customer Requests a Refund

Preconditions: The mode of the MIVM is 'Dispense Item'.

Statements:
Concurrently
    invoke use case: Customer Makes a Selection.
and
    invoke use case: Customer Makes a Payment.
and
    optionally invoke use case: Customer Requests a Refund.
end concurrently.

Whitebox sequence diagram:[†] See Figure 4.1.

Postconditions:
1. Primary Path 1: Customer Buys an Item
   - – The postconditions of use case: Customer Makes a Selection.
   - – The postconditions of use case: Customer Makes a Payment.
   - – The mode of the MIVM is 'Dispense Item'.
2. Alternative Path 2: Customer Requests a Refund
   - – The postconditions of use case: Customer Requests a Refund.

[†] The whitebox sequence diagram largely repeats in graphical form the information in the preceding statements subsection. On typical projects, only one or the other is usually produced and documented. The textual form is usually easier to produce and maintain, but the diagram is typically easier to understand.

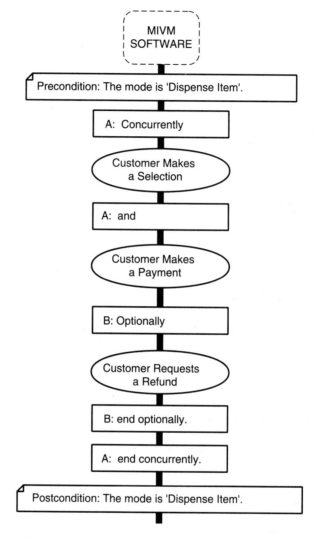

Figure 4.1 Whitebox sequence diagram for the use case: Customer Buys an Item.

4.1.1.1.1 **Customer Makes a Selection**

Description: This whitebox scenario diagram models the interactions between internal objects when a customer selects an item dispenser in the item dispenser assembly.

Requirement verified:
    SYS-R) C-1.1. Customer Makes a Selection

Objects:
- Mandatory:
  - aLetterSelectionButton
  - aNumberSelectionButton
  - currentModeProxy
  - customer
  - customerCredit
  - customerSelection
  - customOperatingSystemCalls
  - customOperatingSystemInterrupts
  - dispenseItemMode
  - mainDisplay
- Optional:
  - If an item is selected and paid for:
    - anItemDispenser
    - anItemStepperMotor
    - customerMessages
    - itemDispenserAssembly
  - If an item is selected and paid for and change is due to the customer:
    - aCoinDispenser
    - aCoinSolenoid
    - coinDispensingPolicy

Preconditions: The mode of the MIVM is 'Dispense Item'.

Statements:
Concurrently
    invoke use case: Customer Selects a Column.
and
    invoke use case: Customer Selects a Row
end concurrently.

Whitebox sequence diagram: See Figure 4.2.

Postconditions:
The postconditions of the use case: Customer Selects a Column.
The postconditions of the use case: Customer Selects a Row.
The mode of the MIVM is 'Dispense Item'.

4.1.1.1.1.1 Customer Selects the Column of an Item

Description: This whitebox scenario diagram models the interactions between internal objects when a customer selects a column of the desired item dispenser in the item dispenser assembly.

Requirements verified:
    SYS-R) C-1.1.1. Customer Selects the Column of an Item
    SW-R) C-1.1.1-1. Customer Selects the Column without Selecting the Item

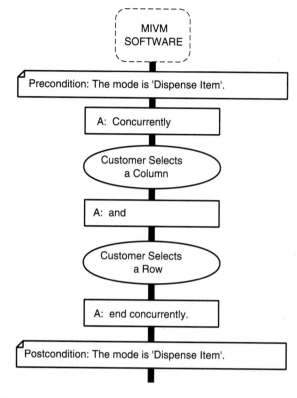

Figure 4.2 Whitebox sequence diagram for the use case: Customer Makes a Selection.

SW-R) C-1.1.1-2. Customer Selects the Item by Selecting the Column
SW-R) C-1.1.1-3. Customer Reselects the Column

Objects:
- Mandatory:
    - aNumberSelectionButton
    - currentModeProxy
    - customer
    - customerCredit
    - customerSelection
    - customOperatingSystemCalls
    - customOperatingSystemInterrupts
    - dispenseItemMode
    - mainDisplay
- Optional:
    - If an item is selected and paid for:
        - anItemDispenser
        - anItemStepperMotor

- customerMessages
- itemDispenserAssembly
- If an item is selected and paid for and change is due to the customer:
  - aCoinDispenser
  - aCoinSolenoid
  - coinDispensingPolicy

Paths:
- Primary paths:
  1. Customer Selects the Column without Selecting the Item
  2. Customer Selects the Item by Selecting the Column
- Alternative Path:
  3. Customer Reselects the Column

Preconditions: The mode of the MIVM is 'Dispense Item'.

Statements:

customOperatingSystemInterrupts	**sends** pressed()	**to** aNumberSelectionButton.
aNumberSelectionButton	**sends** selected(anInteger)	**to** currentModeProxy.
currentModeProxy	**sends** selected(anInteger)	**to** dispenseItemMode.
dispenseItemMode	**sends** selected(anInteger)	**to** customer.
customer	**sends** selected(anInteger)	**to** selection. // of the customer
selection	**sends** columnNotSelected()	**to** location. // of the selection

If columnNotSelected(), **then**

selection	**sends** rowNotSelected()	**to** location. // of the selection

  If rowNotSelected(), **then**

  // Primary Path 1. Customer Selects the Column without Selecting the Item:

selection	**sends** column(anInteger)	**to** location. // of the selection
selection	**sends** display('C ', anInteger)	**to** mainDisplay .
mainDisplay	**sends** displayMain('C ', anInteger)	**to** customOperatingSystemCalls.

  else

  // Primary Path 2. Customer Selects the Item by Selecting the Column:

selection	**sends** column(anInteger)	**to** location. // of the selection

  Invoke use case: Attempt To Dispense.

  end if.

else

// Alternative Path 3. Customer Reselects the Column:

selection	**sends** column(anInteger)	**to** location. // of the selection
selection	**sends** row(null)	**to** location. // of the selection
selection	**sends** display('C ', anInteger)	**to** mainDisplay.
mainDisplay	**sends** displayMain('C ', anInteger)	**to** customOperatingSystemCalls.

end if.

Whitebox sequence diagram: See Figure 4.3.

Postconditions:
1. Primary Path 1. Customer Selects the Column without Selecting the Item:
   - The selection location stores the new column.
   - The main display displays the column of the customer's selection.
   - The mode of the MIVM is 'Dispense Item'.
2. Primary Path 2. Customer Selects the Item by Selecting the Column:
   - The selection location stores the new column.
   - The postconditions of the use case: Attempt to Dispense.
   - The mode of the MIVM is 'Dispense Item'.

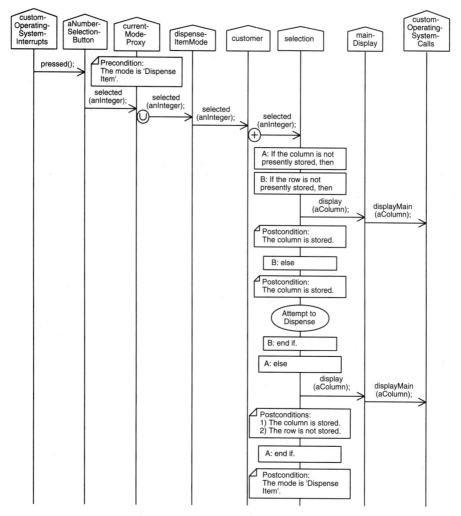

Figure 4.3 Whitebox sequence diagram for the use case:
Customer Selects the Column of an Item.

3. Alternative Path 3. Customer Reselects the Column:
   - The selection location stores the new column.
   - The selection location no longer stores the previous row.
   - The main display displays the column of the customer's selection.
   - The mode of the MIVM is 'Dispense Item'.

4.1.1.1.1.2 Customer Selects the Row of an Item

Description: This whitebox scenario diagram models the interactions between
internal objects when a customer selects a row of the desired item dispenser in
the item dispenser assembly.

Requirement verified:
  SYS-R) C-1.1.2. Customer Selects the Row of an Item
  SW-R) C-1.1.2-1. Customer Selects the Row without Selecting the Item
  SW-R) C-1.1.2-2. Customer Selects the Item by Selecting the Row
  SW-R) C-1.1.2-3. Customer Reselects the Row

Objects:
- Mandatory:
  - aLetterSelectionButton
  - currentModeProxy
  - customer
  - customerCredit
  - customerSelection
  - customOperatingSystemCalls
  - customOperatingSystemInterrupts
  - dispenseItemMode
  - mainDisplay
- Optional:
  - If an item is selected and paid for:
    - anItemDispenser
    - anItemStepperMotor
    - customerMessages
    - itemDispenserAssembly
  - If an item is selected and paid for and change is due to the customer:
    - aCoinDispenser
    - aCoinSolenoid
    - coinDispensingPolicy

Paths:
- Primary Paths:
  1. Customer Selects the Row without Selecting the Item
  2. Customer Selects the Item by Selecting the Row
- Alternative path:
  3. Customer Reselects the Row

Preconditions: The mode of the MIVM is 'Dispense Item'.

Statements:

customOperatingSystemInterrupts	**sends** get(aLetter)	**to** letterSelectionButtons.
customOperatingSystemInterrupts	**sends** pressed()	**to** aLetterSelectionButton.
aLetterSelectionButton	**sends** selected(aLetter)	**to** currentModeProxy.
currentModeProxy	**sends** selected(aLetter)	**to** dispenseItemMode.
dispenseItemMode	**sends** selected(aLetter)	**to** customer.
customer	**sends** selected(aLetter)	**to** selection. // of the customer
selection	**sends** rowNotSelected()	**to** location. // of the selection
If rowNotSelected(), **then**		
selection	**sends** columnNotSelected()	**to** location. // of the selection

If columnNotSelected(), **then**
// Primary Path 1. Customer Selects the Row without Selecting the Item:

selection	**sends** row(aLetter)	**to** location. // of the selection
selection	**sends** display('R ', aLetter)	**to** mainDisplay .
mainDisplay	**sends** displayMain('R ', aLetter)	**to** customOperatingSystemCalls.

else
// Primary Path 2. Customer Selects the Item by Selecting the Row:

selection	**sends** row(aLetter)	**to** location. // of the selection

Invoke use case: Attempt To Dispense.
end if.
else
// Alternative Path 3. Customer Reselects the Row:

selection	**sends** row(aLetter)	**to** location. // of the selection
selection	**sends** column(null)	**to** location. // of the selection
selection	**sends** display('R ', aLetter)	**to** mainDisplay.
mainDisplay	**sends** displayMain('R ', aLetter)	**to** customOperatingSystemCalls.

end if.

Whitebox sequence diagram: See Figure 4.4.

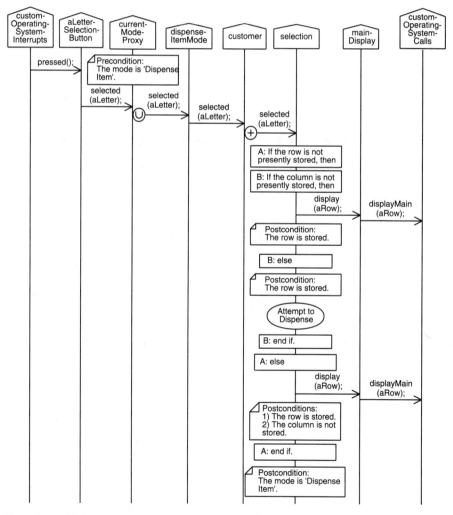

Figure 4.4 Whitebox sequence diagram for the Use Case: Customer Selects the Row of an Item

Postconditions:
1. Primary Path 1. Customer Selects the Row without Selecting the Item:
   - The selection location stores the new row.
   - The main display displays the row of the customer's selection.
   - The mode of the MIVM is 'Dispense Item'.
2. Primary Path 2. Customer Selects the Item by Selecting the Row:
   - The selection location stores the new row.
   - The postconditions of the use case: Attempt to Dispense.
   - The mode of the MIVM is 'Dispense Item'.
3. Alternative Path 3. Customer Reselects the Row:
   - The selection location stores the new row.
   - The selection location no longer stores the previous column.
   - The main display displays the row of the customer's selection.
   - The mode of the MIVM is 'Dispense Item'.

4.1.1.1.2 Customer Makes a Payment

Description: This whitebox scenario diagram models the interactions between internal objects when a customer pays for a selection.

Requirement verified:
    SYS-R) C-1.2. Customer Makes a Payment

Objects:
- Mandatory:
  - currentModeProxy
  - customer
  - customerCredit
  - customerSelection
  - customOperatingSystemCalls
  - customOperatingSystemInterrupts
  - dispenseItemMode
  - mainDisplay
- Optional:
  - If bill inserted:
    - billValidator
  - If coin inserted:
    - coinDispenserAssembly
    - coinValidator
  - If item selected and paid for:
    - anItemDispenser
    - anItemStepperMotor
    - customerMessages
    - itemDispenserAssembly

    – If item selected and paid for and change due customer:
       – aCoinDispenser
       – aCoinSolenoid
       – coinDispensingPolicy ·

Preconditions: The mode of the MIVM is 'Dispense Item'.

Statements:
Concurrently
    invoke use case: Customer Inserts a Valid Bill.
and
    invoke use case: Customer Inserts a Valid Coin.
end concurrently.

Whitebox sequence diagram: See Figure 4.5.

Postconditions:
The postconditions of the use case: Customer Inserts a Valid Bill.
The postconditions of the use case: Customer Inserts a Valid Coin.
The mode of the MIVM is 'Dispense Item'.

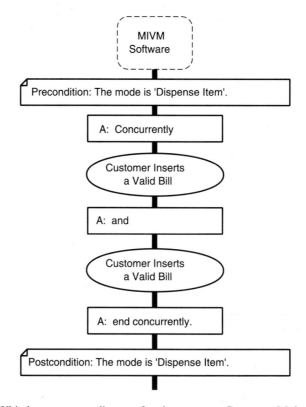

Figure 4.5 Whitebox sequence diagram for the use case: Customer Makes a Payment.

4.1.1.1.2.1 **Customer Inserts a Valid Bill**

Description: This whitebox scenario diagram models the interactions between internal objects when a customer inserts a valid bill into the bill validator.

Requirements verified:
  SYS-R) C-1.2.1. Customer Pays with Valid Bills
  SW-R) C-1.2.1-1. Customer Inserts a Bill when the Item is Selected
  SW-R) C-1.2.1-2. Customer Inserts a Bill when the Item is not Selected

Objects:
- Mandatory:
  - billValidator
  - currentModeProxy
  - customer
  - customerCredit
  - customerSelection
  - customOperatingSystemCalls
  - customOperatingSystemInterrupts
  - dispenseItemMode
  - mainDisplay
- Optional:
  - If item selected and paid for:
    - anItemDispenser
    - anItemStepperMotor
    - customerMessages
    - itemDispenserAssembly
  - If item selected and paid for and change due customer:
    - aCoinDispenser
    - aCoinSolenoid
    - coinDispensingPolicy

Paths:
- Primary Paths:
  1. The Item is Presently Selected
  2. The Item is not Presently Selected

Precondition: The mode of the MIVM is 'Dispense Item'.

Statements:

customOperatingSystemInterrupts	**sends** inserted(aBill)	**to** billValidator.
billValidator	**sends** valid(aBill)	**to** currentModeProxy.
currentModeProxy	**sends** valid(aBill)	**to** dispenseItemMode.
dispenseItemMode	**sends** valid(aBill)	**to** customer.
customer	**sends** add(aBill)	**to** credit. // of the customer
customer	**sends** creditIncremented()	**to** selection. // of the customer
selection	**sends** itemSelected()	**to** location. // of the selection

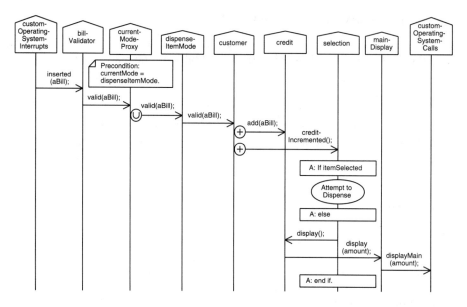

Figure 4.6 Whitebox sequence diagram for the use case: Customer Inserts a Valid Bill.

If itemSelected( ), **then** // Path 1. The Item is Presently Selected
   Invoke use case: Attempt to Dispense.
else // Path 2. The Item is not Presently Selected
    selection   **sends** display( )   **to** credit. // of the customer
    credit   **sends** display(amount)   **to** mainDisplay.
    mainDisplay   **sends** displayMain(amount)   **to** customOperatingSystemCalls.
end if.

Whitebox sequence diagram: See Figure 4.6.

Postconditions:
1. Primary Path 1. The Item is Presently Selected:
   – The postconditions of the use case: Attempt to Dispense.
   – The mode of the MIVM is 'Dispense Item'.
2. Primary Path 2. The Item is Not Presently Selected:
   – The customer's credit stores the new amount.
   – The main display displays the amount of the customer's credit.
   – The mode of the MIVM is 'Dispense Item'.

4.1.1.1.2.2 Customer Inserts a Valid Coin

Description: This whitebox scenario diagram models the interactions between the following internal objects when a customer inserts a valid coin into the coin validator.

Requirements verified:
SYS-R) C-1.2.2. Customer Pays with Valid Coins
SW-R) C-1.2.2-1. Customer Inserts a Coin when the Item is Selected
SW-R) C-1.2.2-2. Customer Inserts a Coin when the Item is not Selected

Objects:
- Mandatory:
  - coinDispenserAssembly
  - coinValidator
  - currentModeProxy
  - customer
  - customerCredit
  - customerSelection
  - customOperatingSystemCalls
  - customOperatingSystemInterrupts
  - dispenseItemMode
  - mainDisplay
- Optional:
  - If item selected and paid for:
    - anItemDispenser
    - anItemStepperMotor
    - customerMessages
    - itemDispenserAssembly
  - If item selected and paid for and change due customer:
    - aCoinDispenser
    - aCoinSolenoid
    - coinDispensingPolicy

Paths:
- Primary paths:
  1. The Item is Presently Selected
  2. The Item is not Presently Selected

Precondition: The mode of the MIVM is 'Dispense Item'.

Statements:

customOperatingSystemCalls	**sends** inserted(aCoin)	**to** coinValidator.
coinValidator	**sends** valid(aCoin)	**to** currentModeProxy.
currentModeProxy	**sends** valid(aCoin)	**to** dispenseItemMode.
dispenseItemMode	**sends** valid(aCoin)	**to** customer.
customer	**sends** add(aCoin)	**to** credit. // of the customer
customer	**sends** creditIncremented()	**to** selection. // of the customer
selection	**sends** itemSelected()	**to** location. // of the selection

If itemSelected(), **then** // Path 1. The Item is Presently Selected
    Invoke use case: Attempt to Dispense.
else // Path 2. The Item is not Presently Selected

selection	**sends** display()	**to** credit. // of the customer
credit	**sends** display(amount)	**to** mainDisplay.
mainDisplay	**sends** displayMain(amount)	**to** customOperatingSystemCalls.

end if.

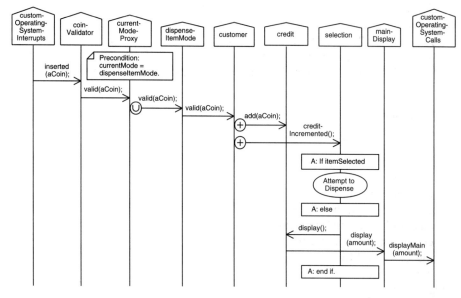

Figure 4.7 Whitebox sequence diagram for the use case: Customer Inserts a Valid Coin.

Whitebox sequence diagram: See Figure 4.7.

Postconditions:
1. Primary Path 1. The Item is Presently Selected:
   - The postconditions of the use case: **Attempt to Dispense.**
   - The mode of the MIVM is 'Dispense Item'.
2. Primary Path 2. The Item is Not Presently Selected:
   - The customer's credit stores the new amount.
   - The main display displays the amount of the customer's credit.
   - The mode of the MIVM is 'Dispense Item'.

4.1.1.1.3 Customer Requests a Refund

Description: This whitebox scenario diagram models the interactions between internal objects when a customer requests a refund.

Requirements verified:

SYS-R) C-1.3. Customer Requests a Refund

Objects:
- Mandatory:
  - currentModeProxy
  - customer
  - customerCredit
  - customerSelection
  - customOperatingSystemInterrupts
  - dispenseItemMode
  - modeButton

- Optional:
  - If change is due to the customer:
    - aCoinDispenser
    - aCoinSolenoid
    - coinDispenserAssembly
    - coinDispensingPolicy
    - customOperatingSystemCalls

Paths:
- Primary Path:
  1. Customer Requests a Refund

Precondition: The mode of the MIVM is 'Dispense Item'.

Statements:

customOperatingSystemInterrupts	**sends** pressed( )	**to** refundButton.
modeButton	**sends** refund ( )	**to** currentModeProxy.
currentModeProxy	**sends** refund ( )	**to** dispenseItemMode.
dispenseItemMode	**sends** refund ( )	**to** customer.
customer	**sends** reset( )	**to** selection. // of the customer

Assertion: selection.location.getColumn( ) = null.
Assertion: selection.location.getRow( ) = null.
Assertion: price = Money.none( );

selection	**sends** refundMinus(price)	**to** credit. // of the customer

Invoke use case: Dispense Change.

Whitebox sequence diagram: See Figure 4.8.

Postconditions:
customer.selection.location.column( ) = null.
customer.selection.location.row( ) = null.
The postconditions of the use case: Dispense Change.
The mode of the MIVM is 'Dispense Item'.

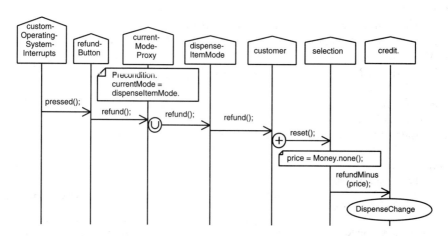

Figure 4.8 Whitebox sequence diagram for the use case: Customer Requests a Refund.

4.1.1.1.4 Attempt To Dispense

Description: This whitebox scenario diagram models the interactions between internal objects when the vending machine attempts to dispense a customer's selection.

Requirements verified:
SYS-R) C-1.4. Attempt to Dispense
SYS-R) C-1.4-1. Item Selected and Paid For
SYS-R) C-1.4-2. Item Selected and Not Paid For
SYS-R) C-1.4-3. Item Not Selected

Objects:
- Mandatory:
  - customer
  - customerCredit
  - customerSelection
  - customOperatingSystemCalls
  - mainDisplay
- Optional:
  - If an item is selected and paid for:
    - anItemDispenser
    - anItemStepperMotor
    - customerMessages
    - itemDispenserAssembly
  - If change is due to the customer:
    - aCoinDispenser
    - aCoinSolenoid
    - coinDispensingPolicy

Paths:
- Primary paths:
  1. The Item is Presently Selected and Paid For
  2. The Item is Presently Selected and Not Paid For
- Alternative path:
  3. Customer Makes an Invalid Selection

Preconditions:
An item has been selected.
The mode of the MIVM is 'Dispense Item'.

Statements:
// Get the customer's credit:

selection	**sends** amount( )	**to** credit. // of the customer

// Get the price of the selection:

selection	**sends** priceAt(location)	**to** itemDispenserAssembly.
itemDispenserAssembly	**sends** get(location)	**to** itemDispensers.
itemDispenserAssembly	**sends** price( )	**to** itemDispenser.

If credit.amount( ) is not less than selection.priceAt(location), **then**
 // Path 1. The Item is Presently Selected and Paid For:

selection	**sends** dispenseAt(location)	**to** itemDispenserAssembly.
itemDispenserAssembly	**sends** get(location)	**to** itemDispensers.
itemDispenserAssembly	**sends** dispense( )	**to** anItemDispenser.
anItemDispenser	**sends** step(360)	**to** aStepperMotor.
aStepperMotor	**sends** dispenseItemFrom(aPort)	**to** customOperatingSystemCalls.

 If customOperatingSystemCalls **throws** InvalidSelectionException, **then**
  // **Alternative Path 3: Customer**
  Invoke use case: Customer Makes an Invalid Selection.
 else

selection	**sends** refundMinus(price)	**to** credit. // of the customer
credit	**sends** dispense(aMoney)	**to** coinDispenserAssembly.

  Invoke use case: Dispense Change.
 end if.
else
 // Path 2. The Item is Presently Selected and Not Paid For:

selection	**sends** display(amountDue)	**to** mainDisplay.
mainDisplay	**sends** displayMain(amountDue)	**to** customOperatingSystemCalls.

end if.

Whitebox sequence diagram: See Figure 4.9.

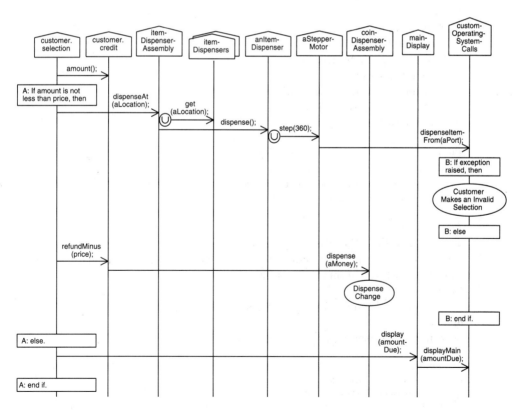

Figure 4.9 Whitebox sequence diagram for the use case: Attempt to Dispense.

Postconditions:
1. Primary Path 1. The Item is Presently Selected and Paid For:
   - An item has been dispensed.
   - The postconditions of the use case: Attempt to Dispense.
   - The mode of the MIVM is 'Dispense Item'.
2. Primary Path 2. The Item is Presently Selected and Not Paid For:
   - The main display displays the amount due.
   - The mode of the MIVM is 'Dispense Item'.
3. Alternative Path 3. Customer Makes an Invalid Selection:
   - The postconditions of the use case: Customer Makes an Invalid Selection.
   - The mode of the MIVM is 'Dispense Item'.

4.1.1.1.4.1 Handle Invalid Customer Selection

Description: This whitebox scenario diagram models the interactions between internal objects when a customer makes an invalid selection.

Requirement verified:
   SW-R) C-1.4.1. Handle Invalid Customer Selection

Objects:
- Mandatory:
  - anItemDispenser
  - anItemStepperMotor
  - customerSelection
  - customOperatingSystemCalls
  - itemDispenserAssembly
  - mainDisplay

Paths:
- Alternative:
  1. No Price has been set for the Selected Item Dispenser
  2. No Item Dispenser exists at the Selected Location

Preconditions:
The mode of the MIVM is 'Dispense Item'.
The MIVM software is presently storing the location (i.e. both the column and the row) of the customer's selection.
Either
   no price has been set for the item dispenser at that location
or
   no item dispenser exists at that location.

Statements:
If selection.getPrice( ) = null, **then**
   // Alternative Path 1. No price has been set for the Selected Item Dispenser:
   theItemDispenser   **throws** InvalidSelectionException   **to** itemDispenserAssembly.
   itemDispenserAssembly   **throws** InvalidSelectionException   **to** selection. // of the customer

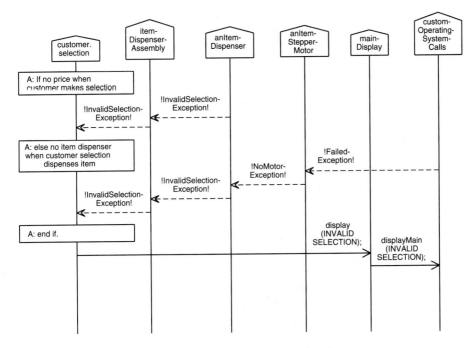

Figure 4.10 Whitebox sequence diagram for the use case:
Handle Invalid Customer Selection.

else if no item dispenser exists at the selected location, **then**
   // Alternative Path 2. No Item Dispenser exists at the Selected Location:

customOperatingSystemCalls	**throws** FailedException	**to** theItemStepperMotor.
theItemStepperMotor	**throws** NoMotorException	**to** theItemDispenser.
theItemDispenser	**throws** InvalidSelectionException	**to** itemDispenserAssembly.
itemDispenserAssembly	**throws** InvalidSelectionException	**to** selection. // of the customer
end if.		
customerSelection	**sends** display('INVALID SELECTION')	**to** mainDisplay.
mainDisplay	**sends** displayMain('INVALID SELECTION')	**to** customOperatingSystemCalls.

Whitebox sequence diagram: See Figure 4.10.

Postconditions:
The mode of the MIVM is 'Dispense Item'.
The MIVM software no longer stores either the column or row of the
   customer's selection.
The main display displays 'INVALID SELECTION'.

4.1.1.2 Dispense Change

Description: This whitebox scenario diagram models the interactions between
internal objects when the coin dispenser assembly dispenses change to the
customer.

Requirements verified:
    SYS-R) C-1.4.2. Dispense Change
    SYS-R) C-1.4.2-1. Credit for Undispensed Change
    SYS-D) C-1.4.2-2. Coin Dispensing Policy

Objects:
- Mandatory:
  - aCoinDispenser
  - aCoinSolenoid
  - coinDispenserAssembly
  - coinDispensingPolicy
  - customOperatingSystemCalls

Paths:
- Primary Path:
  1. Customer's Credit Dispensed without Problem
- Alternative Paths:
  2. Could not Dispense all of the Customer's Credit.
  3. Could not Dispense a kind of Coin

Precondition: The mode of the MIVM is 'Dispense Item'.

Statements:

customer.selection	**sends** refundMinus(price)	**to** credit. // of the customer
credit	**sends** dispense(amount)	**to** coinDispenserAssembly.
coinDispenserAssembly	**sends** dispense(amount)	**to** coinDispensingPolicy.

If credit > Money.none(), **then**
invoke use case: Dispense Quarters.
end if.
If credit > Money.none(), **then**
invoke use case: Dispense Dimes.
end if.
If credit > Money.none(), **then**
invoke use case: Dispense Nickels.
end if.
Invoke use case: Display Greeting.

Whitebox sequence diagram: See Figure 4.11.

Postconditions:
The mode of the MIVM is 'Dispense Item'.
The postconditions of the use case: Dispense Quarters.
The postconditions of the use case: Dispense Dimes.
The postconditions of the use case: Dispense Nickels.
The postconditions of the use case: Display Messages.

4.1.1.2.1 Dispense Quarters

Description: This whitebox scenario diagram models the interactions between internal objects when the vending machine dispenses quarters.

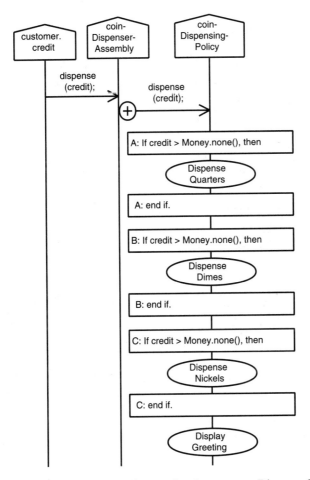

Figure 4.11 Whitebox sequence diagram for the use case: Dispense Change.

Requirement verified:

SYS-D) C-1.4.2.1. Dispense Quarters

Objects:
- Mandatory:
  - aCoinDispenser (holding quarters)
  - aCoinSolenoid (dispensing quarters)
  - coinDispensers
  - coinDispensingPolicy
  - customOperatingSystemCalls

Paths:
- Primary path:
  1. Could Dispense Quarters

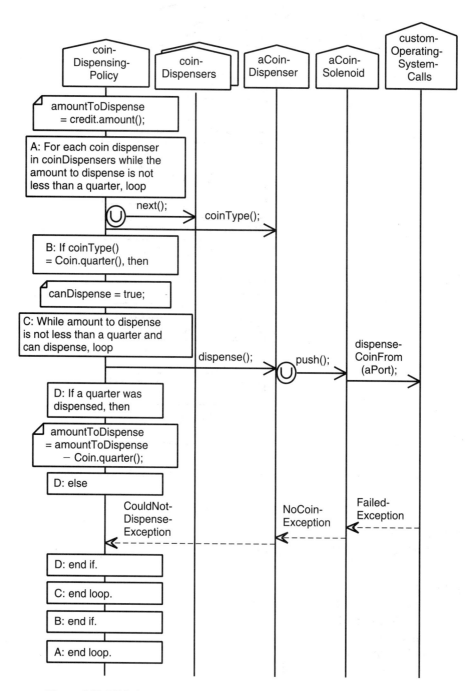

Figure 4.12 Whitebox sequence diagram for the use case: Dispense Quarters.

- Alternative path:
  2. Could not Dispense a Quarter

Precondition: The mode of the MIVM is 'Dispense Item'.

Statements:
Money amountToDispense = customerCredit.amount( );
Boolean canDispense = true;
// Dispense quarters as long as the amount to dispense is at least a quarter and there are more coin dispensers.
For each aCoinDispenser in coinDispensers **while** amountToDispense.isNotLessThan(Coin.quarter( )) **loop:**
  coinDispensingPolicy   **sends** coinType( )   **to** aCoinDispenser.
  If coinType( ) = Coin.quarter( ),   **then**
    canDispense = true;
    /* Dispense quarters from the current coin dispenser as long as the amount to dispense is at least a quarter and
    * the current coin dispenser can dispense quarters. */
    while amountToDispense.isNotLessThan(Coin.quarter( )) **and** canDispense, **loop**
      coinDispensingPolicy   **sends** dispense( )   **to** aCoinDispenser.
      aCoinDispenser   **sends** push( )   **to** aCoinSolenoid.
      aCoinSolenoid   **sends** dispenseCoinFrom(aPort)   **to** customOperatingSystemCalls.
      If a coin was dispensed, **then**
        // Primary Path 1. Could Dispense Quarters:
        amountToDispense = amountToDispense - Coin.quarter( );
      else
        customOperatingSystem   **throws** FailedException   **to** aCoinSolenoid.
        aCoinSolenoid   **throws** NoCoinException   **to** aCoinDispenser.
        aCoinDispenser   **throws** CouldNotDispenseException   **to** coinDispensingPolicy.
        canDispense = false;
      end if.
    end loop.
  end if.
end loop.

Whitebox sequence diagram: See Figure 4.12.

Postconditions:
The mode of the MIVM is 'Dispense Item'.

4.1.1.2.2 Dispense Dimes

Description: This whitebox scenario diagram models the interactions between internal objects when the vending machine dispenses dimes.

Requirement verified:
  SYS-D) C-1.4.2.2. Dispense Dimes

Objects:
- Mandatory:
  - aCoinDispenser (holding dimes)
  - aCoinSolenoid (dispensing dimes)
  - coinDispensers
  - coinDispensingPolicy
  - customOperatingSystemCalls

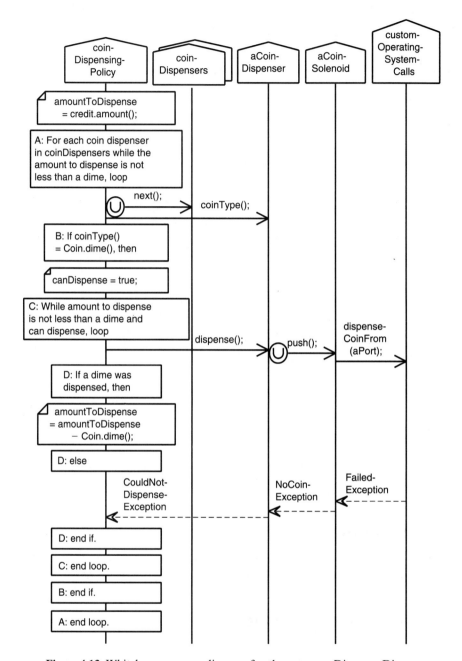

Figure 4.13 Whitebox sequence diagram for the use case: Dispense Dimes.

Paths:

- Primary path:
  1. Could Dispense Dimes

- Alternative path:
  2. Could not Dispense a Dime

Precondition: The mode of the MIVM is 'Dispense Item'.

Statements:
Money amountToDispense = customerCredit.amount( ),
Boolean canDispense = true;
// Dispense dimes as long as the amount to dispense is at least a dime and there are more coin dispensers.
For each aCoinDispenser **in** coinDispensers **while** amountToDispense.isNotLessThan(Coin.dime( )) **loop:**
  coinDispensingPolicy   **sends** coinType( )   **to** aCoinDispenser.
  If coinType( ) = Coin.dime( ), **then**
    canDispense = true;
    /* Dispense dimes from the current coin dispenser as long as the amount to dispense is at least a dime and
    * the current coin dispenser can dispense dimes. */
    while amountToDispense.isNotLessThan(Coin.dime( )) **and** canDispense, **loop**
      coinDispensingPolicy   **sends** dispense( )   **to** aCoinDispenser.
      aCoinDispenser   **sends** push( )   **to** aCoinSolenoid.
      aCoinSolenoid   **sends** dispenseCoinFrom(aPort)   **to** customOperatingSystemCalls.
      If a coin was dispensed, **then**
        // Primary Path 1. Could Dispense Dimes:
        amountToDispense = amountToDispense − Coin.dime( );
      else
        customOperatingSystem   **throws** FailedException   **to** aCoinSolenoid.
        aCoinSolenoid   **throws** NoCoinException   **to** aCoinDispenser.
        aCoinDispenser   **throws** CouldNotDispenseException   **to** coinDispensingPolicy.
          canDispense = false;
      end if.
    end loop.
  end if.
end loop.

Whitebox sequence diagram: See Figure 4.13.

Postconditions:
The mode of the MIVM is 'Dispense Item'.

4.1.1.2.3 Dispense Nickels

Description: This whitebox scenario diagram models the interactions between internal objects when the vending machine dispenses nickels.

Requirement verified:

  SYS-D) C-1.4.2.3. Dispense Nickels

Objects:
- Mandatory:
  - aCoinDispenser (holding nickels)
  - aCoinSolenoid (dispensing nickels)
  - coinDispensers
  - coinDispensingPolicy
  - customOperatingSystemCalls

Paths:
- Primary path:
  1. Nickels dispensed without problem

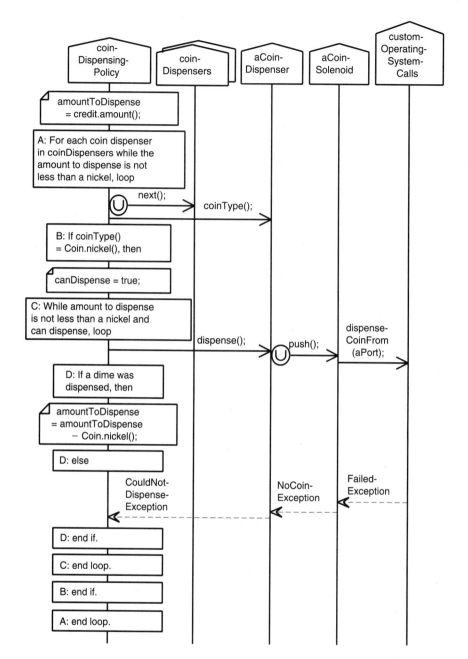

Figure 4.14 Whitebox sequence diagram for the use case: Dispense Nickels.

- Alternative path:
  2. Could not dispense a nickel

Precondition: The mode of the MIVM is 'Dispense Item'.

Statements:
Money amountToDispense = customerCredit.amount( );
Boolean canDispense = true;
// Dispense nickels as long as the amount to dispense is at least a nickel and there are more coin dispensers.
For each aCoinDispenser **in** coinDispensers **while** amountToDispense.isNotLessThan(Coin.nickel( )) **loop:**

  coinDispensingPolicy   **sends** coinType( )   **to** aCoinDispenser.
  If coinType( ) = Coin.nickel( ), **then**
    canDispense = true;
    /* Dispense nickels from the current coin dispenser as long as the amount to dispense is at least a nickel and
    * the current coin dispenser can dispense nickels. */
    while amountToDispense.isNotLessThan(Coin.nickel( )) **and** canDispense, **loop**
      coinDispensingPolicy   **sends** dispense( )   **to** aCoinDispenser.
      aCoinDispenser   **sends** push( )   **to** aCoinSolenoid.
      aCoinSolenoid   **sends** dispenseCoinFrom(aPort)   **to** customOperatingSystemCalls.
      If a coin was dispensed, **then**
        // Primary Path 1. Could Dispense Dimes:
        amountToDispense = amountToDispense - Coin.nickel( );
      else
        customOperatingSystem   **throws** FailedException   **to** aCoinSolenoid.
        aCoinSolenoid   **throws** NoCoinException   **to** aCoinDispenser.
        aCoinDispenser   **throws** CouldNotDispenseException   **to** coinDispensingPolicy.
        canDispense = false;
      end if.
    end loop.
  end if.
end loop.

Whitebox sequence diagram: See Figure 4.14.

Postconditions:
The mode of the MIVM is 'Dispense Item'.

4.1.1.2.4 Display Greeting

Description: This whitebox scenario diagram models the interactions between internal objects when the vending machine displays the appropriate customer greetings.

Requirements verified:
  SYS-D) C-1.4.2.4. Display Greeting
  SYS-D) C-1.4.2.4-1. Thank Customer
  SYS-D) C-1.4.2.4-2. Display Exact Change Warning
  SYS-D) C-1.4.2.4-3. Display Remaining Credit

Objects:
- Mandatory:
  - coinDispenserAssembly
  - customer.credit
  - customer.messages
  - customOperatingSystemCalls
  - mainDisplay

Paths:
- Primary path:
  1. Customer's Credit Dispensed Without a Problem
- Alternative paths:
  2. Could Not Dispense a Kind of Coin
  3. Could Not Dispense All of the Customer's Credit

Precondition: The mode of the MIVM is 'Dispense Item'.

Statements:
String exactChangeWarning = customerMessages.exactChangeWarning( ).
String greeting = customerMessages.greeting( ).
String thanksMessage = customerMessages.thanks( ).

If (customerCredit.getAmount( ) > Money.none( )), **then**
// Alternative Path 1. Customer has credit:
   customerMessages   **sends** display(credit)   **to** mainDisplay.
   mainDisplay   **sends** displayMain(credit).   **to** customOperatingSystemCalls.
else
   customer.messages   **sends** isWarningNeeded( )   **to** coinDispenserAssembly.
   // Determine if the coin dispensers have all kinds of coins:
   For each coinDispenser **in** coinDispensers **loop**
      coinDispenserAssembly   **sends** next( )   **to** coinDispensers.
      coinDispenserAssembly   **sends** coinType( )   **to** coinDispenser.
      coinDispenserAssembly   **sends** haveCoin( )   **to** coinDispenser.
   end loop.
   If coinDispensersHaveAllCoins( ), **then**
      // Primary Path 1. Everything normal:
      customerMessages   **sends** display(thanksMessage)   **to** mainDisplay.
      mainDisplay   **sends** displayMain(thanksMessage)   **to** customOperatingSystemCalls.
      delay 2 seconds.
      customerMessages   **sends** display(greeting)   **to** mainDisplay.
      mainDisplay   **sends** displayMain(greeting)   **to** customOperatingSystemCalls.
   else
      // Alternative Path 2. Coin dispensers do not have all coins:
      customerMessages   **sends** mainDisplay   **to** display(exactChangeMessage).
      mainDisplay   **sends** customOperatingSystemCalls   **to** displayMain(exactChangeMessage).
   end if.
end if.

Whitebox sequence diagram: See Figure 4.15.

Postconditions: The mode of the MIVM is 'Dispense Item'.

4.1.1.3 Service Representatives

This subsection documents all of the whitebox scenario diagrams involving the service representative as the primary actor.

4.1.1.3.1 Service Representative Changes the Mode of the MIVM

Description: This whitebox scenario diagram models the interactions between internal objects when a service representative changes the mode of the vending machine.

Requirements verified:
   SYS-R) SR-1.2. Service Representative Changes the Mode of the MIVM

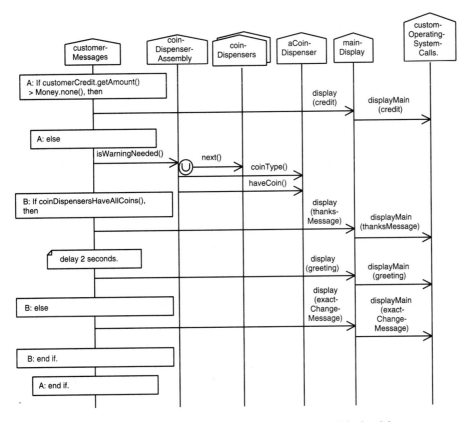

Figure 4.15 Whitebox sequence diagram for the use case: Display Messages.

Paths:
- Primary paths:
  1. Service representative pressed the mode button
  2. Door switch resets the mode

Precondition: None.

Statements:
Either
   Invoke use case: Service Representative Presses the Mode Button
or
   Invoke use case: Door Switch Resets the Mode.

Whitebox sequence diagram: See Figure 4.16.

Postconditions: None.

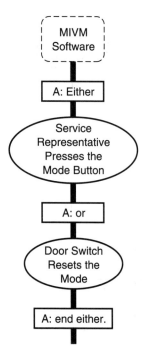

Figure 4.16 Whitebox sequence diagram for the use case: Service Representative Changes the Mode of the MIVM.

4.1.1.3.1.1 Service Representative Presses the Mode Button

Description: This whitebox scenario diagram models the interactions between internal objects when a service representative changes the mode of the vending machine by pressing the mode button.

Requirements verified:
   SYS-R) SR-1.2.1. Service Representative Presses the Mode Button
   SYS-R) SR-1.2.1-1. Change from 'Dispense Item' Mode
   SYS-R) SR-1.2.1-2. Change from 'Set Price' Mode
   SYS-R) SR-1.2.1-3. Change from 'Display History' Mode

Paths:
● Primary paths:
   1. Change from 'Dispense Item' Mode
   2. Change from 'Set Price' Mode
   3. Change from 'Display History' Mode

Precondition: None.

Statements:
ActualMode| initialMode;

customOperatingSystemInterrupts	**sends** pressed( )	**to** modeButton.
modeButton	**sends** changeMode( )	**to** currentModeProxy.

initialMode := currentModeProxy.currentMode( );
// Primary Path 1. Change from 'Dispense Item' Mode:
If initialMode = 'Dispense Item', **then**

currentModeProxy	**sends** canChange( )	**to** dispenseItemMode.
dispenseItemMode	**sends** hasCredit( )	**to** customer.
customer	**sends** getAmount ( )	**to** customerCredit.

  If customerCredit.getAmount( ) > Money.none( ), **then**

dispenseItemMode	**sends** displayMessages( )	**to** customer.
customer	**sends** display(customerCredit.amount)	**to** customerMessages.

  Invoke use case: Display Messages.
  else

dispenseItemMode	**sends** reset( )	**to** customer.
customer	**sends** reset( )	**to** customerSelection.
customerSelection	**sends** display( )	**to** customerCredit.
customerCredit	**sends** customerMessages	**to** display(customerCredit.amount).

  Invoke use case: Display Messages.
  end if.

currentModeProxy	**sends** currentMode(setPriceMode)	**to** currentModeProxy
currentModeProxy	**sends** display('SET PRICE MODE')	**to** mainDisplay.
mainDisplay	**sends** displayMain('SET PRICE MODE')	**to** customOperatingSystemCalls.

end if.
// Primary Path 2. Change from 'Set Price' Mode:
If initialMode = 'Set Price', **then**

currentModeProxy	**sends** reset( )	**to** setPriceMode.
setPriceMode	**sends** reset( )	**to** serviceRepresentative.
serviceRepresentative	**sends** reset( )	**to** serviceRepresentativeSelection.
serviceRepresentative	**sends** reset( )	**to** self.location.
currentModeProxy	**sends** currentMode(displayHistoryMode)	**to** currentModeProxy.
currentModeProxy	**sends** display('DISPLAY HISTORY MODE')	
		to mainDisplay.
mainDisplay	**sends** displayMain('DISPLAY HISTORY MODE')	
		to customOperatingSystemCalls

end if.
// Primary Path 3. Change from 'Display History' Mode:
If initialMode = 'Display History', **then**

currentModeProxy	**sends** coinDispenserAssemblyLoaded( )	**to** serviceRepresentative.
serviceRepresentative	**sends** loaded( )	**to** coinDispenserAssembly.
coinDispenserAssembly	**sends** load( )	**to** coinDispensers.

  For each coinDispenser **in** coinDispensers **loop:**

coinDispensers	**sends** coinType( )	**to** coinDispenser.
coinDispensers	**sends** inserted(coinDispenser coinType)	**to** coinDispenser.

  end loop.

currentModeProxy	**sends** currentMode(dispenseItemMode)	**to** currentModeProxy.
currentModeProxy	**sends** display('DISPENSE ITEM MODE')	**to** mainDisplay .
mainDisplay	**sends** displayMain('DISPENSE ITEM MODE')	
		to customOperatingSystemCalls.

end if.

Whitebox sequence diagrams: See Figures 4.17, 4.18 and 4.19.

Postconditions:
1. Primary Path 1. Change from 'Dispense Item' Mode:
   - The mode of the MIVM is the 'Selecting Column' submode of the 'Set Price' mode.
   - The postconditions of the use case: **Dispense Change.**

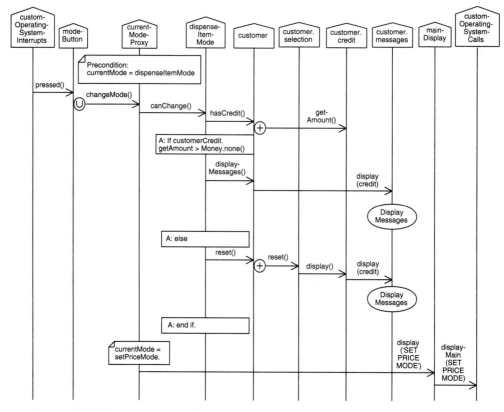

Figure 4.17 Whitebox sequence diagram for primary path: Change from 'Dispense Item' mode of the use case: Service Representative Presses the Mode Button.

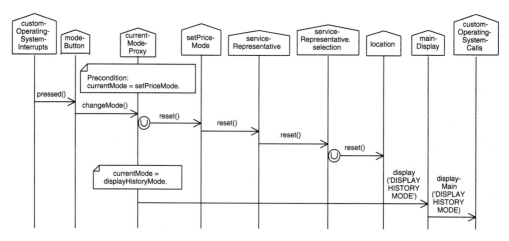

Figure 4.18 Whitebox sequence diagram for primary path: Change from 'Set Price' mode of the use case: Service Representative Presses the Mode Button.

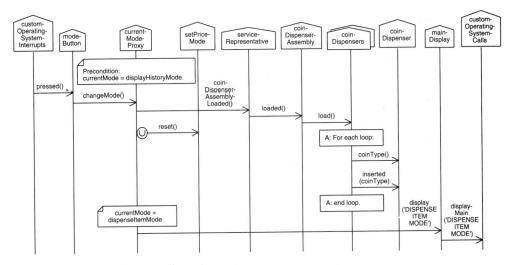

Figure 4.19 Whitebox sequence diagram for primary path: Change from 'Display History' mode of the use case: Service Representative Presses the Mode Button.

2. Primary Path 2. Change from 'Set Price' Mode:
   – The mode of the MIVM is the 'Display History'.
3. Primary Path 3. Change from 'Display History' Mode:
   – The mode of the MIVM is the 'Dispense Item'.

4.1.1.3.1.2 Door Switch Resets the Mode of the MIVM

Description: This whitebox scenario diagram models the interactions between internal objects when a service representative closes and locks the door.

Requirements verified:
  SYS-R) SR-1.2.2. Door Switch Resets the Mode
  SYS-R) SR-1.2.2-1. Door Switch Resets the Service Representative Information
  SYS-R) SR-1.2.2-2. Door Switch Resets the Coin Dispenser Assembly Information

Paths:
● Primary paths:
   1. Change from 'Dispense Item' mode
   2. Change from 'Set Price' mode
   3. Change from 'Display History' mode

Precondition: None.

Statements:
CurrentMode initialMode = currentModeProxy.currentMode();

customOperatingSystemInterrupts	**sends** trip( )	**to** doorSwitch.
doorSwitch	**sends** locked( )	**to** door.
door	**sends** doorLocked( )	**to** currentModeProxy.

// Primary Path 1. Change from 'Dispense Item' Mode:
If initialMode = 'Dispense Item', **then**
  null.
else
  If initialMode = 'Set Price', **then**
  // Primary Path 2. Change from 'Set Price' Mode:

currentModeProxy	**sends** reset( )	**to** setPriceMode.
setPriceMode	**sends** reset( )	**to** serviceRepresentative.
serviceRepresentative	**sends** reset( )	**to** serviceRepresentativeSelection.
serviceRepresentative	**sends** reset( )	**to** this.location( ).

  else
    // Primary Path 3. Change from 'Display History' Mode:
    null.
end if.

currentModeProxy	**sends** coinDispenserAssemblyLoaded( )	**to** serviceRepresentative.
serviceRepresentative	**sends** loaded( )	**to** coinDispenserAssembly.
coinDispenserAssembly	**sends** load( )	**to** coinDispensers.

For each coinDispenser **in** coinDispensers **loop:**

coinDispensers	**sends** coinType( )	**to** coinDispenser.
coinDispensers	**sends** inserted(coinDispenser.coinType)	**to** coinDispenser.

end loop.

currentModeProxy	**sends** currentMode(dispenseItemMode)	**to** currentModeProxy.
currentModeProxy	**sends** display('DISPENSE ITEM MODE')	**to** mainDisplay.
mainDisplay	**sends** displayMain('DISPENSE ITEM MODE')	
		to customOperatingSystemCalls.

end if.

Whitebox sequence diagrams: See Figures 4.20 and 4.21.

Postconditions: The mode of the MIVM is 'Dispense Item'.

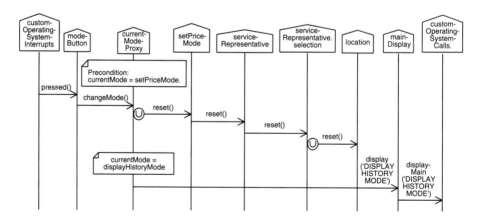

Figure 4.20 Whitebox sequence diagram for primary path: Change from 'Set Price' mode of the use case: Door Switch Resets the Mode of the MIVM.

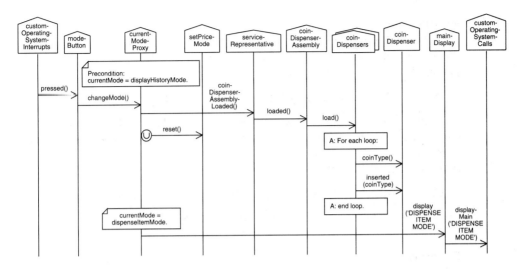

Figure 4.21 Whitebox sequence diagram for primary path: Change from 'Display History' mode of the use case: Door Switch Resets the Mode of the MIVM.

4.1.1.3.2 Service Representative Prices an Item

Description: This whitebox scenario diagram models the interactions between internal objects when a service representative prices the items in an item dispenser in the item dispenser assembly.

Requirement verified:
   SYS-D) SR-1.3. Service Representative Prices an Item

Precondition: The mode of the MIVM is 'Set Price'.

Statements:
Invoke use case: Service Representative Makes a Selection.
Invoke use case: Service Representative Enters a Price.

Whitebox sequence diagram: See Figure 4.22.

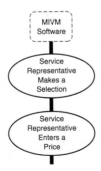

Figure 4.22 Whitebox sequence diagram for the use case:
Service Representative Prices an Item.

Postconditions:
The postconditions of use case: Service Representative Makes a Selection.
The postconditions of use case: Service Representative Enters a Price.
The mode of the MIVM is 'Set Price'.

4.1.1.3.2.1 Service Representative Makes a Selection

Description: This whitebox scenario diagram models the interactions between internal objects when a service representative selects an item dispenser in the item dispenser assembly.
Requirement verified:

SYS-D) SR-1.3.1. Service Representative Makes a Selection

Precondition: The mode of the MIVM is 'Set Price'.

Statements:
Concurrently
    invoke use case: Service Representative Selects a Column
and
    invoke use case: Service Representative Selects a Row
end concurrently;

Whitebox sequence diagram: See Figure 4.23.

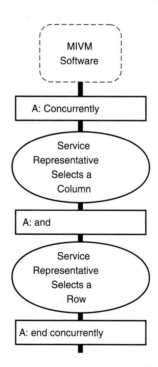

Figure 4.23 Whitebox sequence diagram for the use case: Service Representative Makes a Selection.

Postconditions:
The postconditions of use case: Service Representative Selects a Column.
The postconditions of use case: Service Representative Selects a Row.
The mode of the MIVM is 'Set Price'.

4.1.1.3.2.1.1 Service Representative Selects a Column

Description: This whitebox scenario diagram models the interactions between internal objects when a service representative selects the column of an item dispenser in the item dispenser assembly.

Requirements verified:

SYS-D) SR-1.3.1.1. Service Representative Selects a Column

SYS-D) SR-1.3.1.1-1. Service Representative Selects a Column when the Row is Not Selected

SW-D) SR-1.3.1.1-2. Service Representative Selects a Column when the Row is Selected

SW-R) SR-1.3.1.1-3. Ignore the Refund Button

SW-R) SR-1.3.1.1-4. Handle unexpected Money

Paths:
- Primary path:
1. Select a Column
- Alternative paths:
2. Press a Letter Selection Button
3. Press the Refund Button
4. Handle Unexpected Money

Precondition: The MIVM is in the 'Selecting Column' submode of the 'Set Price' mode.

Statements:
Concurrently
// Primary Path 1. Select a Column:

customOperatingSystemInterrupts	**sends** pressed( )	**to** aNumberSelectionButton.
aNumberSelectionButton	**sends** selected(anInteger)	**to** currentModeProxy.
currentModeProxy	**sends** selected(anInteger)	**to** setPriceMode.
setPriceMode	**sends** selected(anInteger)	**to** serviceRepresentative.
serviceRepresentative	**sends** selected(anInteger)	**to** serviceRepresentative.selection.
serviceRepresentative.selection	**sends** column(anInteger)	**to** this.location.
serviceRepresentative.selection	**sends** display(aColumn)	**to** mainDisplay.
mainDisplay	**sends** displayMain(aColumn)	**to** customOperatingSystemCalls.

and
// Alternative Path 2. Press a Letter Selection Button:

customOperatingSystemInterrupts	**sends** pressed( )	**to** aLetterSelectionButton.
aLetterSelectionButton	**sends** selected(aLetter)	**to** currentModeProxy.
currentModeProxy	**sends** selected(aLetter)	**to** setPriceMode.
setPriceMode	**sends** selected(aLetter)	**to** serviceRepresentative.
serviceRepresentative	**sends** selected(aLetter)	**to** serviceRepresentative.selection.

and
// Alternative Path 3. Press the Refund Button:

customOperatingSystemInterrupts	**sends** pressed( )	**to** refundButton.
refundButton	**sends** refund( )	**to** currentModeProxy.
currentModeProxy	**sends** refund( )	**to** setPriceMode.

and

// Alternative Path 4. Handle Unexpected Money:

customOperatingSystemInterrupts	**sends** inserted(aMoney)	**to** aMoneyValidator.
aMoneyValidator	**sends** valid(aMoney)	**to** currentModeProxy.
currentModeProxy	**sends** valid(aMoney)	**to** setPriceMode.
setPriceMode	**sends** reset( )	**to** serviceRepresentative.
serviceRepresentative	**sends** reset( )	**to** serviceRepresentative.selection.
currentModeProxy	**sends** currentMode(dispenseItemMode)	**to** this.
currentModeProxy	**sends** display ('DISPENSE ITEM MODE')	
		to mainDisplay.
mainDisplay	**sends** displayMain('DISPENSE ITEM MODE')	
		to customOperatingSystemCalls.

Invoke the use case: Customer Pays for a Selection.
end concurrently.

Whitebox sequence diagrams: See Figures 4.24, 4.25, 4.26 and 4.27.

Postconditions:
1. Path 1. Select a Column:
   – The MIVM is in the 'Selecting Row' submode of the 'Set Price' mode.
   – The MIVM software now stores the column of the service representative selection.
2. Path 2. Press an Inappropriate Button:
   – The MIVM is in the 'Selecting Column' submode of the 'Set Price' mode.
3. Path 3. Handle Unexpected Money:
   – The mode of the MIVM is 'Dispense Item'.
   – The postconditions of the use case: **Customer Pays for a Selection.**

4.1.1.3.2.1.2 Service Representative Selects a Row

Description: This whitebox scenario diagram models the interactions between internal objects when a service representative selects the row of an item dispenser in the item dispenser assembly.

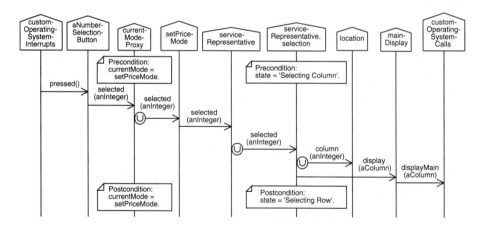

Figure 4.24 Whitebox sequence diagram for primary path: Select a Column of the use case: Service Representative Selects a Column.

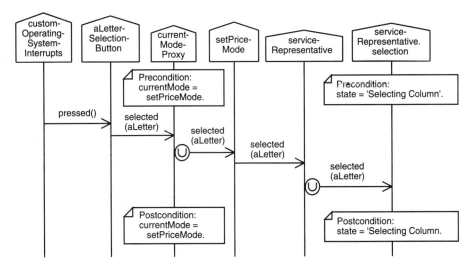

Figure 4.25 Whitebox sequence diagram for alternative path: Press a Letter Selection Button of the use case: Service Representative Selects a Column.

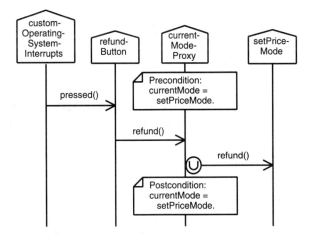

Figure 4.26 Whitebox sequence diagram for alternative path: Press the Refund Button of the use case: Service Representative Selects a Column.

Requirements verified:
   SYS-D) SR-1.3.1.2. Service Representative Selects a Row
   SYS-D) SR-1.3.1.2-1. Service Representative Selects a Row when the Column is Not Selected
   SYS-D) SR-1.3.1.2-2. Service Representative Selects a Row when the Column is Selected
   SW-R) SR-1.3.1.2-3. Ignore the Refund Button
   SW-R) SR-1.3.1.2-4. Handle Unexpected Money

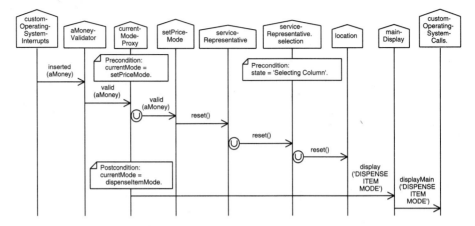

Figure 4.27 Whitebox sequence diagram for alternative path: Handle Unexpected Money of the use case: Service Representative Selects a Column.

Paths:
- Primary paths:
  1. Select a Row
- Alternative paths:
  2. Press a Number Selection Button
  3. Press the Refund Button
  4. Handle Unexpected Money

Preconditions:
The MIVM is in the 'Selecting Row' submode of the 'Set Price' mode.
The column of the service representative selection has been selected.

Statements:
Concurrently

```
// Primary Path 1. Select a Row:
CustomOperatingSystemInterrupts  sends pressed( )                       to aLetterSelectionButton.
aLetterSelectionButton           sends selected(aLetter)                to currentModeProxy.
currentModeProxy                 sends selected(aLetter)                to setPriceMode.
setPriceMode                     sends selected(aLetter)                to serviceRepresentative.
serviceRepresentative            sends selected(aLetter)                to serviceRepresentative.selection.
serviceRepresentative.selection  sends setState('Building Price')       to this.
serviceRepresentative.selection  sends row(aLetter))                    to this.location(.
serviceRepresentative.selection  sends priceAt(aLocation)               to itemDispenserAssembly.
itemDispenserAssembly            sends priceAt(aLocation)               to itemDispensers.
itemDispensers                   sends getPrice( )                      to anItemDispenser.
serviceRepresentativeSelection   sends display(location,price)          to mainDisplay.
mainDisplay                      sends displayMain(location,price)      to customOperatingSystemCalls.
```
and
```
// Alternative Path 2. Press a Number Selection Button:
CustomOperatingSystemInterrupts  sends pressed( )                       to aNumberSelectionButton.
aNumberSelectionButton           sends selected(anInteger)              to currentModeProxy.
currentModeProxy                 sends selected(anInteger)              to setPriceMode.
setPriceMode                     sends selected(anInteger)              to serviceRepresentative.
serviceRepresentative            sends selected(anInteger)              to serviceRepresentativeSelection.
```

and
  // Alternative Path 3. Press the Refund Button:

customOperatingSystemInterrupts	**sends** pressed( )	**to** refundButton.
refundButton	**sends** refund( )	**to** currentModeProxy.
currentModeProxy	**sends** refund( )	**to** setPriceMode.

and
  // Alternative Path 4. Handle Unexpected Money:

customOperatingSystemInterrupts	**sends** inserted(aMoney)	**to** aMoneyValidator.
aMoneyValidator	**sends** valid(aMoney)	**to** currentModeProxy.
currentModeProxy	**sends** valid(aMoney)	**to** setPriceMode.
setPriceMode	**sends** reset( )	**to** serviceRepresentative.
serviceRepresentative	**sends** reset( )	**to** serviceRepresentative.selection.
currentModeProxy	**sends** currentMode(dispenseItemMode)	**to** this.
currentModeProxy	**sends** display ('DISPENSE ITEM MODE')	
		to mainDisplay.
mainDisplay	**sends** displayMain('DISPENSE ITEM MODE')	
		to customOperatingSystemCalls.

  Invoke the use case: Customer Pays for a Selection.
end concurrently.

Whitebox sequence diagrams: See Figures 4.28, 4.29, 4.30 and 4.31.

Postconditions:
1. Path 1. Select a Row:
   - The MIVM is in the 'Building Price' submode of the 'Set Price' mode.
   - The MIVM software now stores the location (i.e. column and row) of the service representative selection.
2. Path 2. Press an Inappropriate Button:
   - The MIVM is in the 'Selecting Row' submode of the 'Set Price' mode.
3. Path 3. Handle Unexpected Money:
   - The mode of the MIVM is 'Dispense Item'.
   - The postconditions of the use case: **Customer Pays for a Selection.**

4.1.1.3.3 Service Representative Enters a Price

Description: This whitebox scenario diagram models the interactions between internal objects when a service representative enters a price for the items in an item dispenser in the item dispenser assembly.

Requirements verified:
  SYS-D) SR-1.3.1.3. Service Representative Enters a Price
  SYS-D) SR-1.3.1.3-1. Accept the Old Price
  SYS-D) SR-1.3.1.3-2. Build the New Price
  SYS-D) SR-1.3.1.3-3. Enter the New Price
  SYS-D) SR-1.3.1.3-4. Handle an Invalid Price
  SYS-D) SR-1.3.1.3-5. Cancel the New Price
  SW-R) SR-1.3.1.3-6. Ignore Inappropriate Buttons
  SYS-D) SR-1.3.1.3-7. Handle Unexpected Money

Paths:
- Primary path:
  1. Enter the New Price

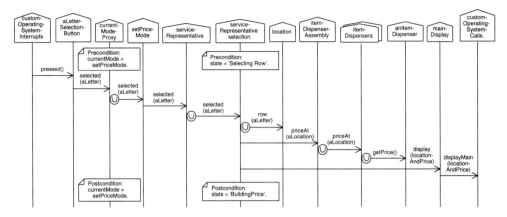

Figure 4.28 Whitebox sequence diagram for primary path: Select a Row of the use case: Service Representative Selects a Row.

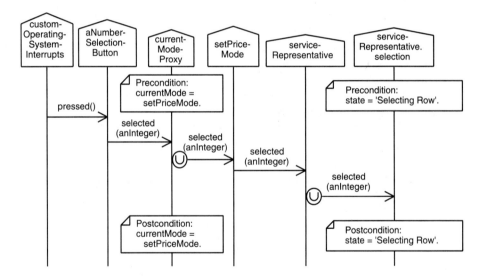

Figure 4.29 Whitebox sequence diagram for alternative path: Press a Number Selection Button of the use case: Service Representative Selects a Row.

- Alternative paths:
  2. Accept the old Common Price
  3. Handle an Invalid Price
  4. Cancel the New Price
  5. Handle an Inappropriate Letter Button
  6. Handle the Refund Button
  7. Handle Unexpected Money

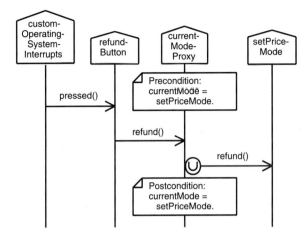

Figure 4.30 Whitebox sequence diagram for alternative path: Press the Refund Button of the use case: Service Representative Selects a Row.

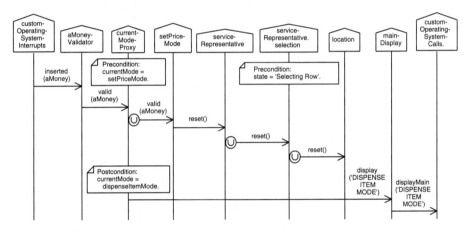

Figure 4.31 Whitebox sequence diagram for alternative path: Handle Unexpected Money of the use case: Service Representative Selects a Row.

Preconditions:
currentModeProxy.currentMode() = setPriceMode.
serviceRepresentativeSelection.getState() = 'Building Price'.

Statements:
Concurrently
  Either
    // Alternative Path 2. Accept the old Common Price:

customOperatingSystemInterrupts	**sends** pressed()	**to** buttonA.
buttonA	**sends** selected('A')	**to** currentModeProxy.
currentModeProxy	**sends** selected('A')	**to** setPriceMode.
setPriceMode	**sends** selected('A')	**to** serviceRepresentative.
serviceRepresentative	**sends** selected('A')	**to** serviceRepresentative.selection.

serviceRepresentative.selection	**sends** reset( )	**to** this.location( ).
serviceRepresentative.selection	**sends** setState('Selecting Column')	**to** this.
serviceRepresentative.selection	**sends** display('ACCEPTED')	**to** mainDisplay.
mainDisplay	**sends** displayMain('ACCEPTED')	**to** customOperatingSystemCalls.

or

   Until the new common price is built **and** accepted **loop:**

     // Build the new common price:

serviceRepresentativeSelection	**sends** price(Money.none)	**to** this.

     Until the new common price is built **loop:**

customOperatingSystemInterrupts	**sends** pressed( )	**to** aNumberSelectionButton.
aNumberSelectionButton	**sends** selected(anInteger)	**to** currentModeProxy.
currentModeProxy	**sends** selected(anInteger)	**to** setPriceMode.
setPriceMode	**sends** selected(anInteger)	**to** serviceRepresentative.
serviceRepresentative	**sends** selected(anInteger)	**to** serviceRepresentative.selection.

     // Update the price:

serviceRepresentative.selection	**sends** appendToPrice(anInteger)	**to** this.
serviceRepresentative.selection	**sends** priceAt(this.getLocation( ),this.getPrice( ))	
		to itemDispenserAssembly.
itemDispenserAssembly	**sends** price(aPrice)	**to** anItemDispenser.
anItemDispenser	**sends** display(this.getLocation( ),this.getPrice( ))	
		to anItemDisplay.

     // Display the new price on the item display:

anItemDisplay	**sends** display(locationAndPrice( ),this.getPort( ))	
		to anItemDisplay.
anItemDisplay	**sends** display (locationAndPrice,aPort)	
		to customOperatingSystemCalls.

     // Display the new price on the main display:

serviceRepresentative.selection	**sends** display(this.locationAndPrice( ))	
		to mainDisplay.
mainDisplay	**sends** displayMain(locationAndPrice)	
		to customOperatingSystemCalls.

   end loop.

   If the service representative presses the 'C' letter button, **then**

     // Alternative Path 4. Cancel the New Price:

customOperatingSystemInterrupts	**sends** pressed( )	**to** buttonC.
buttonC	**sends** selected('C')	**to** currentModeProxy.
currentModeProxy	**sends** selected('C')	**to** setPriceMode.
setPriceMode	**sends** selected('C')	**to** serviceRepresentative.
serviceRepresentative	**sends** selected('C')	**to** serviceRepresentative.selection.
serviceRepresentative.selection	**sends** reset( )	**to** this.location( ).
serviceRepresentative.selection	**sends** setState('Selecting Column')	**to** this.
serviceRepresentative.selection	**sends** display('CLEARED')	**to** mainDisplay.
mainDisplay	**sends** displayMain('CLEARED')	**to** customOperatingSystemCalls.

     Invoke use case: Service Representative Selects a Column.
     Invoke use case: Service Representative Selects a Row.

   end if.

   If the service representative presses the 'E' letter button, **then**

customOperatingSystemInterrupts	**sends** pressed( )	**to** buttonE.
buttonE	**sends** selected('E')	**to** currentModeProxy.
currentModeProxy	**sends** selected('E')	**to** setPriceMode.
setPriceMode	**sends** selected('E')	**to** serviceRepresentative.
serviceRepresentative	**sends** selected('E')	**to** serviceRepresentative.selection.
serviceRepresentative.selection	**sends** isPractical(this.price)	**to** coinDispenserAssembly.

     For each coinDispenser in the coinDispenserAssembly **loop**

coinDispenserAssembly	**sends** coinType( )	**to** aCoinDispenser.

     end loop.

     If coinDispenserAssembly.isPractical(this.price) returns true, **then**

       // Primary Path 1: Enter the New Price:

serviceRepresentative.selection	**sends** priceAt(this.price,this.location)	
		to itemDispenserAssembly.
itemDispenserAssembly	**sends** price(price)	**to** anItemDispenser.

anItemDispenser	**sends** display(this.location( ),this.price( ))	
		to anItemDisplay.
anItemDisplay	**sends** displayItem(this.locationAndPrice( ),this(aPort))	
		to customOperatingSystemCalls.
serviceRepresentative.selection	**sends** display(this.priceAndLocation( ))	
		to mainDisplay.
mainDisplay	**sends** display (this.locationAndPrice( ))	
		to customOperatingSystemCalls.
serviceRepresentative.selection	**sends** setState('SelectingColumn')	**to** this.

```
        else
          // Alternative Path 3. Handle an Invalid Price:
```

serviceRepresentative.selection	**sends** setPrice(Money.none( ))	**to** this.
serviceRepresentative.selection	**sends** display('REJECTED')	**to** mainDisplay.
mainDisplay	**sends** display ('REJECTED')	**to** customOperatingSystemCalls.
serviceRepresentative.selection	**sends** setState('BuildingPrice')	**to** this.

```
        end if.
      end if.
    end loop.
  end either.
and
  // Alternative Path 5. Handle an Inappropriate Letter Button:
```

CustomOperatingSystemInterrupts	**sends** pressed( )	**to** aLetterSelectionButton.
aLetterSelectionButton	**sends** selected(aLetter)	**to** currentModeProxy.
currentModeProxy	**sends** selected(aLetter)	**to** setPriceMode.
setPriceMode	**sends** selected(aLetter)	**to** serviceRepresentative.

```
and
  // Alternative Path 6. Handle the Refund Button:
```

customOperatingSystemInterrupts	**sends** pressed( )	**to** refundButton.
refundButton	**sends** refund( )	**to** currentModeProxy.
currentModeProxy	**sends** refund( )	**to** setPriceMode.
setPriceMode	**sends** refund( )	**to** serviceRepresentative.

```
and
  // Alternative Path 7. Handle Unexpected Money:
```

customOperatingSystemInterrupts	**sends** inserted(aMoney)	**to** aMoneyValidator.
aMoneyValidator	**sends** valid(aMoney)	**to** currentModeProxy.
currentModeProxy	**sends** valid(aMoney)	**to** setPriceMode.
setPriceMode	**sends** reset( )	**to** serviceRepresentative.
serviceRepresentative	**sends** reset( )	**to** serviceRepresentative.selection.
currentModeProxy	**sends** currentMode(dispenseItemMode)	
		to this.
currentModeProxy	**sends** display ('DISPENSE ITEM MODE')	
		to mainDisplay.
mainDisplay	**sends** displayMain('DISPENSE ITEM MODE')	
		to customOperatingSystemCalls.

Invoke the use case: Customer Pays for a Selection.
end concurrently.

Whitebox sequence diagram: See Figure 4.32.

Postconditions:

1. Primary Path 1. Build and Enter the new Common Price:
   – The MIVM is in the 'Selecting Column' submode of the 'Set Price' mode.
   – The MIVM software stores the new location and new price of the service representative selection.
2. Alternative Path 2. Accept the old Common Price:
   – The MIVM is in the 'Selecting Column' submode of the 'Set Price' mode.
   – The MIVM software stores the old location and old price of the service representative selection.

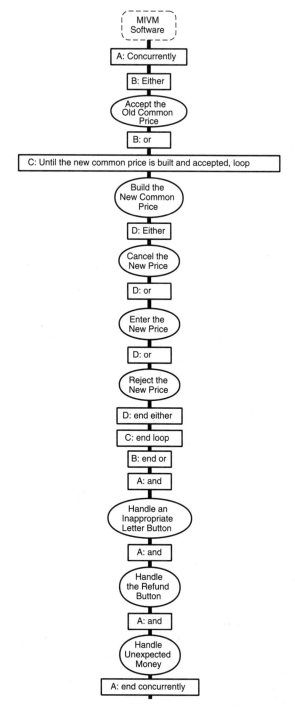

Figure 4.32 Whitebox sequence diagram for the use case:
Service Representative Enters a Price.

3. Alternative Path 3. Build and Reject the new Common Price:
   - The MIVM is in the 'Building Price' submode of the 'Set Price' mode.
   - The MIVM software stores the new location and the old price of the service representative selection.
4. Alternative Path 4 Build and Clear the new Common Price:
   - The MIVM is in the 'Building Price' submode of the 'Set Price' mode.
   - The MIVM software stores the new location and the old price of the service representative selection.
5. Alternative Path 5. Press an Inappropriate Button:
   - The MIVM is in the 'Building Price' submode of the 'Set Price' mode.
   - The MIVM software stores the new location and the partially built new price of the service representative selection.
6. Alternative Path 6. Handle Unexpected Money.
   - The MIVM software no longer stores the location or price of the service representative selection.
   - The mode of the MIVM is 'Dispense Item'.
   - The postconditions of the use case: **Customer Pays for a Selection.**

4.1.1.4 Service Representative Displays History

Description: This whitebox scenario diagram models the interactions between internal objects when a service representative displays the history of the vending machine.

Requirements verified:
  SYS-R) SR-1.4. Service Representative Displays History
  SYS-D) SR-1.4-1. Service Representative Displays the Total Number of Items Sold
  SYS-D) SR-1.4-2. Service Representative Displays the Total Income
  SYS-D) SR-1.4-3. Ignore Inappropriate Buttons
  SYS-D) SR-1.4-4. Handle Unexpected Money

Objects:
- Mandatory:
  - buttonA
  - buttonB
  - currentModeProxy
  - customOperatingSystemCalls
  - customOperatingSystemInterrupts
  - displayHistoryMode
  - itemDispenserAssembly
  - mainDisplay
  - serviceRepresentative

Paths:
- Primary paths:
  1. Display Total Items Sold
  2. Display Total Income
- Alternative paths:
  3. Ignore Inappropriate Buttons
  4. Handle Unexpected Money

Precondition: currentModeProxy.currentMode( ) = displayHistoryMode.

Statements:
Concurrently

    // Primary Path 1. Display Total Items Sold:
    invoke use case: Service Representative Displays Total Items Sold
and
    // Primary Path 2. Display Total Income:
    invoke use case: Service Representative Displays Total Income
and
    // Alternative Path 3. Ignore Inappropriate Buttons:
    ignore inappropriate buttons
and
    // Alternative Path 4. Handle Unexpected Money:
    If money is validated, **then**
        The MIVM software stores the mode as 'Dispense Item', **and**
        invoke use case: Customer Pays for a Selection.
    end if.
end concurrently.

Whitebox sequence diagram: See Figure 4.33.

Postconditions:
1. Primary Path 1. Display Total Items Sold:
   - currentModeProxy.currentMode( ) = displayHistoryMode.
   - The main display displays the total number of items sold by the MIVM.
2. Primary Path 2. Display Total Income:
   - currentModeProxy.currentMode( ) = displayHistoryMode.
   - The main display displays the total income of the MIVM.
3. Alternative Path 3. Ignore Inappropriate Buttons:
   - currentModeProxy.currentMode( ) = displayHistoryMode.
4. Alternative Path 4. Handle Unexpected Money:
   - currentModeProxy.currentMode( ) = dispenseItemMode.
   - The postconditions of the use case: **Customer Pays for a Selection.**

4.1.1.4.1 Service Representative Displays the Total Number of Items Sold

Description: This whitebox scenario diagram models the interactions between internal objects when a service representative requests the display of the total number of items sold by the vending machine.

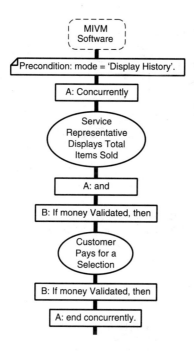

Figure 4.33 Whitebox sequence diagram for the use case:
Service Representative Displays History.

Requirement verified:
SYS-D) SR-1.4-1. Service Representative Displays the Total Number of Items Sold

Objects:
- Mandatory:
  - buttonA
  - currentModeProxy
  - customOperatingSystemCalls
  - customOperatingSystemInterrupts
  - displayHistoryMode
  - itemDispenserAssembly
  - mainDisplay
  - serviceRepresentative

Paths:
- Primary path:
  1. Display total items sold

Precondition: currentModeProxy.currentMode( ) = displayHistoryMode.

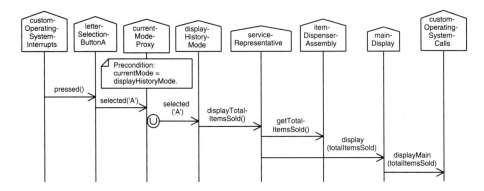

Figure 4.34 Whitebox sequence diagram for the use case: Service Representative Displays the Total Number of Items Sold.

Statements:

customOperatingSystemInterrupts	**sends** pressed( )	**to** buttonA.
buttonA	**sends** selected('A')	**to** currentModeProxy.
currentModeProxy	**sends** selected('A')	**to** displayHistoryMode.
displayHistoryMode	**sends** displayTotalItemsSold( )	**to** serviceRepresentative.
serviceRepresentative	**sends** totalItemsSold( )	**to** itemDispenserAssembly.
serviceRepresentative	**sends** display(totalItemsSold)	**to** mainDisplay.
mainDisplay	**sends** displayMain(totalItemsSold)	**to** customOperatingSystemCalls.

Whitebox sequence diagram: See Figure 4.34.

Postconditions:
currentModeProxy.currentMode() = displayHistoryMode.
The main display displays the total number of items sold from the MIVM.

4.1.1.4.2 Service Representative Displays the Total Income

Description: This whitebox scenario diagram models the interactions between internal objects when a service representative requests the display of the total income from the vending machine.

Requirement verified:
    SYS-D) SR-1.4-2. Service Representative Displays the Total Income

Objects:
● Mandatory:
    − buttonB
    − currentModeProxy
    − customOperatingSystemCalls
    − customOperatingSystemInterrupts
    − displayHistoryMode
    − itemDispenserAssembly
    − mainDisplay
    − serviceRepresentative

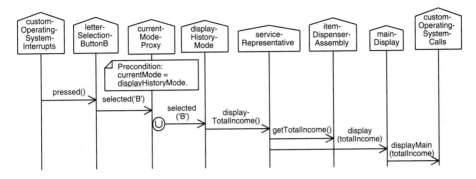

Figure 4.35 Whitebox sequence diagram for the use case: Service Representative Displays the Total Income.

Paths:
- Primary paths:
  1. Display total income

Precondition: currentModeProxy.currentMode() = displayHistoryMode.

Statements:

customOperatingSystemInterrupts	**sends** pressed( )	**to** buttonB.
buttonB	**sends** selected('B')	**to** currentModeProxy.
currentModeProxy	**sends** selected('B')	**to** displayHistoryMode.
displayHistoryMode	**sends** displayTotalIncome( )	**to** serviceRepresentative.
serviceRepresentative	**sends** totalIncome( )	**to** itemDispenserAssembly.
serviceRepresentative	**sends** display(totalIncome)	**to** mainDisplay.
mainDisplay	**sends** displayMain(totalIncome)	**to** customOperatingSystemCalls.

Whitebox sequence diagram: See Figure 4.35.

Postconditions:
currentModeProxy.currentMode() = displayHistoryMode.
The main display displays the total income from the MIVM.

4.2 Class/package testing

The following patterns from the Pattern Language for Object-Oriented Testing (PLOOT)[†] were used during class/package testing:

- *Class as unit.* Classes are the unit of unit testing.
- *Concrete class via instance.* Each concrete class is indirectly tested by first instantiating it to produce an Object Under Test (OUT) which is directly tested.
- *Abstract class via subclass.* Each abstract class is indirectly tested via a concrete test subclass.

[†] Firesmith D.G. (1996) 'Pattern Language for Testing Object-Oriented Software,' *Object Magazine,* **5**(8), SIGS Publications Inc., New York, January, 32–38.

- *Dependency-based testing.* The packages were integration tested bottom-up in terms of dependency, and the classes within each package were class tested bottom-up in terms of dependency. Thus, superclasses were tested before subclasses and server classes were tested before their client classes.
- *Test messages and exceptions.* Test messages and exceptions are used to stimulate objects under test.
- *Test stubs.* Classes are subclassed to produce test stubs for logging messages and raising test exceptions.
- *Assertions and exceptions.* Preconditions, postconditions and class invariants are used to specify required behavior, and exceptions are raised when assertions are violated.
- *Every kind of event in every state.* Every kind of test interaction (message, exception) is exercised in every state.
- *Test cases, scripts and sets as objects.* Test cases, scripts and sets are implemented as objects.
- *Built-in tests.* Unit test cases are built into the classes they test.
- *Use-case testing.* Acceptance test cases were chosen to exercise usage scenarios.
- *Tester interface.* A GUI interface is used to simplify testing.
- *Iterative, incremental, parallel testing.* Testing is preformed in an iterative, incremental manner by developers and teams working in parallel.
- *Automated regression testing.* Regression testing is automated.

4.3 Acceptance testing

In accordance with 'PLOOT: A Pattern Language for Object-Oriented Testing' [Firesmith 1996], acceptance testing of the MIVM software was performed using the use case pattern. As documented in Section 2.5 (Requirements Trace to Verification and Validation Techniques), a test script is developed for each use case documented in Section 1 (Requirements) and test cases are developed for each combination of relevant state and path through the associated use case.

This testing was initially performed on the host hardware using a GUI tester interface layer that accessed test hardware proxy classes representing both client and server device external objects. This testing was then repeated on the target hardware when the software was integrated with the actual hardware actors.

4.3.1 Acceptance test harness

A test harness was developed in order to permit testing of the domain layer classes on the host prior to the existence of the actual hardware devices and custom operating system that would control and be controlled by the vending machine software. As illustrated in Figures 4.36 and 4.37, these test classes were divided into four layers:

- *Developer GUI.* This layer contains the following developer interface objects:
  – customerInterface, which allows the developer to automatically create the vending machine software and related test software.

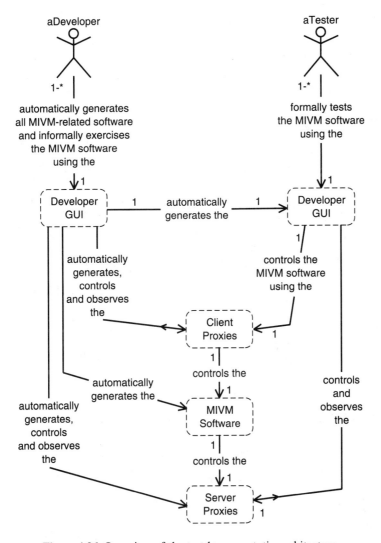

Figure 4.36 Overview of the test harness static architecture.

– developerInterface, which allows the developer to play the role of the customer during manual debugging.
– serviceRepresentativeInterface, which allows the developer to play the role of service representative during manual debugging.
● *Tester GUI.* This layer contains the following user interface and test infrastructure objects allowing the tester to automate the testing process:
– acceptanceTestCases, which store acceptance test cases including oracles.
– acceptanceTestScripts, which consist of a cohesive, executable set of acceptance test cases.

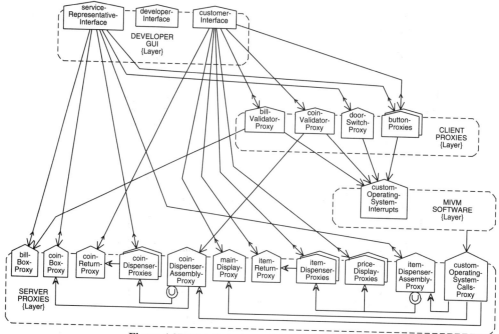

Figure 4.37 Detailed view of the test harness architecture.

- acceptanceTestSets, which consist of a cohesive, executable set of acceptance test sets.
- testerInterface, which allows the tester to automatically perform regression testing of the vending machine software.
- *Client proxies.* This layer contains the following proxy objects representing hardware and software clients of the vending machine software:
  - billValidatorProxy
  - buttonProxies
  - coinValidatorProxy
  - doorSwitchProxy
- *Server proxies.* This layer contains the following proxy objects representing hardware and software servers of the vending machine software:
  - billBoxProxy
  - coinBoxProxy
  - coinDispenserAssemblyProxy
  - coinDispenserProxies
  - coinReturnProxy
  - customOperating-SystemCallsProxy
  - itemDispenserAssemblyProxy
  - itemDispenserProxies
  - itemReturnProxy
  - mainDisplayProxy
  - priceDisplayProxies

4.3.2 *Test harness classes*

The following classes were developed as part of the test harness in order to test the vending machine software:

- ClientProxy:
  - ButtonProxy
  - DoorSwitchProxy
  - MoneyValidatorProxy
    - BillValidatorProxy
    - CoinValidatorProxy
- ServerProxy:
  - CoinDispenserAssemblyProxy
  - DisplayProxy
  - ItemDispenserProxy
  - ItemDispenserAssemblyProxy
  - MoneyBoxProxy
  - ReturnProxy
- Interface classes:
  - CustomerInterface
  - DeveloperInterface
  - ServiceRepresentativeInterface
  - TesterInterface

4.3.2.1 ClientProxy

Description: This abstract class models clients of the software vending machine that act as proxies for the associated hardware devices.

Superclass: Object.

Responsibilities:
- Know the vending machine.
  Collaborator: Vending Machine.

Characteristics:
  Constructor:
  - ClientProxy(VendingMachine aVendingMachine);

  Operations:
    Accessors:
      - public VendingMachine getVendingMachine( ) {...};
      - public void setVendingMachine(VendingMachine aVendingMachine) {...};
  Properties:
    Attributes: none.
    Links:
      - VendingMachine vendingMachine;
    Parts: none.

4.3.2.1.1 ButtonProxy

Description: Instances of this concrete class are clients of the software vending machine that act as proxies for the associated hardware buttons.

Superclass: ClientProxy.

Responsibilities:
- Send the same message to vending machine that would be sent by the operating system when the associated hardware button is pressed.
  Collaborator: Vending Machine.

Characteristics:
  Constructor:
  - ButtonProxy(String anArgument, Symbol aSelector, VendingMachine aVendingMachine) {...};

  Operations:
    Services:
    - public void pressed() {...};
      // Notify the software vending machine that the associated hardware
      // button was pressed.

  Properties:
    Attributes:
    - String argument;
    - Symbol selector;

    Links: none.
    Parts: none.

4.3.2.1.2 DoorSwitchProxy

Description: The single instance of this concrete class is a proxy for the associated hardware door switch.

Superclass: ClientProxy.

Responsibilities:
- Send the same message to vending machine that would be sent by the operating system when the associated hardware door switch is closed.
  Collaborator: VendingMachine.

Characteristics:
  Operations:
    Services:
    - public void closed() {...};
      // Notify the software vending machine that the door has closed.

  Properties:
    Attributes: none.
    Links: none.
    Parts: none.

4.3.2.1.3 MoneyValidatorProxy

Description: This abstract class is a client of the software vending machine that acts as a proxy for the associated hardware money validator.

Superclass: ClientProxy.

Responsibilities:
- Send the same message to vending machine that would be sent by the operating system when the associated hardware bill validator validates a bill. *Collaborator:* Vending Machine.

Characteristics:
  Operations:
    Services:
      - public abstract void valid(Money aMoney);
        // Notify the software vending machine that aMoney has been validated.

  Properties:
    Attributes: none.
    Links: none.
    Parts: none.

4.3.2.1.3.1 BillValidatorProxy

Description: The single instance of this concrete class is a client of the software vending machine that acts as a proxy for the associated hardware bill validator.

Superclass: MoneyValidatorProxy.

Responsibilities:
- Send the same message to vending machine that would be sent by the operating system when the associated hardware bill validator validates a bill. *Collaborator:* Vending Machine.

Characteristics:
  Operations:
    Public services:
      - public void valid(Bill aBill) {...};
        // Notify the software vending machine that aBill has been validated.

  Properties:
    Attributes: none.
    Links: none.
    Parts: none.

4.3.2.1.3.2 CoinValidatorProxy

Description: The single instance of this concrete class is a client of the software vending machine that acts as a proxy for the associated hardware coin validator.

Superclass: MoneyValidatorProxy.

Responsibilities:
- Send the same message to vending machine that would be sent by the operating system when the associated hardware coin validator validates a coin.
  Collaborator: Vending Machine.

Characteristics:
  Operations:
    Public services:
      - public void valid(Coin aCoin) {...};
        //Notify the software vending machine that aCoin has been validated.

  Properties:
    Attributes: none.
    Links: none.
    Parts: none.

4.3.2.2 ServerProxy

4.3.2.2.1 CoinDispenserAssemblyProxy

Description: The single instance of this concrete class is a proxy for the associated hardware coin dispenser assembly.

Superclass: ServerProxy.

Responsibilities:
- Dispense a valid coin.
  Collaborators: none.
- Load with coins.
  Collaborators: none.
- Characteristics:
  Operations:
    Services:
      - public void dispenseDime() throws EmptyException {...};
        // Dispense a dime into the coin return proxy
        // Upon failure, throw Empty Exception with coin = Bill.dime()
      - public void dispenseNickel() throws EmptyException {...};
        // Dispense a nickel into the coin return proxy
        // Upon failure, throw Empty Exception with coin = Bill.nickel()
      - public void dispenseQuarter() throws EmptyException {...};
        // Dispense a quarter into the coin return proxy
        // Upon failure, throw Empty Exception with coin = Bill.quarter()
      - public void load() {...};
        // Load the coin dispenser assembly proxy with coins
  Properties:
    Attributes:
      - int maximumNumberOfNickels;
      - int maximumNumberOfDimes ;
      - int maximumNumberOfQuarters;

- int numberOfNickels;
- int numberOfDimes;
- int numberOfQuarters;

Links:
- CoinReturnProxy coinReturnProxy;

Parts: none.
Entries: none.
Exceptions:
- EmptyException

4.3.2.2.2 DisplayProxy

Description: The instances (e.g. mainDisplay and the item displays) of this concrete class are proxies for the associated hardware displays.

Superclass: ServerProxy.

Responsibilities:
- Display a given string.
  Collaborators: none.

Characteristics:
  Operations:
    Services:
      - public void display(String aString) {...};
        // Display the given string.

  Properties:
    Attributes: none.
    Links: none.
    Parts: none.
    Entries: none.
    Exceptions: none.

4.3.2.2.3 ItemDispenserProxy

Description: The instances of this concrete class are proxies for the associated hardware item dispensers.

Superclass: ServerProxy.

Responsibilities:
- Know the common price of the items it stores.
  Collaborator: none.
- Dispense an item when requested.
  Collaborators: none.

Characteristics:
  Operations:
    Services:
      - public void dispense() {...};

// Dispense an item into the item return.
- public void load() {...};
  // Load the item dispenser with items.

Properties:
Attributes:
- int currentNumber;
- Money price;
- int size;

Links: none.
Parts: none.
Entries: none.
Exceptions:
- EmptyException

4.3.2.2.4 ItemDispenserAssemblyProxy

Description: The single instance of this concrete class is a proxy for the hardware item dispenser assembly.

Superclass: Testable Object.

Responsibilities:
- Dispense item from requested item dispenser.
  Collaborator: ItemDispenserProxy.

Characteristics:
Constructor:
- ItemDispenserAssembly(int numberOfColumns, int numberOfRows)

Operations:
Services:
- public void dispenseAt(Location aLocation) {...};
  // Dispense an item from the item dispenser at the given location.
- public void loadItemDispensers() {...};
  // Load all item dispensers with items.

Properties:
Attributes:
- int numberOfColumns;
- int numberOfRows;

Links: none.
Parts:
- HashTable item Dispensers; // Dictionary of (Location, Item Dispenser)

Entries: none.
Exceptions: none.

4.3.2.2.5 MoneyBoxProxy

Description: The two instances, billBox and coinBox, of this concrete class are proxies for the associated hardware bill and coin boxes.

Superclass: ServerProxy.

Responsibilities:
• Know the amount of money it contains.
  Collaborator: none.

Characteristics:
  Operations:
    Services:
      • public void add(Money aMoney) {...};
        // Add money to any money already in the money box.
      • public void empty() {...};
        // Remove all money from the money box.
  Properties:
    Attributes:
      • Money money.

    Links: none.
    Parts: none.
    Entries: none.
    Exceptions: none.

4.3.2.2.6 ReturnProxy

Description: The two instances, coinReturn and itemReturn, of this concrete class are proxies for the associated hardware returns.

Superclass: ServerProxy.

Responsibilities:
• Hold dispensed objects until emptied.
  Collaborator: none.

Characteristics:
  Operations:
    Services:
      • public abstract void add(Object anObject) {...};
        // Add an object to those objects already in the return.
      • public void empty() {...};
        // Empty the objects out of the return.
  Properties:
    Attributes:
      • Collection contents;

    Links: none.
    Parts: none.
    Entries: none.
    Exceptions: none.

4.3.2.3 Interface classes

4.3.2.3.1 CustomerInterface

As illustrated in Figure 4.38, this presentation object simulates the actual customer interface and allows the tester (playing the role of customer) to interact with and observe the software proxies representing those hardware actors that the real customer will interact with. This aggregate object contains the following action button and eight subpanes:

- *Bill validator.* This subpane allows the tester to insert dollar bills into the bill validator.
- *Coin return.* This subpane allows the tester to observe and take nickels, dimes and quarters dispensed by the hardware coin dispenser proxy and contained in the hardware coin return proxy.
- *Coin validator.* This subpane allows the tester to insert nickels, dimes and quarters into the coin validator.
- *Display.* This subpane allows the tester to observe the messages displayed by the hardware display proxy.
- *Item dispenser assembly.* This subpane allows the tester to observe the

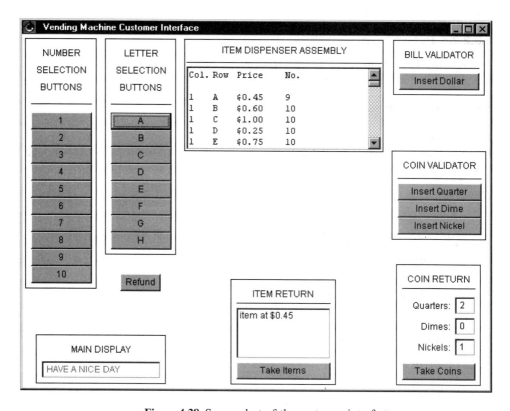

Figure 4.38 Screen shot of the customer interface.

common price and number of items in each hardware item dispenser proxy in the hardware item dispenser assembly proxy.

- *Item return*. This subpane allows the tester to observe and take the items dispensed by the hardware item dispensers and contained in the hardware item return proxy.
- *Letter selection buttons*. This subpane allows the tester to press the letter selection buttons.
- *Number selection buttons*. This subpane allows the tester to press the number selection buttons.
- *Refund button*. This action button allows the tester to request a refund of the money deposited.

4.3.2.3.2 DeveloperInterface

As illustrated in Figure 4.39, this presentation object allows the tester to parameterize the MIVM software. This aggregate object contains two action buttons and the following two subpanes:

- *Coin dispenser*. This subpane allows the tester to set the maximum number of nickels, dimes and quarters that the coin dispenser can hold.
- *Item dispenser assembly*. This subpane allows the tester to set the number of columns and rows in the item dispenser assembly as well as the maximum number of items that an individual item dispenser can hold.
- *OK button*. This action button causes the other layers to be constructed, the Customer Interface and the Service Representative Interface to be opened, and the developer interface to be closed.
- *Quit button*. This action button causes the developer interface to be closed.

4.3.2.3.3 ServiceRepresentativeInterface

As illustrated in Figure 4.40, this presentation object simulates the actual service representative interface and allows the tester (playing the role of service representative) to interact with and observe the software proxies representing those hardware actors that the real service representative will interact with. This aggregate object contains the following three action buttons and two subpanes:

- *Coin dispenser*. This subpane allows the tester to observe, partially load, and completely load the hardware coin dispenser proxy.
- *Door switch*. This action button allows the tester to simulate closing the door.
- *Load item dispenser assembly button*. This action button allows the tester to load the hardware item dispenser assembly proxy.
- *Mode button*. This action button allows the tester to simulate pressing the hardware mode button.
- *Money boxes*. This subpane allows the tester to observe and take the bills and coins in the hardware bill box and coin box proxies.

4.3.2.3.4 TesterInterface

As illustrated in Figure 4.41, this presentation object allows the tester to browse and execute test sets, scripts and cases.

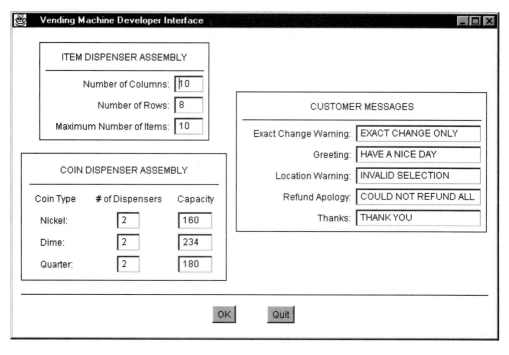

Figure 4.39 Screen shot of the developer interface.

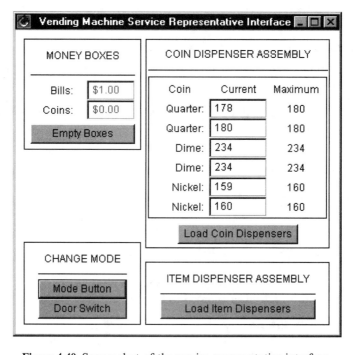

Figure 4.40 Screen shot of the service representative interface.

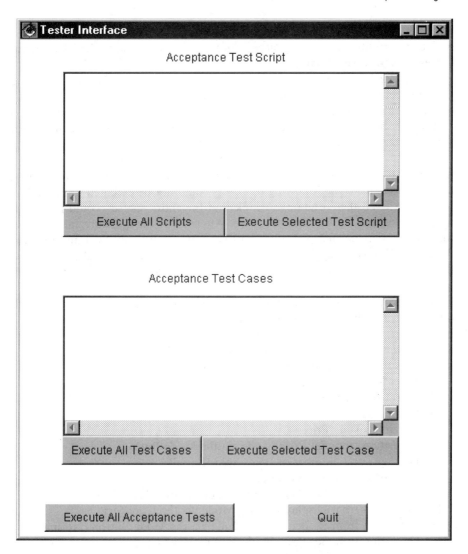

Figure 4.41 Screen shot of the tester interface.

4.3.3 Acceptance test set

The Mark I Vending Machine software has a large amount of state behavior (e.g. modes, state of selection objects). Unfortunately, this means that the preconditions of many of the acceptance test cases are not trivial to establish, especially from the outside. In order to minimize the amount of this test preparation required, the test cases have been ordered so that the postconditions of each successful test case fulfill the preconditions of the following test case. Although this requires that some tests must be successfully passed before other tests can be run, this is acceptable in this case because:

- The total number of acceptance tests is small.
- The preconditions of many acceptance tests can be established by sending messages to server proxies.
- The test order is logical for other reasons (e.g. one must be able to change modes before setting prices before buying items).
- Because the application is under maintenance and in its third version, it is relatively bug free and the acceptance tests are primarily run in batch mode as part of regression testing.

One potential problem with the above approach is that it would appear that if any test case failed, the following test cases could not be executed until the bugs were fixed. Even then, one might think that the entire test set would have to be rerun to prepare for the next test case. After all, if the software fails any test case, then the associated postconditions have not been established and therefore the preconditions of the following test case have not been established. However, this is not so because the test harness can be used to directly establish the preconditions of any test case.

The acceptance test set for the MIVM system consists of and executes the following test scripts and test cases in the following order:

- *Test Script 1 – Set Up the Vending Machine*
  1. Test Initial Mode of the Vending Machine
  2. Enter Valid New Price
  3. Reject Invalid New Price
  4. Cancel New Price
  5. Accept Existing Price
  6. Transition from Set Price Mode via the Mode Button
  7. Display Total Number of Items Sold (Initial)
  8. Display Total Income (Initial)
  9. Transition from Display History Mode via the Mode Button
  10. Transition from Display History Mode via the Door Switch
  11. Transition from Dispense Item Mode via the Mode Button (Normal)
  12. Transition from Set Price Mode via Door Switch
- *Test Script 2 – Use the Vending Machine*
  1. Request Refund
  2. Buy Item (Pay Exactly, Select Column, Select Row)
  3. Buy Item (Overpay, Select Row, Select Column)
  4. Buy Item (Select Column, Underpay, Select Column, Select Row, Overpay)
  5. Buy Unpriced Item
  6. Buy Item (Cannot Make Change)
  7. Buy Item (Credit is Available)
- *Test Script 3 – Service the Vending Machine*
  1. Display Total Items Sold (Items Sold)
  2. Display Total Income (Income Exists)
  3. Service Representative Displays History (Inappropriate Buttons)
  4. Service Representative Displays History (Unexpected Money)

5. Transition from Dispense Item Mode via Mode Button (Could Not Dispense All)
6. Transition from Display History Mode via Door Switch
7. Service Representative Makes a Selection (Refund Button)
8. Service Representative Makes a Selection (Unexpected Money)
9. Service Representative Enters a Price (Unexpected Money)

4.3.3.1 Test script 1 – Set Up the Vending Machine

This test script is intended to discover bugs preventing the service representative from setting up the vending machine for use by customers.

4.3.3.1.1 Test case 1-1 – Test Initial Mode of the Vending Machine

Purpose: Discover any bugs preventing the vending machine from responding properly upon being plugged into an electrical outlet.

Use cases tested:
- Initial State of the MIVM
- Display Greeting – Primary Path: Customer's Credit Dispensed Without a Problem

Establish preconditions:
- Dispenser proxies:
  - Quarter dispenser proxy 1 contains 0 quarters.
  - Quarter dispenser proxy 2 contains 0 quarters.
  - Dime dispenser proxy 1 contains 0 dimes.
  - Dime dispenser proxy 2 contains 0 dimes.
  - Nickel dispenser proxy 1 contains 0 nickels.
  - Nickel dispenser proxy 2 contains 0 nickels.
  - Each item dispenser proxy contains 0 items.
- Display proxies:
  - The main display proxy is blank.
  - Each item display proxy is blank.
- Door switch proxy:
  - Locked.
- Money box proxies:
  - The bill box proxy is empty.
  - The coin box proxy is empty.
- Return proxies:
  - The coin return proxy is empty.
  - The item return proxy is empty.

Execute test case:
1. The tester plugs the MIVM into an electrically outlet.
   Expected responses:
   - Each item display proxy displays its column and row. (No price is displayed because no price has yet been set.)
   - The main display proxy displays 'SET PRICE'.

2. The tester unlocks and opens the door.
   Expected response:
   - None.
3. The tester partially loads each coin dispenser.
   Expected response:
   - Quarter dispenser proxy 1 contains 2 quarters.
   - Quarter dispenser proxy 2 contains 2 quarters.
   - Dime dispenser proxy 1 contains 4 dimes.
   - Dime dispenser proxy 2 contains 3 dimes.
   - Nickel dispenser proxy 1 contains 1 nickel.
   - Nickel dispenser proxy 2 contains 0 nickels.
4. The tester loads each item dispenser.
   Expected response:
   - Each item dispenser proxy contains 10 items.

Evaluate postconditions:
- Dispenser proxies:
  - Quarter dispenser proxy 1 contains 2 quarters.
  - Quarter dispenser proxy 2 contains 2 quarters.
  - Dime dispenser proxy 1 contains 4 dimes
  - Dime dispenser proxy 2 contains 3 dimes.
  - Nickel dispenser proxy 1 contains 1 nickel.
  - Nickel dispenser proxy 2 contains 0 nickels.
  - Each item dispenser proxy contains 10 items
- Display proxies:
  - The main display proxy displays 'SET PRICE'.
  - Each item display proxy displays the location (e.g. '7A') of the corresponding item dispenser.
- Door switch proxy:
  - Locked.
- Money box proxies:
  - The bill box proxy is empty.
  - The coin box proxy is empty.
- Return proxies:
  - The coin return proxy is empty.
  - The item return proxy is empty.

4.3.3.1.2 Test case 1-2 – Enter Valid New Price

Purpose: Discover any bugs preventing the service representative from successfully entering a valid new price, starting by selecting the column of the item dispenser.

Use cases tested:
- Service Representative Selects a Column – Primary Path: The Column is Not Selected
- Service Representative Selects a Row – Primary Path: The Row is Not Selected
- Service Representative Enters a Price – Primary Path: Build and Enter the new Valid Price

- Service Representative Enters a Price – Alternative Path: Press an Inappropriate Button

Establish preconditions:
- Dispenser proxies:
  - Quarter dispenser proxy 1 contains 2 quarters.
  - Quarter dispenser proxy 2 contains 2 quarters.
  - Dime dispenser proxy 1 contains 4 dimes.
  - Dime dispenser proxy 2 contains 3 dimes.
  - Nickel dispenser proxy 1 contains 1 nickel.
  - Nickel dispenser proxy 2 contains 0 nickels.
  - Each item dispenser proxy contains 10 items.
- Display proxies:
  - The main display proxy displays 'SET PRICE'.
  - Each item display proxy displays its column and location, but not its price.
- Door switch proxy:
  - Unlocked.
- Money box proxies:
  - The bill box proxy is empty.
  - The coin box proxy is empty.
- Return proxies:
  - The coin return proxy is empty.
  - The item return proxy is empty.

Execute test case:
1. The tester presses the '1' button.
   Expected response:
   - The main display proxy displays 'COLUMN 1'.
2. The tester presses the 'A' button.
   Expected response:
   - The main display proxy displays 'COL 1 ROW A $0.00'.
3. The tester presses the '4' button.
   Expected response:
   - The main display proxy displays 'COL 1 ROW A $0.04'.
4. The tester presses the '5' button.
   Expected response:
   - The main display proxy displays 'COL 1 ROW A $0.45'.
5. The tester presses the 'E' button.
   Expected response:
   - The main display displays 'ENTERED'.
   - The 1A item display proxy displays '1A $0.45'.
6. The tester presses the '2' button.
   Expected response:
   - The main display proxy displays 'COLUMN 2'.
7. The tester presses the 'B' button.
   Expected response:
   - The main display proxy displays 'COL 2 ROW B $0.00'.

8. The tester presses the '6' button.
   Expected response:
   • The main display proxy displays 'COL 1 ROW A $0.06'.
9. The tester presses the '10' button.
   Expected response:
   • The main display proxy displays 'COL 1 ROW A $0.60'.
10. The tester presses the 'H' button.
    Expected response:
    • Nothing happens.
11. The tester presses the refund button.
    Expected response:
    • Nothing happens.
12. The tester presses the 'E' button.
    Expected response:
    • The main display displays 'ENTERED'.
    • The 2B item display proxy displays '2B $0.60'.

Evaluate postconditions:
• Dispenser proxies:
  – Quarter dispenser proxy 1 contains 2 quarters.
  – Quarter dispenser proxy 2 contains 2 quarters.
  – Dime dispenser proxy 1 contains 4 dimes.
  – Dime dispenser proxy 2 contains 3 dimes.
  – Nickel dispenser proxy 1 contains 1 nickel.
  – Nickel dispenser proxy 2 contains 0 nickels.
  – Each item dispenser proxy contains 10 items.
• Display proxies:
  – The main display proxy displays 'ENTERED'.
  – The 1A item display proxy displays '1A $0.45'.
  – The 2B item display proxy displays '2B $0.60'.
  – All other item display proxies display their column and location, but not their prices.
• Door switch proxy:
  – Unlocked.
• Money box proxies:
  – The bill box proxy is empty.
  – The coin box proxy is empty.
• Return proxies:
  – The coin return proxy is empty.
  – The item return proxy is empty.

4.3.3.1.3 Test case 1-3 – Reject Invalid New Price

Purpose: Discover any bugs preventing the vending machine from rejecting an invalid new price, when the service representative first selected the row of the item dispenser.

Use cases tested:
- Service Representative Selects a Row – Primary Path: The Column is Not Selected
- Service Representative Selects a Column – Primary Path: The Row is Selected
- Service Representative Enters a Price – Alternative Path: Build and Enter the new Invalid Price

Establish preconditions:
- Dispenser proxies:
  - Quarter dispenser proxy 1 contains 2 quarters.
  - Quarter dispenser proxy 2 contains 2 quarters.
  - Dime dispenser proxy 1 contains 4 dimes.
  - Dime dispenser proxy 2 contains 3 dimes.
  - Nickel dispenser proxy 1 contains 1 nickel.
  - Nickel dispenser proxy 2 contains 0 nickels.
  - Each item dispenser proxy contains 10 items.
- Display proxies:
  - The main display proxy displays 'ENTERED'.
  - The 1A item display proxy displays '1A $0.45'.
  - The 2B item display proxy displays '2B $0.60'.
  - All other item display proxies display their column and location, but not their prices.
- Door switch proxy:
  - Unlocked.
- Money box proxies:
  - The bill box proxy is empty.
  - The coin box proxy is empty.
- Return proxies:
  - The coin return proxy is empty.
  - The item return proxy is empty.

Execute test case:
1. The tester presses the 'H' button.
   Expected response:
   - The main display proxy displays 'ROW H'.
2. The tester presses the '10' button.
   Expected response:
   - The main display proxy displays 'COL 10 ROW H $0.00'.
3. The tester presses the '2' button.
   Expected response:
   - The main display proxy displays 'COL 1 ROW 'H' $0.02'.
4. The tester presses the '7' button.
   Expected response:
   - The main display proxy displays 'COL 1 ROW 'H' $0.27'.
5. The tester presses the 'E' button.
   Expected response:
   - The main display proxy displays 'REJECTED'.

Evaluate postconditions:

- Dispenser proxies:
  - Quarter dispenser proxy 1 contains 2 quarters.
  - Quarter dispenser proxy 2 contains 2 quarters.
  - Dime dispenser proxy 1 contains 4 dimes.
  - Dime dispenser proxy 2 contains 3 dimes.
  - Nickel dispenser proxy 1 contains 1 nickel.
  - Nickel dispenser proxy 2 contains 0 nickels.
  - Each item dispenser proxy contains 10 items.
- Display proxies:
  - The main display proxy displays 'REJECTED'.
  - The 1A item display proxy displays '1A $0.45'.
  - The 2B item display proxy displays '2B $0.60'.
  - All other item display proxies display their column and location, but not their prices.
- Door switch proxy:
  - Unlocked.
- Money box proxies:
  - The bill box proxy is empty.
  - The coin box proxy is empty.
- Return proxies:
  - The coin return proxy is empty.
  - The item return proxy is empty.

4.3.3.1.4 Test case 1-4 – Cancel New Price

Purpose: Discover any bugs preventing the service representative from successfully canceling a new price or using the 10 button when building a price.

Use cases tested:

- Service Representative Selects a Column – Primary Path: The Row is Not Selected
- Service Representative Selects a Row – Primary Path: The Column is Selected
- Service Representative Enters a Price – Alternative Path: Build and Cancel the new Price

Establish preconditions:

- Dispenser proxies:
  - Quarter dispenser proxy 1 contains 2 quarters.
  - Quarter dispenser proxy 2 contains 2 quarters.
  - Dime dispenser proxy 1 contains 4 dimes.
  - Dime dispenser proxy 2 contains 3 dimes.
  - Nickel dispenser proxy 1 contains 1 nickel.
  - Nickel dispenser proxy 2 contains 0 nickels.
  - Each item dispenser proxy contains 10 items.
- Display proxies:
  - The main display displays 'REJECTED'.

- The 1A item display proxy displays '1A $0.45'.
- The 2B item display proxy displays '2B $0.60'.
- All other item display proxies display their column and location, but not their prices.
- Door switch proxy:
  - Unlocked.
- Money box proxies:
  - The bill box proxy is empty.
  - The coin box proxy is empty.
- Return proxies:
  - The coin return proxy is empty.
  - The item return proxy is empty.

Execute test case:
1. The tester presses the '1' button.
   Expected response:
   - The main display proxy displays 'COLUMN 1'.
2. The tester presses the 'C' button.
   Expected response:
   - The main display proxy displays 'COL 1 ROW C $0.00'.
3. The tester presses the '1' button.
   Expected response:
   - The main display proxy displays 'COL 1 ROW 'C' $0.01'.
4. The tester presses the '10' button.
   Expected response:
   - The main display proxy displays 'COL 1 ROW 'C' $0.10'.
5. The tester presses the '5' button.
   Expected response:
   - The main display proxy displays 'COL 1 ROW 'C' $1.05'.
6. The tester presses the 'C' button.
   Expected response:
   - The main display proxy displays 'CANCELED'.

Evaluate postconditions:
- Dispenser proxies:
  - Quarter dispenser proxy 1 contains 2 quarters.
  - Quarter dispenser proxy 2 contains 2 quarters.
  - Dime dispenser proxy 1 contains 4 dimes.
  - Dime dispenser proxy 2 contains 3 dimes.
  - Nickel dispenser proxy 1 contains 1 nickel.
  - Nickel dispenser proxy 2 contains 0 nickels.
  - Each item dispenser proxy contains 10 items.
- Display proxies:
  - The main display proxy displays 'CANCELED'.
  - The 1A item display proxy displays '1A $0.45'.
  - The 2B item display proxy displays '2B $0.60'.

- All other item display proxies display their column and location, but not their prices.
- Door switch proxy:
  - Unlocked.
- Money box proxies:
  - The bill box proxy is empty.
  - The coin box proxy is empty.
- Return proxies:
  - The coin return proxy is empty.
  - The item return proxy is empty.

4.3.3.1.5 Test case 1-5 – Accept Existing Price

Purpose: Discover any bugs preventing the service representative from accepting an existing price.

Use cases tested:
- Service Representative Selects a Column – Primary Path: The Row is Not Selected
- Service Representative Selects a Row – Primary Path: The Column is Selected
- Service Representative Enters a Price – Alternative Path: Accept the old Price

Establish preconditions:
- Dispenser proxies:
  - Quarter dispenser proxy 1 contains 2 quarters.
  - Quarter dispenser proxy 2 contains 2 quarters.
  - Dime dispenser proxy 1 contains 4 dimes.
  - Dime dispenser proxy 2 contains 3 dimes.
  - Nickel dispenser proxy 1 contains 1 nickel.
  - Nickel dispenser proxy 2 contains 0 nickels.
  - Each item dispenser proxy contains 10 items.
- Display proxies:
  - The main display proxy displays 'CANCELED'.
  - The 1A item display proxy displays '1A $0.45'.
  - The 2B item display proxy displays '2B $0.60'.
  - All other item display proxies display their column and location, but not their prices.
- Door switch proxy:
  - Unlocked.
- Money box proxies:
  - The bill box proxy is empty.
  - The coin box proxy is empty.
- Return proxies:
  - The coin return proxy is empty.
  - The item return proxy is empty.

Execute test case:
1. The tester presses the '1' button.
   Expected response:
   • The main display proxy displays 'COLUMN 1'.
2. The tester presses the 'A' button.
   Expected response:
   • The main display proxy displays 'COL 1 ROW A $0.45'.
3. The tester presses the 'A' button.
   Expected response:
   • The main display proxy displays 'ACCEPTED'.

Evaluate postconditions:
• Dispenser proxies:
  – Quarter dispenser proxy 1 contains 2 quarters.
  – Quarter dispenser proxy 2 contains 2 quarters.
  – Dime dispenser proxy 1 contains 4 dimes.
  – Dime dispenser proxy 2 contains 3 dimes.
  – Nickel dispenser proxy 1 contains 1 nickel.
  – Nickel dispenser proxy 2 contains 0 nickels.
  – Each item dispenser proxy contains 10 items.
• Display proxies:
  – The main display proxy displays 'ACCEPTED'.
  – The 1A item display proxy displays '1A $0.45'.
  – The 2B item display proxy displays '2B $0.60'.
  – All other item display proxies display their column and location, but not their prices.
• Door switch proxy:
  – Unlocked.
• Money box proxies:
  – The bill box proxy is empty.
  – The coin box proxy is empty.
• Return proxies:
  – The coin return proxy is empty.
  – The item return proxy is empty.

4.3.3.1.6 Test case 1-6 – Transition from Set Price Mode via the Mode Button

Purpose: Discover any bugs preventing the vending machine from successfully transitioning from the set price mode if the service representative presses the mode button.

Use cases tested:
• Service Representative Presses the Mode Button – Primary Path: Change from 'Set Price' Mode

Establish preconditions:
• Dispenser proxies:

- Quarter dispenser proxy 1 contains 2 quarters.
- Quarter dispenser proxy 2 contains 2 quarters.
- Dime dispenser proxy 1 contains 4 dimes.
- Dime dispenser proxy 2 contains 3 dimes.
- Nickel dispenser proxy 1 contains 1 nickel.
- Nickel dispenser proxy 2 contains 0 nickels.
- Each item dispenser proxy contains 10 items.
- Display proxies:
  - The main display proxy displays 'ACCEPTED'.
  - The 1A item display proxy displays '1A $0.45'.
  - The 2B item display proxy displays '2B $0.60'.
  - All other item display proxies display their column and location, but not their prices.
- Door switch proxy:
  - Unlocked.
- Money box proxies:
  - The bill box proxy is empty.
  - The coin box proxy is empty.
- Return proxies:
  - The coin return proxy is empty.
  - The item return proxy is empty.

Execute test case:
1. The tester presses the mode button.
   Expected response:
   - The main display proxy displays 'DISPLAY HISTORY'.

Evaluate postconditions:
- Dispenser proxies:
  - Quarter dispenser proxy 1 contains 2 quarters.
  - Quarter dispenser proxy 2 contains 2 quarters.
  - Dime dispenser proxy 1 contains 4 dimes.
  - Dime dispenser proxy 2 contains 3 dimes.
  - Nickel dispenser proxy 1 contains 1 nickel.
  - Nickel dispenser proxy 2 contains 0 nickels.
  - Each item dispenser proxy contains 10 items.
- Display proxies:
  - The main display proxy displays 'DISPLAY HISTORY'.
  - The 1A item display proxy displays '1A $0.45'.
  - The 2B item display proxy displays '2B $0.60'.
  - All other item display proxies display their column and location, but not their prices.
- Door switch proxy:
  - Unlocked.
- Money box proxies:
  - The bill box proxy is empty.
  - The coin box proxy is empty.

- Return proxies:
  - The coin return proxy is empty.
  - The item return proxy is empty.

4.3.3.1.7 Test case 1-7 – Display Total Number of Items Sold (Initial)

Purpose: Discover any bugs preventing the service representative from displaying the total number of items sold when none have been sold yet.

Use cases tested:
- Service Representative Displays the Total Number of Items Sold

Establish preconditions:
- Dispenser proxies:
  - Quarter dispenser proxy 1 contains 2 quarters.
  - Quarter dispenser proxy 2 contains 2 quarters.
  - Dime dispenser proxy 1 contains 4 dimes.
  - Dime dispenser proxy 2 contains 3 dimes.
  - Nickel dispenser proxy 1 contains 1 nickel.
  - Nickel dispenser proxy 2 contains 0 nickels.
  - Each item dispenser proxy contains 10 items.
- Display proxies:
  - The main display proxy displays 'DISPLAY HISTORY'.
  - The 1A item display proxy displays '1A $0.45'.
  - The 2B item display proxy displays '2B $0.60'.
  - All other item display proxies display their column and location, but not their prices.
- Door switch proxy:
  - Unlocked.
- Money box proxies:
  - The bill box proxy is empty.
  - The coin box proxy is empty.
- Return proxies:
  - The coin return proxy is empty.
  - The item return proxy is empty.

Execute test case:
1. The tester presses the 'A' button.
   Expected response:
   - The main display proxy displays 'ITEMS SOLD: 0'.

Evaluate postconditions:
- Dispenser proxies:
  - Quarter dispenser proxy 1 contains 2 quarters.
  - Quarter dispenser proxy 2 contains 2 quarters.
  - Dime dispenser proxy 1 contains 4 dimes.
  - Dime dispenser proxy 2 contains 3 dimes.
  - Nickel dispenser proxy 1 contains 1 nickel.
  - Nickel dispenser proxy 2 contains 0 nickels.

- Each item dispenser proxy contains 10 items.
- Display proxies:
  - The main display proxy displays 'ITEMS SOLD: 0'.
  - The 1A item display proxy displays '1A $0.45'.
  - The 2B item display proxy displays '2B $0.60'.
  - All other item display proxies display their column and location, but not their prices.
- Door switch proxy:
  - Unlocked.
- Money box proxies:
  - The bill box proxy is empty.
  - The coin box proxy is empty.
- Return proxies:
  - The coin return proxy is empty.
  - The item return proxy is empty.

4.3.3.1.8 Test case 1-8 – Display Total Income (Initial)

Purpose: Discover any bugs preventing the service representative from displaying the total income of the vending machine when no items have been sold yet.

Use cases tested:
- Service Representative Displays the Total Income

Establish preconditions:
- Dispenser proxies:
  - Quarter dispenser proxy 1 contains 2 quarters.
  - Quarter dispenser proxy 2 contains 2 quarters.
  - Dime dispenser proxy 1 contains 4 dimes.
  - Dime dispenser proxy 2 contains 3 dimes.
  - Nickel dispenser proxy 1 contains 1 nickel.
  - Nickel dispenser proxy 2 contains 0 nickels.
  - Each item dispenser proxy contains 10 items.
- Display proxies:
  - The main display proxy displays 'ITEMS SOLD: 0'.
  - The 1A item display proxy displays '1A $0.45'.
  - The 2B item display proxy displays '2B $0.60'.
  - All other item display proxies display their column and location, but not their prices.
- Door switch proxy:
  - Unlocked.
- Money box proxies:
  - The bill box proxy is empty.
  - The coin box proxy is empty.
- Return proxies:
  - The coin return proxy is empty.
  - The item return proxy is empty.

Execute test case:
1. The tester presses the 'B' button.
   Expected response:
   - The main display proxy displays 'INCOME: $0.00'.

Evaluate postconditions:
- Dispenser proxies:
  - Quarter dispenser proxy 1 contains 2 quarters.
  - Quarter dispenser proxy 2 contains 2 quarters.
  - Dime dispenser proxy 1 contains 4 dimes.
  - Dime dispenser proxy 2 contains 3 dimes.
  - Nickel dispenser proxy 1 contains 1 nickel.
  - Nickel dispenser proxy 2 contains 0 nickels.
  - Each item dispenser proxy contains 10 items.
- Display proxies:
  - The main display proxy displays 'INCOME: $0.00'.
  - The 1A item display proxy displays '1A $0.45'.
  - The 2B item display proxy displays '2B $0.60'.
  - All other item display proxies display their column and location, but not their prices.
- Door switch proxy:
  - Unlocked.
- Money box proxies:
  - The bill box proxy is empty.
  - The coin box proxy is empty.
- Return proxies:
  - The coin return proxy is empty.
  - The item return proxy is empty.

4.3.3.1.9 Test case 1-9 – Transition from Display History Mode via the Mode Button

Purpose: Discover any bugs preventing the service representative from successfully transitioning the vending machine from display history mode to dispense item mode when exact change is not required.

Use cases tested:
- Service Representative Presses the Mode Button – Primary Path: Change from 'Display History' Mode
- Display Greeting – Primary Path: Customer's Credit Dispensed Without a Problem

Establish preconditions:
- Dispenser proxies:
  - Quarter dispenser proxy 1 contains 2 quarters.
  - Quarter dispenser proxy 2 contains 2 quarters.
  - Dime dispenser proxy 1 contains 4 dimes.

   – Dime dispenser proxy 2 contains 3 dimes.
   – Nickel dispenser proxy 1 contains 1 nickel.
   – Nickel dispenser proxy 2 contains 0 nickels.
   – Each item dispenser proxy contains 10 items.
 • Display proxies:
   – The main display proxy displays 'INCOME: $0.00'.
   – The 1A item display proxy displays '1A $0.45'.
   – The 2B item display proxy displays '2B $0.60'.
   – All other item display proxies display their column and location, but not
     their prices.
 • Door switch proxy:
   – Unlocked.
 • Money box proxies:
   – The bill box proxy is empty.
   – The coin box proxy is empty.
 • Return proxies:
   – The coin return proxy is empty.
   – The item return proxy is empty.

Execute test case:
1. The tester presses the mode button.
   Expected response:
   • The main display proxy displays 'DISPENSE ITEM' for 2 seconds.
   • The main display proxy displays 'THANK YOU' for 2 seconds.
   • The main display proxy displays 'HAVE A NICE DAY'.

Evaluate postconditions:
 • Dispenser proxies:
   – Quarter dispenser proxy 1 contains 2 quarters.
   – Quarter dispenser proxy 2 contains 2 quarters.
   – Dime dispenser proxy 1 contains 4 dimes.
   – Dime dispenser proxy 2 contains 3 dimes.
   – Nickel dispenser proxy 1 contains 1 nickel.
   – Nickel dispenser proxy 2 contains 0 nickels.
   – Each item dispenser proxy contains 10 items.
 • Display proxies:
   – The main display proxy displays 'HAVE A NICE DAY'.
   – The 1A item display proxy displays '1A $0.45'.
   – The 2B item display proxy displays '2B $0.60'.
   – All other item display proxies display their column and location, but not
     their prices.
 • Door switch proxy:
   – Unlocked.
 • Money box proxies:
   – The bill box proxy is empty.
   – The coin box proxy is empty.

- Return proxies:
  - The coin return proxy is empty.
  - The item return proxy is empty.

4.3.3.1.10 Test case 1-10 – Transition from Dispense Item Mode via the Door Switch

Purpose: Discover any bugs preventing the vending machine from responding properly in the Dispense Item mode when the door is closed and locked.

Use cases tested:
- Door Switch Resets the Mode – Primary Path: Change from 'Dispense Item' Mode
- Display Greeting – Primary Path: Customer's Credit Dispensed Without a Problem

Establish preconditions:
- Dispenser proxies:
  - Quarter dispenser proxy 1 contains 2 quarters.
  - Quarter dispenser proxy 2 contains 2 quarters.
  - Dime dispenser proxy 1 contains 4 dimes.
  - Dime dispenser proxy 2 contains 3 dimes.
  - Nickel dispenser proxy 1 contains 1 nickel.
  - Nickel dispenser proxy 2 contains 0 nickels.
  - Each item dispenser proxy contains 10 items.
- Display proxies:
  - The main display proxy displays 'HAVE A NICE DAY'.
  - The 1A item display proxy displays '1A $0.45'.
  - The 2B item display proxy displays '2B $0.60'.
  - All other item display proxies display their column and location, but not their prices.
- Door switch proxy:
  - Unlocked.
- Money box proxies:
  - The bill box proxy is empty.
  - The coin box proxy is empty.
- Return proxies:
  - The coin return proxy is empty.
  - The item return proxy is empty.

Execute test case:
1. The tester closes and locks the door.
   Expected response:
   - The door switch proxy is locked.
   - The main display proxy displays 'DISPENSE ITEM' for 2 seconds.
   - The main display proxy displays 'THANK YOU' for 2 seconds.
   - The main display proxy displays 'HAVE A NICE DAY'.

Evaluate postconditions:
- Dispenser proxies:
  - Quarter dispenser proxy 1 contains 2 quarters.
  - Quarter dispenser proxy 2 contains 2 quarters.
  - Dime dispenser proxy 1 contains 4 dimes.
  - Dime dispenser proxy 2 contains 3 dimes.
  - Nickel dispenser proxy 1 contains 1 nickel.
  - Nickel dispenser proxy 2 contains 0 nickels.
  - Each item dispenser proxy contains 10 items.
- Display proxies:
  - The main display proxy displays 'HAVE A NICE DAY'.
  - The 1A item display proxy displays '1A $0.45'.
  - The 2B item display proxy displays '2B $0.60'.
  - All other item display proxies display their column and location, but not their prices.
- Door switch proxy:
  - Locked.
- Money box proxies:
  - The bill box proxy is empty.
  - The coin box proxy is empty.
- Return proxies:
  - The coin return proxy is empty.
  - The item return proxy is empty.

4.3.3.1.11 Test case 1-11 – Transition from Dispense Item Mode via Mode Button (Normal)

Purpose: Discover any bugs preventing the vending machine from successfully transitioning from dispense item mode to set price mode if the mode button is pressed when there is no customer credit to refund.

Use cases tested:
- Service Representative Presses the Mode Button – Primary Path: Change from 'Dispense Item' Mode

Establish preconditions:
- Dispenser proxies:
  - Quarter dispenser proxy 1 contains 2 quarters.
  - Quarter dispenser proxy 2 contains 2 quarters.
  - Dime dispenser proxy 1 contains 4 dimes
  - Dime dispenser proxy 2 contains 3 dimes.
  - Nickel dispenser proxy 1 contains 1 nickel.
  - Nickel dispenser proxy 2 contains 0 nickels.
  - Each item dispenser proxy contains 10 items.
- Display proxies:
  - The main display proxy displays 'HAVE A NICE DAY'.
  - Each item display proxy displays its column and location, but not its price.

- Door switch proxy:
  - Unlocked.
- Money box proxies:
  - The bill box proxy is empty.
  - The coin box proxy is empty.
- Return proxies:
  - The coin return proxy is empty.
  - The item return proxy is empty.

Execute test case:
1. The tester presses the mode button.
   Expected response:
   - The main display proxy displays 'THANK YOU' for 2 seconds.
   - The main display proxy displays 'SET PRICE'.

Evaluate postconditions:
- Dispenser proxies:
  - Quarter dispenser proxy 1 contains 2 quarters.
  - Quarter dispenser proxy 2 contains 2 quarters.
  - Dime dispenser proxy 1 contains 4 dimes
  - Dime dispenser proxy 2 contains 3 dimes.
  - Nickel dispenser proxy 1 contains 1 nickel.
  - Nickel dispenser proxy 2 contains 0 nickels.
  - Each item dispenser proxy contains 10 items.
- Display proxies:
  - The main display proxy displays 'SET PRICE'.
  - Each item display proxy displays its column and location, but not its price.
- Door switch proxy:
  - Unlocked.
- Money box proxies:
  - The bill box proxy is empty.
  - The coin box proxy is empty.
- Return proxies:
  - The coin return proxy is empty.
  - The item return proxy is empty.

4.3.3.1.12 Test case 1-12 – Transition from Set Price Mode via Door Switch

Purpose: Discover any bugs preventing the service representative from transitioning the vending machine from the 'Set Price' mode by closing and locking the door.

Use cases tested:
Door Switch Resets the Mode Primary Path: Change from 'Set Price' Mode

Establish Preconditions:
- Dispenser Proxies:
  - Quarter dispenser proxy 1 contains 2 quarters.
  - Quarter dispenser proxy 2 contains 2 quarters.
  - Dime dispenser proxy 1 contains 4 dimes.
  - Dime dispenser proxy 2 contains 3 dimes.
  - Nickel dispenser proxy 1 contains 1 nickel.
  - Nickel dispenser proxy 2 contains 0 nickels.
  - Each item dispenser proxy contains 10 items.
- Display Proxies:
  - The main display proxy displays 'SET PRICE'.
  - Each item display proxy displays its column and location, but not its price.
- Door Switch Proxy:
  - Unlocked.
- Money Box Proxies:
  - The bill box proxy is empty.
  - The coin box proxy is empty.
- Return Proxies:
  - The coin return proxy is empty.
  - The item return proxy is empty.

Execute Test Case:
1. The tester closes and locks the door.
   Expected Response:
   - The door switch proxy is locked.
   - The main display proxy displays 'DISPENSE ITEM' for 2 seconds.
   - The main display proxy displays 'THANK YOU' for 2 seconds.
   - The main display proxy displays 'HAVE A NICE DAY'.

Evaluate Postconditions:
- Dispenser Proxies:
  - Quarter dispenser proxy 1 contains 2 quarters.
  - Quarter dispenser proxy 2 contains 2 quarters.
  - Dime dispenser proxy 1 contains 4 dimes.
  - Dime dispenser proxy 2 contains 3 dimes.
  - Nickel dispenser proxy 1 contains 1 nickel.
  - Nickel dispenser proxy 2 contains 0 nickels.
  - Each item dispenser proxy contains 10 items.
- Display Proxies:
  - The main display proxy displays 'HAVE A NICE DAY'.
  - Each item display proxy displays its column and location, but not its price.
- Door Switch Proxy:
  - Unlocked.
- Money Box Proxies:
  - The bill box proxy is empty.
  - The coin box proxy is empty.

- Return Proxies:
  - The coin return proxy is empty.
  - The item return proxy is empty.

4.3.3.2 Test script 2 – Use the Vending Machine
This test script is intended to discover bugs preventing the customer from buying items from the vending machine.

4.3.3.2.1 Test case 2-1 – Request Refund

Purpose: Discover any bugs preventing the vending machine from responding properly refunding customer credit when sufficient change is available.

Use cases tested:
- Customer Inserts a Valid Bill – Primary Path: An Item is Not Presently Selected.
- Attempt to Dispense – Primary Path: Item Not Paid For.
- Customer Requests a Refund.
- Dispense Quarter – Primary Path: Quarter Dispensed without Problem.
- Display Greeting – Primary Path: Customer's Credit Dispensed Without a Problem.

Establish preconditions:
- Dispenser proxies:
  - Quarter dispenser proxy 1 contains 2 quarters.
  - Quarter dispenser proxy 2 contains 2 quarters.
  - Dime dispenser proxy 1 contains 4 dimes.
  - Dime dispenser proxy 2 contains 3 dimes.
  - Nickel dispenser proxy 1 contains 1 nickel.
  - Nickel dispenser proxy 2 contains 0 nickels.
  - Each item dispenser proxy contains 10 items.
- Display proxies:
  - The main display proxy displays 'HAVE A NICE DAY'.
  - The 1A item display proxy displays '1A $0.45'.
  - The 2B item display proxy displays '2B $0.60'.
  - All other item display proxies display their column and location, but not their prices.
- Door switch proxy:
  - Locked.
- Money box proxies:
  - The bill box proxy is empty.
  - The coin box proxy is empty.
- Return proxies:
  - The coin return proxy is empty.
  - The item return proxy is empty.

Execute test case:

1. The tester inserts a dollar bill in the bill validator.

   Expected response:
   - The bill box proxy contains $1.00.
   - The main display proxy displays 'CREDIT: $1.00'.

2. The tester presses the refund button.

   Expected response:
   - Quarter dispenser proxy 1 contains 0 quarters.
   - Quarter dispenser proxy 2 contains 0 quarters.
   - The coin return proxy contains 4 quarters.
   - The main display proxy displays 'THANK YOU' for 2 seconds.
   - The main display proxy displays 'HAVE A NICE DAY'.

Evaluate postconditions:

- Dispenser proxies:
  - Quarter dispenser proxy 1 contains 0 quarters.
  - Quarter dispenser proxy 2 contains 0 quarters.
  - Dime dispenser proxy 1 contains 4 dimes.
  - Dime dispenser proxy 2 contains 3 dimes.
  - Nickel dispenser proxy 1 contains 1 nickel.
  - Nickel dispenser proxy 2 contains 0 nickels.
  - Each item dispenser proxy contains 10 items.
- Display proxies:
  - The main display proxy displays 'HAVE A NICE DAY'.
  - The 1A item display proxy displays '1A $0.45'.
  - The 2B item display proxy displays '2B $0.60'.
  - All other item display proxies display their column and location, but not their prices.
- Door switch proxy:
  - Locked.
- Money box proxies:
  - The bill box proxy contains $1.00.
  - The coin box proxy is empty.
- Return proxies:
  - The coin return proxy contains 4 quarters.
  - The item return proxy is empty.

4.3.3.2.2 Test case 2-2 – Buy Item (Pay Exactly, Select Column, Select Row)

Purpose: Determine if a customer can buy an item by paying exactly, then selecting the column, and finally selecting the row.

Use cases tested:

- Customer Inserts a Valid Coin – Primary Path: An Item is not Presently Selected

- Customer Selects the Column of an Item – Primary Path: Customer Selects the Column without Selecting an Item
- Customer Selects the Row of an Item – Primary Path: Customer Selects an Item by Selecting the Row
- Attempt to Dispense – Primary Path: Item Paid For
- Display Greeting – Primary Path: Customer's Credit Dispensed Without a Problem

Establish preconditions:
- Dispenser proxies:
  - Quarter dispenser proxy 1 contains 0 quarters.
  - Quarter dispenser proxy 2 contains 0 quarters.
  - Dime dispenser proxy 1 contains 4 dimes.
  - Dime dispenser proxy 2 contains 3 dimes.
  - Nickel dispenser proxy 1 contains 1 nickel.
  - Nickel dispenser proxy 2 contains 0 nickels.
  - Each item dispenser proxy contains 10 items.
- Display proxies:
  - The main display proxy displays 'HAVE A NICE DAY'.
  - The 1A item display proxy displays '1A $0.45'.
  - The 2B item display proxy displays '2B $0.60'.
  - All other item display proxies display their column and location, but not their prices.
- Door switch proxy:
  - Locked.
- Money box proxies:
  - The bill box proxy contains $1.00.
  - The coin box proxy is empty.
- Return proxies:
  - The coin return proxy contains 4 quarters.
  - The item return proxy is empty.

Execute test case:
1. The tester inserts a quarter.
   Expected response:
   - The quarter dispenser proxy 1 contains 1 quarter.
   - The main display proxy displays 'CREDIT: $0.25'.
2. The tester inserts a dime.
   Expected response:
   - The dime dispenser proxy 1 contains 5 dimes.
   - The main display proxy displays 'CREDIT: $0.35'.
3. The tester inserts a nickel.
   Expected response:
   - The nickel dispenser proxy 1 contains 2 nickels.
   - The main display proxy displays 'CREDIT: $0.40'.

4. The tester inserts a nickel.
   Expected response:
   - The nickel dispenser proxy 1 contains 3 nickels.
   - The main display proxy displays 'CREDIT: $0.45'.
5. The tester presses the '1' button.
   Expected response:
   - The main display proxy displays 'COLUMN 1'.
6. The tester presses the 'A' button.
   Expected rsponse:
   - The 1A item dispenser proxy contains 9 items.
   - The item return proxy contains one $0.45 item.
   - The main display proxy displays 'THANK YOU' for 2 seconds.
   - The main display proxy displays 'HAVE A NICE DAY'.

Evaluate postconditions:
- Dispenser proxies:
  - Quarter dispenser proxy 1 contains 1 quarters.
  - Quarter dispenser proxy 2 contains 0 quarters.
  - Dime dispenser proxy 1 contains 5 dimes.
  - Dime dispenser proxy 2 contains 3 dimes.
  - Nickel dispenser proxy 1 contains 3 nickels.
  - Nickel dispenser proxy 2 contains 0 nickels.
  - The 1A item dispenser proxy contains 9 items.
  - All other item dispenser proxies contains 10 items.
- Display proxies:
  - The main display proxy displays 'HAVE A NICE DAY'.
  - The 1A item display proxy displays '1A $0.45'.
  - The 2B item display proxy displays '2B $0.60'.
  - All other item display proxies display their column and location, but not their prices.
- Door switch proxy:
  - Locked.
- Money box proxies:
  - The bill box proxy contains $1.00.
  - The coin box proxy contains $0.00.
- Return proxies:
  - The coin return proxy contains 4 quarters.
  - The item return proxy contains one $0.45 item.

4.3.3.2.3 Test case 2-3 – Buy Item (Overpay, Select Row, Select Column)

Purpose: Discover any bugs preventing a customer from buying an item by overpaying, then selecting the row, and finally selecting the column.

Use cases tested:
- Customer Inserts a Valid Bill – Primary Path: An Item is not Presently Selected

- Attempt to Dispense – Primary Path: Item Not Paid For
- Customer Selects the Row of an Item – Primary Path: Customer Selects the Row without Selecting an Item
- Customer Selects the Column of an Item – Primary Path: Customer Selects an Item by Selecting the Column
- Attempt to Dispense – Primary Path: Item Paid For
- Display Greeting – Primary Path: Customer's Credit Dispensed Without a Problem

Establish preconditions:
- Dispenser proxies:
  - Quarter dispenser proxy 1 contains 1 quarter.
  - Quarter dispenser proxy 2 contains 0 quarters.
  - Dime dispenser proxy 1 contains 5 dimes.
  - Dime dispenser proxy 2 contains 3 dimes.
  - Nickel dispenser proxy 1 contains 3 nickels.
  - Nickel dispenser proxy 2 contains 0 nickels.
  - The 1A item dispenser proxy contains 9 items.
  - All other item dispenser proxies contains 10 items.
- Display proxies:
  - The main display proxy displays 'HAVE A NICE DAY'.
  - The 1A item display proxy displays '1A $0.45'.
  - The 2B item display proxy displays '2B $0.60'.
  - All other item display proxies display their column and location, but not their prices.
- Door switch proxy:
  - Locked.
- Money box proxies:
  - The bill box proxy contains $1.00.
  - The coin box proxy contains $0.00.
- Return proxies:
  - The coin return proxy contains 4 quarters.
  - The item return proxy contains one $0.45 item.

Execute test case:
1. The tester inserts a dollar bill.
   Expected response:
   - The bill box proxy contains $2.00.
   - The main display proxy displays 'CREDIT: $1.00'.
2. The tester presses the 'B' button.
   Expected response:
   - The main display proxy displays 'ROW B'.
3. The tester presses the '2' button.
   Expected response:
   - The 2B item dispenser proxy contains 9 items.
   - The item return proxy contains one $0.45 item and one $0.60 item.

- Quarter dispenser proxy 1 contains 0 quarters.
- Dime dispenser proxy 1 contains 4 dimes.
- Nickel dispenser proxy 1 contains 2 nickels.
- The coin return proxy contains 5 quarters, 1 dime and 1 nickel.
- The main display proxy displays 'THANK YOU' for 2 seconds.
- The main display proxy displays 'HAVE A NICE DAY'.

Evaluate postconditions:
- Dispenser proxies:
  - Quarter dispenser proxy 1 contains 0 quarters.
  - Quarter dispenser proxy 2 contains 0 quarters.
  - Dime dispenser proxy 1 contains 4 dimes.
  - Dime dispenser proxy 2 contains 3 dimes.
  - Nickel dispenser proxy 1 contains 2 nickels.
  - Nickel dispenser proxy 2 contains 0 nickels.
  - The 1A item dispenser proxy contains 9 items.
  - The 2B item dispenser proxy contains 9 items.
  - All other item dispenser proxies contain 10 items.
- Display proxies:
  - The main display proxy displays 'HAVE A NICE DAY'.
  - The 1A item display proxy displays '1A $0.45'.
  - The 2B item display proxy displays '2B $0.60'.
  - All other item display proxies display their column and location, but not their prices.
- Door switch proxy:
  - Locked.
- Money box proxies:
  - The bill box proxy contains $2.00.
  - The coin box proxy contains $0.00.
- Return proxies:
  - The coin return proxy contains 5 quarters, 1 dime and 1 nickel.
  - The item return proxy contains one $0.45 item and one $0.60 item.

4.3.3.2.4 Test case 2-4 – Buy Item (Select Column, Underpay, Select Column, Select Row, Overpay)

Purpose: Discover any bugs preventing a customer from changing his selection when buying an item or preventing the vending machine from warning the customer that exact change is required.

Use cases tested:
- Customer Selects the Column of an Item – Primary Path: Customer Selects the Column without Selecting an Item
- Attempt to Dispense – Primary Path: Item Not Paid For
- Customer Inserts a Valid Coin – Primary Path: An Item is not Presently Selected
- Customer Selects the Column of an Item – Alternative Path: Customer Reselects the Column

- Customer Selects the Row of an Item – Primary Path: Customer Selects an Item by Selecting the Row
- Customer Inserts a Valid Bill – Primary Path: An Item is Presently Selected
- Attempt to Dispense – Primary Path: Item Paid For
- Dispense Quarter   Alternative Path: Could Not Dispense All
- Dispense Dime – Primary Path: Dime Dispensed Without Problem
- Display Greeting – Alternative Path: Could Not Dispense a Kind of Coin

Establish preconditions:
- Dispenser proxies:
  - Quarter dispenser proxy 1 contains 0 quarters.
  - Quarter dispenser proxy 2 contains 0 quarters.
  - Dime dispenser proxy 1 contains 4 dimes.
  - Dime dispenser proxy 2 contains 3 dimes.
  - Nickel dispenser proxy 1 contains 2 nickels.
  - Nickel dispenser proxy 2 contains 0 nickels.
  - The 1A item dispenser proxy contains 9 items.
  - The 2B item dispenser proxy contains 9 items.
  - All other item dispenser proxies contain 10 items.
- Display proxies:
  - The main display proxy displays 'HAVE A NICE DAY'.
  - The 1A item display proxy displays '1A $0.45'.
  - The 2B item display proxy displays '2B $0.60'.
  - All other item display proxies display their column and location, but not their prices.
- Door switch proxy:
  - Locked.
- Money box proxies:
  - The bill box proxy contains $2.00.
  - The coin box proxy contains $0.00.
- Return proxies:
  - The coin return proxy contains 5 quarters, 1 dime and 1 nickel.
  - The item return proxy contains one $0.45 item and one $0.60 item.

Execute test case:
1. The tester presses the '2' button.
   Expected response:
   - The main display proxy displays 'COLUMN 2'.
2. The tester inserts a nickel.
   Expected response:
   - The nickel dispenser proxy 1 contains 3 nickels.
   - The main display proxy displays 'CREDIT: $0.05'.
3. The tester presses the '1' button.
   Expected response:
   - The main display proxy displays 'COLUMN 1'.

4. The tester presses the 'A' button.

   Expected response:
   - The main display proxy displays 'AMOUNT DUE: $0.40'.

5. The tester inserts a dollar bill.

   Expected response:
   - The bill box proxy contains $3.00.
   - The 1A item dispenser proxy contains 8 items.
   - The item return proxy contains two $0.45 items and one $0.60 item.
   - Dime dispenser proxy 1 contains 0 dimes
   - Dime dispenser proxy 2 contains 1 dime.
   - The coin return proxy contains 5 quarters, 7 dimes and 1 nickel.
   - The main display proxy displays 'THANK YOU' for 2 seconds.
   - The main display proxy displays 'EXACT CHANGE ONLY'.

Evaluate postconditions:
- Dispenser proxies:
  - Quarter dispenser proxy 1 contains 0 quarters.
  - Quarter dispenser proxy 2 contains 0 quarters.
  - Dime dispenser proxy 1 contains 0 dimes.
  - Dime dispenser proxy 2 contains 1 dimes.
  - Nickel dispenser proxy 1 contains 3 nickels.
  - Nickel dispenser proxy 2 contains 0 nickels.
  - The 1A item dispenser proxy contains 9 items.
  - The 2B item dispenser proxy contains 9 items.
  - All other item dispenser proxies contain 10 items.
- Display proxies:
  - The main display proxy displays 'EXACT CHANGE ONLY'.
  - The 1A item display proxy displays '1A $0.45'.
  - The 2B item display proxy displays '2B $0.60'.
  - All other item display proxies display their column and location, but not their prices.
- Door switch proxy:
  - Locked.
- Money box proxies:
  - The bill box proxy contains $3.00.
  - The coin box proxy contains $0.00.
- Return proxies:
  - The coin return proxy contains 5 quarters, 7 dimes and 1 nickel.
  - The item return proxy contains two $0.45 items and one $0.60 item.

4.3.3.2.5 Test case 2-5 – Buy Unpriced Item

Purpose: Discover any bugs preventing the vending machine from reacting properly when a customer attempts to buy an unpriced item whereby the customer selects the column and then the row.

Use cases tested:
- Customer Selects the Column of an Item – Primary Path: Customer Selects the Column without Selecting an Item
- Attempt to Dispense – Primary Path: Item Not Paid For
- Customer Selects the Row of an Item   Primary Path: Customer Selects an Item by Selecting the Row
- Attempt to Dispense – Alternative Path: Invalid Customer Selection

Establish preconditions:
- Dispenser proxies:
  - Quarter dispenser proxy 1 contains 0 quarters.
  - Quarter dispenser proxy 2 contains 0 quarters.
  - Dime dispenser proxy 1 contains 0 dimes.
  - Dime dispenser proxy 2 contains 1 dime.
  - Nickel dispenser proxy 1 contains 3 nickels.
  - Nickel dispenser proxy 2 contains 0 nickels.
  - The 1A item dispenser proxy contains 8 items.
  - The 2B item dispenser proxy contains 9 items.
  - All other item dispenser proxies contain 10 items.
- Display proxies:
  - The main display proxy displays 'EXACT CHANGE ONLY'.
  - The 1A item display proxy displays '1A $0.45'.
  - The 2B item display proxy displays '2B $0.60'.
  - All other item display proxies display their column and location, but not their prices.
- Door switch proxy:
  - Locked.
- Money box proxies:
  - The bill box proxy contains $3.00.
  - The coin box proxy contains $0.00.
- Return proxies:
  - The coin return proxy contains 5 quarters, 7 dimes and 1 nickel.
  - The item return proxy contains two $0.45 items and one $0.60 item.

Execute test case:
1. The tester presses the '1' button.
   Expected response:
   - The main display proxy displays 'COLUMN 1'.
2. The tester presses the 'B' button.
   Expected response:
   - The main display proxy displays 'INVALID SELECTION' for 5 seconds.
   - The main display proxy displays 'THANK YOU' for 2 seconds.
   - The main display proxy displays 'EXACT CHANGE ONLY'.

Evaluate postconditions:
- Dispenser proxies:
  - Quarter dispenser proxy 1 contains 0 quarters.
  - Quarter dispenser proxy 2 contains 0 quarters.

- Dime dispenser proxy 1 contains 0 dimes.
- Dime dispenser proxy 2 contains 1 dime.
- Nickel dispenser proxy 1 contains 3 nickels.
- Nickel dispenser proxy 2 contains 0 nickels.
- The 1A item dispenser proxy contains 8 items.
- The 2B item dispenser proxy contains 9 items.
- All other item dispenser proxies contain 10 items.
- Display proxies:
  - The main display proxy displays 'EXACT CHANGE ONLY'.
  - The 1A item display proxy displays '1A $0.45'.
  - The 2B item display proxy displays '2B $0.60'.
  - All other item display proxies display their column and location, but not their prices.
- Door switch proxy:
  - Locked.
- Money box proxies:
  - The bill box proxy contains $3.00.
  - The coin box proxy contains $0.00.
- Return proxies:
  - The coin return proxy contains 5 quarters, 7 dimes and 1 nickel.
  - The item return proxy contains two $0.45 items and one $0.60 item.

4.3.3.2.6 Test case 2-6 – Buy Item (Cannot Make Change)

Purpose: Discover any bug preventing the vending machine from reacting properly when a customer attempts to buy an item whereby the customer reselects the row and there are insufficient dimes and nickels to make change.

Use cases tested:
- Customer Selects the Row of the Item – Primary Path: Customer Selects the Row without Selecting an Item
- Attempt To Dispense – Primary Path: Item Not Paid For
- Customer Selects the Row of the Item – Alternative Path: Customer Reselects the Row
- Customer Selects the Column of the Item – Primary Path: Customer Selects an Item by Selecting the Column
- Customer Inserts a Valid Bill – Primary Path: An Item is Presently Selected
- Attempt To Dispense – Primary Path: Item Paid For
- Dispense Dimes – Alternative Path: Could Not Dispense All
- Dispense Nickels – Alternative Path: Could Not Dispense All
- Display Greeting – Alternative Path: Could Not Dispense All of the Customer's Credit

Establish preconditions:
- Dispenser proxies:
  - Quarter dispenser proxy 1 contains 0 quarters.
  - Quarter dispenser proxy 2 contains 0 quarters.
  - Dime dispenser proxy 1 contains 0 dimes.

- Dime dispenser proxy 2 contains 1 dime.
- Nickel dispenser proxy 1 contains 3 nickels.
- Nickel dispenser proxy 2 contains 0 nickels.
- The 1A item dispenser proxy contains 8 items.
- The 2B item dispenser proxy contains 9 items
- All other item dispenser proxies contain 10 items.
- Display proxies:
  - The main display proxy displays 'EXACT CHANGE ONLY'.
  - The 1A item display proxy displays '1A $0.45'.
  - The 2B item display proxy displays '2B $0.60'.
  - All other item display proxies display their column and location, but not their prices.
- Door switch proxy:
  - Locked.
- Money box proxies:
  - The bill box proxy contains $3.00.
  - The coin box proxy contains $0.00.
- Return proxies:
  - The coin return proxy contains 5 quarters, 7 dimes and 1 nickel.
  - The item return proxy contains two $0.45 items and one $0.60 item.

Execute test case:
1. The tester presses the 'B' button.
   Expected response:
   - The main display displays 'ROW B'.
2. The tester presses the 'A' button.
   Expected response:
   - The main display displays 'ROW A'.
3. The tester presses the '1' button.
   Expected response:
   - The main display displays 'AMOUNT DUE: $0.45'.
4. The tester inserts a dollar.
   Expected response:
   - The bill box contains $4.00.
   - The 1A item dispenser proxy contains 7 items.
   - The item return proxy contains three $0.45 items and one $0.60 item.
   - Dime dispenser proxy 2 contains 0 dimes.
   - Nickel dispenser proxy 1 contains 0 nickels.
   - The coin return proxy contains 5 quarters, 8 dimes and 4 nickels
   - The main display displays 'THANK YOU' for 2 seconds.
   - The main display displays 'COULD NOT REFUND ALL' for 2 seconds.
   - The main display displays 'CREDIT: $0.30'.

Evaluate postconditions:
- Dispenser proxies:
  - Quarter dispenser proxy 1 contains 0 quarters.
  - Quarter dispenser proxy 2 contains 0 quarters.

- Dime dispenser proxy 1 contains 0 dimes.
- Dime dispenser proxy 2 contains 0 dimes.
- Nickel dispenser proxy 1 contains 0 nickels.
- Nickel dispenser proxy 2 contains 0 nickels.
- The 1A item dispenser proxy contains 7 items.
- The 2B item dispenser proxy contains 9 items.
- All other item dispenser proxies contain 10 items.
- Display proxies:
  - The main display proxy displays 'CREDIT: $0.30'.
  - The 1A item display proxy displays '1A $0.45'.
  - The 2B item display proxy displays '2B $0.60'.
  - All other item display proxies display their column and location, but not their prices.
- Door switch proxy:
  - Locked.
- Money box proxies:
  - The bill box proxy contains $4.00.
  - The coin box proxy contains $0.00.
- Return proxies:
  - The coin return proxy contains 5 quarters, 8 dimes and 4 nickels.
  - The item return proxy contains three $0.45 items and one $0.60 item.

4.3.3.2.7 Test case 2-7 – Buy Item (Credit is Available)

Purpose: Discover any bug preventing the vending machine from reacting properly when a customer attempts to buy an item whereby credit is available.

Use cases tested:
- Customer Selects the Row of an Item – Primary Path: Customer Selects the Row without Selecting an Item
- Attempt To Dispense – Primary Path: Item Not Paid For
- Customer Selects the Column of an Item – Primary Path: Customer Selects an Item by Selecting the Column
- Customer Inserts a Valid Coin – Primary Path: An Item is Presently Selected
- Attempt To Dispense – Primary Path: Item is Paid For
- Display Greeting – Alternative Path: Could Not Dispense a Kind of Coin

Establish preconditions:
- Dispenser proxies:
  - Quarter dispenser proxy 1 contains 0 quarters.
  - Quarter dispenser proxy 2 contains 0 quarters.
  - Dime dispenser proxy 1 contains 0 dimes.
  - Dime dispenser proxy 2 contains 0 dimes.
  - Nickel dispenser proxy 1 contains 0 nickels.
  - Nickel dispenser proxy 2 contains 0 nickels.

- The 1A item dispenser proxy contains 7 items.
- The 2B item dispenser proxy contains 9 items.
- All other item dispenser proxies contain 10 items.
- Display proxies:
  - The main display proxy displays 'CREDIT: $0.30'.
  - The 1A item display proxy displays '1A $0.45'.
  - The 2B item display proxy displays '2B $0.60'.
  - All other item display proxies display their column and location, but not their prices.
- Door switch proxy:
  - Locked.
- Money box proxies:
  - The bill box proxy contains $4.00.
  - The coin box proxy contains $0.00.
- Return proxies:
  - The coin return proxy contains 5 quarters, 8 dimes and 4 nickels.
  - The item return proxy contains three $0.45 items and one $0.60 item.

Execute test case:
1. The tester presses the 'B' button.
   Expected response:
   - The main display displays 'ROW B'.
2. The tester presses the '2' button.
   Expected response:
   - The main display proxy displays 'AMOUNT DUE: $0.30'.
3. The tester inserts a quarter.
   Expected response:
   - Quarter dispenser proxy 1 contains 1 quarter.
   - The main display proxy displays 'AMOUNT DUE: $0.05'.
4. The tester inserts a nickel.
   Expected response:
   - Nickel dispenser proxy 1 contains 1 nickel.
   - The 2B item dispenser proxy contains 8 items.
   - The item return proxy contains three $0.45 items and two $0.60 items.
   - The main display proxy displays 'THANK YOU' for 2 seconds.
   - The main display proxy displays 'EXACT CHANGE ONLY'.
     // The dime dispenser proxy is empty.

Evaluate postconditions:
- Dispenser proxies:
  - Quarter dispenser proxy 1 contains 1 quarter.
  - Quarter dispenser proxy 2 contains 0 quarters.
  - Dime dispenser proxy 1 contains 0 dimes.
  - Dime dispenser proxy 2 contains 0 dimes.
  - Nickel dispenser proxy 1 contains 1 nickel.
  - Nickel dispenser proxy 2 contains 0 nickels.
  - The 1A item dispenser proxy contains 7 items.

- The 2B item dispenser proxy contains 8 items.
- All other item dispenser proxies contain 10 items.
- Display proxies:
  - The main display proxy displays 'EXACT CHANGE ONLY'.
  - The 1A item display proxy displays '1A $0.45'.
  - The 2B item display proxy displays '2B $0.60'.
  - All other item display proxies display their column and location, but not their prices.
- Door switch proxy:
  - Locked.
- Money box proxies:
  - The bill box proxy contains $4.00.
  - The coin box proxy contains $0.00.
- Return proxies:
  - The coin return proxy contains 5 quarters, 8 dimes and 4 nickels.
  - The item return proxy contains three $0.45 items and two $0.60 items.

4.3.3.3 Test script 3 – Service the Vending Machine

This test script is intended to discover bugs preventing the service representative from servicing the vending machine.

4.3.3.3.1 Test case 3-1 – Display Total Items Sold (Items Sold)

Purpose: Discover any bugs preventing the service representative from displaying the total number of items sold, when the number is positive.

Use cases tested:
- Service Representative Presses the Mode Button – Primary Path: Change from 'Dispense Item' Mode.
- Service Representative Presses the Mode Button – Primary Path: Change from 'Set Price' Mode.
- Service Representative Displays History – Primary Path: Display Total Items Sold

Establish preconditions:
- Dispenser proxies:
  - Quarter dispenser proxy 1 contains 1 quarter.
  - Quarter dispenser proxy 2 contains 0 quarters.
  - Dime dispenser proxy 1 contains 0 dimes.
  - Dime dispenser proxy 2 contains 0 dimes.
  - Nickel dispenser proxy 1 contains 1 nickel.
  - Nickel dispenser proxy 2 contains 0 nickels.
  - The 1A item dispenser proxy contains 7 items.
  - The 2B item dispenser proxy contains 8 items.
  - All other item dispenser proxies contain 10 items.
- Display proxies:
  - The main display proxy displays 'EXACT CHANGE ONLY'.
  - The 1A item display proxy displays '1A $0.45'.
  - The 2B item display proxy displays '2B $0.60'.

– All other item display proxies display their column and location, but not their prices.
- Door switch proxy:
  – Locked.
- Money box proxies:
  – The bill box proxy contains $4.00.
  – The coin box proxy contains $0.00.
- Return proxies:
  – The coin return proxy contains 5 quarters, 8 dimes and 4 nickels.
  – The item return proxy contains three $0.45 items and two $0.60 items.

Execute test case:
1. The tester unlocks and opens the door.
   Expected response:
   - Nothing happens.
2. The tester presses the mode button.
   Expected response:
   - The main display proxy displays 'THANK YOU' for 2 seconds.
   - The main display proxy displays 'SET PRICE'.
3. The tester presses the mode button.
   Expected response:
   - The main display proxy displays 'DISPLAY HISTORY'.
4. The tester presses the 'A' button.
   Expected response:
   - The main display proxy displays 'TOTAL ITEMS: 5'.

Evaluate postconditions:
- Dispenser proxies:
  – Quarter dispenser proxy 1 contains 1 quarter.
  – Quarter dispenser proxy 2 contains 0 quarters.
  – Dime dispenser proxy 1 contains 0 dimes.
  – Dime dispenser proxy 2 contains 0 dimes.
  – Nickel dispenser proxy 1 contains 1 nickel.
  – Nickel dispenser proxy 2 contains 0 nickels.
  – The 1A item dispenser proxy contains 7 items.
  – The 2B item dispenser proxy contains 8 items.
  – All other item dispenser proxies contain 10 items.
- Display proxies:
  – The main display proxy displays 'TOTAL ITEMS: 5'.
  – The 1A item display proxy displays '1A $0.45'.
  – The 2B item display proxy displays '2B $0.60'.
  – All other item display proxies display their column and location, but not their prices.
- Door switch proxy:
  – Unlocked.
- Money box proxies:

- The bill box proxy contains $4.00.
- The coin box proxy contains $0.00.
- Return proxies:
  - The coin return proxy contains 5 quarters, 8 dimes and 4 nickels.
  - The item return proxy contains three $0.45 items and two $0.60 items.

4.3.3.3.2 Test case 3-2 – Display Total Income (Income Exists)

Purpose: Discover any bugs preventing the service representative from displaying the total income of the vending machine, when items have been sold.

Use cases tested:
- Service Representative Displays History – Primary Path: Display Total Income

Establish preconditions:
- Dispenser proxies:
  - Quarter dispenser proxy 1 contains 1 quarter.
  - Quarter dispenser proxy 2 contains 0 quarters.
  - Dime dispenser proxy 1 contains 0 dimes.
  - Dime dispenser proxy 2 contains 0 dimes.
  - Nickel dispenser proxy 1 contains 1 nickel.
  - Nickel dispenser proxy 2 contains 0 nickels.
  - The 1A item dispenser proxy contains 7 items.
  - The 2B item dispenser proxy contains 8 items.
  - All other item dispenser proxies contain 10 items.
- Display proxies:
  - The main display proxy displays 'TOTAL ITEMS: 5'.
  - The 1A item display proxy displays '1A $0.45'.
  - The 2B item display proxy displays '2B $0.60'.
  - All other item display proxies display their column and location, but not their prices.
- Door switch proxy:
  - Unlocked.
- Money box proxies:
  - The bill box proxy contains $4.00.
  - The coin box proxy contains $0.00.
- Return proxies:
  - The coin return proxy contains 5 quarters, 8 dimes and 4 nickels.
  - The item return proxy contains three $0.45 items and two $0.60 items.

Execute test case:
1. The tester presses the 'B' button.
   Expected response:
   - The main display proxy displays 'TOTAL INCOME: $2.55'.

Evaluate postconditions:

- Dispenser proxies:
  - Quarter dispenser proxy 1 contains 1 quarter.

- Quarter dispenser proxy 2 contains 0 quarters.
- Dime dispenser proxy 1 contains 0 dimes.
- Dime dispenser proxy 2 contains 0 dimes.
- Nickel dispenser proxy 1 contains 1 nickel.
- Nickel dispenser proxy 2 contains 0 nickels.
- The 1A item dispenser proxy contains 7 items.
- The 2B item dispenser proxy contains 8 items.
- All other item dispenser proxies contain 10 items.
- Display proxies:
  - The main display proxy displays 'TOTAL INCOME: $2.55'.
  - The 1A item display proxy displays '1A $0.45'.
  - The 2B item display proxy displays '2B $0.60'.
  - All other item display proxies display their column and location, but not their prices.
- Door switch proxy:
  - Unlocked.
- Money box proxies:
  - The bill box proxy contains $4.00.
  - The coin box proxy contains $0.00.
- Return proxies:
  - The coin return proxy contains 5 quarters, 8 dimes and 4 nickels.
  - The item return proxy contains three $0.45 items and two $0.60 items.

4.3.3.3.3 Test case 3-3 – Service Representative Displays History (Inappropriate Buttons)

Purpose: Discover any bugs preventing the vending machine from ignoring inappropriate buttons when in the 'Display History' mode.

Use cases tested:
- Service Representative Displays History – Alternative Path: Ignore Inappropriate Buttons

Establish preconditions:
- Dispenser proxies:
  - Quarter dispenser proxy 1 contains 1 quarter.
  - Quarter dispenser proxy 2 contains 0 quarters.
  - Dime dispenser proxy 1 contains 0 dimes.
  - Dime dispenser proxy 2 contains 0 dimes.
  - Nickel dispenser proxy 1 contains 1 nickel.
  - Nickel dispenser proxy 2 contains 0 nickels.
  - The 1A item dispenser proxy contains 7 items.
  - The 2B item dispenser proxy contains 8 items.
  - All other item dispenser proxies contain 10 items.
- Display proxies:
  - The main display proxy displays 'TOTAL INCOME: $2.55'.
  - The 1A item display proxy displays '1A $0.45'.
  - The 2B item display proxy displays '2B $0.60'.

- All other item display proxies display their column and location, but not their prices.
- Door switch proxy:
  - Unlocked.
- Money box proxies:
  - The bill box proxy contains $4.00.
  - The coin box proxy contains $0.00.
- Return proxies:
  - The coin return proxy contains 5 quarters, 8 dimes and 4 nickels.
  - The item return proxy contains three $0.45 items and two $0.60 items.

Execute test case:

1. The tester presses the 'C' button.
   Expected response:
   - Nothing happens.
2. The tester presses the '1' button.
   Expected response:
   - Nothing happens.
3. The tester presses the refund button.
   Expected response:
   - Nothing happens.

Evaluate postconditions:

- Dispenser proxies:
  - Quarter dispenser proxy 1 contains 1 quarter.
  - Quarter dispenser proxy 2 contains 0 quarters.
  - Dime dispenser proxy 1 contains 0 dimes.
  - Dime dispenser proxy 2 contains 0 dimes.
  - Nickel dispenser proxy 1 contains 1 nickel.
  - Nickel dispenser proxy 2 contains 0 nickels.
  - The 1A item dispenser proxy contains 7 items.
  - The 2B item dispenser proxy contains 8 items.
  - All other item dispenser proxies contain 10 items.
- Display proxies:
  - The main display proxy displays 'TOTAL INCOME: $2.55'.
  - The 1A item display proxy displays '1A $0.45'.
  - The 2B item display proxy displays '2B $0.60'.
  - All other item display proxies display their column and location, but not their prices.
- Door switch proxy:
  - Unlocked.
- Money box proxies:
  - The bill box proxy contains $4.00.
  - The coin box proxy contains $0.00.
- Return proxies:
  - The coin return proxy contains 5 quarters, 8 dimes and 4 nickels.
  - The item return proxy contains three $0.45 items and two $0.60 items.

4.3.3.3.4 Test case 3-4 – Service Representative Displays History (Unexpected Money)

Purpose: Discover any bugs preventing the vending machine from properly handling unexpected money that is validated when the vending machine is in the 'Display History' mode.

Use cases tested:
- Service Representative Displays History – Alternative Path: Handle Unexpected Money
- Attempt To Dispense – Primary Path: Item Not Paid For

Establish preconditions:
- Dispenser proxies:
  - Quarter dispenser proxy 1 contains 1 quarter.
  - Quarter dispenser proxy 2 contains 0 quarters.
  - Dime dispenser proxy 1 contains 0 dimes.
  - Dime dispenser proxy 2 contains 0 dimes.
  - Nickel dispenser proxy 1 contains 1 nickel.
  - Nickel dispenser proxy 2 contains 0 nickels.
  - The 1A item dispenser proxy contains 7 items.
  - The 2B item dispenser proxy contains 8 items.
  - All other item dispenser proxies contain 10 items.
- Display proxies:
  - The main display proxy displays 'TOTAL INCOME: $2.55'.
  - The 1A item display proxy displays '1A $0.45'.
  - The 2B item display proxy displays '2B $0.60'.
  - All other item display proxies display their column and location, but not their prices.
- Door switch proxy:
  - Unlocked.
- Money box proxies:
  - The bill box proxy contains $4.00.
  - The coin box proxy contains $0.00.
- Return proxies:
  - The coin return proxy contains 5 quarters, 8 dimes and 4 nickels.
  - The item return proxy contains three $0.45 items and two $0.60 items.

Execute test case:
1. The tester inserts a dollar bill.
   Expected response:
   - The bill box proxy contains $5.00.
   - The main display proxy displays 'DISPENSE ITEM' for 2 seconds.
   - The main display proxy displays 'CREDIT: $1.00'.

Evaluate postconditions:
- Dispenser proxies:
  - Quarter dispenser proxy 1 contains 1 quarter.
  - Quarter dispenser proxy 2 contains 0 quarters.

- Dime dispenser proxy 1 contains 0 dimes.
- Dime dispenser proxy 2 contains 0 dimes.
- Nickel dispenser proxy 1 contains 1 nickel.
- Nickel dispenser proxy 2 contains 0 nickels.
- The 1A item dispenser proxy contains 7 items.
- The 2B item dispenser proxy contains 8 items.
- All other item dispenser proxies contain 10 items.
- Display proxies:
  - The main display proxy displays 'CREDIT: $1.00'.
  - The 1A item display proxy displays '1A $0.45'.
  - The 2B item display proxy displays '2B $0.60'.
  - All other item display proxies display their column and location, but not their prices.
- Door switch proxy:
  - Unlocked.
- Money box proxies:
  - The bill box proxy contains $5.00.
  - The coin box proxy contains $0.00.
- Return proxies:
  - The coin return proxy contains 5 quarters, 8 dimes and 4 nickels.
  - The item return proxy contains three $0.45 items and two $0.60 items.

4.3.3.3.5 Test case 3-5 – Transition from Dispense Item Mode via Mode Button (Could Not Dispense All)

Purpose: Discover any bugs preventing the vending machine from displaying the correct message when it transitions from 'Dispense Item' mode via the mode button.

Use cases tested:
- Service Representative Presses the Mode Button – Alternative Path 4: Could Not Dispense All

Establish preconditions:
- Dispenser proxies:
  - Quarter dispenser proxy 1 contains 1 quarter.
  - Quarter dispenser proxy 2 contains 0 quarters.
  - Dime dispenser proxy 1 contains 0 dimes.
  - Dime dispenser proxy 2 contains 0 dimes.
  - Nickel dispenser proxy 1 contains 1 nickel.
  - Nickel dispenser proxy 2 contains 0 nickels.
  - The 1A item dispenser proxy contains 7 items.
  - The 2B item dispenser proxy contains 8 items.
  - All other item dispenser proxies contain 10 items.
- Display proxies:
  - The main display proxy displays 'CREDIT: $1.00'.
  - The 1A item display proxy displays '1A $0.45'.
  - The 2B item display proxy displays '2B $0.60'.

- All other item display proxies display their column and location, but not their prices.
- Door switch proxy:
  - Unlocked.
- Money box proxies:
  - The bill box proxy contains $5.00.
  - The coin box proxy contains $0.00.
  - Return proxies:
  - The coin return proxy contains 5 quarters, 8 dimes and 4 nickels.
  - The item return proxy contains three $0.45 items and two $0.60 items.

Execute test case:

1. The tester presses the mode button.

   Expected response:
   - Quarter dispenser proxy 1 contains 0 quarters.
   - Nickel dispenser proxy 1 contains 0 nickels.
   - The coin return proxy contains 6 quarters, 8 dimes and 5 nickels.
   - The main display proxy displays 'THANK YOU' for 2 seconds.
   - The main display proxy displays 'COULD NOT REFUND ALL' for 2 seconds
   - The main display proxy displays 'CREDIT: $0.70'.

Evaluate postconditions:

- Dispenser proxies:
  - Quarter dispenser proxy 1 contains 0 quarters.
  - Quarter dispenser proxy 2 contains 0 quarters.
  - Dime dispenser proxy 1 contains 0 dimes.
  - Dime dispenser proxy 2 contains 0 dimes.
  - Nickel dispenser proxy 1 contains 0 nickels.
  - Nickel dispenser proxy 2 contains 0 nickels.
  - The 1A item dispenser proxy contains 7 items.
  - The 2B item dispenser proxy contains 8 items.
  - All other item dispenser proxies contain 10 items.
- Display proxies:
  - The main display proxy displays 'CREDIT: $0.70'.
  - The 1A item display proxy displays '1A $0.45'.
  - The 2B item display proxy displays '2B $0.60'.
  - All other item display proxies display their column and location, but not their prices.
- Door switch proxy:
  - Unlocked.
- Money box proxies:
  - The bill box proxy contains $5.00.
  - The coin box proxy contains $0.00.
- Return proxies:
  - The coin return proxy contains 6 quarters, 8 dimes and 5 nickels.
  - The item return proxy contains three $0.45 items and two $0.60 items.

4.3.3.3.6 Test case 3-6 – Transition from Display History Mode via Door Switch

Purpose: Discover any bugs preventing the service representative from transitioning the vending machine from the 'Display History' mode by closing and locking the door.

Use cases tested:
- Service Representative Presses the Mode Button – Primary Path: Change from 'Dispense Item' Mode
- Service Representative Presses the Mode Button – Primary Path: Change from 'Set Price' Mode
- Door Switch Resets the Mode – Primary Path: Change from 'Display History' Mode
- Display Greeting – Alternative Path: Could Not Dispense a Kind of Coin

Establish preconditions:
- Dispenser proxies:
  - Quarter dispenser proxy 1 contains 0 quarters.
  - Quarter dispenser proxy 2 contains 0 quarters.
  - Dime dispenser proxy 1 contains 0 dimes.
  - Dime dispenser proxy 2 contains 0 dimes.
  - Nickel dispenser proxy 1 contains 0 nickels.
  - Nickel dispenser proxy 2 contains 0 nickels.
  - The 1A item dispenser proxy contains 7 items.
  - The 2B item dispenser proxy contains 8 items.
  - All other item dispenser proxies contain 10 items.
- Display proxies:
  - The main display proxy displays 'CREDIT: $0.70'.
  - The 1A item display proxy displays '1A $0.45'.
  - The 2B item display proxy displays '2B $0.60'.
  - All other item display proxies display their column and location, but not their prices.
- Door switch proxy:
  - unlocked.
- Money box proxies:
  - The bill box proxy contains $5.00.
  - The coin box proxy contains $0.00.
- Return proxies:
  - The coin return proxy contains 6 quarters, 8 dimes and 5 nickels.
  - The item return proxy contains three $0.45 items and two $0.60 items.

Execute test case:
1. The tester presses the '2' button.
   Expected Response:
   - The main display displays 'COLUMN 2'.
2. The tester presses the 'B' button.
   Expected Response:
   - The 2B item dispenser proxy contains 7 items.

- The item return proxy contains three $0.45 items and three $0.60 items.
- The main display displays 'THANK YOU' for 2 seconds.
- The main display displays 'COULD NOT REFUND ALL' for 2 seconds.
- The main display displays 'CREDIT: $0.10'.

3. The tester presses the 'A' button.

   Expected Response:
   - The main display displays 'ROW A'.

4. The tester presses the '1' button.

   Expected Response:
   - The main display displays 'AMOUNT DUE: $0.35'.

5. The tester inserts a quarter.

   Expected Response:
   - Quarter dispenser proxy 1 contains 1 quarter.
   - The main display displays 'AMOUNT DUE: $0.10'.

6. The tester inserts a dime.

   Expected Response:
   - Dime dispenser proxy 1 contains 1 dime.
   - The 1A item dispenser proxy contains 6 items.
   - The item return proxy contains four $0.45 items and three $0.60 items.
   - The main display displays 'THANK YOU' for 2 seconds.
   - The main display proxy displays 'EXACT CHANGE ONLY'.

7. The tester opens and unlocks the door.

   Expected Response:
   - The door switch proxy is unlocked.

8. The tester presses the mode button.

   Expected Response:
   - The main display proxy displays 'SET PRICE'.

9. The tester presses the mode button.

   Expected Response:
   - The main display proxy displays 'DISPLAY HISTORY'.

10. The tester closes and locks the door.

    Expected Response:
    - The door switch proxy is locked.
    - The main display proxy displays 'DISPENSE ITEM' for 2 seconds.
    - The main display proxy displays 'THANK YOU' for 2 seconds.
    - The main display proxy displays 'HAVE A NICE DAY'. (The software assumes that the coin dispenser assembly was loaded before the door was closed and locked.)

Evaluate postconditions:
- Dispenser proxies:
  - Quarter dispenser proxy 1 contains 1 quarter.
  - Quarter dispenser proxy 2 contains 0 quarters.
  - Dime dispenser proxy 1 contains 1 dime.
  - Dime dispenser proxy 2 contains 0 dimes.
  - Nickel dispenser proxy 1 contains 0 nickels.

- Nickel dispenser proxy 2 contains 0 nickels.
- The 1A item dispenser proxy contains 6 items.
- The 2B item dispenser proxy contains 7 items.
- All other item dispenser proxies contain 10 items.
- Display proxies:
  - The main display proxy displays 'HAVE A NICE DAY'.
  - The 1A item display proxy displays '1A $0.45'.
  - The 2B item display proxy displays '2B $0.60'.
  - All other item display proxies display their column and location, but not their prices.
- Door switch proxy:
  - Locked.
- Money box proxies:
  - The bill box proxy contains $5.00.
  - The coin box proxy contains $0.00.
- Return proxies:
  - The coin return proxy contains 6 quarters, 8 dimes and 5 nickels.
  - The item return proxy contains four $0.45 items and three $0.60 items.

4.3.3.3.7 Test case 3-7 – Service Representative Makes a Selection (Refund Button)

Purpose: Discover any bugs preventing vending machine from ignoring the refund button when the service representative is making a selection.

Use cases tested:
- Service Representative Presses the Mode Button – Primary Path: Change from 'Dispense Item' Mode
- Service Representative Makes a Selection – Alternative Path: Press the Refund Button

Establish preconditions:
- Dispenser proxies:
  - Quarter dispenser proxy 1 contains 1 quarter.
  - Quarter dispenser proxy 2 contains 0 quarters.
  - Dime dispenser proxy 1 contains 1 dime.
  - Dime dispenser proxy 2 contains 0 dimes.
  - Nickel dispenser proxy 1 contains 0 nickels.
  - Nickel dispenser proxy 2 contains 0 nickels.
  - The 1A item dispenser proxy contains 6 items.
  - The 2B item dispenser proxy contains 7 items.
  - All other item dispenser proxies contain 10 items.
- Display proxies:
  - The main display proxy displays 'HAVE A NICE DAY'.
  - The 1A item display proxy displays '1A $0.45'.
  - The 2B item display proxy displays '2B $0.60'.

– All other item display proxies display their column and location, but not their prices.
• Door switch proxy:
   – Locked.
• Money box proxies:
   – The bill box proxy contains $5.00.
   – The coin box proxy contains $0.00.
• Return proxies:
   – The coin return proxy contains 6 quarters, 8 dimes and 5 nickels.
   – The item return proxy contains four $0.45 items and three $0.60 items.

Execute test case:
1. The tester opens and unlocks the door.
    Expected response:
    • The door switch proxy is unlocked.
2. The tester presses the mode button.
    Expected response:
    • The main display proxy displays 'SET PRICE'.
3. The tester presses the refund button.
    Expected response:
    • Nothing happens.

Evaluate postconditions:
• Dispenser proxies:
   – Quarter dispenser proxy 1 contains 1 quarter.
   – Quarter dispenser proxy 2 contains 0 quarters.
   – Dime dispenser proxy 1 contains 1 dime.
   – Dime dispenser proxy 2 contains 0 dimes.
   – Nickel dispenser proxy 1 contains 0 nickels.
   – Nickel dispenser proxy 2 contains 0 nickels.
   – The 1A item dispenser proxy contains 6 items.
   – The 2B item dispenser proxy contains 7 items.
   – All other item dispenser proxies contain 10 items.
• Display proxies:
   – The main display proxy displays 'SET PRICE'.
   – The 1A item display proxy displays '1A $0.45'.
   – The 2B item display proxy displays '2B $0.60'.
   – All other item display proxies display their column and location, but not their prices.
• Door switch proxy:
   – Locked.
• Money box proxies:
   – The bill box proxy contains $5.00.
   – The coin box proxy contains $0.00.
• Return proxies:
   – The coin return proxy contains 6 quarters, 8 dimes and 5 nickels.
   – The item return proxy contains four $0.45 items and three $0.60 items.

4.3.3.3.8 Test case 3-8 – Service Representative Makes a Selection (Unexpected Money)

Purpose: Discover any bugs preventing vending machine from properly handling unexpected money that is validated when the service representative is making a selection.

Use cases tested:
- Service Representative Selects a Column – Primary Path: Service Representative Selects the Column without Selecting an Item
- Service Representative Makes a Selection – Alternative Path: Handle Unexpected Money
- Attempt To Dispense – Item Not Paid For

Establish preconditions:
- Dispenser proxies:
  - Quarter dispenser proxy 1 contains 1 quarter.
  - Quarter dispenser proxy 2 contains 0 quarters.
  - Dime dispenser proxy 1 contains 1 dime.
  - Dime dispenser proxy 2 contains 0 dimes.
  - Nickel dispenser proxy 1 contains 0 nickels.
  - Nickel dispenser proxy 2 contains 0 nickels.
  - The 1A item dispenser proxy contains 6 items.
  - The 2B item dispenser proxy contains 7 items.
  - All other item dispenser proxies contain 10 items.
- Display proxies:
  - The main display proxy displays 'SET PRICE'.
  - The 1A item display proxy displays '1A $0.45'.
  - The 2B item display proxy displays '2B $0.60'.
  - All other item display proxies display their column and location, but not their prices.
- Door switch proxy:
  - Locked.
- Money box proxies:
  - The bill box proxy contains $5.00.
  - The coin box proxy contains $0.00.
- Return proxies:
  - The coin return proxy contains 6 quarters, 8 dimes and 5 nickels.
  - The item return proxy contains four $0.45 items and three $0.60 items.

Execute test case:
1. The tester presses the '1' button.
   Expected response:
   - The main display proxy displays 'COLUMN 1'.
2. The tester inserts a dime.
   Expected response:
   - Dime dispenser proxy 1 contains 2 dimes.

- The main display proxy displays 'DISPENSE ITEM' for 2 seconds.
- The main display proxy displays 'CREDIT: $0.10'.

Evaluate postconditions:
- Dispenser proxies:
  - Quarter dispenser proxy 1 contains 1 quarter.
  - Quarter dispenser proxy 2 contains 0 quarters.
  - Dime dispenser proxy 1 contains 2 dimes.
  - Dime dispenser proxy 2 contains 0 dimes.
  - Nickel dispenser proxy 1 contains 0 nickels.
  - Nickel dispenser proxy 2 contains 0 nickels.
  - The 1A item dispenser proxy contains 6 items.
  - The 2B item dispenser proxy contains 7 items.
  - All other item dispenser proxies contain 10 items.
- Display proxies:
  - The main display proxy displays 'CREDIT: $0.10'.
  - The 1A item display proxy displays '1A $0.45'.
  - The 2B item display proxy displays '2B $0.60'.
  - All other item display proxies display their column and location, but not their prices.
- Door switch proxy:
  - Locked.
- Money box proxies:
  - The bill box proxy contains $5.00.
  - The coin box proxy contains $0.00.
- Return proxies:
  - The coin return proxy contains 6 quarters, 8 dimes and 5 nickels.
  - The item return proxy contains four $0.45 items and three $0.60 items.

4.3.3.3.9 Test case 3-9 – Service Representative Enters a Price (Unexpected Money)

Purpose: Discover any bugs preventing vending machine from properly handling unexpected money that is validated when the service representative is entering a price.

Use cases tested:
- Customer Requests a Refund
- Dispense Dimes – Primary Path: Dimes Dispensed without Problem
- Display Greeting – Alternative Path: Could Not Dispense a Kind of Coin
- Service Representative Presses the Mode Button – Primary Path: Change from 'Dispense Item' Mode
- Service Representative Selects a Column – Primary Path: Service Representative Selects the Column without Selecting an Item
- Service Representative Selects a Row – Primary Path: Service Representative Selects an Item by Selecting the Row

- Service Representative Enters a Price – Alternative Path: Handle Unexpected Money
- Attempt To Dispense – Primary Path: Item not Paid For

Establish preconditions:
- Dispenser proxies:
  - Quarter dispenser proxy 1 contains 1 quarter.
  - Quarter dispenser proxy 2 contains 0 quarters.
  - Dime dispenser proxy 1 contains 2 dimes.
  - Dime dispenser proxy 2 contains 0 dimes.
  - Nickel dispenser proxy 1 contains 0 nickels.
  - Nickel dispenser proxy 2 contains 0 nickels.
  - The 1A item dispenser proxy contains 6 items.
  - The 2B item dispenser proxy contains 7 items.
  - All other item dispenser proxies contain 10 items.
- Display proxies:
  - The main display proxy displays 'CREDIT: $0.10'.
  - The 1A item display proxy displays '1A $0.45'.
  - The 2B item display proxy displays '2B $0.60'.
  - All other item display proxies display their column and location, but not their prices.
- Door switch proxy:
  - Locked.
- Money box proxies:
  - The bill box proxy contains $5.00.
  - The coin box proxy contains $0.00.
- Return proxies:
  - The coin return proxy contains 6 quarters, 8 dimes and 5 nickels.
  - The item return proxy contains four $0.45 items and three $0.60 items.

Execute test case:
1. The tester presses the refund button.
   Expected response:
   - Dime dispenser proxy 1 contains 1 dime.
   - The coin return proxy contains 6 quarters, 9 dimes and 5 nickels.
   - The main display proxy displays 'THANK YOU' for 2 seconds.
   - The main display proxy displays 'HAVE A NICE DAY'.
2. The tester presses the mode button.
   Expected response:
   - The main display proxy displays 'SET PRICE'.
3. The tester presses the '1' button.
   Expected response:
   - The main display proxy displays 'COLUMN 1'.
4. The tester presses the 'B' button.
   Expected response:
   - The main display proxy displays 'COL 1 ROW B $0.00'.

5. The tester presses the '5' button.

   Expected response:
   - The main display proxy displays 'COL 1 ROW B $0.05'.
6. The tester inserts a quarter.

   Expected response:
   - The quarter dispenser proxy 1 contains 2 quarters.
   - The main display proxy displays 'DISPENSE ITEM' for 2 seconds.
   - The main display proxy displays 'CREDIT $0.25'.

Evaluate postconditions:

- Dispenser proxies:
  - Quarter dispenser proxy 1 contains 2 quarters.
  - Quarter dispenser proxy 2 contains 0 quarters.
  - Dime dispenser proxy 1 contains 1 dime.
  - Dime dispenser proxy 2 contains 0 dimes.
  - Nickel dispenser proxy 1 contains 0 nickels.
  - Nickel dispenser proxy 2 contains 0 nickels.
  - The 1A item dispenser proxy contains 6 items.
  - The 2B item dispenser proxy contains 7 items.
  - All other item dispenser proxies contain 10 items.
- Display proxies:
  - The main display proxy displays 'CREDIT: $0.25'.
  - The 1A item display proxy displays '1A $0.45'.
  - The 2B item display proxy displays '2B $0.60'.
  - All other item display proxies display their column and location, but not their prices.
- Door switch proxy:
  - Locked.
- Money box proxies:
  - The bill box proxy contains $5.00.
  - The coin box proxy contains $0.00.
- Return proxies:
  - The coin return proxy contains 6 quarters, 9 dimes and 5 nickels.
  - The item return proxy contains four $0.45 items and three $0.60 items.

4.3.3.4 Requirements trace from paths to acceptance test cases

4.3.3.4.1 Customer requirements trace

Table 4.1 Requirements trace from customer use case paths to acceptance test cases.

Customer use case	Use case path	Acceptance test case(s)
Customer Buys an Item	N/A	N/A
Customer Makes a Selection	N/A	N/A
Customer Selects the Column of an Item	PP1. Customer Selects the Column without Selecting an Item	2-2, 2-4, 2-5
	PP2. Customer Selects an Item by Selecting the Column	2-3, 2-6, 2-7, 3-6
	AP3. Customer Reselects the Column	2-4
Customer Selects the Row of an Item	PP1. Customer Selects the Row without Selecting an Item	2-3, 2-6, 2-7, 3-6
	PP2. Customer Selects an Item by Selecting the Row	2-2, 2-4
	AP3. Customer Reselects the Row	2-6
Customer Makes a Payment	N/A	N/A
Customer Inserts a Valid Bill	PP1. An Item is Presently Selected	2-4, 2-6
	PP2. An Item is Not Presently Selected	2-1
Customer Inserts a Valid Coin	PP1. An Item is Presently Selected	2-7, 3-6
	PP2. An Item is Not Presently Selected	2-2, 2-3, 2-4
Customer Requests a Refund	N/A	2-1, 3-10
Attempt To Dispense	PP1. Item Paid For	2-2, 2-3, 2-4, 2-6, 2-7, 3-6
	PP2. Item Not Paid For	2-1, 2-2, 2-3, 2-4, 2-5, 2-6, 2-7, 3-4, 3-6, 3-9, 3-10
	AP3. Invalid Customer Selection	2-5
Handle an Invalid Customer Selection	AP1. Invalid Selection	2-5
Dispense Change	N/A	N/A
Dispense Quarters	PP1. Quarters Dispensed Without Problem	2-1, 2-3
	AP2. Could Not Dispense All	2-4
Dispense Dimes	PP1. Dimes Dispensed Without Problem	2-3, 3-10
	AP2. Could Not Dispense All	2-6
Dispense Nickels	PP1. Nickels Dispensed Without Problem	2-3
	AP2. Could Not Dispense All	2-6
Display Greeting	PP1. Customer's Credit Dispensed Without a Problem	1-1, 1-10, 1-11, 2-1, 2-2, 2-3
	AP1. Could Not Dispense a Kind of Coin	2-4, 2-7, 3-6, 3-7
	AP2. Could Not Dispense All of the Customer's Credit	2-6

4.3.3.4.2 Service representative requirements trace

Table 4.2 Requirements trace from service representative use case paths to acceptance test cases

Service representative use case	Use case path	Acceptance test case(s)
Service Representative Services the MIVM	N/A	N/A
Initial State of the MIVM	PP1: Initial State of the MIVM	1-1
Service Representative Changes the Mode of the MIVM	N/A	N/A
Service Representative Presses the Mode Button	PP1. Change from 'Dispense Item' Mode	1-11, 1-12, 3-1, 3-7, 3-8, 3-10
	PP2. Change from 'Set Price' Mode	1-6, 3-1, 3-7
	PP3. Change from 'Display History' Mode	1-9
	AP4. Could Not Dispense All	3-5
Door Switch Resets the Mode	PP1. Change from 'Dispense Item' Mode	1-10, 3-6
	PP2. Change from 'Set Price' Mode	1-12
	PP3. Change from 'Display History' Mode	3-7
Service Representative Prices an Item	N/A	N/A
Service Representative Makes a Selection	AP1. Press the Refund Button	3-8
	AP2. Handle Unexpected Money	3-9
Service Representative Selects a Column	PP1. Service Representative Selects the Column without Selecting an Item	1-2, 1-4, 1-5, 3-9, 3-10
	PP2. Service Representative Selects an Item by Selecting the Column	1-3
Service Representative Selects a Row	PP1. Service Representative Selects the Row without Selecting an Item	1-3
	PP2. Service Representative Selects an Item by Selecting the Row	1-2, 1-4, 1-5, 3-10
Service Representative Enters a Price	PP1. Build and Enter the new Common Price	1-2
	AP2. Accept the old Common Price	1-5
	AP3. Build and Reject the new Common Price	1-3
	AP4. Build and Cancel the new Common Price	1-4
	AP5. Press an Inappropriate Button	1-2
	AP6. Handle Unexpected Money	3-10
Service Representative Displays History	PP1. Display Total Items Sold	1-7, 3-1
	PP2. Display Total Income	1-8, 3-2
	AP3. Ignore Inappropriate Buttons	3-3
	AP4. Handle Unexpected Money	3-4

Appendix A

Glossary

The following glossary has been largely adapted from the *OPEN Modeling Language (OML) Reference Manual:*[†]

abstract class   Any incomplete class that therefore cannot be used to instantiate semantically meaningful instances.
   Kinds: deferred class.
actor   Any external that models a role played by a human.
aggregate   Any modeling element that has other modeling elements of the same metatype as collaborating parts that form a structure.
   Example: a car engine consists of pistons, cylinders, spark plugs, etc. and these component parts have specific interpart relationships.
   Contrast with: container.
aggregate state   Any general state that has specialized substates.
aggregation   The specialized kind of referential relationship that captures the logical relationship that exists from an aggregate (whole) to its component parts.
   Comments: Because the aggregate is [partially] defined in terms of its component parts in the object paradigm, the parts are visible to the aggregate and the aggregate can therefore delegate some of its responsibilities to its parts (i.e. one can navigate from the aggregate to its parts). Aggregations provide an example of the practical use of abstraction. Initially, the modeler can work at a higher, blackbox level of abstraction, deferring consideration of the encapsulated, lower level parts until later.
   Kinds: bi-directional aggregation.
assertion   Any business rule that is a constraint on the property values of an object.
   Kinds: invariant, precondition, postcondition.
association   Any referential relationship that represents a general structural dependency relationship between kinds of things (e.g. class, type). A class or type of corresponding linkages between instances.
associative   The stereotype of an object, class, type, or role, the primary responsibilities of which is to associate or link two other model elements.
   Example: a marriage between two persons, a contract between a buyer and a seller.
asynchronous message   Any message involving two threads of control that do not synchronize during message passing.

[†] Firesmith D.G., Henderson-Sellers B. and Graham I. (1997). *OPEN Modeling Language (OML) Reference Manual.* SIGS Books/Cambridge University Press.

Comment: Neither the sender nor the receiver of the message is blocked by having to wait for the other.

atomic state   Any state that is not decomposed into substates.

attribute   Any descriptive property.

Comments: An attribute is usually hidden, but may be visible. An attribute provides the only reference to an internal hidden object, the life span of which matches that of the object of which it is an attribute. An attribute may reference only a single object.

bi-directional aggregation   The shorthand convention representing the rare case in which a unidirectional aggregation relationship and a semi-strong inverse association/linkage exists, allowing the part to know about and sends messages to the aggregate.

Comments: Bi-directional aggregation is used in the Mediator pattern. Note that bi-directional aggregation does not mean that the part contains the aggregate, but merely that there is a reason to model a semi-strong inverse relationship (i.e. is a part of) back to the aggregate.

bi-directional association   Any class or type of bi-directional linkages.

bi-directional linkage   The shorthand way of expressing the combination of two one-way linkages between peers, whereby each of the corresponding one-way links is the semi-strong inverse of the other and the corresponding operations in the peers ensure referential integrity.

binary unidirectional dependency relationship   Any relationship between two model elements that is directed in the direction of dependency from client to server (i.e. dependent).

Kinds: definitional relationship, invokes relationship, precedes relationship, referential relationship, transitional relationship, uses relationship.

blackbox sequence diagram   Any sequence diagram, the purpose of which is to document the sequence of interactions between externals and the blackbox system or software application involved in a single path of a use case.

Comment: A blackbox sequence diagram treats the application as a blackbox and is used to capture user-oriented requirements, verify the context diagram, and document an acceptance test case.

characteristic   Any resource or feature that characterizes something.

Kinds partitioned by parent: external characteristic, object characteristic, package characteristic, package class characteristic.

Kinds partitioned by level: class-level characteristic, instance-level characteristic.

Kinds partitioned by inheritance: deferred characteristic, effective characteristic, overridden characteristic.

class   Any definition of a single kind of instance. Optionally, a class can be used to instantiate instances that capture the same abstraction and have the same or similar characteristics. A class consists of an interface of one or more types that are implemented by one or more implementations. (Note that the terms type and class are not synonymous. A type is not an instance and does not provide an implementation. A class is an instance of a metaclass, contains one or more types, and does provide an implementation.)

Kinds partitioned by kind of instance: object class, object metaclass, package class, scenario class.

Kinds partitioned by instantiability: abstract class, concrete class.

classification   Any 'is a' definitional relationship(s) from an object (instance) to one of its classes, types or roles.

Kinds: conforms to, instance of, plays the role of.

class implementation   Any declaration of hidden characteristics that [partially] implements the associated class by implementing one or more of the types of a class.

Kinds: external class implementation, object class implementation, package implementation.

class-level characteristic   Any characteristic of a class as a whole rather than its instances.

Example: constructor operations (e.g. new in Smalltalk) are class-level operations.

class responsibility collaborator card (CRC)   A kind of index card used as a simple, manual upperCASE tool, the purpose of which is to document the responsibilities and associated collaborators for a class of objects, packages, or externals.

Kinds: object CRC card, package CRC card, role responsibility collaborator card.

client external   Any external that depends on the current application.

collaboration diagram   Any interaction diagram in the form of a graph, the purpose of which is to document the potential collaboration of a package of classes and objects in terms of the messages and exceptions they may send and raise.

Comments: If the associations, linkages, aggregation arcs and containment arcs on package diagrams are viewed as roads connecting the classes and objects, then the messages and exceptions on the collaboration diagrams can be viewed as the traffic on those roads. Collaboration diagrams typically have the same nodes and topology as the corresponding package diagrams, but the arcs are labeled with messages and exceptions rather than with static relationships. In many cases, especially in concurrent situations, the ordering of this message and exception 'traffic' is important. Thus, the arcs on collaboration diagrams can be optionally labeled with sequence numbers. (If the sequence of interactions is important, sequence diagrams are typically used instead of collaboration diagrams.)

Kinds: internal collaboration diagram, package collaboration diagram, scenario collaboration diagram.

collaborator   Any server on which the thing documented by the responsibility collaborator card depends in order to fulfill its associated responsibility.

common global data   Any application-internal data that is not stored as a property of some object.

common global operation   Any application-internal operation that is not stored as an operation of some object.

common global operations   Any logically or physically cohesive collection of common global operations.

concrete class Any complete class that therefore can be used to instantiate semantically meaningful instances.

concurrent object Any object that is *inherently* capable of running concurrently (i.e. simultaneously) with other objects because it contains, either directly or indirectly, one or more of its *own* threads of execution. (OML does not use the terms active and passive as synonyms for concurrent and sequential because concurrent objects (e.g. some objects containing tasks in Ada95) can be passive, only using their thread to protect themselves from corruption due to simultaneous access.)

Comment: An object may be concurrent because:

1. It directly has its own thread of execution (e.g. an object in the Actor language).
2. One or more of its attributes, parts, or entries are concurrent.
3. One or more of its operations are directly concurrent (i.e. have their own inherent thread of execution).

configuration diagram Any semantic net, the purpose of which is to document the configuration of an application, layer, or subdomain in terms of its component layers, subdomains and packages respectively, their visibility (i.e. encapsulation), and the dependency relationships among the component parts.

Comment: Aggregation is documented by nesting if the number of components is small and by using aggregation arcs if the number of components is large. Although this is typically one of the first diagrams to be started when using the OPEN method, it is also one of the last to be completed because of the iterative and incremental nature of the object-oriented development cycle. This diagram is used to communicate with domain experts, business analysts, customers, managers and architects.

Kinds: software configuration diagram, system configuration diagram.

conforms to The classification relationship from an instance to one of its types.

container Any modeling element that contains other modeling element of the same metatype that do not form a structure.

Example: a car trunk (boot) can contain many items and these items do not have relationships.

Kinds: heterogeneous container, homogeneous container.

containment The special form of referential relationship that captures the logical relationship that exists from container to its component entries.

Comment: Because the container holds its entries in the object paradigm, the entries are visible to the container.

context diagram Any specialized semantic net, the purpose of which is to document the context of a blackbox application, layer or subdomain in terms of its externals and the semantically meaningful relationships between them (e.g. associations, aggregation, inheritance).

Comment: A context diagram is typically one of the first diagrams developed using the OPEN method. This diagram is used to communicate with domain experts, business analysts, customers, managers and architects.

Kinds: software context diagram, system context diagram.

controller The stereotype of an object, class, type or role, the primary responsibilities of which involve the detailed controlling of its servers.

coordinator The stereotype of an object, class, type or role, the primary responsibilities of which involve the coordination of its collaborating servers.

deferred characteristic Any characteristic that has a current declaration but does not have a complete current implementation.

deferred class Any abstract class that declares the existence of one or more characteristics that must be implemented by its descendants prior to instantiation.

definitional relationship Any binary unidirectional dependency relationship that either defines one modeling element in terms of another modeling element of the same metatype or indicates that one modeling element conforms to or was instantiated from the definition of another modeling element of different metatype.

Kinds: classification, inheritance.

deployment diagram Any semantic net, the purpose of which is to document the structure of hardware on which an application runs and the [static] allocation of the software to the hardware.

direct external Any external that interacts directly with the current application.

discriminant Any value of a property of the parent class that is used to differentiate the members of a partition of child classes.

distribution unit Any package, the components of which are guaranteed to be allocated to a processor or process as a group.

Comments: Distribution units have the trait 'location'. Members of the same distribution unit communicate locally, whereas members of different distribution units may communicate remotely if distributed to different processors or processes.

drop-down box Any optional rectangular node attached to the bottom outside of its parent node, used to display a subset of the information stored about its parent node based on a selection of traits.

effective characteristic Any characteristic that has a current declaration and also has a complete current implementation.

entry Any property of a container that references an object contained by the container.

Comment: An entry is usually hidden, but may be visible. An object is typically an entry of only one container at a time. The life span of an entry is usually not that of its container, but could be. The entries of a container do not reference each other and the container (e.g. a car trunk) provides any organization.

exception Any abnormal interaction consisting of an object which models an exceptional or error condition that is raised by an operation in order to notify a client that the condition (e.g. an assertion has been violated) has occurred.

exceptional transition Any transition caused by an exception or exception handler.

external characteristic Any characteristic of an external (i.e. any property, operation or assertion).

external class Any class, the instances of which are externals.

external class implementation Any class implementation that [partially] implements an external class.

external object Any instance of an external class that uses its characteristics to model a single thing that is *external* to the current application and is important to document during modeling (e.g. because it interacts with the application or implies the existence of a corresponding object inside the application).
Kinds partitioned by degree removed: direct external, indirect external.
Kinds partitioned by kind of thing modeled: actor, hardware external, other external, persistent memory external, software external.
Kinds partitioned by direction of dependency: client external, peer external, server external.

generalization Any generalized node at the parent end of a specialization arc.

group transition Any transition to or from a superstate.

guard condition Any condition (either Boolean or of enumeration type) that must evaluate properly in order for the trigger to cause the corresponding transition to fire.

hardware external Any external that models a hardware device, either with or without significant processing power.

heterogeneous container Any container that contains entries of multiple types.

homogeneous container Any container that contains entries of a single type.

implementation inheritance The whitebox inheritance that is used for the purpose of reusing implementation. Polymorphic substitutability is not guaranteed.

indirect external Any external that interacts indirectly with the current application via other externals.

information holder The stereotype of an object, class, type, or role, the primary responsibilities of which is to store information.

inheritance The definitional relationship from a child to one of its parents, whereby the child is formed as a possibly extended and modified union of its parent(s).
Comment: Inheritance is a way of creating new definitions (e.g. subtype, subclass or derived class) in terms of one or more existing definitions (e.g. supertype, superclass or base class).
Kinds: implementation inheritance, interface inheritance, specialization.

inheritance diagram Any semantic net, the purpose of which is to document the static structure of all or part (e.g. branch) of an inheritance graph.

instance Any uniquely identified model of a single thing, whereby the model is defined by one or more classes and conforms to one or more types.
Kinds: linkage, object, package instance.

instance-level characteristic Any characteristic of an instance of a class rather than the class as a whole.
Example: initialization operations that set the values of the properties of an instantiated object are instance-level operations.

instance of   The classification relationship from an instance to one of its classes.

interaction   Any form of communication sent by one instance to another.
  Kinds: exception, message.

interaction diagram   Any diagram, the purpose of which is to document the interactions either among externals and the application or among objects and classes within [part of] the application. The nodes of an interaction diagram represent either things or their time lines, and the arcs of the graph represent the interactions between nodes.
  Kinds: collaboration diagram, sequence diagram.

interfacer   The stereotype of an object, class, type or role, the primary responsibilities of which involve the detailed controlling of its servers.

interface inheritance   The blackbox inheritance that implies only interface conformance (subtyping), but not specialization.

internal collaboration diagram   Any collaboration diagram, the purpose of which is to document the potential collaboration of operations within an individual class or object, in terms of control flow (i.e. message passing, exception raising) and object flow (the reading and writing of properties within the class or object).

internal non-OO database   Any application-internal non-object-oriented (e.g. relational, network, hierarchical) database, database table, file, etc.

invariant   Any assertion concerning a class that must hold both before and after the execution of all of its operations.

invokes relationship   The binary dependency relationship between two scenario classes whereby the server scenario class is invoked at a specific point in the execution of the client scenario class.

layer   Any large, horizontal package used as a strategic architectural unit of design.

layer diagram   Any semantic net, the purpose of which is to document the software architecture of an application or the software allocated to a processor.
  Comment: A layer diagram is typically one of the first diagrams developed using the OPEN method. This diagram is used to communicate with domain experts, business analysts, customers, managers, and architects.

leaving transition   Any transition that causes the object to leave its pre-transition state and transition to its post-transition state.

link   Any property that references an external object via a linkage relationship.
  Comments: Although the link is usually hidden, the object it references is not. Multiple links in multiple objects may reference the same object.

linkage   Any referential relationship that represents a general structural dependency relationship between individual things (e.g. object, external, package).
  Kinds: bi-directional linkage, observer linkage, TBD linkage, unidirectional linkage.

logical package   Any requirements analysis-level or logical design-level package.

logical property   Any property that implements a responsibility for knowing by representing a query that can be made of its object or class.

Comment: A logical property it typically implemented by an operation that returns a copy or reference to an object that results from either referencing one or more physical properties, calculating the returned value, or sending messages to servers.

logic box Any box used on sequence diagrams to represent the logic of the interactions.

Kinds: branch, concurrency, critical region, loop.

mechanism Any scenario class consisting of a mid-sized pattern of collaborating roles, the cooperative behavior of which provides a desired functional abstraction.

mechanism diagram Any scenario class diagram, the purpose of which is to document one or more mechanisms, any associated objects or classes, and the semantically important relationships between them.

message Any normal interaction sent from one object to another.

Kinds: asynchronous message, sequential message, synchronous message.

multiobject Any homogeneous collection of objects that are instances of the same class or type.

multiplicity The potential number of things. (Multiplicity is often confused with cardinality, which is defined as the current *actual* number of things.)

Kinds: multiplicity of an aggregate, association, class, container, multiobject, package, package instance.

multiplicity of an aggregate The potential number of the aggregate's component parts.

multiplicity of an association The potential number of objects that are involved at each end of the association.

multiplicity of a class The potential number of the class's instances.

multiplicity of a container The potential number of entries in the associated container.

multiplicity of a multiobject The potential number of objects in the associated collection.

multiplicity of a package The potential total number of package characteristics (e.g. object classes, types, packages) in the package.

multiplicity of a package instance The potential total number of package instance characteristics (e.g. objects, classes, package instances, roles) in the package instance.

normal transition Any transition caused by a message or operation.

notifier The stereotype of an object, class, type or role, the primary responsibilities of which involve the forwarding of messages to one or more servers.

Comment: A notifier may either pass on the notification without change or may translate the notification so that it makes sense to the server.

object Any uniquely identified abstraction that uses its *characteristics* to model a single thing that is important in the current application. In order to be a complete abstraction, an object captures all of the essential characteristics (i.e. *properties, behavior* and *rules*) of the thing being modeled while ignoring the thing's non-essential, diversionary details.

Kinds: concurrent object, external object, internal object, sequential object.

object characteristic   Any characteristic of an object (e.g. property, operation or assertion).

object class   Any object that is also a class, the instances of which are objects.
Kinds: external class, internal class.

object class implementation   Any class implementation that [partially] implements an object class.

object CRC card   Any CRC card, the purpose of which is to document the responsibilities of a class of objects.

object flow   The shorthand way of representing on a class-internal collaboration diagram the sending of read or write accessor messages (typically to self) referencing the associated property, thereby resulting in the flow of object represented by that property.
Comment: Analogous to the term 'data flow' on a traditional data flow diagram.

object interface   The externally visible characteristics of an object.

object implementation   The encapsulated hidden characteristics of an object.

object metaclass   Any class, the instances of which are object classes.

object operation   Any functional abstraction that models a discrete activity, action or behavior that is performed by an object, typically in response to a message. An operation consists of a *signature* (i.e. interface) and a *method* (i.e. implementation).

object type   Any type of object. An object conforms to an object type if and only if its interface is consistent with the type (i.e. the set of characteristics in the interface of the object is a superset of the set of characteristics declared by the type).

observer association   Any class or type of observer linkages.

observer linkage   The specialized kind of bi-directional linkage which captures a pattern related to the observer pattern from the patterns book by the Gang of Four (Gamma *et al.*, 1995).

other external   Any external that is not an actor, hardware external, persistent memory external or software external.

overridden characteristic   Any characteristic, the current implementation of which hides a previous implementation.
Kinds: refined characteristic, replaced characteristic.

package   Any class, the instances of which are package instances.
Kinds: distribution unit, layer, logical package, physical package.

package characteristic   Any characteristic of a package (i.e. any object class, object type or role).

package collaboration diagram   Any specialized collaboration diagram, the purpose of which is to document the potential collaboration of a package of blackbox classes etc. (or package instance of objects etc.) in terms of the messages and exceptions they may send and raise.

package CRC card   Any CRC card, the purpose of which is to document the responsibilities of a class of packages.

package diagram   Any semantic net, the purpose of which is to document the static structure of a package or mechanism of collaborating objects or roles respectively in terms of the semantically meaningful relationships between them.

package implementation   Any class implementation that [partially] implements a package.

package instance   Any instance of a package, consisting of a cohesive collection of collaborating objects, classes, packages, and optionally non-object-oriented software such as common global data and common global operations. Any instance of a package.
Comments: Packaging is also used to control size and complexity by providing a unit of modularity larger than a class. A package instance is usually used to encapsulate the software that is typically developed as a unit by a small team layer, but it is also used to capture the implementation of a pattern, a layer, a subdomain, or a distribution unit.

package instance characteristic   Any characteristic of a package instance (i.e. any object, multiobject, object class, package, common global data, common global operation).

package type   Any type of package. A package conforms to a package type if and only if its interface is consistent with the type (i.e. the set of public characteristics in the interface of the package is a superset of the set of characteristics declared by the type).

part   Any property of an aggregate that references a component of the aggregate.
Comment: The aggregate usually, but not always, hides its component parts. An object is typically a part of only one aggregate at a time. The life span of a part is usually that of its aggregate, but need not be. At least some of the parts of an aggregate reference each other, thus creating a structure (e.g. a car engine) that depends on the correct interaction of its parts. The life of a part is usually, but not always, confined to that of its aggregate. As a counterexample, a car engine may be reused meaning that it may exist after the first car exists but before the second car exists.
Example: the switch on a motor as a visible, public part of the motor.

path   Any contiguous list of referential relationships that are involved in a single scenario.
Comment: A scenario class may have multiple paths, each of which may be traversed by multiple scenarios of the scenario class.
Kinds: primary path, secondary path.

peer external   Any external that is both a client external and a server external.

persistent memory external   Any external that models some persistent memory (e.g. a file, a database, a relational database table, a tape, a disk).

physical package   Any physical design-level or coding-level package (e.g. distribution unit).

physical property   Any property consisting of a named reference to an object. (A property is different from the object it references. A property that does not reference an object is called a dangling property and represents either an error in the model or a reference that is temporarily uninitialized.)

postcondition   Any assertion that must hold after the execution of the associated operation.

precedes relationship   The binary dependency relationship between two scenario classes whereby the server scenario class must complete execution before the server scenario class is permitted to begin execution.

precondition Any assertion that must hold before the execution of the associated operation.

primary path Any path through a given scenario class that is relatively important and commonly traversed.

property Any kind of characteristic capturing a static aspect of its encapsulating object or external.

Comments: All properties are either logical or physical. Logical properties are used during requirements analysis and logical design, whereas physical properties are used during physical design, forward engineering to code and reverse engineering from code. A property is assumed to be logical unless explicitly annotated as physical.

Kinds partitioned by kind: attribute, entry, exception, link, part.

Kinds partitioned by level of abstraction: logical property, physical property.

referential relationship Any binary unidirectional dependency relationship whereby one modeling element refers to another.

Kinds partitioned by level: association, linkage.

Kinds partitioned by directionality: bi-directional, observer, TBD, unidirectional.

Kinds partitioned by meaning: aggregation, containment.

refined characteristic Any overridden characteristic, the current implementation of which delegates to its previous implementation (e.g. using the pseudo-variable super).

remaining transition Any transition that causes the object to remain in its pre-transition state while also transitioning to its post-transition state.

Comment: This changes the situation from a single pre-transition state to multiple post-transition states.

replaced characteristic Any overridden characteristic, the current implementation of which replaces its previous implementation.

responsibility Any purpose, obligation or required capability of the instances of a class of objects, packages or externals.

Comment: A responsibility is typically implemented by a cohesive collection of one or more characteristics.

Kinds: a responsibility for doing, a responsibility for knowing, a responsibility for enforcing.

role Any partial declaration of the interface and implementation of an object, the declared characteristics of which are required to fulfill a cohesive set of responsibilities. Any object that exhibits the declared characteristics, regardless of its class, is said to play the role.

scenario Any specific, contiguous set of interactions that is not completely implemented as a single operation within an instance or class. Any instance of a scenario class.

Kinds: usage scenario.

scenario class Any class, the instances of which are scenarios.

Kinds: mechanism, task script, use case.

scenario class diagram   Any diagram, the purpose of which is to document a set of collaborating scenario classes and the invocation and precedes relationships between them.

Kinds: mechanism diagram, task script diagram, use case diagram.

scenario collaboration diagram   Any specialized collaboration diagram, the purpose of which is to document the collaboration of blackbox classes and objects involved in a scenario in terms of the messages and exceptions they may send and raise.

scenario type   Any type of object that declares the externally visible aspects of a scenario class, typically including name, parameters (if any), preconditions, and postconditions.

secondary path   Any path through a given scenario class that is not of primary importance and less commonly traversed. Secondary paths are often variants of a primary path that provide exception handling.

semantic net (SN)   Any diagram, the purpose of which is to document the static structure of a cohesive collection of related things (e.g. externals, classes, objects, packages) connected by the semantically meaningful relationships (e.g. associations, aggregation, inheritance) between them.

Comments: The semantic net is the most important and most widely used diagram type in the OPEN method.

Kinds: collaboration diagram, context diagram, deployment diagram, inheritance diagram, layer diagram, package diagram.

sequence diagram   Any interaction diagram in the form of a 'fence' diagram, the purpose of which is to document the sequence of interactions among either externals and the application or among objects within [part of] the application.

Kinds: blackbox sequence diagram, whitebox sequence diagram.

sequential message   Any message (e.g. Smalltalk, C++) involving only one thread of control that is temporarily passed from the sender to the receiver, thereby blocking the sender until the server's operation(s) are completed.

sequential object   Any object that is not *inherently* capable of running concurrently (i.e. simultaneously) with other objects because it does not contain, either directly or indirectly, one or more of its *own* threads of execution.

sequential transition   Any single transition from and to a single [sub]state. A sequential transition does not increase or decrease the number of concurrent states.

server external   Any external on which the current application depends.

service provider   The stereotype of an object, class, type or role, the primary responsibilities of which involve providing one or more services to its clients.

software configuration diagram   Any configuration diagram, the purpose of which is to document a software application.

software context diagram   Any context diagram, the purpose of which is to document the context of a cohesive collection of software (e.g. an entire software application, a layer or a subdomain within the application).

software external   Any external that models software (e.g. a legacy application).

specialization (1) the definitional relationship from a more specialized node (child) to a more general node (parent), whereby the child is a kind of its parent(s), (2) any specialized node at the child end of a specialization arc.

start state Any atomic state of an object or class upon instantiation and initialization.

state Any equivalence class of property values used to represent a status, situation, condition, mode or life-cycle phase of an instance during which certain rules of qualitative behavior apply. (Note that all properties need not influence the qualitative behavior of objects. In fact, many objects do not exhibit any significant state behavior at all and therefore do not need a state transition diagram.) A state typically lasts for a significant period of time. OML recognizes the following kinds of state:

Kinds partitioned by level of aggregation: aggregate state, atomic state.

Kinds partitioned by level of transitions: start state, stop state.

Kinds partitioned by role: substate, superstate.

state transition diagram (STD) Any diagram consisting of a directed graph of states (nodes) connected by transitions (directed arcs), the purpose of which is to specify the common *qualitative* (i.e. whether or not an operation executes or which path of a logic branch is taken) behavior of the instances of a class. (Although guard conditions are also graphed as nodes, they are best considered a part of the transition they control.)

Comment: A state transition diagram describes the potential life history of objects of a given class, in terms of the ways they respond to interactions (messages from, exceptions raised by) other objects.

stereotype Any subtype of the associated model element's metatype.

Kinds: associative, controller, coordinator, information holder, interfacer, notifier, service provider, structurer.

stop state Any terminal state from which the object or class cannot transition.

structurer The stereotype of an object, class, type or role, the primary responsibilities of which involve maintaining referential relationships with one or more servers.

subclass Any class that inherits from another class.

substate Any state that specializes another state (its superstate).

Comments: Note that the equivalence classes of property values of substates partition (i.e. form a disjoint cover of) the equivalence class of their superstates. A substate therefore inherits the outgoing group transitions of its superstate.

subtype Any type that inherits from another type.

superclass Any class from which another class inherits.

superstate Any aggregate state that is specialized by its substates. A superstate has a default starting substate to which incoming group transitions point.

supertype Any type from which another type inherits.

synchronous message Any message (e.g. Ada rendezvous) that synchronizes two threads of control, thereby potentially blocking either the sender or the receiver until both are ready to interact.

synchronous transition Any single transition from or to multiple [sub]states. A synchronous transition increases or decreases the number of concurrent states.

system configuration diagram Any configuration diagram, the purpose of which is used to document the configuration of an entire system consisting of hardware, software, wetware (people) and paperware (documentation).

system context diagram Any context diagram, the purpose of which is to document the context of an entire system consisting of hardware, software, wetware (people) and paperware (documentation).

task script Any scenario class that defines a business process, possibly independent of any application.

task script diagram Any scenario class diagram, the purpose of which is to document one or more task scripts, any associated externals, and the semantically important relationships between them.

TBD association Any class or type of TBD linkages.

TBD linkage Any linkage, the directionality of which is yet To Be Determined (TBD).

trait Any specific information about a particular modeling element, typically documented in the element's drop-down box (e.g. its description, its responsibilities, its public protocol, its assertions, its characteristics of a class).

trait kind Any general kind of information about a modeling element (e.g. 'description', 'responsibilities', 'public protocol', 'assertions', 'characteristics', 'stereotypes'); a class of traits.

transition Any change in state. Because states are defined in terms of property values, a change in state is typically of such short duration compared to a state as to be instantaneous.
Kinds partitioned by level of aggregation: group transition.
Kinds partitioned by cause type: exceptional transition, normal transition.
Kinds partitioned by concurrency: sequential transition, synchronous transition.
Kinds partitioned by impact on pre-transition state: leaving transition, remaining transition.

transitional relationship Any relationship in which one state transitions or transforms into another.

trigger Anything that causes a state transition by changing the associated state property values. Most state modeling techniques refer to triggers as events, without specifying what they are in terms of object-oriented concepts.

type Any declaration of visible characteristics that form all or part of the interface of a single kind of instance that conforms to the type.
Kinds: object type, package type, scenario type.

unidirectional association Any class or type of unidirectional linkages.

unidirectional linkage Any one-way linkage from a client on a server and is implemented as a link property of the client that is maintained by operations of the client. (Note that the client and the server may be the same.)

usage scenario Any scenario that captures a complete functional abstraction that provides something of value to the users of the application.

use case Any scenario class that defines a general, requirements-level way of using an application described in terms of interactions between the blackbox application and its externals. A class of usage scenarios.

use case diagram Any scenario class diagram, the purpose of which is to document one or more use cases, any associated externals that either use or are used by them, and the semantically important relationships between them.

uses relationship The binary dependency relationship between an external and a scenario class.

utility The scope of usage for which a modeling element is intended: application-specific, domain-specific, general purpose.

whitebox sequence diagram Any sequence diagram, the purpose of which is to document the sequence of interactions among objects and classes involved in a single mechanism, design pattern, or [partial] path of a use case.

Comment: A whitebox sequence diagram treats the application as a whitebox, showing the interactions among its internal objects. It is used to capture user-oriented requirements, verify the context diagram, and document an acceptance test case.

Appendix B

UML documentation

This appendix includes example diagrams, illustrating how relevant parts of the documentation would look if documented using the Unified Modeling Language (UML). A complete comparison of OML vs UML is beyond the scope of this book; for a more detailed comparison, see Appendix 3 in the *OPEN Modeling Language (OML) Reference Manual.*[†] The main differences between this UML documentation and the original OML/COMN documentation is that UML has:

- an emphasis on detailed design issues,
- a hybrid, data-driven philosophy, historically oriented towards C++ and relational database technology,
- less-intuitive icons,
- different terminology.

B.1 Class diagrams

UML uses *class diagrams* in those situations in which OML uses semantic nets. Unlike OML semantic nets, which were derived from the field of artificial intelligence, UML class diagrams are modified and extended entity relationship attribute diagrams derived from data modeling and relational database design.

B.1.1 Context diagrams

Although UML does not explicitly have a context diagram, one can use UML class diagrams as context diagrams. Whereas OML emphasizes natural-language labels, UML emphasizes the use of roles on associations, whereby roles are essentially the names of references (links) that partially implement the association. Figure B.1 below is the UML version of Figure 2.1.

B.1.2 Layer and configuration diagrams

UML uses class diagrams to show the dependencies between packages. Because UML does not have the concept of layers, UML does not have layer diagrams. Unlike OML, the relationships between the layers and packages are listed merely as unlabeled dependencies. Figure B.2 below is the UML version of Figure 3.1.

[†] Firesmith D.G., Henderson-Sellers B and Graham I. (1997). *OPEN Modeling Language (OML) Reference Manual.* SIGS Books/Cambridge University Press.

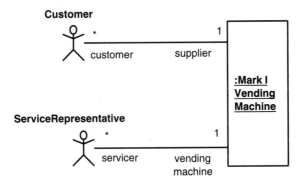

Figure B.1 Example UML context diagram.

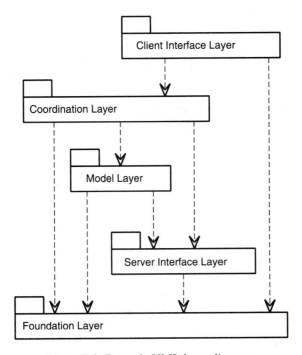

Figure B.2 Example UML layer diagram.

B.1.3 *Class diagrams*

UML uses class diagrams rather than semantic nets to document the static architecture of related classes. Whereas OML emphasizes natural-language labels, UML emphasizes the use of roles on associations, whereby roles are essentially the names of references (links) that partially implement the association. UML also emphasizes the viewpoint that classes can be

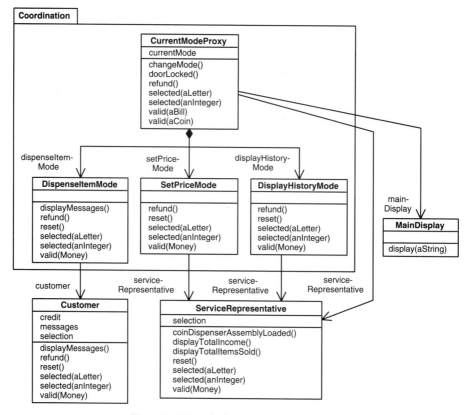

Figure B.3 Example UML class diagram.

characterized in terms of the attributes and operations they define. Finally, UML promotes the use of a solid diamond to represent by-value composition, whereby the lifespan of the part coincides with that of the whole. (OML does not emphasize such implementation-level information, but provides the designer with stereotypes if so desired. OML also provides a separate tombstone icon to represent coincident lifespans.) Figure B.3 below is the UML version of Figure 3.15.

B.1.4 Inheritance diagrams

There are several differences between UML and OML in how they document inheritance:

- UML does not use dropdown boxes to document the characteristics that are inherited.
- UML uses a less intuitive symbol for inheritance that does not distinguish between specialization, interface and implementation inheritance.
- UML uses a 'lollipop' icon to represent types that does not provide any way to document the characteristics they define.

Figure B.4 below is the UML version of Figure 3.17.

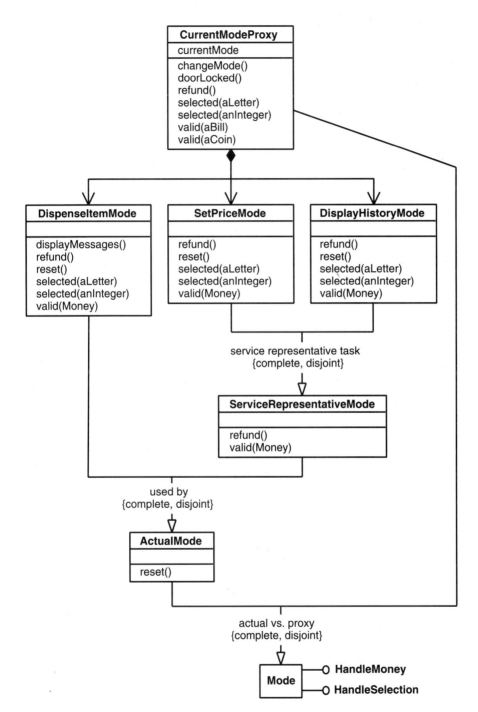

Figure B.4 Example UML inheritance diagram.

B.2 Use case diagrams

The following are some of the differences between UML and OML regarding use case diagrams:

- UML uses stick figures to represent all actors on use case diagrams.
- UML does not allow multiple levels of actors on use case diagrams.
- UML uses the term 'uses' instead of 'invokes'.
- UML does not support the 'precedes' relationship.

Figure B.5 below is the UML version of Figure 2.3.

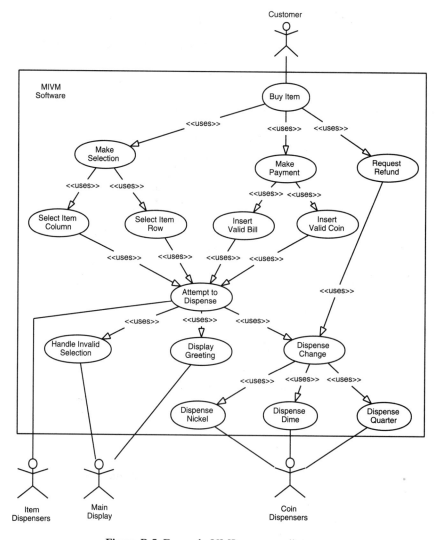

Figure B.5 Example UML use case diagram.

B.3 Interaction diagrams

Both OML and UML use interaction diagrams to document the interactions between objects and classes. Both OML and UML decompose interaction diagrams into collaboration diagrams and sequence diagrams.

B.3.1 Collaboration diagrams

Although both OML and UML draw collaboration diagrams as graphs of collaborating objects, OML and UML take very different approaches to collaboration diagrams:

- OML uses collaboration diagrams to document potential interactions. Additionally:
  - OML documents exception handling on its collaboration diagrams.
  - The scope of OML collaboration diagrams (i.e. package, instance) is different from the scope of OML sequence diagrams (i.e. task script, use case, mechanism).
- UML uses collaboration diagrams to document a specific sequence of interactions. Additionally:
  - UML does not document exception handling on its collaboration diagrams.
  - UML collaboration diagrams have the same scope and purpose as sequence diagrams, making one of them essentially redundant. UML collaboration diagrams are also much more difficult to understand than UML sequence diagrams.
  - UML does not have a collaboration diagram for documenting class or object-internal collaborations.

Figure B.6 below is the UML version of Figure 4.6.

B.3.2 Sequence diagrams

Although both OML and UML draw sequence diagrams as fence diagrams, OML and UML are quite different in their capabilities:
- OML is far more powerful, allowing the modeler to document more information (e.g., multiple paths, assertions, logic) on fewer diagrams.
- OML has time lines for objects, classes, roles, types, and CIRTs.
- OML uses a separate notation for messages and exceptions.
- OML uses logic boxes to express branching (if-then, if-then-else, case), looping, critical regions, and concurrent mechanisms.
- OML keeps the annotations for aggregation, containment, and membership.
- OML uses notes for preconditions and postconditions.
- UML restricts sequence diagrams to interactions between objects.
- UML treats exceptions as a kind of message.
- UML only supports simple branching, but not case branching, looping, critical regions and concurrent mechanisms.

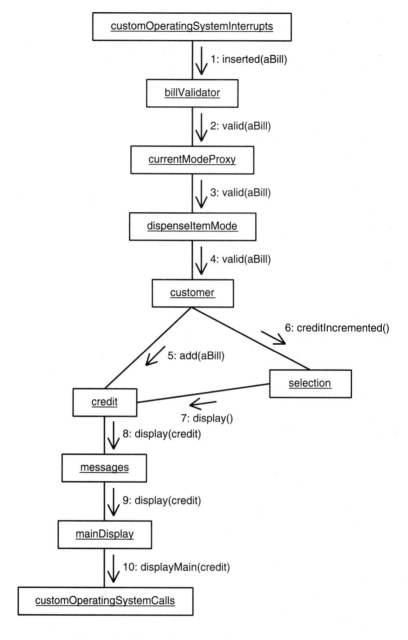

Figure B.6 Example UML collaboration diagram.

- UML does not keep the annotations aggregation and composition.

Figure B.7 below is the UML version of Figure 4.12.

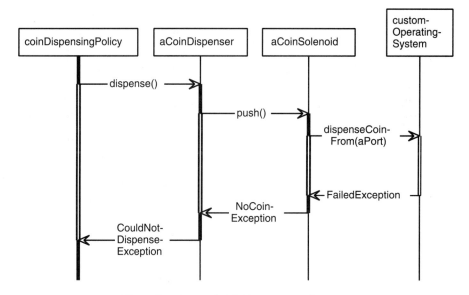

Figure B.7 Example UML sequence diagram.

B.4 State transition diagram

UML uses Harel State Charts, whereas OML uses a state transition diagram with extensions drawn from Embley, Kurtz and Woodfield, the ROOM method, and Firesmith. The major differences between the two approaches highlighted by the following diagram are:

- The UML State Chart labels its transitions with 'events' whereas OML remains more object-oriented by labeling its transitions with interactions (i.e. messages and exceptions).
- UML uses a dot notation for start states and substates, whereas OML uses the stereotype {start}. The OML approach is less cluttered and easier to understand when states have multiple substates.
- UML does not draw visible substates on the boundary of their superstates, making the encapsulation of states less obvious.
- UML labels transitions with their guards thus scattering the information about guards, whereas OML uses a guard icon that makes the guard and its result more clear.

Figure B.8 below is the UML version of Figure 3.34.

B.5 Activity diagrams

UML uses activity diagrams as a form of state machine documenting a procedure. OML does not include such diagrams because:

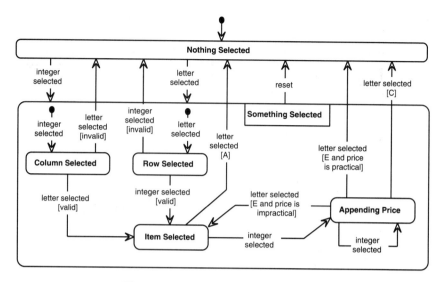

Figure B.8 Example UML State Chart

- The diagrams emphasize functional decomposition.
- The scope of the diagram includes operations and states from many different classes.
- The diagrams are therefore not object-oriented.

B.6 Component diagrams

UML uses component diagrams to document the dependencies between physical components such as source code components, binary code components and executable components. While this may be possibly useful when dealing with hybrid languages where compilation units do not match classes, these diagrams are relatively useless for pure OO languages such as Java, Smalltalk and Eiffel. OML therefore does not support component diagrams.

Appendix C

Smalltalk documentation

This appendix includes examples, illustrating how some of the documentation would look if designed for Smalltalk. The main differences between this Java design and the original Smalltalk design include:

- Smalltalk naming conventions
- Smalltalk's lack of typing
- Smalltalk's lack of operation overloading based on the type of the parameters
- Smalltalk's lack of Java interfaces

This appendix includes the following examples:

- a package collaboration diagram
- a whitebox sequence diagram
- an inheritance diagram showing Java interfaces
- an internal collaboration diagram
- a state transition diagram
- a class specification

C.1 Package collaboration diagram

Figure C.1 is a Smalltalk version of the Java-specific Figure 3.26. The only differences between these two figures are:

- Figure C.1 uses Smalltalk syntax and naming conventions for messages and exceptions.
- Because Smalltalk is not strongly typed, it does not support overloading. Therefore, overloaded messages on Figure 3.26 (e.g. `selected(aLetter)` and `selected(anInteger)`) are given different names on the Smalltalk diagram (`letter: aLetter` and `integer: anInteger`).

C.2 Whitebox sequence diagram

Figure C.2 is the Smalltalk version of the Java-specific Figure 4.24. The only differences between these two figures are:

- Figure C.2 uses Smalltalk syntax and naming conventions for messages.
- Because Smalltalk is not strongly typed, it does not support overloading. Therefore, the overloaded Java message `selected(anInteger)` is given a different name `integer: anInteger`.
- The state of the serviceRepresentativeSelection is an instance of class Symbol in Smalltalk rather than a static variable of type `int` in Java.

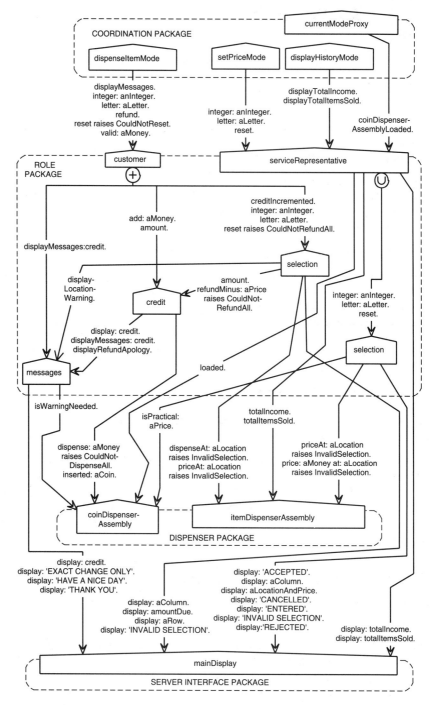

Figure C.1 Smalltalk package collaboration diagram for the role package.

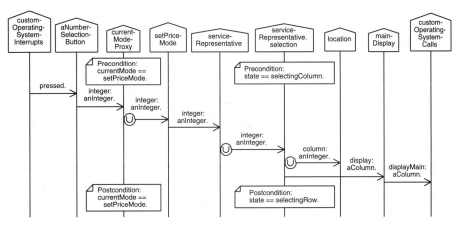

Figure C.2 Smalltalk whitebox sequence diagram for the primary path: Select a Column of the use case: Service Representative Selects a Column.

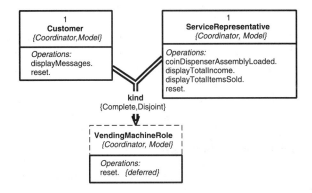

Figure C.3 Smalltalk inheritance diagram for the Role class.

C.3 Inheritance diagram

Figure C.3 is the Smalltalk version of the Java-specific Figure 3.35. The only differences between these two figures are:

- Figure C.3 uses Smalltalk syntax and naming conventions for messages.
- Because Smalltalk is not strongly typed, it does not support overloading. Therefore, the overloaded Java message selected(anInteger) is given a different name integer: anInteger.
- Because Smalltalk does not support interfaces, types are handled informally.

C.4 Internal collaboration diagram

Figure C.4 is the Smalltalk version of the Java-specific Figure 3.37. The only differences between these two figures are:

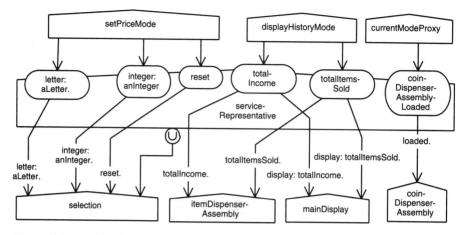

Figure C.4 Smalltalk internal collaboration diagram for the ServiceRepresentative class.

- Figure C.4 uses Smalltalk syntax and naming conventions for messages.
- Because Smalltalk is not strongly typed, it does not support overloading. Therefore, the overloaded Java message `selected(anInteger)` is given a different name `integer: anInteger`.
- Because Smalltalk does not support interfaces, types are handled informally.

C.5 State transition diagram

Figure C.5 is the Smalltalk version of the Java-specific Figure 3.34. The only differences between these two figures are:

- Figure C.5 uses Smalltalk syntax and naming conventions for messages.
- Because Smalltalk is not strongly typed, it does not support overloading. Therefore, the overloaded Java message `selected(anInteger)` is given a different name `integer: anInteger`.

C.6 Class specification for the ServiceRepresentative class

Description: The single instance, serviceRepresentative, of this concrete class models a human service representative by supporting his or her tasks of pricing items and displaying history.

Stereotype: Coordinator.

Utility: Application-specific.

Superclass: VendingMachineRole.

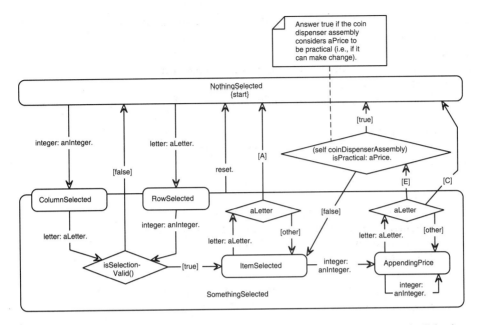

Figure C.5 Smalltalk state transition diagram for the ServiceRepresentativeSelection class.

Responsibilities:

R1. Know the service representative s selection.
    Collaborator: ServiceRepresentativeSelection.
R2. Display history information.
    Collaborators: ItemDispenserAssembly, MainDisplay.
R3. Load the coin dispenser assembly.
    Collaborator: CoinDispenserAssembly.

Constructor:
coinDispenserAssembly: aCoinDispenserAssembly
itemDispenserAssembly: anItemDispenserAssembly
mainDisplay: aMainDisplay
serviceRepresentativeSelection: aSelection.

Characteristics:
  Public services:
  • coinDispenseı AssemblyLoaded.
    'Notify the coin dispenser assembly that it has been loaded.'
  • displayTotalIncome.
    'Display the total income of the vending machine to the service representative.'
  • displayTotalItemsSold.

'Display the total items sold by the vending machine to the service representative.'

- reset.

'Reset the customer credit and customer selection.'

- integer: anInteger.

'Update the column or build the price of the service representative selection.'

- letter: aLetter.

'Update the row of the service representative selection.'

Properties:

Attributes: none.

Links:

- coinDispenserAssembly 'CoinDispenserAssembly'
- itemDispenserAssembly 'ItemDispenserAssembly'
- mainDisplay 'MainDisplay'

Parts: none.

Entries:

- selection 'ServiceRepresentativeSelection'

Exceptions: none.

Appendix D

Tailoring guidelines

The preceding documentation of the vending machine software contains all of the information one would desire if one were to develop, review or maintain the application. However, this documentation was developed primarily for training purposes; on real projects, one never has unlimited resources in terms of either time or staffing to document everything that would be useful to document and iterate over that documentation to ensure its quality. Developers and their management therefore have to decide, on a project-by-project basis, how much documentation is cost-effective and practical. Unfortunately, without an accepted content and format standard and complete examples, developers do not usually know what they are implicitly tailoring out when they produce less than complete documentation. A major objective of this book has been to provide them with a maximal baseline from which they can logically back off for practical reasons.

Except for projects developing applications that are life or business critical (e.g. military projects, avionics, medical systems, banking software), few will produce documentation as complete as the vending machine documentation. Given that not all parts of the documentation are equally valuable, what should the developer consider mandatory and what should the developer consider optional or even excessive? The following table provides tailoring guidelines, not requirements, that may need to be modified, depending on the project requirements, corporate culture, and availability and capabilities of CASE tools.

Some of the redundant information in the documentation becomes much less of a development and maintenance burden if it is stored in a CASE tool and is automatically generated by a documentation tool.

Table D.1 Tailoring guidelines for other applications.

Documentation components	Priority	Comments
Description of the application	High	Such a high-level description is crucial to those new to the project.
Context diagrams	High	These diagrams are quite cost-effective because they are few in number and help developers both understand the application and identify objects.
Use case diagrams	Medium	Although few in number, these diagrams can promote a functional decomposition mindset. Avoid excessively decomposing the use cases.

Table D.1 (Continued)

Documentation components	Priority	Comments
External object specifications	Medium	These specifications help modelers understand and design the corresponding internal objects.
Use case specifications	Medium	Textual requirements may be deleted if the use case captures the requirements in an effective manner. The list of externals can be derived from either the use case statements or the blackbox sequence diagrams. The assertions and statements are redundant with the blackbox sequence diagrams, so one or the other may be deleted.
Blackbox sequence diagrams	Medium	The blackbox sequence diagrams are redundant with the associated assertions and statements, so one or the other may be deleted.
Quality requirements	Medium	If these are deleted, developers may fail to adequately consider them in their designs, producing applications that are more difficult and expensive to maintain.
Requirements trace to classes	Medium	Requirements traces are very useful to ensure that all of the requirements are met, but are also difficult and expensive to maintain. They may be deleted in the documentation if adequately reviewed and adequate, automated regression tests are maintained.
Layer diagram	Medium	This diagram should probably not be deleted because there is only a small number to produce and they provide an important overview of the entire application. On small projects such as the vending machine, this diagram may be redundant with the configuration diagram.
Configuration diagram	Optional	This diagram may be redundant with the layer diagram on small projects having only one package per layer. However, on larger projects, this diagram provides a good road map to either the application or its layers.
Package diagrams	High	These diagrams capture the static architecture at the highest level of abstraction, and provide an excellent overview of the architecture. Because there are relatively few of these diagrams and they are critical to the quality of the design, they should probably not be tailored out, even though there is some overlap between them and the package collaboration diagrams.
Package collaboration diagrams	Medium	These diagrams provide an excellent overview of the dynamic architecture of the package. They are, however, somewhat redundant with the package diagrams and especially the whitebox sequence diagrams. However, they have a different scope from the whitebox sequence diagrams, should be developed first, and should therefore not be considered to be merely a summary of the whitebox sequence diagrams that can be automatically generated from them.
Design decisions and rationale	Medium	This subsection is very useful for helping readers understand higher-level design choices that are not obvious from individual classes.

Table D.1 (Continued)

Documentation components	Priority	Comments
Requirements trace from the classes	Optional	This trace is the reverse of the previous trace, and may well be deleted if not deemed cost-effective (especially if not supported automatically by a documentation tool).
Previous architectures	Optional	While not explicitly needed to document the current architecture, this subsection typically provides useful information that helps prevent future maintenance from going down previously-rejected false paths.
Class summaries	Medium	These provide a nice overview of the classes in the layer, but are redundant with the information in the class specifications and may be deleted if necessary.
Class specifications	Medium	Capturing the class descriptions and responsibilities is high priority. However, most of the rest of the class specifications are redundant with either the code or the internal collaboration diagrams, and can therefore be deleted. These should be developed and maintained in javadoc rather than paper form. One should consider the readability of the code when making this decision, because certain languages (e.g. Eiffel, Smalltalk, Java) are more self-documenting than others (e.g. C++).
Internal collaboration diagrams	Optional	These diagrams should only be developed for those objects with non-trivial interactions among their characteristics.
State transition diagrams	Optional	These diagrams should only be developed for the relatively small number of classes that have significant state behavior.
Path specifications	Medium	The assertions and statements are redundant with the whitebox specifications, so that one or the other can be deleted if necessary. If exceptional paths and exceptions are ignored, the resulting software is likely to be far less complete and robust.
Whitebox sequence diagrams	Medium	These diagrams provide the best way to visualize the flow of control and to verify that the use cases are properly implemented. However, there can be many of these diagrams, they can be hard to maintain without adequate CASE tool support. They are also redundant with the assertions and statements in the associated path specifications, so that one or the other can be deleted if necessary.
Distribution diagram	Optional	This diagram need only be developed if the application is distributed or if the application interfaces with multiple hardware devices. This diagram may be redundant with the software context diagram.

Appendix E

CD-ROM contents

The CD-ROM contains the following two directories:

1. Java – the Java directory contains the Java MIVM source code, byte code, associated html and text documentation, and a 32-bit Java Runtime Environment.
2. Smalltalk – the Smalltalk directory contains source code for the MIVM software written in VisualWorks Smalltalk.

E.1 Java code

The Java directory contains the following subdirectories:

- javadoc – this subdirectory contains hypertext documentation of the Java packages and classes generated by the Javadoc tool. It duplicates much of the textual information in the design documentation section of the book in an easy-to-navigate, quick reference format.
  - Api_users_guide.html This file describes how to use the documentation.
  - packages.html This file provides a hyper-linked list of the MIVM packages and is a good place to start browsing.
  - tree.html This file provides the MIVM class inheritance hierarchy.
  - AllNames.html This file provides a hyper-linked list of all MIVM fields and methods.
  - A file for each class and interface.
- jarfile – this subdirectory is a jar (Java archive) containing the compiled bytecodes of the MIVM software.
- jre – this subdirectory contains a 32-bit Windows version of the Java Runtime Environment.
- source – this subdirectory contains the Java source code. Import these files into your favorite Java development environment for easy browsing. They become the starting point for enhancement of the MIVM application (e.g. allowing service representatives to modify the customer messages).

The Java directory also contains the following files:

- mivm.bat – double clicking on this file brings up MIVM software as a Java application.
- mivm.html – double clicking on this html file brings up the MIVM software as a Java applet.
- mivm.ico – this file contains an icon representing a vending machine that can be used as the icon for the start menu representing the MIVM application.

- readme.html – this file contains important information in html format for users of the Java directory.
- readme.txt – this file contains important information in text format for users of the Java directory.

Windows 95/NT users

If you have a browser that is fully compatible with the Java 1.1 specification, you can just open the mivm.html file and the Java MIVM will start as an applet. To test the Java application of the Mark I Vending Machine, run the 'mivm.bat' batch file in this directory. You may also copy the contents of this directory to your hard drive and execute from there. If the application works but the applet does not, the browser probably does not support the 1.1 specification.

Other platforms/advanced users

If you have a browser that is fully compatible with the Java 1.1 specification, you can just open the mivm.html file and the Java MIVM will start as an applet. A Java 1.1 interpreter (virtual machine) is required to run the Java MIVM. Once you have an appropriate port of the interpreter installed on your machine (ports for Solaris and links to other ports can be found on Sun Microsystems' Java pages at http://java.sun.com), add this directory to your CLASSPATH (refer to the interpreter documentation on the procedure for accomplishing this). You can then launch the DeveloperInterface with a command such as:

- jre mivm.test.gui.Developer.DeveloperInterface.
- java mivm.test.gui.Developer.DeveloperInterface.

E.2 Smalltalk code

The Smalltalk directory contains the following subdirectories:

- The complete source code for the vending machine software including test software (e.g. developer, customer, and service representative interface windows, hardware proxies). This software was written in VisualWorks Smalltalk from ParkPlace/Digitalk under ENVY. It consists of a file for each package that was filed out.

Index